The United States In History

By James T. *Thompson* Shotwell

SIMON AND SCHUSTER : NEW YORK : 1956

TO MARGARET

CONTENTS

vii

FOREWORD

This volume is not history but a commentary on it, notes along the margin of a theme too vast and too magnificent to be crowded into a few pages of hurried text. Many things are left out of it that should be there, but the literature of United States history is now rich, varied, and rapidly growing, and to it the thoughtful reader will turn. Here he will find the personal outlook of one who has been privileged to watch from a corner of the stage itself the greatest drama of all history unfold its tragic course, through blunderings and heroic enterprises to a goal still hidden from us. For the past, with which this story mostly deals, offers no sure guide to a future whose outlines are forever changing under the urging impact of science. Here, on the threshold of tomorrow, our survey stops. But the inspiration of the search for peace and freedom, which has guided us through history, still remains.

J. T. S.

December 1955

Sail on, O Ship of State,
Sail on, O Union strong and great!
Humanity with all its fears,
With all its hopes of future years,
Is hanging breathless on thy fate.

—LONGFELLOW

THE UNITED STATES
IN HISTORY

———◆◆◆———

CHAPTER I

BEFORE HISTORY

For untold centuries America lay waiting, like an empty
stage, for the drama of human history to begin. No one
was here to watch the Rocky Mountains push their gleam-
ing peaks against the sky, or the rivers turn new courses
seaward when blocked by the glacial drifts, or the wet sea
floor dry out into the magnificent stretches of the prairies.
Throughout millions of geological years the continent had
been storing the richest possessions the earth could bestow,
in soil and mines and the power of tumbling waters. But
man himself came late. If there were a clock of the universe ticking off the years instead of the seconds, the last
few minutes of the dial would cover all the recorded past,
and the last few seconds all the record of America. But
the origins of human life reach far beyond history. Scientists are today recovering glimpses of it from traces left
by early man in that greatest of all museums, the earth
itself, and from a study of savage peoples who are still
living as our ancestors may have lived in those far-off ages.

1. *Man's Earliest Home*

Piecing fragments of knowledge together, we are beginning to see the pattern of what is called "prehistory." It is
a puzzling pattern, but through it run the same red thread
of war, the black threads of ignorance and superstition,
and the white threads of knowledge, which also are

woven by the loom of time into the rich fabric of our civilization. The prehistory of America paralleled that of Asia and Europe, just as its later history did. This country of ours, set in magnificence and beauty, "from sea to shining sea," contains the heritage of all the ages, and its destiny is in harmony with all that mankind has achieved and dreamed about the world over.

Early man must have been a great traveler. He left traces of his weapons, his bones, and the marks of his crude handiwork in places as far apart as Java and western Europe. He hunted in the islands of the southern Asiatic seas before they were detached from the mainland and in the forests of Africa before it was separated from Europe. But the earliest remains which have been found so far are those in eastern Asia, and it seems likely that the cradle of the human race was that part of the world where most people live today. The vastest of all mountain ranges runs through the heart of Asia, "the roof of the world," as it has been called. East and south of it are the lush river valleys of China, India, and Babylonia, the homes of great civilizations. But north and west of it are deserts, where the Mongol tribesmen hunted and fought, a constant danger and scourge for the civilized. This was the first chapter of history, long before the days of Greece or Rome. It was also the prehistory of America, for the first Americans were Asiatics.

2. *Asia and America*

No one knows how or when these first immigrants came to America. The easiest way was over the Bering Strait, where their frail canoes may have been fishing, or by the stepping stones of the Aleutian Islands, which push out to the very edge of Asia. It was no great movement of conquest, we may be sure, for there was never food for many at a time. But they must have begun coming more than ten thousand years ago, for their remains have been found in the track of their camps which are that old. They were not all alike. They differed in language, in looks, and in manner of life. The last to come, the Athabascas of the north and their kin the Apaches of the south, resembled the Mongols most. In the forest fastnesses, the Indians of the northeast lost some of the squint which had protected their eyes from the desert sun, but their weather-beaten skin, stretched tightly across the cheekbones, kept its protective copper coloring. It was not a face for laughter, that of the Mongol or the American Indian. Hunter and hunted, where food was scarce and protection lacking, he fought his tribal wars with relentless ferocity.

The Indian of the north never conquered the wilderness, because he lacked the metal tools with which to work. Hatchets of chipped stone are good enough for hunting, along with bow and arrow, but they are poor implements for cutting down trees. So the forests were left for the wild beasts as the preserves of food supply, over which rival tribes fought wars of extermination. Such life called for cunning, courage, and endurance; but it did not lead to settlement or the development of the arts. Not inferior to the white man in mental equipment, the Indian was conquered by the wilderness, which kept him unchanged throughout the centuries. When our fathers found him here, he was likely much the same as when he left his Asiatic home in the prehistoric period.

3. *The American Babylonia*

But in America, as in Asia, the southland produced civilization. Yucatan was like Babylonia, a land of temples and rich culture, where astronomy was studied and time reckoned on stone calendars, which are the marvel of scientists today. The highly gifted Mayas burned and slashed the tropic jungles to build the first civilization in the Americas. But they, and the Toltecs who succeeded them, were overrun over a thousand years ago by a poor Indian tribe which settled in what was then swampy lake country where the City of Mexico now stands. These were the Aztecs, fresh arrivals from the north. They dug up the rich soil from the lake bottom and gardened it in floating baskets, growing corn, beans, sweet potatoes, and fruit. Out on the hills, veins of copper, gold, and silver ran through the rocks, and their metalworkers added to both the power and splendor of their priestly kings. Warlike and superstitious, they sacrificed thousands of victims to their gods. It was Babylonia in the New World.

Nor does this romance of history stop here. For down in the Andes of Peru the Incas even outrivaled the Aztecs in wealth. One wonders what would have happened if the white man had not come. Would the Americans have worked out their own civilization? Perhaps not. Already the last wave of Asiatics, the Apaches, was reaching down to Mexico. They had reached the Rio Grande country when Francisco Coronado met them, a thousand years after Attila, their greatest kinsman, had ravaged the Western world.

Probably if the white man had not come, America would have remained about what it was when its history began with the era of European discovery.

CHAPTER II

---◆---

THE AMERICAN SAGA
AND THE MIDDLE AGES

There was a saga of America before its history began, an epic like that which Homer sang of the wandering Ulysses. It was the story of Leif Ericson, son of the discoverer of Iceland and Greenland, Eric the Red, and of their kinsmen and followers, who came in open boats across the northern seas to a far-off shore which they named Vinland. The memory of this great adventure, which ranks high among the exploits of brave men, was kept alive in Iceland and in Denmark in the *Saga of Eric the Red*. This must have been widely known in its time, for a German monk, Adam of Bremen, visiting Denmark some sixty years later, made reference to it in his history. But three centuries passed before it was written down, to be accepted in our day as the first chapter in the long story of the discovery of America.

•

1. *Restless Europe*

The peoples of Europe have always been restless. From earliest time, dim movements of barbaric tribesmen kept sweeping down from the forest lands of the north to the sunny Mediterranean, destroying civilizations and then rebuilding them, for others to destroy again. Finally, breaking the bulwark of mighty Rome, which held them back for centuries, they drove onward, plundering, bringing the Dark Ages with them.

But some came by boats, over stormy seas to the bays, on *viks* as they called them, along the coasts of France and Britain. These Vikings were Norsemen, fair-complexioned, with yellow hair undarkened by the northern sun and eyes bluer than the seas they sailed. But they were as cruel as they were stalwart; and they were as feared as they themselves were fearless. They did not pause on the edge of the Atlantic, but pushed out to Ireland and beyond, first to Iceland and Greenland, and then to America.

2. The First Discovery of America

It was the year 1000 when Leif Ericson, sailing from Norway to the newly discovered Greenland, was blown by storms to a "land of which he had never heard before," where there were "self-sown wheat fields and vines growing." This short phrase is the first description of America in the literature of Europe. Although he himself never returned to the shore he had discovered, the stories which he brought back to the firesides of his seagoing kinsmen in Iceland and bleaker Greenland stirred them to plan the first expedition to America; and in two years' time his kinsman Thorfinn Karsefni, a name for Americans to remember, set forth with 160 followers in four ships to found the first European colony in the New World. First, they coasted along the shore of Labrador. Then, turning southward along sandy banks and bays, they passed "a fine country, with mountains thereabouts" and finally reached Vinland itself, "where no snow came and all of their livestock lived by grazing ... where every

brook was full of fish . . . and where there were great
numbers of animals of all kinds in the woods, and where,
alongside the wheat fields, wherever there was hilly
ground, there were vines. . . . One morning early they
looked about them and saw a great number of skin canoes
. . . filled with swarthy men and ill-looking, and the hair
of their heads was ugly. They had great eyes and were
broad of cheek." This is the first description of America
and of the American Indians. These were harmless at
first but next year came back in war bands, fighting with
war slings. "It now seemed clear to Karsefni and his people that although the country thereabouts was attractive,
their life would be one of constant dread and turmoil by
reason of the inhabitants of the country, so they prepared
forthwith to leave and determined to return to their own
country." Disputes among themselves hastened the decision and, sailing away, they left America unvisited by
any European for almost five hundred years.

Such are the meager outlines of one of the greatest tales
ever told. Other Norsemen followed across the trackless
waters to the west and south, but the story of their wan-
derings was soon lost to memory, so that we do not know
who built the stone cairns on the New England coast, or
whether there were expeditions to the heart of the continent coming by Hudson Bay. It is said that a sword found
in the wilderness north of Lake Superior was of Viking
make, and there are strange Norse letters carved on stone
found in Minnesota. What nameless pioneering heroes
were these? Some day the earth may yield more traces
of this and other sagas of the North, but even then this
first chapter of the history of the discovery of America
will always remain like the faint echo of a distant song.

3. *Europe Keeps Looking to the East*

One reason that no echo of the Norsemen's exploits was awakened in Europe was that it had always looked to the East as the home of fabulous wealth and splendor. Before the great days of Greece and Rome, the empires of Egypt and Babylonia, Assyria and Persia had come and gone, leaving the remains of their magnificence for the Greek soldiers of Alexander to gaze upon, and the Roman legions to plunder. No wonder that the ancient world felt the lure of Asia, and that the center of the Roman Empire itself moved from Rome to Constantinople.

When a new empire of the East arose, that of the Mohammedans, feudal Europe, poverty-stricken, isolated, mobilized its forces in the Crusades to win not only the Holy Land, but also the wealth and treasure of the Moslem world. The returning crusaders brought their tapestries to hide the bare walls of their castles, and silks and jewels to adorn their courts. The lure of Asia continued.

More important still, ships began to ply the Mediterranean. From fishing huts on a marshy shore rose Venice, Queen of the Adriatic, filling her stores with the rich goods of the bazaars of western Asia. Her rival, Genoa, bred hardy sailors to trade at Constantinople and beyond. Over the Alps the merchants came once more along the old Roman roads or by new pathways through the forests to the fairs of rising cities. Thus Asia helped Europe to reach modern times.

4. *The Need for Gold*

Under the shadow of great cathedrals and in the halls of monasteries, schools revived learning, and kings employed lawyers to spread their justice among the people. Thus the anarchy of feudal lords made way for the nations of today, but the rulers needed gold to pay their soldiers and to maintain their state and majesty. Politics was becoming a business, the business of kings.

From the thirteenth century to the nineteenth the need for money grew; but even more the demand for luxury—the silks and spices of the Orient—increased. Thus the Mediterranean cities built the splendors of the Renaissance on the produce of the oriental trade and the new industries which it stimulated.

But the caravan routes were difficult and coastal shipping dangerous, and if a better way could be found to reach the distant East, it would bring wealth, not only to the ruling class, but to the merchants in towns and cities as well.

It was to find this better way that Christopher Columbus sailed west to reach the East and found America.

CHAPTER III

———◆◆———

THE OLD WORLD FINDS THE NEW

From beyond recorded time the traders of Asia came and
went in overland caravans with goods for Babylon and the
bazaars of the Near East. But the distance was long, the
risks were great, and each camel's pack only a bale or two.
So, when the Mediterranean traders gathered these goods
for the markets of Rome and the cities and courts of medieval Europe, the cost was high and only the richest could
purchase them. But water-borne freight is cheap, for a single
ship can carry the cargoes of many beasts of burden, and
the profits are great, as the merchants of Genoa and Venice
showed by the wealth which made them rivals of the king-
doms of western Europe, and by the use of their fleets in
the last Crusades.

1. *Portugal Leads*

The crusaders' zeal combined with the lure of Asia to
cause the Commercial Revolution, which moved the center of Europe to the countries fringing the Atlantic, as the
trackless oceans were charted by improvements in the
compass and the mariner's astrolabe. The caravans could
then turn to the seas, but Africa lay like a road block to
the Orient, almost five thousand miles long, and if, as men
were beginning to believe, the world was round, the short-
est way lay to the west. Then America was discovered—

another road block for Europe to find the way through or around, and then finally to accept as a richer prize than all the wealth of Asia and a new home for mankind.

The charm of romance lies over the history of the great explorers. It was an era in which Portugal led. Prince Henry the Navigator, looking westward from his tower at Sagres by Cape Saint Vincent—that southernmost cape of Europe, jutting into the Atlantic—studied his maps and sent out his seamen to the newly discovered Azores and down the coast of Africa. When, at the opening of the sixteenth century, Vasco da Gama, following Bartholomeu Dias' route around the Cape of Good Hope of a few years earlier, reached India, Venice was ruined, as the caravels of Portugal brought the spices of Asia to the wharves of Lisbon. The seaway had won over the land routes. A revolution in human affairs was to follow.

2. *Christopher Columbus, Student Adventurer*

Christopher Columbus, a student adventurer, was born in the old trading city of Genoa. He had had his imagination stirred by the story of Marco Polo, the Venetian who, in the thirteenth century, had traveled the overland route to far-off China and who, in his old age, had set forth the narrative of that great romance while a prisoner of the Genoese. Columbus, fired with the ambition to reach Asia by sea, traveled to Portugal and settled there for a while, marrying the daughter of one of Prince Henry's sea captains. He talked with the old sea dogs of their voyages, while he made maps and charts for a livelihood. He was present at the ceremonial reception by King John of Portugal to Bartholomeu Dias, upon his return from the discovery of the Cape of Good Hope, but the Portuguese king would not supply him with ships for his own enterprise. It was only after eight years of failure, which would have discouraged any less stouthearted man, that he finally found a patron in Queen Isabella of Spain, who offered to supply him with ships and men. In January 1492, the Queen sent for him to come to Granada, just when that last stronghold of the Moslems surrendered to her and her husband Ferdinand. His eyes feasted on the Alhambra, the symbol in western Europe of that great epoch of Mohammedan culture which had been built up on the trade of the land routes with Asia. But even he, with all his dreams, could hardly have divined that he was destined to strike a greater blow at Islam than the victorious army of Spain as sea routes supplanted caravans.

3. *A New Date in History*

Armed with a royal letter of introduction to the Grand Khan of Cathay, as China was then termed, Columbus set sail on August 3, 1492, at eight o'clock in the morning, with his three small ships, the *Santa Maria*, the *Pinta*, and the *Niña*. The trade winds blew steadily across the weedy sea plains of the Sargasso Sea, ominously steady. Mutiny showed its head. He quelled it. Land birds were sighted, and at two o'clock on the morning of Friday, October 12, a sailor on the *Niña* sighted land. The same morning they rowed ashore and, holding the royal banner of Spain, they knelt while Columbus took possession of the newly found land, naming it San Salvador, in honor of the Holy Savior. It was a new date in the history of mankind.

But this was not Asia, nor even the mainland of a new continent. It was one of the outer Bahamas, today called

Watling Island. Leaving it, the three little ships sailed on, past island after island which lifted their green palms above the blue waters of the Caribbean Sea. They were not the spice islands of India, although Columbus thought they were and gave the natives the name they still bear, "Indians."

4. *Columbus the Colonizer*

No sooner had Columbus returned to Spain and told his great story at the Spanish court than the whole country was astir at the news. Ferdinand and Isabella gave him almost royal honors, seating him beside them like a king. Cheering crowds followed him in the streets. Nobles vied with each other for the chance to sail with him on his next voyage, hoping to share with him the spices and silks of China and India and to bring back some of the treasures of "golden-roofed" Japan. Gaily they sailed away, fifteen hundred of them in seventeen vessels, not only sailors and adventurers, but colonists as well: the first chapter of one of the greatest stories of history, that of the migration to America.

In his first voyage Columbus had not thought of colonizing, but his flagship, the *Santa Maria*, was wrecked on Christmas Eve, 1492, on the coast of Haiti (Hispaniola), and, as the *Pinta* had left him, he could not take the wrecked crew back to Spain on the little *Niña*. So he built a fort with the ship's timbers and sailed off, leaving the first white settlement in the New World. But the settlers tortured the natives for gold, and when Columbus returned all the Spaniards had been killed and the fort was in ruins. Undismayed, he planted his second colony on the same swampy, unhealthy shore, and then left it to suffer from hunger and disease and the hostility of the natives, while he sailed on in the vain quest for Asia. It was no longer as a triumphant admiral that he returned to Spain; from now on, failure dogged his great achievements and darkened his renown. On his third voyage he touched the coast of South America without knowing it. Then bitter intrigue triumphed, and he was sent home in chains. Released and his titles restored, his indomitable will unbroken, he sailed on his fourth and last voyage; but it added nothing to either wealth or fame, and he died in poverty and neglect two years after the death of his protectress, Queen Isabella. History has few such tragic lives to record.

But it was Columbus himself who was the first to sully the bright story of Spain in the New World when, unable to bring back to Europe the wares of the Orient, he sent home five shiploads of islanders as slaves and forced those at the colony to pay tribute like serfs. Thus the discoverer of America linked it to the Old World by oppression. But it should be recorded that the first strong protest against the enslavement of the natives came from a noblehearted Spanish priest, Bartolomé de Las Casas, "The Apostle of the Indians."

5. America

In 1497, a year before Columbus touched the coast of the mainland, another Italian claimed to have discovered it. This was Amerigo Vespucci; and the popularity of the published accounts of his "travels" won for him the greatest of all titles to fame; no one else ever had a continent named after him. The same year another seaman of Italian blood, John Cabot, sailed with an English crew along the coast of the New World, from Hudson Bay to Florida; but more than a century passed before the English followed to plant their colonies there, and no land bears the name of Cabot.

For years after its discovery, America lay like an unwelcome obstacle on the pathway to India and the East. Cabot's purpose, like that of Columbus, was to find a way to the court of the Great Khan. Time after time sailors tried to find their way through it or around it. The English hunted vainly for the elusive Northwest Passage. Even as late as 1609, two years after Jamestown was founded, Henry Hudson hoped that the noble river which bears his name was an arm of the Western Sea, and turned back disappointed when the tidal stream narrowed down, by Albany. Then he searched the waters of the frozen northern bay, from which no tidings of him ever came back.

Meanwhile, however, Spanish explorers had discovered in the New World itself untold treasure, richer than any dream of the Orient.

CHAPTER IV

———◆———

MANKIND'S SECOND CHANCE

Four hundred years ago, in Europe as well as in Asia, there was little hope for liberty for the average man of courage and goodwill. The ambitions of a ruling class and the times alike conspired against liberty of conscience, liberty of speech, liberty of the person, liberty of economic opportunities. Wars, dynastic and religious, had exhausted both the substance and the tolerance of the old world.

Then came one of the great ironies of history—rulers needed to find gold to pay their armies and increase their power over the common man. The seamen they sent out to find that gold, found instead the way of escape for the common man from those rulers. What they found over the western horizon was not the silk and the jewels of Cathay, but mankind's second chance—a chance to create a new world, after it almost spoiled an old one.

> —Franklin D. Roosevelt at the rededication
> of the Statue of Liberty

1. *They Came Seeking Gold*

In earliest times and throughout antiquity, gold was too precious for common circulation. Even the Greeks used it mostly as ornament or treasure. War rather than commerce distributed it. Gold was extremely rare throughout the Middle Ages and even at the dawn of modern times, when a penny was the wage of a workingman; the new supplies of gold and silver which the Spanish explorers found in Mexico and Peru caused, more than any other single thing, the rise of modern times. More gold and silver came from America in a single generation than all Europe had in the entire Middle Ages. Bankers and merchants began to supplant the feudal lords, and the moneyed or middle class began to demand the right to decide what taxes to pay and in other ways to assert their rights to share in governing themselves. Thus the treasure of the New World helped to overthrow the Middle Ages and the tyrannies of warring kings.

Gold! It was the prize of statesmen and kings, and the struggle for it sent Spanish galleons overseas and English sea hawks after them. Cortes in Mexico and Pizarro in Peru plundered undreamed-of treasures. For gold De Soto toiled through the swamps of Florida and the forests beyond, and Coronado reached north from Mexico to the Colorado. For gold Drake sailed around the Horn up the coast of California, passing the Golden Gate in the mists, and further north took possession of our western coast in the name of Queen Elizabeth. But the British waited a long time before they followed up that exploration, and meanwhile the Spanish came in and held California.

2. *They Came Seeking Freedom for the Common Man*

Force and violence marked the path of all the early history of mankind. War brought slavery and oppression. The first of all laws was the right of the powerful, but slowly, throughout the ages, the common man won the right to be free and safeguarded his freedom in courts of law and parliaments.

These institutions of freedom and justice developed more strongly in England than on the continent of Europe. The liberties of the Magna Charta, won from King John in the thirteenth century, were never wholly lost; and when, in the seventeenth century, the English people overthrew the despotism of the Stuart kings, they drew up a Bill of Rights which asserted those ideals of justice and self-government which were shared by the English settlers who came to the bleak New England coasts and there carried on the great tradition of the liberties of Englishmen.

Holland, although a smaller country, had shared equally in this great movement of human freedom, and the Dutch settlers sturdily upheld the principles of liberty in the New World.

The French were slower to achieve their freedom and it was not until after the American Revolution had been fought and won that the principles of liberty, equality, and fraternity were emblazoned on the banners of France.

3. *They Came Seeking Religious Freedom*

"The sounding aisles of the dim woods rang to the anthem of the free."

The history of religion holds the strangest paradox. The fires of persecution have lighted the path of high ideals and exalted faith. Down to our own time even the religion based on the principles of universal charity was haunted by the same attitude toward the heretic and unbeliever that had marked the practices of primitive taboo. Intolerance was shared by Protestant and Catholic alike, and its practice varied only with the depth of conviction and the strength of the secular arm to root out with unrelenting force those who did not share the orthodoxy practiced by their fellows.

Although America was, from the first, a land of refuge from persecution, the Puritans of Massachusetts still believed that persecution was right, when it was rightly applied; and in this the Old Testament was the chief guide. The death penalty was to be inflicted, not only for murder, but for idolatry, blasphemy, and witchcraft. The burning of witches casts a lurid light across the page of Colonial history, stained also by the blood of Quakers and others who insisted on worshiping God in their own way. Thus those who had suffered in the Old World from religious bigotry brought it with them to the New.

But beyond the fringe of the woods there was a chance of escape. Thus the settlement of Rhode Island was founded as an asylum for religious liberty, when Roger Williams and five companions, fleeing from Boston, founded Providence, looking out over the blue waters of Narragansett Bay.

Farther west, the Dutch of the Hudson Valley never shared the intolerance of the Puritans. Although no people had suffered more than their ancestors from religious persecution, they were the first people of Europe to establish religious toleration; and those who came to the New World shared this generous ideal.

The Quakers of Pennsylvania were stronger still in their assertion of tolerance because of their belief that true religion is found in each man's relation to God by an "inner light" that illumines his soul. The Catholics of Maryland gave tolerance to others because of the need to

secure it for themselves. The cavalier society and squirearchy of the southern plantations were tolerant in propor-
tion as worldly interests took the upper hand.

Slowly but steadily the freedom which the individual
found in America and the enforced mingling of neighbors
in the settlements made for religious tolerance, without,
however, lessening the essentially religious basis of the
common life.

4. *They Came Seeking Livelihood*

There were no fabled cities of Cathay on the North Atlantic Coast. There were not even gold and silver as in
Mexico and Peru. There was only a wilderness to tame;
and yet, in course of time, it offered the richest prize of
all to those who tamed it, for it was illimitable and inex-
haustible, a continent as the homeland of a nation. As the
ringing ax kept forever opening new farm lands to the
sun, it opened as well new light on the nation's pathway
—the truth that lasting wealth comes not as the spoil of
conquest, but as the result of labor; wealth in body and
mind as well as in possessions, for hardships breed strength
and temper the steel of courage, without which no people
is great.

New England's poor and rock-strewn fields were
helped out by harvests of the sea when those on land
failed, for the early New Englanders, settled along a hundred bays, were also seagoing people. Then richer lands
were found along the river valleys, like the Connecticut,
and settlements grew into towns. But for long the fur
trade was a richer source of livelihood than farming.
Along the Hudson, the Dutch had great plantations, but
they were less important to them than the trading posts of

Nieuw Amsterdam (New York) and Beverwyck (Beaver Town, now Albany).

More inviting was the rich farming country along the seaboard on the middle and southern coast. The strange new article of luxury for Europe, tobacco, was worth many gold mines. Great estates grew rich, worked in part by indentured English and slave labor. On the uplands, further inland, settlers, mostly Scotch-Irish, pushed the frontier back in desperate frontier wars.

Never was there such a migration of homeseekers. The land of freedom was also the land of opportunity. Across the Appalachian Mountain range, which paralleled the sea coast from Maine to Georgia, lay the illimitable prairies, watered by rivers greater than any in Europe. Never since Babylonia, the granary of the ancient world, had richer soil been broken by the plow for wheat and corn; and under great stretches of it or pocketed in the hills lay mineral wealth for the generations that followed. Here was mankind's second chance, and it drew the greatest of all migrations in a steadily increasing tide for three centuries, until our own day. From every land they came, and thus America became the melting pot, or rather the crucible, in which is destined to be fused all of those living and enduring interests of mankind upon which a higher civilization can be based.

But the land of opportunity was also a land of danger and hardship for the pioneers. America began with the heroic age, one kept alive in song and story for all time to come.

CHAPTER V

———◆◆◆———

THE CONQUISTADORS
AND THE HERITAGE OF SPAIN

The history of America, like that of Europe, began with a Homeric Age, one which combined in heroic proportions feats of chivalry with barbaric ruthlessness. The odyssey of Leif Ericson, that Ulysses who rode the "sounding furrows" of the northern seas, was but a mere episode of adventure and had long been forgotten when, five centuries later, the other heroes of the New World epic fought in the harbors of the Caribbean and over the mountains to the capitals of native kings. The treasures, which the Spaniards took from the palaces and temples of Mexico and Peru, far outshone the golden hoards of the Greek kings, but the marauding bands led by Cortes and Pizarro had all the semibarbarous qualities of Achilles or Hector. It was as if the moral influences of Christendom had gone for naught, and the world was still at the threshold of history.

In spite of these dark beginnings, the work of the conquistadors proved permanent, as colonists and the Catholic church established a Latin culture over all Central and South America. The rise of English sea power, which challenged the might of Spain, never reached this vast cultural empire.

1. *From Piracy to Sea Power*

The prowess of these plunderers of the New World was not seriously contested for long by the natives, whom they despoiled. Coats of mail and weapons of Toledo steel brought certain victories. But the real test came when the Spaniards tried to ship their booty home; for the nations not under Spanish power regarded it as plunder to be shared by anyone who could take it. Raiding the harbors where the Spanish ships were loading, and attacking them on their way, the freebooting sailors of northern Europe carried on a piratical war, in which the English led, and which reached its climax in the defeat of the Spanish Armada. Again, there were exploits to match the greatest in the annals of war, but cruelty, as well as daring, was unrestrained.

The English had no such great ships as the Spanish, but they excelled in seamanship and their little ships could hit and run, while the great Spanish galleons lumbered on. Sir John Hawkins and Sir Francis Drake and their fellow sea dogs performed incredible feats. Drake's *Golden Hind*, in which he made the voyage around the world, was no larger than a coastwise schooner, yet he captured the greatest Spanish treasure ship in the Pacific and brought back immense spoil to his delighted Queen Elizabeth. In his slow, massive way, Philip II planned to strike back with the greatest invasion by sea that the world had ever seen. Gathering in the harbors of Spain a vast naval armament from all the countries which his power or his money could reach, to sail under the Spanish flag alongside the Spanish men-of-war, he prepared for the attack on England. But the English sea dogs hounded the shipping, and Drake sailed boldly into the harbor of Cádiz and destroyed the ships assembled there. It was not until 1588 that the Great Armada was ready. Its destruction by the English sealed the fate not only of Spain but of Europe and America as well.

2. *If Philip Had Won*

The Marxian theory of history will have hard work to
deal with the problem: what would have happened if
Philip had won? The consequences would certainly have
been a very different history of the modern world than
that which actually happened. In North America, as yet
almost uncolonized, the result would certainly have been
a Latin culture, with all the resiliency which that culture
has shown whenever it has been given a chance to develop.

As for Europe, Philip used the plunder of the New
World less for himself or his court than to restore the
crumbling Middle Ages, to dominate Christendom by
controlling the Mediterranean, checking the ambition of
France, waging a land crusade against the heretic Netherlands and a sea crusade against heretic England, while in
Spain itself the Moors were extirpated and the fires of the
Inquisition purged the land of all freedom of thought.
The power of this monolithic state lay in its soldiery, the
mightiest since Roman days, in the inflexible mind of its
coldly calculating monarch in whom all power was concentrated, and in the wealth of the New World to pay
the costs of his great plan. Fortunately for Europe, for
his failure was Europe's gain, he knew nothing of economics at the very time when commercial capital was
bringing new wealth to other lands, and Spain grew
poorer instead of richer as the gold poured in from overseas, because of restrictions on trade and the costs of war.
But the fallacies of Philip, although visible now in the
perspective of history, were by no means so clear in the
sixteenth century; and the thought that his great career

would be checked by the steady heroism of the Dutch and the daring of the English seemed incredible.

3. *The Latin Model*

Although Spain failed to dominate modern Europe, it did succeed in those parts of America which it colonized. This fact is proof that there was more than spoliation in the Spanish conquests. Beginning as plundering expeditions, they ended in the creation of new civilizations, all of which bore, and still bear, the stamp of Hispanic institutions and culture. As in the mother country, the two dominant forces were military and religious. A feudal regime oppressed and enslaved the natives, held as peons on great estates, living in poverty and ignorance, or worked to death in the mines to keep up the declining output of silver. Only in the magnificence of their churches were the populace given glimpses of treasures such as the conquerors had taken for their own. The ruling class lived like grandees in town or country.

In politics as in economic and social life, the Spanish model was followed, a rigid political structure, ruled without compromise by the persons or party in power. The one check on authoritarianism was not in political debate but in the constant threat of revolution, of which there have been many in Latin America. The greatest phrase in parliamentary usage in the British Commonwealth and the United States, "the loyal opposition," is practically meaningless in Latin-American politics. The opposition must be loyal to itself. Though patriotism demands union against external enemies, it does not call for co-operation with hostile politicians at home to enable them to succeed if their success but strengthens their power. This is the logic of Latin-American politics everywhere. The illogical English tradition of compromise, to make things work even where we do not think they are the best that can be devised, is the key to true democratic government.

Not all of this difference between the authoritarianism of Latin America and the democracies of the United States and the British Commonwealth is due to history. The problems of government have been different. Nowhere in North America has there been so large a native population to be fitted within the framework of the state. And it had no political experience of its own to challenge the rule of the conquerors, who continued to look to Europe for ideas and ideals. This meant that the revolutions which broke the ties with Spain were motivated more by what was happening in Europe than by any great social overturn in America. The freedom for which Bolívar the Liberator fought was home rule. In one way, that was all that Washington fought for, but it was home rule of a different kind. The realization of democracy in Latin America has been the aim of wholly different movements, a century after Simón Bolívar.

CHAPTER VI

THE ENGLISH COLONIES AND THE FRENCH

The Homeric Age of Central and South America had no more relation to the history of the United States and Canada than the struggle on the windy plains of Troy had to the Athens of Pericles—indeed far less. For the conquistadors, North America was a disappointment. They searched in vain in the desert approaches to California and the swamps of Florida for a northern El Dorado to rival that fabled but elusive country of gold which gleamed like a mirage before the explorers of the Andes; but the exploits of Coronado and De Soto belong with those of Cortes and Pizarro and their followers and successors. They left little but a half-forgotten romance alongside the more sober history of the north.

That history opened with almost a complete blank for the century so crowded with events in Latin America. The chief aim of the few explorers of the North Atlantic Coast was to find a northern way through or around the great land mass, so as to outflank the Spaniards or Portuguese in their prior claims upon the Orient. Then came one of the great surprises of history, when the conquest of the continent itself opened the pathway to greater wealth than all of Asia, and to a new era in the history of freedom.

1. *The Dream of a French Empire*

The history of freedom profits from the mistakes of kings. The greatest mistake in the history of France was

29

the attempt of Louis XIV to extend his empire in Europe instead of overseas. It is true that throughout history this absorption in European struggles for power has always marked French politics; but after the defeat of Spain, the gateways were open in both America and Asia for world power, and there were valiant leaders at hand to act as proconsuls of empire. But both soldiers and settlers were few, and the money that might have equipped fleets and armies for the Saint Lawrence or in India went to pay troops on the eastern frontiers of France or to furnish luxuries for the king and his court. The palace of Versailles remains as the lasting monument to lost empires overseas.

The French came first to America in little fleets of cod-fishers from Brittany to the banks of Newfoundland. Already, a few years after the conquest of Mexico by Hernando Cortes (1521), in the early sixteenth century, Jacques Cartier of the fishing port of Saint-Malo explored in several voyages the Gulf of Saint Lawrence and the Saint Lawrence River and took possession of the country in the name of the king. But it was not until France was under the "merchant king," Henry IV of Navarre, that the founder of New France, Samuel de Champlain, began his great career. At first he cherished the hope that the great waterway was the road to China, as the name of the rapids which barred his path—La Chine —bears witness. But in other explorations he charted Lake Ontario and Georgian Bay as well as the lake that bears his name, and colonists, few but sturdy, settled along the Saint Lawrence.

Though neither the hoped-for passage to Asia was discovered nor gold or silver found, a source of wealth was developed in the fur trade. In the chilly houses of Europe, furs were in great demand among those who could afford such luxuries. Everywhere on the American frontiers, the first to explore the wilderness were the hunters and trappers; but the furs of the cold north country were the best of all. The *coureurs de bois*, a roving race of adventurers, drawn from every level of society, and intermixed with Indians, gave a gay note of romance to the French advance. Jesuit missionaries shared with the trappers the dangers of the wilderness, and their record of heroism is unsurpassed in the history of the martyrs. The explorations reached far from the Saint Lawrence when Father Jacques Marquette and Louis Jolliet got to the upper waters of the Mississippi, and Robert de La Salle traced it to its mouth in the swamps and forests of Louisiana.

The guiding spirit in this great enterprise was the governor of New France, Count de Frontenac. Soldier and statesman, he foresaw that the fate of the continent would be decided in wars with the English colonists on the east of the far-flung empire of France. The friendly Indians were wisely dealt with and the Iroquois held in check. A line of forts reached over to the Mississippi. From Quebec to New Orleans, Louis was to be king.

Frontenac's foresight was justified in the century which followed, when the forts by the thin French settlements furnished a far-flung defense against both hostile Indians and the English colonists to the south and east. For England's war with Spain was followed by an intermittent hundred years' war with France that included the dynastic War of the Grand Alliance of William of Orange against Louis XIV, the War of the Spanish Succession, the War of the Austrian Succession, and the Seven Years' War; and all of these lay behind the continued fighting of the French and Indian Wars on the American frontier.

In the final test, France failed to second its great colonial leaders. Few settlers came, and their loyalty was to the old France rather than to the new one. At the most not more than a hundred thousand French had to hold the line against a million and a half English colonists. The brilliant strategists who had planted the line of forts from the Saint Lawrence down the Ohio to the Mississippi were left ill-supported by the government at home. Finally, the dream of empire wholly passed away in the British capture of Quebec and Montreal and the French surrender of Canada. From 1763 to 1776 the whole of the vast Atlantic coast land was British.

2. *The English Colonies*

A gleam of romance lights the first pages of the history of the English colonies, romance quite different from that of the Spaniards or the French, and quickly turned to prose. It began four years before the defeat of the Armada, when expeditions sponsored by Sir Walter Raleigh made temporary settlements on the central section of the Atlantic Coast, named Virginia in honor of the Virgin Queen. In spite of their failure, the same marshy shoreland was chosen for the first successful colony, founded in 1607 at Jamestown, under James I; but when disaster threatened, these young gentlemen, having as yet no slaves to work for them, flexed their muscles to the ax and spade, and the great solution for America was found—work. The town was laid out with a little street of huts, a fort, and a church, while thickets and woods were cleared for garden and farm.

Captain John Smith, writing to England in the name of his fellow settlers, asked that they should be sent "carpenters, husbandmen, fishermen, blacksmiths, masons and diggers up of roots." Later on, William Byrd, founder of a great Virginia family, followed John Smith's admonitions by pouring ridicule upon the idlers who expected to live in luxury without work. Realism, which abounds in English history, was never more soundly stated or applied. The result was the incredible growth of prosperity as the farm lands of Virginia produced, among other things, the one new product of which Europe was becoming an ever-increasing consumer, tobacco. Then cotton began its reign, as the tidewater estates grew wealthy in their favored economy, with ships loading at private wharves in an ever-expanding commerce, bringing in slaves, destined in the years ahead to falsify the whole basis of society so promising in its beginnings.

The gay temper of these New World cavaliers was not shared by the Puritans, whose first little ship, the *Mayflower*, landed on the bleak New England shore in December 1620. They had shown their stamina in giving up their English homes for conscience' sake, seeking refuge in the one country of Europe where religious toleration was practiced, Holland. This little settlement of artisans and businessmen was only the beginning of a great Puritan exodus. By 1630 there were already two thousand of them in the rapidly growing towns of Boston and Salem. While the soil was poor, the sea was rich with cod, and, as a reminder of its importance, a golden codfish still surmounts the state capitol at Boston.

The Puritans accepted the rigors of pioneer life as the conditions which enabled them to safeguard, in their own democratic way, their right to their own religion. Work was not the curse of Eden but the way to win it back. So the fishermen and the seafaring population of the coast and the farmers of the rocky New England fields made a hardy race of settlers. On the frontier, adventuring into the wilderness, but clearing as they went, they showed their respect for intelligence by setting up the first system of popular education in the world. This, with the founding of Harvard College, was mainly for religious instruction, but there was a thrifty sense of its value for this world as well.

Midway along the Atlantic Coast, the greatest harbor and river were settled by the Dutch, equally sturdy in holding their own, proud of the great role played by their little nation in challenging the might of Spain and France, and, when the fortunes of war with England went against them, loyally if reluctantly accepting their place in the colony of New York. Many of them had been Huguenot refugees who had sought asylum in the land of toleration, Holland, and they added a sturdy strain to the colonial life of the New World. But they were far behind the English in the institutions of freedom, with their semi-feudal baronies along the Hudson and their absence of representative government.

Along the middle coast, there were German and other Continental settlers seeking freedom from oppression and finding both freedom and contentment. Outstanding among their neighbors were the Quakers of Pennsylvania and New Jersey, following upon William Penn's treaty with the Indians and building their own commonwealth under his benign guidance. Their ideals of peace were never sullied by lack of thrift, for a good Christian must also be a good member of his society. The busy seaport of Philadelphia soon began to rival Boston and New York as a center of commerce.

The southern colonies had their peculiar economy. Although Jamestown began with the accent on work, it was not long until a leisured class was living on great estates. Farther south, where cotton was already on its way to becoming "king," slavery was increasing ominously. The life of the planters was a mixture of English squirearchy and slaveholding autocracy. On the uplands, behind the tidewater lands, the Scotch-Irish added another strain, stern, uncompromising, daring, born to hardship, but rising to power. To the south lay Georgia, settled by the poorer Englishmen, for whom the philanthropist James Oglethorpe arranged a home, which could also serve to hold back the Spanish of Florida.

By the end of the seventeenth century, all these colonies along the Atlantic seaboard came under English rule, but the political ties of each with England did not bind the colonies together into an "American nation" for almost another hundred years. Cross-country travel was difficult owing to the lack of good roads. The lure of the Old World was greater than the attractions of neighbors with less to offer in culture or luxury. From the first, however, there were three forces making for common nationality, the hard, unending task of hewing homes out of the wilderness; the sharing of the dangers of frontier wars; and, for most of them, the political heritage of English freedom.

It was this last influence in Colonial history which was destined to be decisive. From the first, the English settlers had shown their political-mindedness. The little company on the *Mayflower* had its own compact before landing.

The Massachusetts Bay Company's charter, brought with its first settlers, gave legal title to the first English commonwealth abroad. Even a few years earlier, the first charter of Virginia had declared that its settlers were to have all the rights of Englishmen, the protection of Magna Charta and the common law. In both colonies the legislatures grew in power and in 1639 the freemen of a new colony, Connecticut, drew up the first constitution written by the settlers themselves. A quarter of a century later, Rhode Island became almost a republic under the Crown. The framework of Colonial government varied somewhat, but all followed a general model. Naturally, they developed an alert public opinion to assert the colonists' insistence on their rights, especially when the royal governors seemed careless of them. But, in spite of strains and stress, their loyalty could be counted on as long as the colonists felt their security imperiled in the French and Indian Wars.

3. *The Great Duel Ends*

While the great duel between the English and French in America was linked with wars in Europe, the seaboard colonists were chiefly embittered against the French because of their share in massacres by their Indian allies. After the early Colonial days, the fighting shifted from New England to the hinterland that lay between the waterways of the Hudson and Saint Lawrence, over to Lake Ontario. There, the rival confederacies of Algonquins and Iroquois furnished savage allies for each side. The frontiersmen took their place alongside the redcoats in attacking the French through the outlying screen of ambush and forest fighting, but they were not present at the last act of the great drama. William Pitt, England's great war minister, decided to strike directly at the French citadel of Quebec, and there, on the Plains of Abraham, English and French regular troops, lined up as on parade, in the manner best approved in the military manuals, fired volleys at each other in a contest of discipline and marksmanship. Both generals, Wolfe and Montcalm, were killed, but the French broke and ran, and the New World empire of France was at an end. There were still some other posts to overrun, as at Montreal, but the century-long conflict for sovereignty on the Eastern seaboard of the continent was over.

CHAPTER VII

THE STRUGGLE
FOR INDEPENDENCE

For the Old World the overseas colonies were "possessions" to be exploited, both by the colonists and by the
mother countries which held the title to the land by discovery and conquest. But the colonists from England brought
with them traditions of self-government. Even in the cabin
of the *Mayflower*, they made their "compact" as free men
and citizens of their own community. The colonies varied
in the extent of their rights, but as they grew in wealth and
population they grew increasingly self-reliant and conscious of their rights as Englishmen to the liberties which
had been won in the great revolution which established
the limited monarchy in England. When they refused to
pay taxes imposed on them without their consent, they
found an obdurate king in George III and a servile Parliament which refused to listen to their protests, even when
championed by its greatest statesman, William Pitt, Earl
of Chatham. So opposition became rebellion, and rebellion,
revolution.

Thus a new nation was born, drawing its inspiration from
the rights of Englishmen and the school for freedom in pioneer life, dedicated to the maintenance of liberty and the
institutions of democracy.

1. *The New British Empire*

In the year 1763 Great Britain became a world empire, by
the surrender to it of the French overseas empires in Amer-

ica and India. But the cost of wars and the burden of empire were heavy. The national debt reached a height unknown in history, and the island kingdom, with a population of a few millions, had to maintain a large fleet and a standing army to protect its far-flung frontiers. It, therefore, seemed right that the colonists should pay their share of this protection. The colonists thought so, too. But who was to determine what their fair share should be? This raised the central question in all English history, and it had been decided in the century-long struggle for freedom from royal tyranny: the people who paid should say how much, by their control of taxation. For the power to vote money is the power to govern.

The issue was raised at once. In 1764, the first year of the new British Empire, three momentous acts were passed. The smuggling of foreign goods by New England merchants was put down and the seas patrolled to enforce the law. The largest investor in this illegal trade was John Hancock, of Boston, whose name was to lead the others on the Declaration of Independence. The second act settled a standing army of ten thousand men to maintain the laws of the mother country and enforce its acts—a violation of one of the most fundamental rights won by the English people against the Stuart kings. The third measure was the Stamp Act, extending to the colonies this apparently easy way of collecting taxes. Surprised by the vehement protests of the colonists, Parliament withdrew the act, but asserted its right to pass it.

Two systems of government were in open conflict. The ideals of freedom, on which the British constitution had been founded, were now championed by the colonists, strengthened by the restless vigor of life in the New World. At home, the Mother of Parliaments, at this fateful hour, failed to apply to its empire overseas the very principles upon which it was founded. By an incredible turn in its long and noble history, the guardian of liberty became an instrument of tyranny under a king too vain and too stupid to understand what he was doing.

2. The New American Nation

The colonies differed greatly among themselves—Puritan, commercial New Englanders, the country gentry of Virginia along the seacoast, and the sturdy, pioneering settlers of the interior. There were Tory Royalists in New York and Philadelphia and on great estates; there were radicals working their way up from poverty on the farms and in the workshops. But a common sense of human rights ran through the whole people, responding quickly to the call of committees of safety and correspondence, binding them together in the first national movement. In the Virginia House of Burgesses the ringing eloquence of Patrick Henry and the sober but stern voice of Thomas Jefferson challenged the authority of the home government, and in Massachusetts Samuel Adams led the rising resistance. In the next ten years, things went from bad to worse, and finally, in 1774, the First Continental Congress took the necessary measures for joint action by the colonies, while events moved ominously toward war.

3. Rebellion, Then Revolution

On April 19, 1775, at Lexington, a small village between Boston and Concord, the "embattled farmers" fired at the marching redcoats "the shot heard round the world." At least it was heard throughout the colonies. The Second

Continental Congress, meeting in Philadelphia, enrolled twenty thousand volunteers, and George Washington was appointed commander. Before he could arrive in Cambridge, however, the Battle of Bunker Hill had been fought.

From New England the tide of war swept over all the colonies and north into Canada, and with it a compelling sense that they were no longer rebels against a tyrannical government, but the founders of a new nation, free and independent. Virginia led, both in its own convention and in the Continental Congress, linked closely with Massachusetts. Finally, on July 4, 1776, the Declaration of Independence, framed mostly in Jefferson's words, proclaimed the advent of the United States of America. Boldly, it challenged, not merely the tyranny of George III, but the public opinion of the world. Neither time nor the changed circumstances of future centuries will ever blot from the memory of mankind these imperishable words:

> We hold these truths to be self-evident that all men are created equal; that they are endowed by their Creator with certain unalienable Rights; that among these are Life, Liberty and the pursuit of Happiness. That to secure these rights, Governments are instituted among Men, deriving their just powers from the consent of the governed. . . .

On such a basis, the United States of America was founded. The usurpations of George III had shown him to be a tyrant, "unfit to govern a free people," and Parliament had refused redress.

> WE, THEREFORE, the Representatives of the United States of America, in General Congress, Assembled, appealing to the Supreme Judge of the world for the rectitude of our

intentions, do, in the Name and by Authority of the good People of these Colonies, solemnly publish and declare, That these United Colonies are, and of Right ought to be Free and Independent States. ... And for the support of this Declaration, with a firm reliance on the protection of Divine Providence, we mutually pledge to each other, our Lives, our Fortunes, and our sacred Honor.

Independence had been proclaimed; it had still to be won on the field of battle, and the war was going badly for the Revolution. It was not until Christmas 1776 that Washington, driven out of New York and over the Delaware, turned back to overwhelm his pursuers in 'surprise attacks. He held them at bay, while the British lost their chance to conquer the Hudson Valley by the defeat of General John Burgoyne at Saratoga. This proved to be the turning point of the war, for France, convinced at last that the colonists had a chance, came in as an ally. This was also the very time, however, when Washington's fortunes seemed at lowest ebb, after the defeat at Brandywine and during the terrible winter at Valley Forge. Through the months and years which followed, the indomitable spirit of their commander steeled the Revolutionary army to battle against all odds. Finally, the French, with both fleet and army, joined in the attack upon the beleaguered army of General Charles Cornwallis at Yorktown, and forced his surrender on October 19, 1781. The bells of Philadelphia rang out their message of victory. The war of the "embattled farmers" was not quite over, but the outcome was settled. By the Treaty of Paris, signed on September 3, 1783, Great Britain acknowledged the United States as a sovereign nation.

CHAPTER VIII

——◆——

THE CONSTITUTION

"We, the people of the United States, in order to establish a more perfect Union, establish justice, insure domestic tranquillity, provide for the common defense, promote the general welfare, and secure the blessings of liberty to ourselves and to our posterity, do ordain and establish this Constitution for the United States of America."

In these words, remembered and treasured by succeeding generations, the Preamble to the Constitution defined the purposes of the government of a free people, in whose name the Founding Fathers spoke.

The creation of a federal state was a great new experiment, a supreme test of statesmanship, for the Old World offered no models to go by. That the compromise in sovereignty between the central government and the governments of the states was not completely accepted was made clear by disputes of the next half century and the tragedy of the Civil War. But the nation survived and the Constitution was preserved and strengthened as "the supreme law of the land."

1. *The Articles of Confederation*

On June 7, 1776, Richard Henry Lee of Virginia introduced three resolutions in Congress, which mark the first milestone in the history of the United States. They were: (1) that the thirteen colonies were and ought to be free and independent; (2) that foreign alliances should be made; and (3) that steps be taken to adopt a general plan of confederation. Within a week Congress took action. On June 11, only one day after the appointment of the committee to draft the Declaration of Independence, a committee was set up to prepare a plan for the constitution of the United States. Under the pressure of war the alliance was becoming a nation. It now had to form a state. But the task proved too hard for speedy action and it was not until November 1777 that the Articles of Confederation were adopted. This first constitution made of the union a mere league of states; the powers of Congress were limited to little more than foreign affairs, coinage, posts, and roads. Its revenues were to be requisitioned upon the states, not upon individuals. There was no separate executive; the president of Congress was to hold office for one year, and he had no veto power. There was no federal judiciary. The "Union" was only a "firm league of friendship," in which each state retained "its sovereignty, freedom and independence." Only near the end was it stated that "the Union shall be perpetual." It read like an afterthought.

2. *The Constitution*

For ten years the young republic lived under this weak confederacy, but it was rapidly falling into anarchy, with no sanction to its laws, with commerce between the states blocked by conflicting regulations and customs dues, and a currency practically worthless. Therefore, by 1787, Congress approved a call for a convention "for the sole and express purpose of revising the Articles of Confederation" to remedy its defects and "render the federal constitution adequate to the exigencies of Government and the preservation of the Union." But the convention which met in Philadelphia in May 1787, or a majority of it, saw clearly that a wholly new form of government was needed, and four months later, by what amounted to a revolutionary act, it submitted to conventions within the states, instead of to their legislatures, the text of an entirely new constitution.

It was a document without parallel in history. But while there were no models to go by in the shaping of the federal union for the new nation—for even Switzerland, that miracle of democratic statesmanship, had not yet achieved its final form—yet no other form of government was possible. The makers of the Constitution did not have a blank paper to write on; for each of the thirteen colonies had history behind it, and throughout most of that history had acted on its own. The pattern of the past was clear, a system of commonwealths was already at hand; no other system could be invented than that which built the nation within a federal framework. Moreover, it was the only framework fitted to be applied to the expanding nation, as new communities were founded along the ever-moving frontier, for it both recognized local liberties along with responsibility for law and order and drew from the contact with the daily life of the common man lessons for national statesmanship.

The Constitutional Convention was composed of men with profound convictions. While the Federalists, as they were called, insisted on the need for a strong national union, with an effective government, their democratic, or "Republican," opponents voiced the fear of domination by large states over the smaller ones and by commerce and capital over farmers and artisans. It was a division which, in one form or another, has lasted through all the history of the Republic. Fortunately, the members of the Constitutional Convention were more than brilliant debaters or narrow partisans; they combined their convictions with the vision of statesmanship, profiting from the wise and experienced diplomacy of Benjamin Franklin, the studied arguments of James Madison, and the calm, judicious temper of the chairman, George Washington. Wisely, the Founding Fathers carried on their debates in secrecy. Fortunately, Madison, "the Father of the Constitution," kept careful notes, which were published half a century later, and we can follow the battle between the large and small states point by point until the final compromise was reached on Franklin's proposal that membership in the Senate should be based on equality of the states, but in the lower house on population.

Next to the jealous rivalry of the states came the safeguards against the tyranny of government. The prerogatives of the federal government were divided by "the separation of the powers" among the executive, legislative, and judicial branches. This was the lesson drawn from English history by the French jurist Montesquieu. His history was faulty, for in England Parliament became both executive and legislative. But the American system of "checks and balances" was the very heart of the plan of federal government for that "more perfect union" which Washington hailed as the culmination of the long struggle for freedom: the president to conduct foreign affairs and to administer the laws passed by the Congress, and the Supreme Court and a federal judiciary to safeguard the country against any violation of the Constitution.

3. *The Bill of Rights*

The great debate on the Constitution was carried on out-side the Convention as well as within it. In the *Federalist Papers*, a series of some eighty-five long articles published in New York between October 1787 and May 1788, Hamilton, Madison, and Jay expounded and supported with classic eloquence the principles on which the new government was founded. But powerful as these papers were in logic and in practical statesmanship, they were in support of decisions most of which were already taken or concerned with acts already done. Quite different was the work of those who, while accepting the Constitution as a necessary structure for government, demanded that it include as well definite guarantees of the rights of citizens against any possible tyranny by government, guarantees of freedom of religion, speech, and the press, and the protection of life, liberty, and property by due process of law.

The Bill of Rights has a history of its own. In the first of all American constitutions, that of Virginia, which preceded the Declaration of Independence by a short time, George Mason, deeply imbued with English ideas of freedom, inserted a Bill of Rights, prefaced by a chal-lenge like that of the Declaration of Independence, that "all men . . . have certain inherent rights of which they cannot by any Compact deprive or divest their posterity; among which are life and liberty with the means of ac-quiring and possessing property, and pursuing and obtain-ing happiness and safety." Bills of rights, such as that to which these ringing words are a prelude, were incorpo-rated in the constitutions of seven of the revolting colo-nies. There was therefore a widespread trend toward these ideas, and when Madison sent the text of the Constitution to Jefferson, then minister to France, Jefferson wrote back that "a Bill of Rights is what the people are entitled to against every government on earth." The *Federalist*, in its eighty-fourth number, came out squarely for a bill of rights, and finally, on June 8, 1789, Madison himself rose in Congress to propose the first of ten amendments, which, rapidly adopted, became, when duly ratified, a substantial part of the original Constitution.

4. *The Supreme Court Becomes Supreme*

All history shows that the structure of the state, however well and truly made, is never complete, for it must be adjustable to an ever-changing world. It is for this reason that the British, practicing the most realistic statesmanship, matured through centuries of experience, have held to an unwritten constitution, and that the Constitution of the United States, which began its history by adding to the original document ten amendments in a Bill of Rights, safeguarding the citizen against government itself, has, by further amendment and interpretation remained a vital organ of the will of a nation at grips with destiny, and not the rigid embodiment of outworn issues. But how could the Constitution serve as the symbol and embodiment of sovereignty if there were any doubt about where sovereignty lay? How build the allied colonies into a state capable of making treaties with other sovereign nations and yet preserve local governments in the framework of the provinces?

The Constitution takes for granted the division of the powers of government into three separate organs, executive, legislative, and judicial, but, while it defines the functions of each of them, it wisely avoids any detailed provisions for their interrelations. It was apparently taken for granted at first that as their functions were parallel, each acting within its own field, their place in the structure of government would also be parallel. But views along this line, while strongly held by Jefferson and the anti-Federalists, were countered by decisions of the Supreme Court itself, under the leadership of one of the greatest jurists and statesmen in the history of the United States, John Marshall, chief justice from 1801 until his death in 1835. By a liberal interpretation of the Constitution, he established the right of the Court to be the final judge of the constitutionality of all acts of federal and state governments and thus made it the guardian of the rights and the freedom of the citizen. The impress of Marshall's mind on the subsequent history of the Constitution is unparalleled in the history of modern law.

CHAPTER IX

THE NEW NATION

The wilderness was sovereign when the white man came.
It had overcome the Indian and made him its creature. Our
fathers accepted its challenge and with ringing ax cut their
clearings for the homes of a pioneering people. Danger
surrounded but never daunted them, until from sea to sea
they won sovereignty over soil and river, mountain and
plain, for themselves and their children's children.

But a nation is more than its homes, more than its farms
and cities. It is the living past, the unremembered things
that wear their grooves in the minds of men, like the rocks
in a glacial drift, as well as the conscious purpose and act
registered in history. It is, therefore, not strictly accurate
to speak of America as a new nation, for it brought rich
and varied experiences from the Old World to mingle with
those of the New. Yet, it was not long, seldom more than
a generation, before a new type of mind began to be molded
by the changed conditions of life in a land so unlike the
homeland of Europe. Even in feature as well as in manner,
the American emerged on the great stage of world history,
at first hardly aware of what had taken place, then self-
reliant in the mastering of his fate.

1. *The Conquest of a Continent*

Everywhere along the frontier the settlers took up the
challenge of the continent. From the forests of Canada
to the uplands of Georgia they moved steadily westward

along the trails where the hunter and the trapper had first penetrated the wilderness. They pierced the Appalachians at every pass from the Cherry Valley by the Mohawk to the Cumberland Gap that opened into the bluegrass country of Kentucky, to meet in the rich river basin of the Ohio. With no one to rely on but themselves, they faced undaunted the lurking dangers of hostile Indians and the hardships and sufferings of pioneer life, clearing the forests for their fields and planting settlements along the pathway of their advance. Some of their leaders had names that will be forever legendary in the romance of America. Such a one was the pathfinder Daniel Boone. Some of those born in the log cabins by the clearings were destined to play great parts in the nation's history; and some to make history for all time, like Abraham Lincoln.

As the settlers came pouring through the Appalachians down the rivers and overland in an ever-growing invasion, clearing the forests and draining the swamps, they found some of the richest farm lands in the world. But to make these safe for settlement, new Indian wars had to be fought, like those of Colonial days. In the presidency of Washington, who had been an Indian fighter in his youth, Anthony Wayne defeated the Indians and forced them to give up the territory now in the state of Ohio. But the whole territory from the Great Lakes to the Ohio and Mississippi, the old Northwest, was not cleared of danger until the final defeat of the last great chieftain, Tecumseh, in the War of 1812. Then the tide of migration gathered momentum; villages grew into towns and towns into cities, among them Chicago. Beyond the forests lay the wide prairies, mostly treeless except in the river courses, an unending stage for new dramas of endurance and adventure, creased with the wagon wheels of caravans moving ever farther west.

2. The Louisiana Purchase

Into the long reaches of the Mississippi Valley the wagons of the pioneers kept pushing the frontier westward with ever-increasing strength. The Ohio River became an artery of trade. The settlers planted their log cabins mile by mile along the river fronts and the newly opened roads. But the Mississippi itself was not free, for it was a boundary river, and beyond it, the Spanish, then the French, held it and the territory west of it over to the Rocky Mountains, while the great port New Orleans was in French hands.

In 1803 this vast territory, as large as western Europe, was bought from Napoleon by President Jefferson, approximately a million square miles for less than three cents an acre. Thirteen states of the Union were to be carved out of it, and New Orleans, the Queen City of the South, opened the gateway of commerce for the lands across the Alleghenies until the Erie Canal was built some twenty years later, and then the railroads began to span the river valleys east and west.

3. The War of 1812

England, in her desperate struggle with Napoleon, searched American ships for English sailors. Napoleon did the same, but the British navy was supreme at sea and was guilty of impressing several thousand American seamen. An embargo against British trade and nonintercourse acts failed to bring redress. Both Jefferson and his successor, Madison, were opposed to war, but the war hawks of the frontier states, led by Henry Clay, were eager for the conquest of Canada and forced a declaration of war on Great Britain, against the bitter opposition of the New Englanders whose commerce was profiting from the European war and who were jealous of the rising political power of the new Middle West.

The invasion of Canada failed, but left Canadians with a bitter memory. The government buildings at York (Toronto) were burned and in retaliation the British burned the Capitol at Washington.

The battles at sea were memorable for heroic exploits, but the greatest naval victory was won on the peaceful waters of Lake Erie, where Commodore Perry defeated a small British fleet. At New Orleans, Jackson's frontiersmen defeated the British veterans who had fought against Napoleon. The war settled nothing and the treaty left the issues still unsettled except for the fact that Canada remained apart from the United States.

The futility of the war led, however, to a great experiment in enduring peace along an undefended frontier. Although forts were held for years at strategic points, the Great Lakes were disarmed, and, as years went on, this symbol of mutual confidence was extended over the whole three thousand miles of frontier—three thousand miles of lake and river, of prairie and mountain range, without a soldier, without a gun, except in the joint maintenance of a common peace—a model of international good will for all mankind.

4. *The Settlement of the Great Plains and the Far Northwest*

The great age of the explorers was not over yet. Although settlements had sprung up on the pathway of La Salle and Père Marquette, the discoverer of the Mississippi, in the continent beyond it the earlier heroism of the East was repeated when Lewis and Clark led their expeditions over the Rockies half a century before those far-off regions were settled .

As it had been in the East, the fur traders pushed their posts into the wilderness, and great companies competed with each other from Hudson Bay on the north to Saint Louis on the south. Fighting or mingling with the Indians, the hunters and trappers led the advance; following them came the settlers with their ox-drawn caravans and other wagons. On many a lonely battlefield the Indians ambushed the invaders and fought savagely to stop the westward movement, which, with steady, irresistible, glacierlike power, pushed them from the richest lands that lay along the line of advance. The old buffalo ranges became cattle ranches and then fenced fields of wheat and corn. For the cattlemen were only the scouts of a nation, and the sod cabins that dotted the plains were made into homes by the heroic men and women who shared the hardships and perils of pioneer life.

Beyond the mountains, north of Spanish California, lay the Oregon country, held by the early traders of the Columbia River against their rivals of the Hudson's Bay Company, awaiting the opening of the trail from the East, along whose route Mormons wrote their epic of sturdy fortitude.

5. Manifest Destiny

Missouri was at the parting of the two trails, the Oregon to the north and the Santa Fe to the southwest. Here Thomas Benton gave the country its vision of the "manifest destiny" of a free nation to the Rockies and beyond, but instead of his ideal of peaceful expansion, there were two wars with Mexico, one between Mexico and Texas and one between Mexico and the United States. The heroic sacrifices of the Texans in the Alamo were avenged at the Battle of San Jacinto, and the Republic of Texas, which had declared its independence of Mexico in 1836, was admitted into the United States by Congress in 1845. But boundary disputes brought the next war with the United States. The invasions of Mexico ended in the capture of its heroically defended capital; while the conquest of California and some further changes in the frontier gave the United States its continental boundaries.

The Mexican War left Mexico with bitter resentment, long remembered; but in the treaty of peace there was a provision which went even further than any formal treaty with Canada: all future disputes between Mexico and the United States should be settled by arbitration. This clause in the Treaty of Guadalupe Hidalgo was to be of value in crises in the twentieth century.

6. California

A touch of romance lay upon the origins of California. There was the memory of Spain in sunlit hills and in mission bells calling across the great estates. There were gracious manners of an Old World society strangely at variance with those of the hardy pioneers who came over the Rockies into the sunlit valleys between the mountains and the sea. The war with Mexico brought American sovereignty to California and, by the strangest chance, in the very year of the Treaty of Guadalupe Hidalgo, 1848, pebbles of gold were picked out of the gravelly bed of Sutter Creek, near Sacramento. The news traveled fast and far, and the gold rush of 1849, by land and by sea, changed California with magic swiftness. San Francisco grew almost overnight to a city of fabulous happenings. Every California stream was washed for gold and every outcropping of rock tapped by the hammer of the prospector. There was also wealth in the rich soil and in the merchandising of goods for careless spenders. In 1850 California entered the Union as a "free" state, to balance the possible extension of slavery through the territories east of it. In 1869 a golden spike, driven into a railroad tie, joined the Central Pacific Railway of California with the Union Pacific from the east, and California entered fully into the history of the United States.

CHAPTER X

A NATION DIVIDED

Steadily, unchecked, irresistible, the movement of the American people spread their homes over the vast reaches of the continent; but midway in its career, the heroism of this great exploit was turned into a tragic struggle, which will forever darken and yet glorify the annals of America. The conflict had been long in the making. Time and time again the far-flung fabric of federal union had to stand the strain of diverse interests: frontiersmen against the "money power" of the seaboard cities, the agrarian South against the industrialized North. Already, in Washington's Farewell Address, secession was first of those listed in the warnings of dangers confronting the republic. "It is of infinite moment that you should properly estimate the immense value of your national union to your collective and individual happiness; that you should cherish a cordial, habitual and immovable attachment to it; accustoming yourselves to think and speak of it as the palladium of your political safety and prosperity; watching for its preservation with jealous anxiety; discountenancing whatever may suggest even a suspicion that it can in any way be abandoned, and indignantly frowning upon the first dawning of every attempt to alienate any portion of our country from the rest or to enfeeble the sacred ties which now link together the various parts."

1. *Sovereign States or Sovereign Nation*

The "first dawning" of disruptive politics was not long delayed. Aaron Burr's conspiracy to set up a state of his own in the Louisiana Territory was followed shortly by threats from New England that it might forcibly resist President Madison's Nonintercourse Act, by which he hoped to avoid war with England. But these were minor incidents in the current of American history. Much more serious was the cleavage between North and South as revealed in the fight over the tariff—which was bitterly opposed by the South. It rallied to the support of South Carolina's threat to nullify the federal law, while the North equally rallied behind Daniel Webster's famous call to the loyalty for which Washington had pleaded: "Liberty and Union, now and forever, one and insepara- ble." Meanwhile, behind these debates in Congress, the power of the central government was quietly but firmly defined and established by the greatest of American ju- rists, John Marshall, who held the office of chief justice of the Supreme Court from 1801 to 1835 and made it "the living voice of the Constitution" both in strengthen- ing the federal government and in safeguarding the rights and liberties of the citizens against abuse of its power. Never was politics more soundly based upon the rule of law; and never has history more clearly shown that the rule of law is not enough unless it guarantees the rights of all. And slaves were, in the great essentials of civilized life, outside the law. Here, then, lay the gravest issue of all.

2. The Fundamental Issue, Slavery

It is one of the most incredible facts of history that a na- tion created as the home for freedom became the last home for slavery in the Western world. There had been no slavery in England since the early Middle Ages, and in 1772 the courts held that any slave setting foot on the soil of England was freed. The era of the French Revolution ended slavery on the Continent. But in the colonies slavery continued, and it grew to terrible proportions in the southern states, prospering by the inventions in cotton manufacture and sugar production. The greatest of the Founding Fathers, at least, were opposed to it: Washington, whose slaves were emancipated in his will, and Jefferson, who drafted the plan for keeping slavery out of the Northwest Territory—an act which probably was to save the Union in the Civil War. But the South, with its great estates, could only keep its balance of power with the growing industries of the North if it were allowed to expand as the lands opened up across the Mississippi. To head off the threatening conflict of interests between the free-soilers and slaveowners, in the Compromise of 1820 Missouri was admitted as a slave-owning state to balance the entry of Maine, while slavery was prohibited in the Louisiana Purchase north of Missouri's southern boundary. John Quincy Adams wrote in his diary, "I take it for granted that the present question is a mere preamble, a title page to a great tragic volume." The day of decision was postponed, but the issue grew as the nation expanded, and the territory taken from Mexico had to be brought into balance by the Compromise of 1850. It was passed by Congress after the greatest debates in its history, by the greatest debaters, John Calhoun, Henry Clay, and Daniel Webster, whose voices were to be heard no more, while the Fugitive Slave Law stirred the embers of conflict into flames in the North. The effort of Stephen Douglas to compromise once more by squatter sovereignty was no solution, and the final word was spoken by Abraham Lincoln, when, addressing the convention which nominated him in 1858, he said, "A house divided against itself cannot stand. I believe this government cannot permanently endure half slave and half free."

Nevertheless, the secession movement, led at first by South Carolina, swept over the states of the Deep South, where "Cotton was king" and slavery a basic fact in economic life. In February 1861 delegates of these states met in Montgomery, Alabama, and formed a provisional government for the "Confederate States of America," electing Jefferson Davis President. The final constitution, adopted in March, was largely copied from the constitution of the United States, only expressly maintaining state sovereignty. The Border states, of which the most important was Virginia, hesitated to join, but when the Federal Government called on them for troops to suppress the rebellion, Robert E. Lee of Virginia became commander in chief of the Confederacy forces.

3. War

Lincoln's Inaugural Address gave the country the measure of the man to whom its destinies were entrusted in the hour of crisis. He denied any thought of disturbing the institutions of the South, but declared that he must uphold the laws of the nation. "In your hands, my dissatisfied fellow-countrymen, not in mine, is the momentous issue of civil war. . . . You have no oath registered in heaven to destroy the government, while I have the most solemn one to 'preserve, protect and defend it.' " The common memories of the North and South were "mystic chords stretching from every battlefield and patriot grave to every living heart and hearthstone all over this broad land." But before dawn on April 12, 1861, the Confederates at Charleston fired on Fort Sumter in its harbor and forced its surrender the next day. From that hour until the final scene of Lee's surrender at Appomattox, the country suffered four years of the terrible scourges of civil war.

The hopes of the Confederacy ran high as Lee and his lieutenants—"Stonewall" Jackson, James Longstreet, Jeb Stuart, and others—outfought the northern armies. But his invasion of Maryland was turned back on the bloody field of Antietam, and then Lincoln judged the time had come to issue his Emancipation Proclamation freeing the slaves in all states "in rebellion against the United States." The war for the Union could now also be a crusade for freedom, and the "Battle Hymn of the Republic" a marching song with a new meaning. Then the tragedy deepened, as Lee and Jackson threw back the northern armies at Fredericksburg and Chancellorsville, until finally the flood tide of the Confederacy was rolled back across the wheat fields of Gettysburg, carpeted with the dead. On the day after the battle, Grant took Vicksburg and, as Lincoln put it, "the Father of Waters flowed untroubled to the sea." Gratefully, Lincoln revived the old New England institution of a day of Thanksgiving, setting it on the last Thursday of November.

Though terribly defeated, the South fought on, but when Sherman marched three hundred miles through Georgia, from Atlanta to the sea, and Grant, unmoved by the slaughter of his troops in the Wilderness, moved around Richmond and captured it, Lee surrendered at Appomattox. It was April 9, 1865. On the fourteenth of April Lincoln was shot. The nation's rejoicing over victory was turned into mourning for the lost leader.

The meaning of the conflict had been expressed for all time in the immortal words of the Gettysburg Address:

> Fourscore and seven years ago our fathers brought forth on this continent a new nation, conceived in liberty and dedicated to the proposition that all men are created equal. Now we are engaged in a great civil war, testing whether that nation or any nation so conceived and so dedicated, can long endure. We are met on a great battlefield of that war. We have come to dedicate a portion of that field, as a final resting-place for those who here gave their lives that that nation might live. It is altogether fitting and proper that we should do this. But, in a larger sense, we cannot dedicate—we cannot consecrate—we cannot hallow—this ground. The brave men, living and dead, who struggled here, have consecrated it, far above our poor power to add or detract. The world will little note, nor long remember, what we say here, but it can never forget what they did here. It is for us the living, rather, to be dedicated here to the unfinished work which they who fought here have thus far so nobly advanced. It is rather for us to be here dedicated to the great task remaining before us—that from these honored dead we take increased devotion to that cause for which they gave the last full measure of devotion—that we here highly resolve that these dead shall not have died in vain—that this nation, under God, shall have a new birth of freedom—and that government of the people, by the people, for the people, shall not perish from the earth.

4. The Aftermath of the War

The aftermath of civil war is always a moral catastrophe for the victors as well as for the defeated. So it was in the English Restoration after Cromwell's day, in the Bourbon "white terror" after the red terror of the French Revolution, in the cruelties of the Holy Alliance in its suppression of republicanism and of the reactionaries in the suppression of revolutionary movements in Europe in 1848. But as the "War between the States" drew to a close, it looked at first as though the laws of history might not apply here. General Grant's generous terms at the surrender of the southern armies at Appomattox, where there was no humiliation and the officers and men were to take their horses home "for the spring plowing," were matched by all of Lincoln's words in his noble Second Inaugural—"with charity for all and malice toward none" —and his charge to his Cabinet the very day he was shot, "I hope there will be no persecution. . . . We must extinguish resentments if we expect harmony and union." But the promise of such high statesmanship was completely lost in the saddest episode of United States history, a highhanded "reconstruction" of the South, which lasted for a decade and more and left a much deeper resentment than the war itself.

The South showed little opposition to the first phase of northern rule, that by generals of the occupying army; for the war had made it familiar with military necessities. But in the years that followed there were two unpardonable blunders. One was the imposition of civilian rule by "carpetbag" politicians, often corrupt and seldom fit company for the cultured southern families. But the most serious problem was what to do about the Negroes. Here, Lincoln had been ready to do what other nations had done, compensate the slaveowners for the loss of their property; but they had not had to do this after a war which had cost the country so much in blood and treasure—the point which makes Lincoln's offer unique. The

South did not expect generosity, but it had a right to expect that the Negroes should be prepared for citizenship before it was granted to them. This is what the North did not do, passing at once from the Thirteenth Amendment to the Constitution, abolishing slavery, in 1865, to the Fourteenth the next year, making all native-born persons citizens with equal rights under the law. Although the North as a whole was not vindictive in its treatment of the South, the "radicals" in Congress were; and angered in their helplessness, the southerners took the law in their own hands in the Ku-Klux Klan and other vigilante movements. By a law of nature, the children who grew up under Reconstruction were more bitter than the wartime generation. It was not until a new industrial era gave new interests to the whole country that the wounds of war and misrule were slowly healed. Again, we find here a law of nature, important to be kept in mind in the cold war against communism: the one sure way to end animosities is to acquire new interests which lead to a new outlook on life.

CHAPTER XI

FROM ISOLATION TO WORLD POWER

Until the closing years of the nineteenth century the people of the United States felt isolated from the rest of the world. The oceans were still perilous and shipwrecks frequent. For the children of the immigrants, Europe was far away, and Asia hardly more than a name. Absorbed in the conquest of the continent, in sectional disputes and civil war, they concentrated upon the task of building a single nation out of its varied elements and left the nations of the Old World to solve their problems in their own way. For the builders of a nation must keep at their own tasks, great or small, and not turn aside from them to lose themselves in adventures that distract their attention and lessen their strength. The greatest of all nation building was that which was linking up the scattered homes of newly opened countrysides, providing schools and churches as their first need, preserving order and establishing law based on the precepts of the past and their own experience of pioneer life.

1. *Isolation*

There are two forces today that are contending for the mastery over the civilized world. One is the force of nationalism, deep-rooted in common loyalties and in the prejudices that spring from the soil of wars and antagonisms; the other is the force of community interests that build through the nation into the structure of an ordered world. The one is strong with all the past; the other, with strength untried, looks to the future.

Until the twentieth century it was only nationalism that counted. "Internationalism" was an insubstantial dream, held only by altruists, and even at times a term of reproach. It played no part in the stern business of politics. Then, as we shall see, the age of science began to change both time and space, creating new problems within and between nations; but although Americans took a major part in this greatest of all changes in human affairs, their political outlook remained held to the past, held within the framework of two gigantic geographic facts, the continent and the Atlantic. History has quite properly concentrated on the former, for it is the stage on which the drama was played, but the history of the Atlantic has never been written, although it was equally important, in a negative way. One has only to think what it would have meant to America if the wide reaches of the Atlantic, which mark its eastern frontier, were as narrow as the Rhine. Even the Channel protected England from invasion in the wars of the European continent. The Atlantic was America's shield and protection. It kept Europe far away, to become a nostalgic memory to those who left it never expecting to see it again, and a romantic dream to the native-born, brought up on Washington Irving and Sir Walter Scott.

The isolation of distance was not enough, however, even in Washington's day, to ensure detachment from such great European movements as the French Revolution and the wars resulting from it. Sympathy for France as the former ally brought grave disorders, which in turn called out stern measures of repression. It was with this

critical episode directly in mind that Washington's Farewell Address was issued, warning the American people
not to become involved in the political affairs of European
nations, because "our detached and distant situation invites and enables us to pursue a different course" from
theirs.

This text became the classic statement of American isolation, generally quoted out of its historical context as
an axiomatic, unalterable maxim for the guidance of later
generations. It was strengthened by other utterances of
the Founding Fathers. There is no other nation in the
world which begins its instruction in history by a recital
of a declaration of independence. Washington's precepts
were welded into a political program in Jefferson's First
Inaugural (1801). The Napoleonic Wars were then at
their disruptive height, overthrowing the established
order throughout continental Europe, but in America,
the new, great experiment of federal government, "the
world's best hope," was "kindly separated by nature and
a wide ocean from the exterminating havoc of one quarter
of the globe . . . [in] a chosen country, with room enough
for our descendants to the thousandth and thousandth
generation." With such a challenge and with the resources of the continent to meet it, it is small wonder that
Americans should from time to time protest that they did
not see what they had to do with "abroad."

2. The Eagle's Flight

It would be a misreading of history, however, to think
of the doctrine of isolation as purely negative. Although
the forces making for it were so strong as to make any
other outlook secondary, yet, as President Charles Eliot

of Harvard used to point out, the spirit of adventure, so strong from the days of the earliest settlers, was never lost by the American people—the last people in the world to accept barriers, natural or artificial, to the achievement of their "manifest destiny." Isolation was but another form of nationalism; upon the whole, the safest form of that most vital of political doctrines.

It was, therefore, not inconsistent that, in the year 1782, before the treaty of peace was signed with Great Britain, the United States should choose as its emblem the American eagle. The choice was meaningful. Eagles had been symbols of sovereignty all through history; but this was no fanciful creation of heraldry, it was the bird of the wilderness. Its westward flight had already begun; but, free as the air it rode, it followed no single course, and from time to time its shadow fell across northern or southern frontiers. We have already seen how ready it was to strike in the War of 1812, eagerly urged by the war hawks of the Middle West. Canada, the most intimate neighbor, was long suspect as a British colony and in its turn long suspected imperialist designs from across the border. It was not until after the Civil War that the strategy of peace between the two nations was finally worked out—forever. War with Mexico left much stronger animosities, with little effort at international understanding. In neither case did the United States develop a conscious and consistent foreign policy. Through the nineteenth century it had only one, the Monroe Doctrine, itself a document of isolation extending over the nations of the New World as a guarantee of freedom from interference by the nations of Europe.

3. *The Monroe Doctrine*

The history of the Monroe Doctrine carries us back almost to that same era of the French Revolution which lay behind the isolationist admonitions of Washington and Jefferson; but this time the warning was addressed not to the people of the United States but to the governments of Europe, or rather the reactionary governments which had joined the Holy Alliance to wipe out every last trace of liberal thought or institutions. The repression was especially cruel in Spain, and when it was proposed to extend it to America to crush the revolutionary movement which had begun in the Spanish colonies as a result of Napoleon's conquest of Spain itself, the threat was met by the message to Congress of President James Monroe on the second of December, 1823. After the familiar disclaimer of interference in European affairs, the message proceeded to its constructive doctrine of the solidarity of interest of the Americas:

In the wars of the European powers in matters relating to themselves we have never taken any part, nor does it comport with our own policy so to do. It is only when our rights are invaded or seriously menaced that we resent injuries and make preparations for our defense. With the movements in this hemisphere we are, of necessity, more immediately connected, and by causes which must be obvious to all enlightened and impartial observers. The political system of the allied powers [those in the Holy Alliance] is essentially different in this respect from that of America. . . . We owe it, therefore, to candor, and to the amicable relations existing between the United States and those powers, to declare that we should consider any attempt on their part to extend their system to any portion of this hemisphere as dangerous to our peace and safety.

This most American of documents was prompted in the first place by George Canning, the British Foreign Secretary, out of his intense opposition to the Holy Alliance. But he did not go far enough for Monroe, because he did not come out for independence of the Spanish colonies, and John Quincy Adams, President Monroe's Secretary of State, was opposed to having the United States "come in as a cock-boat in the wake of the British man-of-war." It should be added, however, that throughout the nineteenth century the only effective police force in the Atlantic against a possible combination of European powers was the British navy.

The section of the message dealing with the Spanish colonies was preceded by one directed to the head of the Holy Alliance himself, the Tsar Alexander I. Russia was warned not to extend its empire across the Pacific by colonizing the American coast, because "the American continents, by the free and independent condition which they have assumed and maintained, are henceforth not to be considered as subjects for future colonization by any European powers." The British government, said Monroe, had already acceded to a proposal similar to that now made to Russia, "to arrange by amicable negotiation the respective rights and interests of the two nations on the northwest coast of this continent." The final settlement of the Alaska boundary was long delayed, but ultimately carried through.

4. Peace with the Americas

The Monroe Doctrine was a shield against external aggression, but the Latin-American states did not use their newly won independence to further peace among themselves. On the contrary, their sensitiveness about national sovereignty kept them apart and caused constantly recurring hostilities. Even the efforts of Simón Bolívar, the liberator of the northern countries, and José de San Martín, the liberator of the south, clashed in the crisis of their careers. But there was one point on which their rival nationalisms were agreed, opposition to the extension of United States interests in Latin America. As time went on, the war with Mexico, followed later by expeditions in Caribbean countries, the war with Spain, and the acquisition of the Panama Canal Zone, all seemed to point in one direction, American imperialism. Even peaceful penetration by United States business was suspect, because it sometimes invoked government intervention to maintain concessions too freely granted.

Over against this trend toward unfriendliness and misunderstanding, an implement of good will was finally hammered into shape, the Pan-American Congress, out of which came the Pan-American Union. The origins can be traced back to the effort of Bolívar to unite the Spanish colonies against Spain, an effort which failed as did most other proposals until the conference called by Secretary James Blaine in Washington in 1889. It was in this conference that international law, which had always accepted war as a legitimate instrument of politics, was challenged with the revolutionary principle that conquest does not give title to territory, a principle later invoked by Secretary of State Henry Stimson in Manchuria.

Stresses and strains continue between the American nations, and will probably always continue, but North and South America were drawn closer together by the "good-neighbor" policy of President Franklin Roosevelt. The general principle was set forth in his First Inaugural:

> In the field of world policy I would dedicate this nation to the policy of the good neighbor—the neighbor who resolutely respects himself, and because he does so, respects the rights of others—the neighbor who respects his obligations and respects the sanctity of his agreements in and with a world of neighbors.

Secretary Cordell Hull gave these words definite application in signing the Anti-War Pact of the Montevideo conference of 1933 and in giving Cuba complete control of its foreign affairs a year later. By these and other acts, culminating in the grant of full independence to the Philippines on July 4, 1946, the United States has cleared away from its record all traces of "imperialism."

But the policy of the "good neighbor" is not by any means limited to the renunciation of policies of exploitation. It insists upon a respect for our rights as well. It therefore calls for co-operation on the part of the other nations concerned. All history shows that nothing is to be gained by surrendering legitimate rights. It is in the interests of civilization as a whole that nations of higher culture should extend their influence to those which are less advanced, provided that the method used is one that can be welcomed by the beneficiary as that of friendly helpfulness. Mere renunciation of one nation's claims upon another may be interpreted as a sign of weakness, which opens the door to further violations. Therefore, in definitely giving up intervention, the United States is evidently faced with a situation which calls for international co-operation upon the part of the whole American neighborhood of states whenever disorder or anarchy threatens the acknowledged rights of foreigners.

In short, the policy of the "good neighbor" is really that of the "good neighborhood." It does not mean the pursuit of generous and high ideals by any one member of the community of nations, or by nations acting individually. They must give one another some guarantee that the liberal policies will be maintained under ordinary circumstances and not be subject to every shifting current of domestic politics. Political credit rests upon the same basis as credit in finance, a calculable stability of policy and a confidence that policies begun will be consistently carried out. There can be no guarantee of this by the unilateral statement of any one administration, for it cannot control the acts of its successor. Thus, for example, Secretary Elihu Root's liberal and far-sighted policies were succeeded by the "dollar diplomacy" of Secretary Philander Knox. While there is no way to ensure with absolute certainty that nations will not turn back upon themselves, there is much less likelihood of this happening if they have agreed to accept a consistent procedure to cover all, or even most, questions or disputes arising out of their mutual relations.

But, while Secretary Hull was urging the good-neighbor policy at Montevideo, one of the most terrible wars in Latin-American history was being waged between Bolivia and Paraguay, the "Chaco War," and the international peace machinery failed because the League of Nations tried one way and the United States another, and their cross-purposes made both ineffective. The final lesson, not learned at the time, was that the forces for peace, like those for war, must have unity in command. The good neighborhood is world-wide.

5. *The Nation to the North*

It is a strange fact that the problem of war and peace in the Americas is generally stated in terms that leave out Canada. The reason for this is that the problem has been solved. Peace is taken for granted practically to the same extent as peace within the United States itself. This sense of security is undoubtedly justified by the conditions. War between Canada and the United States is not only unthinkable but impossible. Would the Middle West stand for a conquest that would bring in the competition of the vast grain fields of the northwest, or would eastern commerce welcome the untrammeled rivalry of the great waterways of the north? To the extent that the causes of war are economic, there is guarantee of peace in Canadian-American relations that can hardly be paralleled in other parts of the world. There is a further guarantee of peace in the billions of dollars of American money invested in Canadian industries, the largest single movement of capital from one country to another in the world. But this has not always been the case. The emphasis upon a century of peace—now almost a century and a quarter —ignores the fact that that long stretch of peaceful relations was not without very serious crises. The War of 1812 left its scars on both sides of the border. More than once the Canadians scented the danger of American invasion and Great Britain strengthened the defenses of the provinces at those points where invasion might be expected. Contrary to popular belief, the "three thousand miles of undefended frontier" has had its military establishments. This was particularly true during and after the Civil War, when resentment against Great Britain was running strong in the North for her attitude toward the southern states. The Fenian invasions of Canada in 1866 at Niagara and on the Quebec border have long been forgotten south of the line, but they left their mark on Canadian nationalism. Nevertheless, the same period which saw the settlement of the *Alabama* claims by arbitration saw the British redcoats march down from the Citadel of Quebec, and of the British Imperial Army on this continent only a mere handful remained. This means that throughout the whole history of the Dominion of Canada, from 1867, its defense has been left to itself—because no defense was needed. Even the naval harbors on the Atlantic and Pacific are no longer planned as operative bases. Peace between Canada and the United States is taken for granted.

Upon the whole, this situation has been left the way in which Anglo-Saxon nations like it best, that is, without too definite an effort to define it or embody it in institutions. The neighbors think they understand each other, although this is not always the case. Canadians get a certain satisfaction from the poor opinion which many of them entertain of American national morality, and Americans have not taken much trouble to correct these opinions. All in all, things run along just about as they do between neighbors in town or countryside. In short, here is a "good neighborhood."

In 1867, a new nation, Canada, was formed out of the provinces of British North America. Its provinces were held together in a federation, which bore a new title in history, "Dominion." In structure, the "Confederation," as the Canadians termed it, resembled that of the federal union of the United States, but all the governments within it, both of the Dominion and of its provinces, were modeled on the constitution of Great Britain, with parliaments supreme, under the august symbol of the Crown. There was pride in being a member of a great empire, a child of the "Mother of Parliaments," and loyalty to the imperial connection was shared by French and British Canadians alike. But there was a sturdy sense of Canadian nationality, a people governing themselves and allowing no interference with their freedom.

The task confronting this young nation was more difficult than that of its great southern neighbor; for its prairie provinces were separated from the eastern ones by a thousand miles of rocky wilderness north of the Great Lakes, and the Canadian Rocky Mountains barred the pathway to the Pacific with fewer passes than those that led to Oregon or California. It was by a miracle of creative effort that the railroads were flung across the wilderness in the northwest and over the Rockies to the Pacific. But the prize was great: the wilderness yielded harvests of gold and silver and almost every kind of ore; mighty rivers awaited the harnessing of their power; by the discoveries of science, the wheat fields were carried three hundred miles farther north and then, in these last days, beneath the prairie, some of the richest oil fields of the continent were linked to the east by a triumph of engineering.

Canada, created by an act of faith, faces the future confident and strong; its vast resources in the hands of a nobly nurtured people hold the promise of world power in the future.

Across the undefended frontier, railroads interlace the economies of the two North American nations. Each country is not only the other's greatest customer but its closest friend, sharing common ideals of freedom, though under variant sovereignties.

6. *The Flag Goes Overseas*

In 1898 a Cuban revolt against the outworn sovereignty of Spain brought the United States into its first war overseas. Not only was the American fleet dominant in the Caribbean, but the Philippines were taken. At the same time, August 1898, Hawaii, in the mid-Pacific, was annexed. So the United States, reaching the fringe of the Orient, began the strangely new chapter of its history as a colonial power, a chapter opening with the splendid episode of education for the Philippines and then their national independence.

More than a generation earlier, Commodore Matthew Perry had opened the sealed secrets of Japan to the Western World. Then, as China lay a tempting prize to imperialist and commercial powers, the United States insisted that trade with it should be through an open door with equal privileges for all.

Thus the United States, in becoming a world power, did not depart from the fundamental principles of equal opportunities and democracy in trade.

CHAPTER XII

---◆---

THE PROBLEMS OF DEMOCRACY

From the close of the Civil War to the opening of the twentieth century was a troubled period of American history. Material advances continued at an ever-increasing pace. The resources of the continent were the prize of its conquest. From the struggle of man against nature to the harnessing of nature's powers against itself, from the straggling settlements planted by the pioneers to the position of world power, America was challenging the future by its achievements of the past. But this theme of greatness had been only half the story; for the moral and spiritual life of a nation is the final test of its power to endure. It is here, rather than in its material achievements, however great, that we have the surest test of the vitality of the Republic.

1. *A Nation's Morality*

There can be no doubt about the moral stamina of the earliest settlers, nor about their insistence upon the virtues of personal integrity and Christian charity. But life in the New World brought new tests for character and for society. With only themselves to rely upon, the colonists bred a rugged individualism that was impatient of restraint and keen to take advantage of every favoring circumstances. As the nation grew, this meant an increasing

78

cleavage between rich and poor. While neighborly kindliness remained an ideal at every stage and in every society, the conscience of America was troubled, and finally, in the last years of the nineteenth century, challenged the complacent gospel of success by a movement of reform, still going on.

Unfortunately, the history of morals is the most difficult to trace, because there is little to record when things go well, and the evidence is therefore chiefly that of violations or of reform movements protesting against conditions which may have long been taken for granted. The real history of morals goes beyond this negative evidence of evil to balance it with the things that have made life worth living for most people most of the time. All history shows that this pursuit of happiness—for so we have defined it—can only reach its goal if it recognizes that the greatest good for the individual lies in sharing the common good of his fellows. This is the Golden Rule, laid down as the fundamental guide to conduct in all the great religions. Its secular counterpart was set forth in the basic principles of the Roman law, embodying the best thought and varied experiences of the ancient world: "Justice is the fixed and constant purpose to give every man his due." But what is "his due"? The answers given to this question constitute the positive side of the history of morals.

The English, with their practical bent, realized that we have here a question which can never be finally answered, because its terms vary with the changing conditions of life; so the common law, derived from actual experience, avoided rigid definition; and representative government became increasingly the guardian of the rights and welfare of the citizen. No sections of the English people were more aware of this political inheritance than those who drew up the *Mayflower* compact and established government in the colonies. The winning of the continent, far from offering an escape from these fundamental moral and political interests, brought them to the fore in a new setting. Though at times they were obscured by crises, they were never absent from the deeper currents of history; for it has always been characteristic of the American mind to see public issues in moral terms.

Morals in politics is not the same, however, as moralizing in politics, which is a trend shared by nations generally. It is by the actual conduct of affairs and not by protestations of good intentions that a people should be judged. This is a distinction made familiar in the criticism of Soviet Russia; it is also a test of our own history, and of all others. For politics is the mirror of actuality, however clouded or distorted it may seem.

2. *Politics before the Civil War*

At first the history of American politics resembled that of England. The liberties of the English people were won in a struggle that centered on the rights of property, as well as of persons, the insistence of propertied men that they should have control of the nation's business, public as well as private. There were, of course, other assertions of the rights of the citizen against the tyranny of the Crown, but, since it was the new middle class which put the revolution through, it inevitably mirrored the interests of property as a basis of political power. This was clearly set forth in the works of John Locke, who so profoundly influenced the leaders of thought in the colonies. But, while in England the propertied class became and remained for over a century a ruling Whig oligarchy, in

America any such possible tendencies were checked, as the Republic became more and more democratic in temper and in policy.

The issue was fought out in the long debate, theoretical and political, between the Federalists led chiefly by Alexander Hamilton, and the anti-Federalists, largely inspired by Thomas Jefferson. The Federalists' demand for a strong central government won out, to all appearances, in the Constitution, but then efforts to consolidate the nation's finances under federal auspices failed. The line-up was both regional and economic, for the centers of wealth were in the cities and the battle for existence was mostly waged in the back country. Those who had mortgaged farms tried to hold the money power in check. Thus the Democratic party was developed as a voice for social justice, invoking the great names of Jefferson and Jackson, and holding power during most of the early mid-nineteenth century. But these issues were secondary to another one, that of the place of slavery in the expanding nation. Here was a moral issue if there ever was one, yet it came to the American people in confusing terms, involving the nature of the federal union and the guarantee of property. To put the case the other way round, the question of slavery was not so much one of slaves as of slaveowners. It was creating a chasm between the moral, social, and economic life of North and South, which gave such meaning to Lincoln's phrase that a nation cannot live half slave and half free. Although the war was fought to preserve the Union, the Battle Hymn of the Republic was a hymn to freedom.

3. *Politics after the Civil War*

Not only in the South but in the North as well, the war marked a dividing line in American history. After its defeat in battle, the Confederacy suffered the evils and indignities of the Reconstruction era, in sad contrast to Grant's generous terms at the surrender. The North, robbed of Lincoln's leadership and conscious of the evils it had suffered, sullied the history of its victory either by connivance at the humiliation of the South or indifference to it as it turned from the tragic drama of the war to the interrupted epic of peace. Here a greater epoch awaited it than any in the past, but also one which was to test its moral stamina by the very extent of its material success.

Although the nation had not come out of the war unscathed, youth was still in its veins, pulsing, tireless, bold, sure of itself, and taking adventure in its stride. Success was taken for granted, either in its grasp or just beyond it, forever beckoning its onward march. It was but natural, therefore, that the successful man became the ideal of young and old. The "land of illimitable opportunity" was the term applied to it in all the languages of Europe. But the nation at grips with so great a destiny was not seldom ruthless in its impatience to win. Its generous instincts— and no people were ever more generous at heart—were not sufficient guides to conduct in the competitive life of men or communities faced with hardship or with the lure of wealth for the clever or strong. The dominant political thought of England in the first half of the nineteenth century, after the Industrial Revolution, that of *laissez faire*, to keep business free from politics, was still more deeply grounded in the United States. But in the last decades of the century the country faced new conditions as the continent filled up. There were fewer and fewer open spaces; and, at the same time, the tide of immigrants reached its height of almost a million a year. Every ship that came from Europe was loaded with workers and their families ready to start work for lower wages than were native-born Americans and depressing their standard of living as hard times followed the good in ominous sequence. It was taken for granted that the building of railroads should be largely paid for by the public domain, but movements of protest from the farmers against the "money power" of capital, familiar since the days of Andrew Jackson, reached their climax in the Populist movement and found eloquent expression in the democracy of William Jennings Bryan. In the cities, with their growing slums, political corruption had its shame exposed by Lincoln Steffens and the "muckrakers." Labor unions were organized into the American Federation of Labor by the statesmanlike work of Samuel Gompers. But the left wing was impatient of the slow progress of collective bargaining, and strikes and riots marked the path of labor warfare from Massachusetts to Oregon.

Upon the whole, the country kept to the middle path that looked to the ideals of Jefferson, and the conscience of the country was slow to respond to political "interference" with the natural economic laws. Finally, however, it was stirred by a movement for reform, which although discounted and opposed at every turn, became the genuine voice and vital spirit of America at the greatest era of its history.

4. *The New Freedom*

This new movement has commonly been known by a misleading term, that of a political "deal"—the Square Deal of Theodore Roosevelt, the New Deal of Franklin D. Roosevelt, the Fair Deal of Harry Truman—and, in so far as politics rests on compromise, a sound basis on the whole, the term may stand. But Woodrow Wilson, that master of style, had a truer sense of its place in history when he termed it the "New Freedom." For freedom is another name for justice; the perfect balance of the rights of the individual and those of his fellows, the Golden Rule in practice. The movement which embodied this ideal has been obscured by partisan politics, which concentrates on details or on personalities in leadership, or which attempts to discount or frustrate it. But it is more than an episode or a passing phase of history; it marks a definite advance in the outlook of America. It is the expression of the moral life of a nation intent upon ensuring justice in an imperfect world.

The awakening was an unhappy one for those who had led sheltered lives in the quiet respectability of the nineteenth-century middle class, and even those who were not so well off but did not wish to see the well-ordered past disturbed. But public opinion was shocked when the revolts of labor in Pittsburgh or Chicago were put down in blood, and supported against reactionaries in Congress the mobilization of labor itself as a new force, as yet not in politics, but with possibilities. The crusading muckrakers used their pens as swords against entrenched corruption in local governments and exploitation by high finance. History has not yet paid full tribute to this movement, which struck such a powerful blow at that complacent, yet fundamentally false philosophy of life that regarded mere wealth or power, however attained, as the measure of success and the model for the young.

It would be wrong, however, to regard the era of reform as purely American. The long struggle for social legislation in Great Britain then reached its climax in Lloyd George's battle cry that the one enemy was poverty. Even reactionary Bismarck brought social legislation to Germany, and France, in its slow, traditional, but steady pace, moved into the new era. Humanity was on the march, not merely because of its leaders, but because of the Industrial Revolution, which forced it out of the old grooves, which were deep with ancient wrongs and were leading to the dead end of revolution if reforms were not at hand.

This chapter of our history was twice interrupted by wars not of our choosing. Both world wars, however, became under American leadership crusades for freedom. Whatever judgment history may record of them, it can never deny the purpose for which America poured out its blood and treasure, accepting a challenge it can never refuse.

CHAPTER XIII

---◆◆◆---

WAR IN EUROPE

In the summer of 1914 a pistol shot in the streets of the remote Balkan city of Sarajevo broke the brittle structure of the peace of Europe, when the heir of the Austro-Hungarian Empire, Franz Ferdinand, was murdered by Serbian terrorists. Austria struck at Serbia, confident of support by Germany; Russia mobilized its vast armies to protect the menaced South Slavs, drawing in its allies, France and reluctant Great Britain; and Europe moved with the deadly timetable of the general staffs into the greatest war so far in its history.

It will never be possible now, after two world wars, to realize how the coming of the war in Europe in the first week of August 1914 shocked the conscience of the civilized world. In spite of the fact that it was preceded by a number of ominous crises, when peace seemed to hang by a thread, the actual outbreak struck with a tragic force unparalleled by any event in Western history, at least since the wars of the French Revolution. With the prodigious growth of the arts of peace in commerce and industry, men of good will everywhere had begun to write of war among the nations of the Christian world as "unthinkable." This feeling, so widely shared, was expressed in unforgettable terms by Sir Edward Grey, British foreign minister, when in the dusk of the evening of the third of August, as the lamplighter passed in the street below, he said in a phrase that has become historic, "The lamps are going out all over Europe; we shall not see them lit again in our lifetime." The next day England declared war. The Continent was already in flames.

1. *War*

Sir Edward Grey's premonition was realized to the full in the years that followed, but in the opening weeks and months of the war it was apparently not widely shared in Britain. In the country that had escaped unscathed from the dangers of the Spanish Armada and of Napoleon's threat of invasion, it seemed to the ordinary citizen as if this were another Continental war in which Britain would play its traditional role of sending an expeditionary force, as it had done in the days of Marlborough and Wellington, while remaining safe at home behind the bulwark of the British fleet. With imperturbable confidence in the outcome, shopkeepers and businessmen hung out the sign "business as usual" and the slogan was widely lived up to. In France, however, the sense of universal tragedy dominated public opinion as the German invasion swept nearer and nearer to Paris in the attempt—which almost succeeded—to encircle and destroy the armies of Joffre. Although this fate was averted by the "Miracle of the Marne," and the little English expeditionary force grew to an army sufficiently strong to hold the western flank from the Aisne to the Channel, the war in the trenches which followed maintained a perpetual horror for four long years, with no apparent escape from its malignant tragedy. On the eastern front there was equal victory and stalemate for the Central Powers when the Russian armies were overrun at Tannenberg, but in the years which followed the slow-moving might of Russia denied ultimate victory to its invaders.

To the military mind, as developed in the iron clamp of Prussian history, there was something supremely inspiring in this spectacle of men marching to a rendezvous with death; but the death that was waiting for them and which they sought to inflict upon their enemies was not that of the high drama of war but of multiple assassination in the sordid, vermin-infested setting of trench warfare. The world was aghast at such a spectacle, which seemed to revive the worst horrors of barbarism. Nor was this progressive degeneration merely physical. Both at the front and at home the fighting nations became steadily more callous and less responsive to the ideals of peacetime. The impact of the war reached to the innermost recesses of the mind of everyone involved in it, and this meant practically everyone in the Western world.

The fact of this universal involvement made the struggle in Europe a world war even while the actual combatants were limited to the two European alliances, for there was no true neutrality anywhere, no matter how much the neutral nations—and especially the United States—tried to hold aloof. Not only were there moral issues involved which affected deeply all right-minded men, but the war itself revealed the fact that the political boundaries of nations were by no means their true frontiers. The commercial and industrial revolutions had created economic ties and dependencies which extended all over the world. Raw materials for clothes or weapon had to be sought in Asia or America, to supplement the small supplies of the European homeland. War industries sprang up on neutral soil to meet this new imperious demand. And so the area of conflict widened over the seven seas.

2. *Causes of the War*

There are always two causes for a war: the conditions which feed antagonisms; and the men who turn these antagonisms into violence. The mere existence of conditions charged with explosive possibilities is not enough in itself to bring war; the responsibility for actually starting the conflagration among nations rests with a few men in control of their governments. There have been times when the conditions seemed headed for a conflict, but war did not happen because those in power managed to keep the hostile forces in check. Europe had witnessed one of the best examples of this in the last year of the nineteenth century when the imperial designs of France and England clashed in the Sudan, and Kitchener forced the French explorer Marchand to haul down the tricolor at Fashoda, where he had planted it as a symbol of French sovereignty over all central Africa. In France the "insult to the flag" roused memories of century-long warfare with Britain for its colonial empire, and anti-British feeling was so strong that had the French fleet been in the Channel, war might have happened over night. But sober statesmanship prevented the outbreak of a war which, had it happened, would have seemed to the historian to be the logical continuation of the agelong colonial duel between France and England. Instead, England and France became good friends in the *Entente Cordiale*, recognizing their common interests in maintaining the balance of power in Europe, which was then being threatened by the rising might of Germany and Austria's interference in the Balkans.

The balance of power had been the key to Britain's European policy throughout all modern history, from the days of the Spanish Armada to those of the "splendid isolation" of the great era of Queen Victoria. By a strange paradox, the chief Continental advocate of the balance of power was Bismarck himself after he had achieved the unification of Germany. But when in 1890 Kaiser William II dismissed him from his chancellorship and by increased armaments began to challenge Great Britain on the sea and France and Russia on the land, the balance of power ceased to be a guarantee of peace and became the preoccupation of those who were planning the strategy of a future war. The balance of power is at bottom a military concept based upon the weight and power of armaments. It has little relation to the peacetime interests of nations in the upbuilding of their industry and commerce. It is still a vital principle in international conflicts and can serve the cause of peace if, under the aegis of a world organization, it is invoked to check an aggressor. Unfortunately, prior to World War I no such international organization existed. The only international measures taken to meet the growing menace in the race of armaments due to the Industrial Revolution were the Hague conferences on disarmament, the first of which was called in 1899 by Tsar Nicholas II, later the ill-fated victim of the Russian Revolution. This met with polite but ineffective support among the nations; but the second Hague conference (in 1907) went beyond the codification of the laws of war to point the way to peaceful means for settling disputes in a court of arbitration. Thus the first tentative steps were taken to erect a substitute for war. But in the United States, in spite of the brilliant advocacy of Root and Taft, the plan for international arbitration was weakened in the Senate, so as not to apply to any but minor questions. This was the only general organization of peace prior to World War I.

3. *Total War*

The laws of war drafted by the Hague conferences were
ignored by the belligerents in their life-and-death struggle on land and sea. They had been designed to "make
war civilized" by safeguarding civilians and property
from its ravages and by outlawing the newer kinds of
weapons. All of these provisions were violated as Europe
became one vast armed camp, with peacetime industries
turned into munitions works, open cities bombarded
by howitzers and Big Berthas, and ships being sunk at sea
without warning. On the western front death made a no
man's land along the trenches from the Alps to the North
Sea, in the sacred dust of Verdun and the bleak reaches
of the Somme, long stretches of which are "forever England." Even more death and destruction marked the path
of the armies on the eastern front. The flower of the
youth of the civilized world was sacrificed; ten million
died in battle or from disease caused by the war. If that
army of the dead were drawn up in ghostly phalanxes, it
would reach, shoulder to shoulder, eight columns deep,
from New York to Chicago; and if it were to pass in one
last solemn Armistice Day review, ten hours a day, the
lilacs would be in bloom before it ended.

Such an orgy of destruction called for supplies from
all over the world. Germany, as the leading industrial
nation in Europe, had been the first to see this need, and,
while it organized its resources at home, systematically
plundered northern France, the industrial section of the
country, of everything that could be useful to it in the
war. So complete and thorough was the plundering that
even six months after the war was over, there was still no
smoke from any factory chimney in the territory that

had been occupied by the Germans, while it lay like a
pall over industrial Germany along the lower Rhine. But
Europe itself could not meet the imperious needs of a
war that had been revolutionized by science and industry,
and the war at sea took on the ruthless character of that
on land, with international law and the "freedom of the
seas" disavowed and American rights callously violated.
Then the United States, long restive under neutrality,
entered the war.

CHAPTER XIV

THE AMERICAN CRUSADE
AND THE PEACE

It is a fearful thing to lead this great peaceful people into war, into the most terrible and disastrous of all wars, civilization itself seeming to be in the balance. But the right is more precious than peace, and we shall fight for the things which we have always carried nearest our hearts—for democracy, for the right of those who submit to authority to have a voice in their own Government, for the rights and liberties of small nations, for a universal dominion of right by such a concert of free peoples as shall bring peace and safety to all nations and make the world itself at last free. To such a task we can dedicate our lives and our fortunes, everything that we are and everything that we have, with the pride of those who know the day has come when America is privileged to spend her blood and her might for the principles that gave her birth and happiness and the peace which she has treasured. God helping her, she can do no other.

—Woodrow Wilson's War Message, 1917

1. *From Neutrality to War*

There could be no doubt as to United States policy in the early months of the war in Europe. It could only be neutrality. History made it inevitable; President Wilson made it a moral issue in his call for neutrality in thought

as well as in action. This issue, however, was soon seen
to have been wrongly drawn; Americans could not be
indifferent to so vast and terrible a conflict. If the issues
were clearly seen to be either moral or vital, it could not
be "too proud to fight." Nevertheless, for almost three
tragic years of European death and destruction, the
United States was held to the policy of neutrality. President Wilson, holding sternly to his principles, described
it as a "nation fit beyond all others to exhibit the fine
poise of undisturbed judgment, the dignity of self-con-
trol, the efficiency of dispassionate action; a nation that
neither sits in judgment upon others nor is disturbed in its
own counsels." In the election of 1916, the President was
re-elected on the slogan, "He kept us out of war." Yet
six months later he led the country into it. Why?

The reason is not to be found in any change in Wilson's principles or those of the nation. In the critical
months of the early winter of 1916–17, the warring nations, in response to Wilson's demands, revealed their
true character and war aims, and it was at once clear that
German militarism, ruthless in war and unscrupulous in
diplomacy, was planning a world dominance in which
there would be no peace or security for freedom-loving
peoples. This meant, and the Germans verified it by their
acts, that the United States could no longer remain neutral. Germany challenged our rights at sea by unrestricted
submarine warfare, and in defense of those rights, we
took up the challenge of a militarism that was threatening
to dominate both sea and land.

On April 6, 1917, Congress declared war on Germany,
responding to Wilson's call "to accept the gauge of battle with this natural foe to liberty . . . to fight for the
ultimate peace of the world and for the liberties of its

peoples, the German people included; for the right of nations great and small and the privileges of men everywhere to choose their way of life and obedience. The world must be made safe for democracy." This shining ideal thus proclaimed was destined to be sullied by disillusionment and indifference, partisan strife and national antagonisms, leading to a second world war, to appear again in the darkest hour of peril in the variant forms of the Atlantic Charter, and then again, against the menace of a third world war, to inspire the free world with a new resolve to defend and hold inviolate its heritage of liberty.

But freedom is more than a defense against tyranny. Peace had to be organized, by the common consent of nations—something never tried before in all their history. The League of Nations, in which this inspiring effort was attempted, was the political embodiment of America's purpose in the war. That purpose had been spelled out in Wilson's message: "We desire no conquest, no dominion. We ask no indemnities for ourselves, no material compensation for the sacrifices we shall freely make. We are but one of the champions of the rights of mankind. We shall be satisfied when these rights have been made secure as the faith and the freedom of nations can make them."

In the famous Fourteen Points these principles were applied to the peace settlement, along with the destruction of arbitrary power and the establishment of an organization to check aggression. "What we seek is the reign of law based on the consent of the governed and sustained by the organized opinion of mankind." And again: "Peoples and provinces are not to be bartered about from sovereignty to sovereignty as if they were chattels or pawns in a game, even the great game, now forever discredited, of the balance of power, but every territorial settlement involved in this war must be made in the interest and for the benefit of the populations concerned."

In the months that followed, the war was won but the peace was lost.

2. *The Great Crusade*

Unprepared for war, the United States met the emergency by a gigantic mobilization of public spirit and national energy. Fears of national disunity were quickly dispelled, and the isolationist Middle West was the first to fill its quota of the draft. Two million soldiers, taken from the ranks of peace, were hurriedly molded into an expeditionary force, and for the first time an American army invaded Europe. On the battle line, from the Alps to the Channel, the French army at Verdun, the British along the Somme, had checked the German advance, but it was threatening the Marne when the Americans turned it back at Château-Thierry and through the embattled forest of the Argonne. On the western front the Canadians broke the Hindenburg line, but when the defeated German soldiers fell back over the Rhine they were greeted as victors; such was the power of nationalism for self-delusion. Meanwhile the American navy helped to subdue the menace of the submarine and joined with the British to keep control of the seas. The final and total defeat of the Central Powers was due to the blockade as much as to the fighting on the long front lines of battle.

3. *Peace Settlements*

After the soldiers came the statesmen and the diplomats
to shape a new era out of the ruins of the old. Three great
empires had fallen, Hohenzollern, Hapsburg, and Ro-
manov, and a new map had to be drawn on which place
had to be found for the liberated nations along the east
from the Baltic to the Aegean. Bolshevist Russia sought
no conquest of land, but international communism fought
for power in desperate revolutions in Vienna, Budapest,
and Berlin. Although the threat of revolution in France
was never serious, Prime Minister Clemenceau took no
chances, and, on the first of May, Labor Day in Europe, ·
bivouacked sixty thousand troops on the streets of Paris
to make sure that there would be no repetition of the
Commune uprising after the Franco-Prussian War. But
the Paris peace conference ignored the threat of communism and rebuilt Europe on the old-time basis of nationalism, only on a new model of "self-determination" with a
restored Poland, a new Czechoslovakia, a new Yugo-
slavia, an enlarged Rumania and Greece. Austria, once
the proud center of the Continent, accepted its fate; but
in Germany undying resentment reigned, ultimately to
lead, through Hitler's strident voicing of it, to World
War II.

Few documents in history have been more battled over
than the peace treaties of the peace conference. Unques-
tionably there were blunders and mistakes with cruel
consequences. Some of these could have been avoided if
the enemy states had been invited to present their case,
instead of having to accept a dictated peace; but the Germans themselves contributed to this by their own complete failure in diplomacy when given a chance to speak.

The other chief fault on the side of the Allies was that the treaties covered so many fields that, though most of them were well and fairly treated by themselves, the whole was greater than the sum of the parts when all was put together.

The final judgment of history will have to take into account more than the analysis of the technique of diplomacy, however. For what happened at Paris was but a single act in a much larger drama, one which stretches back to the Middle Ages and reaches forward through the era of science and mobilized industry to envisage new and untried forms of political and economic relations within and among nations. The peace treaties had to deal with facts for which they were not responsible, but which, because registered in them, are thought of as their handiwork. For example, the fall of the Hapsburg monarchy took place months before the Treaties of Saint Germain and Trianon were signed, and the documents in which the new sovereignties were recognized embodied, however blunderingly, the inescapable facts of war and revolution. It was impossible to draw this new map of Europe without doing injury to the vested interests of former governments and peoples. But it was also inevitable that the dispossessed would exploit the injury as a political slogan and a diplomatic weapon for years to come. Therefore, for the sake of all concerned, the new frontiers should have been drawn with at least equal consideration for the rights of the ex-enemy states. This could only have happened by a negotiated peace; for, however fair-minded the experts on one side of a dispute, they can rarely see the full merits of those on the other. Lacking the benefit of impartial debate, the peace conference made the inevitable mistake of yielding too much to the insistence of those able to present their case at Paris. In the adjustment of the German-Polish frontier, in the extent of the territories taken from Hungary, and in the extension of Italian sovereignty to the Brenner Pass, wrongs were perpetrated and gross injustices done. But neither Germany nor Hungary was without blame in such matters in the past, and to charge mistakes like these to the Wilsonian principle of "self-determination" is to ignore the lessons of history.

4. *What Germany Forgot*

The greatest blunder in the Treaty of Versailles was the way in which it treated the question of reparations for war damages to be paid by Germany. In the first place, it made it a penalty for Germany's "guilt" in causing the war; and then it left the total amount unsettled, while making reference to impossibly large sums in the future. The result was that opposition to the *Dictat von Versailles* became a religion in Germany. As a result of the blockade, the mass of the civilian population was suffering privation, leaving the scars of war in every German home. Unrest and discontent were shared by capital robbed of its income, and by labor suffering from unemployment. Then came the final blow, national bankruptcy, in which one paid a billion marks for a postage stamp. The blame for this was all laid on reparations; the other nations were all to blame. Actually, Germany had a lower rate of taxation in those years than either France or Britain, both of which met the costs of war with courage, although both had been sorely stricken. What Germany forgot was what the war itself cost it, for, confident of victory, it could—so its military leaders held

—place the burden on the conquered. Actually, the costs to Germany, during the war itself, reached the appalling sum of something in the neighborhood of fifty billion dollars reckoned in money value at the close of the war, more than double that amount now. And this does not include the economic cost to the German people in the exhaustion of human material and resources, deterioration of plants, capital displacement, and credit disturbance in what was then the most highly industrialized country of the world. Add all this in, and the total would be almost as much as, if not more than, the cost to the government.

These are the facts that Germany forgot when it placed all the blame for its sufferings on the reparations of the peace treaty.

5. The Tradition of Militarism

So far we have been tracing the war and its aftermath in the material fortunes of the German people. But, as we have seen, even more disastrous was the ultimate effect upon its spiritual life. This is more difficult to trace than the economic postwar history, for opinions and morals are the hardest to trace of all human possessions. Although on the one hand they are rooted in habit and immemorial custom and therefore are in some ways more stable than material property, on the other hand at times they seem almost to be shifted from their base by the storm pressures of emotion. Nowhere is this dual character of a nation's outlook more evident than in Germany in the postwar years, as the following short sketch will show.

As the war drew to a close the German people found that the fortitude and desperate effort of four years of totalitarian struggle had brought them not only defeat but utter exhaustion. The continuance of the blockade throughout the cruel winter of 1918–19 drove them still further to despair. In their eyes there seemed no reason for the continuance of the blockade unless it was intended to crush them still further and bring them to a state of absolute powerlessness. The fact that peace had not yet been made and that Europe was living under the terms of a truce called an Armistice seemed to them but a quibble on the part of the Allied Powers, for no one really believed that Germany could take up arms again after having laid them down. The fact that the meeting of the Allies and associated powers in Paris was popularly known as a peace conference further strengthened the feeling that the war was over, although it did not legally come to a close until the Treaty of Versailles was ratified in the following winter.

Under these conditions, the long delay in sending food to the half-starved Germans strengthened their sense of suffering by adding to it the feeling that all the world was still their enemy. The blockade was ultimately removed in March, some nine months before the treaty was finally ratified and peace definitely established, but the damage to the spirit of the German people had already been done. A psychosis of self-pity swept over it, which was destined to grow rather than lessen as the postwar years failed to restore prosperity to a world that had been both ruined and shellshocked by the war.

This state of mind was aggravated by Germany's isolation from the rest of the world—a state of affairs which continued to a surprising degree during the first years after the war. While this was chiefly due to the barriers to international trade caused by a poor or worthless currency, it was also due to the trend of German education of the prewar days, which had concentrated upon the great themes of German political unification and the triumphs of German science. No other nation had more to be proud of in the years which had just passed into history before the great catastrophe of World War I. German nationalism was wounded at the height of its pride, and when self-centered nationalism is so beaten down and humiliated, it takes defeat doubly to heart because it has never developed the capacity, nor even the wish, for understanding how other people have suffered from the effects of the war. This leads directly toward a pathological state of mind which is ready to believe that the nation is a victim—and it goes without saying, an innocent one—of the special malice of its foes.

The Hohenzollern kingship of Prussia was the legacy of the crusading Knights of the Teutonic Order. A feudal landowning aristocracy along that frontier maintained the military tradition from that day on. The rigid discipline and sense of duty in army training furnished an example as well for the civilian bureaucracy, which, from the days of the Great Elector, proved to be an invaluable instrument of peacetime autocratic rule. Bureaucracy and militarism therefore worked hand in hand serving the same ends. And when the forces of liberalism and democracy began to speak a different language, from 1848 to 1862, the old order found a champion in Bismarck who, by browbeating the Prussian Diet and deliberately choosing the way of "blood and iron" instead of "speeches and resolutions," determined the course of German history, with fateful consequences for all the world. Bismarck himself was fully conscious, at the time, of the epochal importance of the decision. As he urged his king, William I, to defy parliament by appealing to him as the first officer of the Prussian army, his mind went back to the days of Charles I of England, a king who never swerved from his duty, but "sealed his royal intent with his blood."

The heir of that historic event was Adolf Hitler, for not only did Bismarck win but he taught the German people to lose confidence in themselves, as a people lacking in political capacity. No nation can honestly say that of itself, because political capacity is not the gift of race but an outgrowth of circumstances and breeding. It must be remembered, however, that Bismarck himself, as long as he was in power, held in check the militarism he had invoked, and that the first principle of his statesmanship was to maintain civilian control of policies of state. Unfortunately for Germany there was but one Bismarck.

6. *The Displacement of the War*

This militaristic background of German history was certain to come to the fore in the aftermath of the war, both in the fanatic protest against "war guilt" and in the failure to analyze the effect of war on the conditions of peacetime living. But it must be borne in mind that this failure was shared by the other nations as well, for nowhere else was any such study undertaken. Indeed, no such study had ever been made of any war in history, for historians had concentrated either upon military events or the political repercussions of war, with but casual attention to the way in which war had affected the economic and social life, not only of the belligerent nations, but of others which did not seem directly involved. It was to study this problem that the *Economic and Social History of the*

War was undertaken under the auspices of the Carnegie Endowment for International Peace. This vast survey, prepared in collaboration with statesmen and specialists in all the countries of Europe, culminated in one conclusion: in the world of science and industry war had ceased to be a calculable instrument of national policy as it was—more or less—as recently as the days of Bismarck. This conclusion has now been driven home in the thinking of the Western world by the development of atomic and other weapons of mass destruction; but in the years immediately following World War I it was by no means clearly seen. Its full significance was pointed out by the present writer in an address in Berlin in March 1927, given in the presence of the heads of governments of the German Reich and Prussia, in which it was stated that war had passed out of the relatively static past into the era of dynamics; that its economy combines the two techniques of peace and destruction, both of which are progressively modified by every new invention and discovery, so that war becomes as uncertain in its direction as in its intensity or its spread. This being the case, it is no longer a safe instrument for statesmen to employ. Victor and victim may suffer a common disaster. Its effects reach into the unformed future and rob the savings of generations yet unborn. Time as well as space levels its barriers to the march of destruction. This new dynamic world, the creation of human intelligence, containing as it does the most precious things in our heritage, has no other defense against it once it is loosed than that which endangers it as well. Such are the phenomena of war as revealed by a study of the tragic years 1914–18. However, it is equally clear from this analysis that these phenomena are not merely incidental and temporary; they are typical and more and more true as civilization develops.

What then? In so far as war is no longer calculable, it is a crime to engage in it. Shall we then leave the world as it is, with no other method of ensuring change? By no means. Fortunately, that was not the alternative which this analysis suggested. The dynamic processes of peace offer the fitting means of redress without the dislocation of war, for we can now work out the method by which to subserve the means of justice or secure the aims of national policies, which formerly were entrusted to the forces of war.

CHAPTER XV

THE ORGANIZATION OF PEACE

Of all the contradictions of history, and it is a web woven of contradictions, the greatest is this: Christendom, claiming to be based on the teachings of the gospel of peace, used war to the uttermost in the relation of nation with nation. The contradiction began in the days of the Church Fathers, in dealing with the problem of military service to Rome. Augustine solved it, as far as it was ever solved by theologians, by drawing a line between just and unjust wars; the just wars being those in defense of established authority. The test became meaningless in the modern era of sovereign national states, each of which could apply it in its own behalf. International law could do nothing to prohibit wars under such a regime, and limited itself to lessening their evils. The one alternative to force in disputes beyond the reach of diplomacy to settle was arbitration, and it was not permitted to deal with matters of vital interest, the very issues on which wars are fought. This was the setting for the Hague conferences, in which the peace movement culminated prior to World War I.

1. *The League of Nations*

A new start had to be made based on a denial of the free right of a nation to go to war in violation of the interests of the community of nations. The League of Nations, in which this principle was embodied, was designed by a few leaders of thought in Great Britain and France, as well as in the United States, but the real creator of it was the war itself, which had revealed the inevitability of some such alternative for war, if civilization were to escape the death of anarchy. The organization of peace, on a permanent basis, had become an inescapable necessity.

History offered no models for those drafting the Covenant, only a few, hastily drawn wartime sketches. Yet in six months' time, the Commission on the League of Nations at the Paris peace conference, under Wilson's chairmanship, wrote the constitution for the League, which adjusted the forces of nationalism to great and small powers alike, capable of diplomacy without intrigue and of power without violence. It was a *tour de force* without parallel in the history of diplomacy.

The most revolutionary clause in the Covenant was Article 11, which boldly proclaimed that "any war or threat of war, whether immediately affecting any of the Members of the League or not, is hereby declared a matter of concern to the whole League, and the League shall take any action that may be deemed wise and effectual to safeguard the peace of nations." In these sweeping terms, the Covenant denied the free right of sovereign states to use war as the instrument of policy. The right to go to war, the age-old "argument of kings" and the very touchstone of sovereignty for the national states, was now to be questioned whenever invoked, and the "anarchy tempered by war" to be ended by the community of nations in its own interest.

To implement this great ideal it was necessary to have a permanent organization, and to make it real it had to have representatives from all member nations in an as-

sembly and to organize for action in a council, in which
the Great Powers dominated, with agencies for nonpolitical activities and an international secretariat. Such,
in short, was the structure of the League of Nations, a
structure so inevitable that when, over twenty years later,
the United Nations was created, it reproduced practically
the same framework, although those who worked on the
first draft, of whom the writer was one, sincerely tried to
change the model.

The failure of the League to prevent World War II
has led to the entirely mistaken conclusion—especially in
the United States—that it had little or nothing to its credit
during the interwar years. On the contrary, it intervened
in some forty-four international disputes, none of which
could find settlement outside the League, and some of
them held the threat of war, in addition to its contributions to the unsolved problem of disarmament. The
method used was "conciliation," bringing the pressure
of nations not party to a dispute to calm the hot temper
of the disputants and apply cool reason to the solution.
"The spirit of Geneva" became a byword in the foreign
offices of Europe.

In this connection, we come upon one of the strangest
paradoxes in history. For the European nations, basing
policy upon the ever-shifting balance of power, never
used, in their international relations among themselves,
the one article of the Covenant which kept us out of the
League, Article 10, in which the members of the League
undertook "to respect and preserve as against external
aggression the territorial integrity and existing political independence of all Members of the League." This had
been Wilson's own article, in his opinion "a Monroe Doctrine for the world." But the European nations saw, in

the collective guarantee of the *status quo*, a possible freezing of the terms of the peace settlement, and avoided any use of it.

On at least one occasion, the League stopped a war that had already begun. It was in the Balkans, from which the war had started in 1914. In October 1925, Greek forces crossed the Bulgarian-Macedonian frontier and at once the Bulgarian government sent in an appeal to the League of Nations. It was a week end and some of the leading officials were away, so several hours were lost, during which the Greek invasion was proceeding. This point must be mentioned because it brought up at once the importance of having quick action to meet an emergency. Within an hour after receipt of the appeal, Aristide Briand, as chairman of the Council, telegraphed to Sofia and Athens exhorting both parties to cease further action and withdraw their troops behind their own frontiers. The Council was summoned at once to meet in Paris, and it met three days later, members coming by airplane so as not to lose time. At the Council meeting, the Greek government, not having replied as yet, was given an ultimatum of twenty-four hours for an unconditional order for withdrawal of its troops to Greek soil.

The action of the Council, which followed along the lines of its previous procedure, was to create a commission of inquiry which should go to the Macedonian frontier. For this purpose, and in order to gain time, it "requested" Great Britain and Italy to send to Macedonia such officers as they had within reach and to keep the Council informed of the military situation.

Having thus secured a truce, the Council then appointed a commission of inquiry to investigate the whole situation, decide where the responsibility lay, and indi-

cate the terms of settlement. The commission reported in
due time, in the course of the following winter, and its
report was adopted by the Council and carried out by
the disputing governments.

The League had succeeded in stopping a recognized
aggression after the initial overt act had been committed.
The League had been justified as an instrument for the
preservation of peace between small powers; the question remained whether it would be equally successful
when a great power was involved.

2. *The International Labor Organization*

The League of Nations was more than a grand alliance
against war; there were other dangers to be guarded
against in plague and disease, other obstacles to be overcome in attitudes of mind, ignorance and prejudice, in
economic disorders and barriers to trade, in exploitation
and social injustices. The League pioneered in all these
fields, and the story of its efforts contains some of the
noblest chapters in the history of our time, as, for instance, Dr. Fridtjof Nansen's work in eastern Europe and
Russia against the plague and typhus. But in this short
sketch of a great theme, we must limit ourselves to the
one body which survived the war and still stands as a
leader in social betterment, the International Labor Organization.

The origins of this unique body explain its meaning.
During the Paris peace conference, bolshevist revolutions,
spreading from Russia, were raging in Berlin, Vienna, and
Budapest. It was as a counter to this danger of communism and of the Socialist International that the International Labor Organization was set up, to bring the move-

ments for social reform within the law, by peaceful agreements shared in by workers and employers as well as by governments. In order to make these arrangements more than "pious resolutions," the I.L.O., after months of study, draws them up as "draft conventions" or treaties for the governments to consider. Owing to its federal form of government, however, the United States receives these only as "recommendations" to be dealt with as its Constitution provides.

It will be seen from this slight sketch that the attacks made on the I.L.O. by reactionaries in the United States, as disguised international communism, are completely unjustified. The fact that a satellite state like Czechoslovakia, which joined under Thomas Masaryk, is still a member is unimportant in view of its impotence against the great majority of nations from the free world. What is important is the record: by 1956, 1,531 ratifications of 104 conventions were voted. The one which best illustrates how the United States can gain by this international action is that which practically forced all other maritime nations to accept the conditions of the La Follette Seaman's Act, establishing the eight-hour day at sea. But American interest and sympathy are even more deeply engaged by the application of I.L.O. standards to the social legislation of Japan, preventing child labor in the mills. No longer are little girls of six taken from farms for what was almost slave labor in industry. The beneficent action of the I.L.O. thus reaches throughout the world. The United States should cherish carefully and proudly its membership in this bulwark of social justice through freedom. In 1944 it issued a declaration at a meeting in Philadelphia in which it took responsibility for much of the social-welfare work formerly carried on by the League of Nations. Some of this, however, belongs more properly with the United Nations, and the boundaries between the two organizations are being worked out. The important thing is to make sure that the work goes on.

3. *Disarmament*

Nowhere was the vitality—and confusion—of the peace movement more evident than in the slogan, "The way to peace is by disarmament and the way to disarm is to disarm." Taking this half-truth at face value, Secretary of State Charles Evans Hughes called the Washington conference on naval disarmament for November 1921, and, with a dramatic move almost outrivaling the drama of war, proposed in the name of the United States that the great sea powers should not only halt the building of battleships but should actually destroy a percentage of those already built, and that they should henceforth keep to an agreed ratio. The race in armaments was to give way to co-operation in limiting and lessening the chief instrument of sea power. Never before had any government taken so bold a step in this most delicate of all questions of international relations.

The challenge to the imagination of the world which lay in the act of Secretary Hughes was destined to influence the whole direction of the peace movement for the next twelve years. The spectacle that it offered—in anticipation of the fact—of nations towing battleships out to sea and sinking them in the cause of international good will was much more absorbing than the dull routine of discussion in the bodies of the League of Nations or of argument in courts or arbitration tribunals. In fact, success or failure in disarmament became, for most people, including most statesmen, the acid test of the peace movement itself. The authority of men like Lord Grey of Fallodon was invoked to prove that the race in armaments had been the prime cause of World War I, a theory widely shared in a grossly exaggerated form.

The Washington conference cut through the whole armament problem by a mathematical formula: the ratio of capital ships was set for the United States, Great Britain, and Japan at $5 : 5 : 3$, with lower ratios for other nations. Equations like these impose upon the mind with the force of a conclusion that seems final and inescapable; and spurred on by the general acclaim, an effort was made at Geneva to apply the same method to land armies. But no sooner was the proposal made than the unreality of the whole method of disarmament by arithmetic became apparent. A few troops behind a well-protected frontier are easily the equivalent of a much larger attacking force in the open. There is no way of getting rid of geography in the problem of disarmament. Moreover, there is no $5 : 5 : 3$ in chemical warfare, and science changes the value and power of armaments overnight.

Twelve years of effort to apply and extend the Washington-conference method ended in Japan's renunciation of the limitation of its naval armaments that had been agreed to, and the other sea powers followed suit. Then Germany, which had been arming in defiance of the treaty provisions, withdrew from the disarmament conference at Geneva and the long futile chapter was interrupted by war itself, to be resumed again under less favorable circumstances. Nothing in history has been more clearly proved than that the problem of armament is primarily one of national security—the lesson which, as we have seen, had been hammered home at Geneva, both in the Assembly of the League and in the disarmament conferences. The United States, however, continued rigidly along the lines laid down by Secretary Hughes, both because of its specious appeal to public opinion and because opposition to membership in the one organization for collective security, the League of Nations, had become more deeply entrenched, as is always the case when abstention becomes a habit.

4. The Protocol of Geneva

The Convenant of the League of Nations did not prohibit war as a last resort if the Council of the League failed to settle a dispute. In that case, it provided that "the Members of the League reserve to themselves the right to take such action as they shall consider necessary for the maintenance of right and justice," a diplomatic circumlocution for the right to go to war. This "gap in the Covenant," as it was termed, weakened the guarantee of peace through the League, which from its early days had always been held to be the essential prerequisite of disarmament. In the Assembly of 1924 this all came to a head in the framing of an addition, or Protocol, to the Covenant, which proclaimed a war of aggression to be an international crime. But what was the test of aggression? Every nation in going to war insists that it is merely defending its rights. The Assembly found the solution in the draft of an unofficial American committee, that a nation was an aggressor if it went to war in violation of its obligation to take the case to court. The Protocol of Geneva used this test to outlaw aggressive war, and outlined in detail how it should be applied. This was the high-water mark in the history of the League, the one time when it was proudly aware of its mission to guarantee peace by denying the right to war. It was the longest step ever taken by the League or any other body to "outlaw war"—to use a phrase then current in the United States. It had the support of all the Continental nations, members of the League, and even in Germany there was a strong movement of public opinion in its favor. Unfortunately, however, both for the League and for the rest of the world, in the autumn of 1924 a Conservative government came into power in Great Britain, utterly out of sympathy with the basic principles of the Protocol, which made membership in the League an ironclad obligation to join in prevention of war anywhere in the world. The British Conservatives claimed that "a definite obligation" to maintain peace anywhere in the world was contrary to established British policy; that it interfered with sovereignty in a way which had never happened before. With the British rejection of the Protocol, the League was apparently left weaker than before because it was evident that the British government could not be counted upon to carry out any of the other equally general obligations of the Covenant. The Assembly in 1925, therefore, started over again with the problem of disarmament, setting up a preparatory committee for a disarmament conference, which continued to work uninterruptedly but unsuccessfully until Germany withdrew at the opening of World War II.

5. The Treaties of Locarno

Instead of the general obligation of the Protocol, Great Britain eagerly took up a suggestion from Germany that there should be regional treaties of peace around its frontiers, guaranteed by Great Britain and Italy. This proposal was embodied in the Treaties of Locarno of August 1925. These treaties were linked with the Protocol by the same test of aggression which the American committee had contributed at Geneva, namely, the resort to arms instead of submitting a dispute to peaceful settlement under the aegis of the League or alongside it. History was to show that the British reliance upon the Locarno policy instead of the Protocol of Geneva was the gravest blunder, not only in its own history, but in that of our time. After the rearmament of Germany, Hitler then tested the regional guarantees one by one, and one by one they broke down. The first step was the invasion of the Rhineland. It was tested first of all when Britain found ample excuse for the German action in the recovery of German territory. Lacking support by the British, the French also remained inactive. The next step around the frontier was Hitler's invasion of Austria, and although this was a much more serious violation of Locarno, the arguments in its favor were sufficiently familiar and nothing was done. Next came Czechoslovakia and at Munich it was at last evident that regional security was a fraudulent formula for the peace of Europe. Finally, after the betrayal of Czechoslovakia, when the whole strategic position was absolutely in Germany's favor, Britain and France went to war on the last violation of the regional guarantees, that of Poland.

6. *The Renunciation of War*

It was fitting that the challenge to the disarmament policies of the United States should come from the European

statesman who had been the foremost champion of the
League of Nations, Aristide Briand, foreign minister of
France. He had been deeply distressed at the popular
American charge of French militarism, due to the refusal
of war-stricken France to disarm except as its security
was safeguarded by joint international guarantee. To
clarify the whole situation, he proposed, on April 6, 1927,
ten years after the United States had entered the war, that
the two nations, and as many others as wished to do so,
should not limit themselves to lessening armaments but
should join in a solemn pledge to renounce "war as the
instrument of national policy." His meaning of this
phrase was made clear by reminding Washington that
"the renunciation of war as an instrument of national policy is a conception already familiar to the signatories of
the Covenant of the League of Nations and the Treaties
of Locarno." But this formula did not suit Secretary of
State Frank Kellogg, who, under the influence of Sen-
ator William Borah, insisted that the proposal cover all
wars without distinction; yet, at the same time they reserved the "inherent right of self-defense." As most modern wars are fought as defensive wars, the American
emendation of the Briand offer made it practically meaningless. The popular movement to "outlaw war," a movement hostile to the League, had insisted that it was impossible to distinguish between aggression and defense; yet
it also insisted on Secretary Kellogg's accepting Briand's
offer. In August 1928, in a solemn ceremony at the Quai
d'Orsay, the Paris Peace Pact was signed by fifteen nations. The State Department evidently failed to note that
the nations did not renounce all wars, but only "war as an
instrument of national policy," which was what Briand
had originally proposed. Briand's words, on the occasion

of the signing, drove the lesson home, except for those who did not listen: "We have proclaimed peace; that is good, but it is not enough. Now we want to organize it." This the United States refused to do, falling back on the old-time mood of isolation. As the shadows of a new war darkened the world, the greatest industrial nation again sought safety in neutrality. But again it learned in sacrifice and tragedy that the crime of war, in the era of science and industry, reaches over all mankind. This lesson has now been reaffirmed in the cold war with international communism. While the Kellogg-Borah formula is all but forgotten, the Briand proposal is now dominant in the policies of western European nations, urgently supported by the United States. The eras of Richelieu and Bismarck are over. The late Count Sforza of Italy, thoughtful and experienced statesman, restated the conclusion of Briand in unqualified terms: "War as an instrument of national policy is an anachronism in the nations of western Europe."

CHAPTER XVI

WOODROW WILSON

We must pause here to turn from the tumultuous current of great events to consider the problem: what will be the place in history of the man, who, more than any other, led the United States out of isolation and marked out a path for it to follow in the new great era of today and tomorrow.

It is one of the mysteries of history that the stature of great men is seldom fully seen by their contemporaries. The three whose monuments now stand in Washington as witness to a nation's reverent admiration, Washington, Jefferson and Lincoln, were all vilified in their day. It is too soon to measure the length of the shadow which Woodrow Wilson will cast in the long perspectives of history. The fact that in the postwar years his policies were disavowed is now to be balanced against a growing appreciation of his statesmanship in domestic as well as in foreign affairs. Whatever the ultimate judgment on this may be, the historian must recall the unique character of Wilson's leadership at the time of his greatest influence on the warring nations. The tribute which follows, written by the author as a member of the American Delegation to Negotiate Peace at the Paris Peace Conference, although now it may seem extravagant, is a fair statement of the conviction of those who followed Wilson's leadership.

"It is not too much to say that future generations will never be able to know what Woodrow Wilson meant to the world throughout the year 1918. At a time when the moral forces of humanity were surrendering to bleak despair, he summoned them again to action. When the war had become mere meaningless carnage, he stated the purposes of nations in terms which won homage from both sides of the front. In the darkest hour of disillusionment, he rallied the forces of civilization from their helpless involvement in universal destruction to a task not of rebuilding the outworn structure of the past but of creating a world community of which mankind had until then hardly dared to dream. Never before had any single individual in secular history been able to exert an influence like this. It was a world leadership, for which he himself had not been ready in the earlier years of the war, and from which, by heredity and training his mind at first had sought to escape by insisting upon America's isolation and tradition of neutrality. Even from that distance, however, and even while claiming pride in America's aloofness from the struggle, he had made himself an exponent of the submerged peace forces of the world and had upheld with persistent tenacity the power of the idea against that of brute force, securing from the belligerent governments statements of their war aims which their own peoples had been unable to extract from them. But it was not until America entered the World War that the real power of his thought struck home with full force and effect. Even though subsequent events might falsify the ideal for which he stood, it was then the one guiding beacon in an almost universal night.

"Cynics who, through the early years of the war, while America was still neutral, mocked at Wilson's phrases, watched with amazed bewilderment the effect of those embattled words during the period of our belligerency. When the Allies, in their distress, were ready to barter their very cause for mercenary troops from the Orient to the Mediterranean, and the war was becoming meaningless except as the collapse of civilization, Wilson recalled the moral purposes at stake, and he alone restated them for all the world.

The phrase, "to make the world safe for democracy," was destined to be battered by the war itself and by the cynicism of succeeding years into a thing of cant and hypocrisy, but the historian must recognize the fact that it was a better, soberer and more valid slogan of crusade than any other which has ever animated so many diverse forces as in 1917. Compared with it, the "Liberty, Equality and Fraternity" of the French Revolution was vague and undefined, however vibrant its appeal to a Europe that had not yet had experience in responsible government. The war continued to be fought for other things than the inspiration of such a message, but without it the intervention of America would not have brought that temper and undivided strength which it carried into the battlefields of Europe. The German military and naval heads, unmindful of Bismarck's warning of the power of moral "imponderables," and utterly miscalculating our capacity for action, employed their last full measure of force on land and sea and by unlimited submarine warfare and on the thin front by Amiens all but conquered; but our armies had been preceded by the force of Wilson's words, which shared with the blockade in the overthrow of the Hapsburgs and Hohenzollerns. At the close of the war the name of Woodrow Wilson stood out above all others in the world.

"But it was one thing to secure the adoption of a program by nations at war when the immediate ends to be attained by its adoption were so obvious as to silence the opposition of all but the most belligerent and reactionary elements of public life; it was another thing to translate these principles into a working program for the confused counsels of peace-time politics. Yet the only hope for the permanent establishment of peace on the Wilsonian terms lay in securing co-operation, first on the part of the Allies, and then upon that of the Central Powers, to make these terms substantially their own. Neither Wilson nor House expected to find a full measure of this co-operation in the war-time gov-

ernments of Europe; their faith was in the outlook of the
common man, a faith which linked their ideals with those
of the American and French Revolutions through Jeffersonian democracy. In any case, Wilson was always on his
guard when dealing with his European colleagues. Indeed,
the records show that he even distrusted them unjustly at
times; it is an utterly wrong perspective of history which
presents the American participation in the Peace Conference as the only liberalizing agent there. No one nation has
a monopoly of the ideas of progress. . . .

"Nevertheless, the program set for the Conference of
Paris was that of President Wilson. If it was difficult to
translate these principles into terms suitable for the conditions imposed upon the great Powers by the war and by
the conflicting interests of their past history, it was still
more difficult to set up new states to do this untried thing.
For the liberated peoples did not bring to the understanding of this program of neighborliness and cooperation
among nations anything of that experience in government
which the older nations could contribute. Never was the
adage more perfectly exemplified that "servitude is the
worst of all schools for freedom." "Self-determination"
was already shaping itself in flamboyant supernationalism
and reveling in the oppression of the conquered. So un-
lovely were some of these exhibitions of vindictiveness
that, had Wilson been the sentimental politician which his
enemies have charged, he would have been tempted time
and again to deny his major thesis of Jeffersonian democracy and frankly stop the processes of emancipation. For
not having done so he earned the undying enmity of those
ex-enemy states which had applied his philosophy to their
own emancipation but not to that of their neighbors. By
revolution they had overthrown imperialism at home, but
their newly freed democracies felt cheated of their birthright when Wilson held them to the test of granting free-

dom to those peoples whose enmity they feared when it could no longer be controlled in the accustomed way.

"To those new states as well as to the old, Wilson presented a challenge which accepted nationalism but turned it against itself. Had Germany triumphed, the *pax Germanica* which it would have imposed upon the conquered would have resembled in some degree the *pax Romana*, a peace held down by garrisons in the danger zones of Europe, or at least a Holy Alliance with William in the place of Alexander. Wilson's conception was the opposite of this. There was nothing in it of universal empire, no effort to retrace the processes of history. Instead of this he accepted the historic heritage of the modern age, with all its diversity of states and governments, seeking only to prevent its trend toward international anarchy by applying a device familiar to American thinking, a "Monroe Doctrine for the World," which would give a corporate guaranty against interference by reactionary and imperialistic powers. The supreme tragedy lay in the fact that it was his own country which led in the renunciation of this endeavor to apply its experience to solve the disorders of an unbalanced world." *

This tribute to Wilson was written as a challenge to those who had forgotten what it was like when greatness dwelt among us. But for the historian, this is only half of the record; for the causes of the failure lay in the very nature of the exploit and in the character and outlook of the President who directed it. The dominant theme of American history, isolation from foreign affairs, could be broken down temporarily by the impact of war, but it was strengthened by the emotional reaction once the fighting stopped. Wilson's heroic effort to counter this

* J. T. Shotwell, *At the Paris Peace Conference* (New York: The Macmillan Company, 1937), pp. 20-24.

movement, destined to destroy all his plans, had been lost before it began by his partisan battle with the Republican party leaders, who then could capitalize the postwar disillusionment to win their case.

The final judgment of history will undoubtedly be that Wilson was greatly in the wrong for allowing party politics to mar the conduct of world affairs; but it cannot stop there. For Wilson in this regard but shared the common outlook of politicians and the public generally, although in the tough fiber of his mind there was an added obstacle to compromise. The blame for the ultimate failure to align the United States with the forces that made for organization of peace falls upon the nation as a whole. The weakness of a democracy lies in the very principle that gives it strength, freedom of debate, for debates are not really free when the issues with which they deal are distorted by prejudice and rancor. Then they merely divide the nation while confusing it. It was this danger to the Republic which was Washington's chief concern as a statesman. Throughout his whole presidency he sought to hold political divisions within bounds and in his Farewell Address laid his deep concern for national unity upon the conscience of his countrymen, reminding them that "with slight shades of difference you have the same religion, manners, habits, and political principles," and that "one of the expedients of party . . . is to misrepresent the opinions and aims of others. You cannot shield yourselves too much against the jealousies and heart-burnings which spring from these misrepresentations; they tend to render alien to each other those who ought to be bound together by fraternal affection."

The warning of Washington was addressed to a small but vital democracy. The tragedy of Wilson's failure was a warning to all the world that the organization of international peace called for a better, more mature organization of democracy itself. The history of Europe was to reinforce this lesson, and, at the same time, to make it infinitely more difficult, as the problems of domestic politics became interlocked with those of other nations. In this way the era of Wilson brought the problems of Washington into the arena of world affairs. The solution can only be found in Washington's way.

CHAPTER XVII

THE GREAT DELUSION

The years between the two world wars already lie in dark shadow across the lengthening perspective of United States history. The heights of great adventure were left behind, and the nation, losing its place as a leader among other nations in the most difficult hour of their postwar readjustment, sank to the level of sheer materialism. Science harnessed to mass production seemed to offer illimitable power to improve the conditions of life. But the economic cost of the war had now to be liquidated; in the world of credit it could be postponed for ten years, but then it came with a disaster comparable to the war itself. The citadels of capital crumbled like hollow shells. The army of the unemployed was greater than that of the war, some twelve million of them. More bitter even than the sense of material loss was that of frustration. Liberal thought had lost its way in its avoidance of responsibility. American opinion was uneasy and uncertain. When recovery came, it concentrated on reforms at home, but it still cherished the delusion of safety through isolation, although the rest of the world was, by that time, aflame in World War II. Pearl Harbor was the tragic end of an era not so much of disillusionment as delusion.

War between the great nations of today is not over when the firing ceases. Even where resentment dies, the displacements caused by the war are carried on by the disruption of the world of business, the losses or ill-based gains of markets, and the feverish life of the world of credit—where war costs lodge. The first effect of World War I, as of most wars, was a delusion of prosperity as the vacuum created by the war losses was filled by the vast, undreamed of capacity for production for war, turned to the service of peace. But it was not long before the nations began to meet their most pressing needs out of their own depleted resources and their hurriedly and partially restored industries. To prevent their "dumping" their products in the United States market, Congress raised the tariff higher than it had ever been; yet, after the relatively slight depression of 1921, huge investments went abroad where gains seemed high, although the war debts, in billions of dollars, were still unsettled.

The first to bear the cost of this economic dislocation were the farmers of the Middle West, faced with whole-sale bankruptcy when the wartime market for wheat suddenly ended. But in the nation at large, the new methods of mass production in industry continued to give the impression of prosperity, and an orgy of speculation and spending reached its height under President Herbert Hoover. Then, in October 1929, almost overnight, the whole edifice of credit crumbled to pieces. Mortgages fell due with no purchasers, banks went bankrupt, millions of investors lost the savings of a lifetime. In a few weeks' time securities had shrunk by forty billion dollars from their fantastic boom-time prices. But that was only the beginning. Factories and business houses closed, and millions of unemployed were in the streets. There was starvation in a land of plenty. Ten years had elapsed since Armistice Day had thrilled the world with a new hope; but the last battle had still to come, fought out, not only on the farms of the Middle West, where the arsenals of wheat which had nourished the embattled nations were now in ruins, but also, as the disaster spread back to Europe, in the continued march of financial disaster, until the central bastion of international credit, the British gold standard, was forced to yield.

The Great Depression, lasting a decade, was so evidently a consequence of the economic displacement of the war that it would seem impossible for anyone to fail to see it, yet that is what most economists did, until long after the event, following the traditional, classical economists of the nineteenth century, especially John Stuart Mill. In two massive volumes, *Recent Social Trends*, prepared by leading economists under the direction of a commission appointed by President Hoover, there is only one casual reference to the influence of the war. In view of this fact, the author inserts here his contrary opinion, as set forth in his Report to the Trustees of the Carnegie Endowment for International Peace, in 1932:

> What the world has suffered from is not a cycle of good and bad times but an abnormality in the cycle which produced vast excesses in both prosperity and adversity. The extremes in both cases have outrun all calculations based upon the economic experience of the past; the explanation for them must therefore lie in something outside that experience. This apparently is the impact of the World War upon the structure of organized society. Nevertheless, this underlying cause has not been brought to the fore in much of the discussion concerning the economic crisis of these last years. On the contrary, the discussions have been chiefly concerned with what are in reality fallacies of the post-war period.
>
> There is abundant excuse for this failure to think through to the basic economic effects of the war on the part of those

who are studying the depression in order to find the way out, for those who shape policies must deal with the re-adjustment of a post-war peacetime situation. But this concentration of interest upon securing sounder present measures in finance and trade, however much it may be justified by the pressing exigencies of the hour, should not blind us to the fact that it excludes the vital and determining element from the discussion: the effect of the war upon credit. Credit is not solely a matter of finance; it depends on a basic confidence in the ordered progress of civilization. This confidence was so shaken by four years of war that many doubted if it could be rebuilt in anything like its former strength. To the surprise of the world, after a short interval of crisis and uncertainty, confidence returned in even larger measure than before. The surprise bred fallacies. The world of business acquired a belief in the invincible march of progress, relying upon the vastly increased capacity for production which had come about through the new industrial processes, and forgetting that the consumption market, although temporarily enlarged by the exhaustion of supplies, was fundamentally lessened by the war and its consequences. The apparent ease with which the immediate damage of the war was repaired gave an added impetus to the conception that the world of industrial credit was no longer held to the iron law of the economic cycle of prosperity and depression. The theories of economic science seemed disproved. The idea began to be advanced that the day of accounting could be indefinitely postponed by increased production, and refinanced indefinitely against still more distant futures.

The fever of speculation engendered by this superficial reading of the situation was undoubtedly a chief element in increasing the evil. Never, not even in the South Sea Bubble, was there worse gambling with fictitious values than in 1928 and 1929. But speculation alone is not a sufficient cause for the peculiar extent and depth of this depression. Fictitious values can be cleared out of the way by liquidation and, if the economic structure is sound, normal conditions begin to reassert themselves even during the period of readjustment. The real values remain, although they may be transferred in part to other hands than those of their former owners, by bank foreclosures on speculating debtors or by the purchases by conservative citizens in forced sales. Society also may profit generally from the cheaper prices of the liquidating period. Something more than speculation must be at the root of a phenomenon like that which has held the world in its grip throughout the depression years.

Post-war tariff policies have also to be borne in mind in measuring the effects of the war, for they, too, are a contributing cause of the depression. It is true that not all tariffs are symbols of economic maladjustments, for some have enabled industries to make a start which ultimately proved their value in the coordinated economic life of the nation. But the tariffs of the post-war period, including our own, are of a different kind. They are frankly directed against the foreigner in order to prevent economic aggression and invasion. The whole conception is that of conflict. Every nation has been turning itself into a beleaguered city trusting for safety to its tariff walls. At last, even the classical home of free trade, England itself, yielded to the impulse. All this has happened, too, at the very moment when industry has developed mass production on a scale that cannot profitably be maintained without foreign markets.

This is the picture of the chief peacetime causes of the depression. It must be admitted that the facts present a terrible indictment against the mismanagement of capital, trade and industry. But history teaches that, even with these handicaps, the world might get along and start on its way to recovery if there were no other obstacles in its path —for it must be remembered that the world's accumulation of wealth in the past and its progress in social welfare and

general prosperity were secured in the face of folly and
ignorance at almost every stage of the advance. Seldom
have politicians been persuaded by economists to correct
their prejudices by a knowledge of economic laws. And
economists, themselves, have not seldom misled the world
by giving the semblance of law to the prejudices of their
own time. If, in spite of all these handicaps, the application
of science to power enormously increased the wealth of the
world and raised the standard of living, there is no reason
why the same process should not, without too long delay,
have dealt with the forces of disaster now let loose upon
society. In short, if the crisis of the depression was due to
peacetime maladjustments, readjustment could be secured
by peacetime forces, without reducing the whole world to
impotence.

But what is missing in this picture? It is the first and fundamental cause which set the whole disturbance going: the
World War. The sooner we realize that fact, the better we
shall be prepared to apply the proper remedies. For the
remedies are not entirely economic; they must be political
as well, and of a kind to prevent a recurrence of the cause.

It is no mere figure of speech to describe the economic
depression as a part of the war. Modern war is an industry
of destruction, and a world war is mass destruction which
affects not only all nations but all parts of all nations. The
actual fighting is but one element of the conflict. Battles
are but the dramatic climax of a vast and tragic upheaval
which destroys the accumulated values of society behind
the lines and in quiet homes thousands of miles away from
the front as effectively as the armies destroy the towns and
cities in the area of actual fighting. The blockade which
ultimately brought defeat to the Central Powers affected
as well the neutral world, from Holland to Argentina. It
was this worldwide involvement which made the struggle
of 1914–1918 unique in history, rather than the mere extent of the battle lines that stretched for hundreds of miles

across Europe. The first of all lessons that the world war taught us was the extent of the interdependence of industrialized nations. No one before had guessed the extent of that interdependence, and even then its full import was not clearly seen, because along with the losses entailed came compensating benefits to the non-belligerents in increased prices for such goods as they were permitted to supply, and a temporary enhancement of their prosperity.

The fact which seems to have escaped adequate analysis is that modern war extends as far in time as it does in space —that it reaches out into the future even further than over land and sea, and destroys the prosperity of years to come as well as of those gone by. When the world of modern business goes to war it mobilizes the forces of credit at the same time that it mobilizes the army and navy. In the stress of such times the future seems illimitable, or at least it offers the chance to multiply many times over the capacities of any given moment. These potentialities of the future are sucked into the maelstrom of destruction, and this entails a much greater loss than that resulting from the actual destruction by contending armies. Warring nations mortgage their future during the period of the fighting, and if the fighting continues the mortgage must be rewritten time and time again, until every last item of possible recovery is thrown into the crucible. This is what happened in the four years of the World War.

Yet it is hard to keep such facts in mind, for the destruction of the future shows no visible ruins at the time of action. There is no inherent difference between the destruction of property already in our possession and property which is to be the result of future labor. But when a long period of time intervenes between the action and its consequences, so many other things may happen in the interval that we lose sight of the initial cause, or consciously endeavor to forget and to create antidotes for our misfortunes so that we may escape the otherwise inevitable effect.

Although the future which the World War ravaged was a
vaster field than even that great area of devastated Europe
on which the actual battles were fought, nevertheless in its
long reaches over the coming years of life and work, of
savings and property, there were no burning cities or plundered fields, no visible sign of the presence of the destructive forces. Yet just as the "Big Berthas" of the battlefront
reached out over peaceful lands to scatter their destruction
at distant points, so the process of modern war reaches beyond the immediate present to scatter its ravages in distant
years. The interval of peace makes the whole process seem
utterly unreal—and doubly so, in this case, because the generation that fought the war did its best to forget it as soon
as it possibly could.

It is this difference between the physical destruction on
the battlefield or in the track of an invasion and the equally
actual destruction of capital, of credits drawn against the
future, which underlay so much of the disputes concerning
reparations. France and Belgium could show the consequences of war and claim full reparation for the visible and
obvious damage. Even in the last negotiations prior to the
Lausanne Conference, there was universal assent to the
claim that this kind of damage must be repaired, no matter
what happened to the rest. It was the direct damage of the
battlefront which remained the unconditional part of German reparations, and anyone who has seen the desolated
fields of northern France, the sites of cities leveled to deserts of mud or chalk in Flanders or Picardy, will understand why the claim was granted. But while the French of
the devastated area had put their savings into houses, factories and towns which were destroyed on the spot where
they stood, the people of the rest of the belligerent world
contributed their material sacrifices in other ways. Some of
their savings went in taxes, some in loans and patriotic contributions. The things which this money bought were
never to be the property of those who paid for them, unless

one thinks of safety or victory as property. They were things which no one wanted in times of peace, instruments of destruction or salvage. By incredible effort and unlimited borrowings which gutted the edifices of credit, the war was kept going far beyond the capacity of any single generation to repay.

The fallacy of war finances did not disappear with the war itself. When peace came, the belligerent nations were so largely depleted of both supplies and the machinery of production that they momentarily stimulated industry and commerce by the market created by the vacuum. Only those nations which had their economic possibilities completely destroyed, such as Austria and Hungary, were forced to bankruptcy in the years immediately following the war. Even they were able to secure credits from the rest of the world to put off the day of reckoning. For the most part, the warring nations absorbed their armies into their industries with a success which was, after all, surprising in view of the immense task which the demobilization involved and the vast readjustments of economic life which suddenly had to be made. But this process of the return to normal peace conditions could be carried on only by still further borrowing from the last source of credit left in the world. Fortunately for the time when this need arose, but unfortunately for the period following, enough of this credit was available, chiefly in the United States, to carry through the first depression of 1921, except in the case of Germany. Yet this mortgaging of the future was the undoing of the United States, for it drained the country's last resources of liquid capital for investment to make possible the reestablishment of business throughout the world. At the height of our spending in this great enterprise of rehabilitation, we had put outside of the frontiers of the United States an equivalent of all the liquid assets of New England outside Massachusetts, or a half a dozen of those states which lie along the fringe of the Rocky Mountains, or of that vast empire which covers the southwestern states of Texas, Arizona, and New Mexico. This huge export of our accumulated wealth drained the savings of more than one generation in the fallacious hope of finding profit for it in the future.

The financial evils of the postwar period were increased by the fact that we had been profiteers of the European war prior to our entry into it. War economy is essentially wasteful, for the goods which protect life and property must be had at any cost. The United States became an arsenal for warring Europe, especially for the *Entente* powers. Prices and wages reached fabulous amounts. Thus suddenly enriched, the country was in the mood for spending, and those who never before had known the difference between stocks and bonds became speculators in a money market that was in its most dangerously speculative phase. Bankers who should have been conservative advisers of their clients became salesmen for investments of which they knew little beyond what the prospectuses told them. The fever of financial expansion distorted all sense of the fundamentals of economic life. This orgy of speculation was undoubtedly the direct cause of the panic of November 1929, but behind it lay the continuing influence of the war showing itself in the twofold aspect of a distorted moral and economic outlook on the part of the investor, and of the destruction beyond a capacity for quick recovery on the part of the debtor.

The conclusion is that the wealth of nations not only

rests upon the healthful functioning of the economic processes, but also that the reverse holds true as well: the peace movement is a fundamental part of the economy of nations. The only solid guarantee of continuing prosperity lies in the strengthening of those instruments of international policy which are the substitutes for war: arbitration and the World Court for the settlement of disputes, and the conference method of the League of Nations and the United Nations.

CHAPTER XVIII

THE ERA OF
FRANKLIN D. ROOSEVELT

The historians of the nineteenth century, who raised historical research to a science, dealt with the long perspectives of the past but paused at the threshold of their own times. In the American universities, the history of the United States stopped with the Civil War; it was only in the twentieth century that, greatly daring, it reached through Reconstruction to the war with Spain. The reason for not dealing with more recent events was that it was too soon to pass judgments on them, because we are too close to them to see their relative importance and may be more biased than we know. Yet Thucydides, the greatest historian of the ancient world, deliberately chose as his theme a war in which he had played a part, "believing that it would be great and memorable above any previous war"; and the events of today are infinitely greater than those of the Athens of Pericles.

1. *De Profundis*

The keynote to modern history was given in three revolutions for liberty, in England, America, and France. But all of them were incomplete, limited to securing the freedom of the citizen and his property against the tyranny of government. The revolutionary theory common to all of them was shaped by the logical French mind with the formula *laisser aller*—let things go; do not interfere with the individual in his rights. The nonpropertied classes in Europe, practically ignored during the first half of the nineteenth century, slowly won recognition by reform and revolution, breeding communism on their extreme left wing. In America, although there were voices of discontent from the first, they were lost in the vast spaces of "the land of illimitable opportunity" until the land was filled up with immigrants and new empires of industry and capital were formed. The awakening of the conscience of the nation to its unfinished task of securing social justice for all, in the days of William Jennings Bryan, Theodore Roosevelt, and Woodrow Wilson, marked a new day, as we have seen, in the outlook of politics. But the Founding Fathers, while safeguarding political freedom in the Constitution, especially in the Bill of Rights, left social legislation to the states, so the federal government was limited to little more than interstate matters and the general denial of discriminatory monopolies. Within this narrow framework, President Hoover proposed lending—not giving—money to states and cities for relief and a modest program of federal works to lessen unemployment. His Reconstruction Finance Corporation, authorized by Congress in January 1932, made emergency loans to business, but these and other similar measures fell far short of the need, although the government deficit piled up to almost two and one-half billion dollars, with income steadily declining.

This was the situation when Franklin Delano Roosevelt became president. There can be no doubt that Hoover had all history behind him in attempting to meet the crisis without extending the scope of government;

and it is equally clear that Roosevelt could not have rebuilt the shattered fabric of credit without full government support. In the eyes of conservative Republicans
this was revolutionary and would only make matters
worse, as the ship of state, having lost its moorings, would
become a complete wreck. President Hoover's intem-
perate prophecy, that "grass would grow in the streets of
a hundred cities, a thousand towns" if the tariff was lowered, was echoed in nationwide warnings against Roosevelt's New Deal policies. But, in spite of the boldness in
conception, the New Deal was not conceived by its cre-
ators as a revolutionary doctrine. It subscribed to no new
theories, either political or economic. It was designed to
save rather than destroy the capitalist system. But though
both political parties had a common purpose, the bitterness in their conflict on policies was accentuated by the
difference in temperament of their leaders, the one cau-
tious and convinced that business would recover best
with the least amount of government interference, the
other confident in his ability to improvise "bold persistent
experimentation" and to mobilize public opinion in his
support. Looking back to that hour of decision when
Roosevelt took command, across over twenty years,
mostly spent under the New Deal, it seems clear that over
and above its emergency legislation, it inaugurated reforms long overdue, as in social security, the strengthening of the financial structure, and public works programs:
but it is now equally clear, in the light of the present reaction, that these great achievements would have
been more solidly based if there had been an effort to enlist the support of those who followed Hoover. After all,
the greatest New Deal organization, the Federal Emergency Relief Administration (FERA), had a forerunner,

although an inadequate one, in Hoover's Reconstruction Finance Corporation (RFC). But practical politics triumphed over statesmanship, partisan antagonisms were sharpened on both sides; the conservative forces were charged with being "economic royalists"—a term of opprobrium especially bitter in the minds of economic sufferers; and the New Dealers were charged with socialism, a term meant to be equally opprobrious.

The judgment of history is that this injection of extreme, vituperative antagonism into the heart of a great national crisis is a sign of political immaturity. Washington warned against it as the greatest danger to the stability of the Republic, and, as president, he held out against it in the nonpartisan character of his Cabinet. It is true that he suffered from partisan attack, and that partisanship finally won out; but the vision of statesmanship remains, putting the nation above party. It was the same vision which inspired Lincoln to rise above the passions of war "with charity for all and malice toward none." Again the extremists won, this time with disastrous consequences. The conflicting opinions over the New Deal touched almost as deep springs of national feeling, for both sides felt that it marked a turning point away from the "rugged individualism" of the past to an era of greater government control in the national economy. But the solution of the controversy was not to be found, as Machiavelli would have advised, in the discrediting of opponents, but in that open-minded judgment which makes the decisions of statesmanship lasting. The proof of this is already evident, twenty years later, when, planning to prevent another depression, the anti-New Deal administration of President Eisenhower proposed a program of public works which, while largely based on the Hoover plan for local instead of federal management, include as well provisions for national action that definitely recall the plans of the New Deal to meet the menace of unemployment.

The New Deal program fell into three divisions: relief, recovery, and reform. Relief to meet immediate needs reached over five million families and cost some five billion dollars. Among its many activities, that of the Civilian Conservation Corps providing work for the young won wide popular approval; many others were criticized as "boondoggling" or doing unnecessary things. But miles of roads were built and thousands of schoolhouses and other public buildings erected. The recovery program broadened and continued public works and helped transportation and agriculture. To meet the costs, the dollar was devalued by cutting its gold content down to 59 per cent of its former value. The reform program was animated by one purpose: to give a sense of security to a nation that had suddenly learned what it was to have lost the means of livelihood. The farmers were to have guarantees for the marketing of their produce, labor to have fair conditions of employment, child labor to be forbidden, and a vast scheme of social-security insurance was put into operation similar to those in European countries. The keynote to this reform had been given in Roosevelt's First Inaugural, that "the only thing we have to fear is fear itself," for there can be no doubt that in offering guarantees against disaster, the chief cause of fear was removed. But did the remedy weaken the moral fiber of the nation? Did the new sense of security tend to destroy the incentive for enterprise and initiative? Did the federal control of so vast an undertaking, however beneficent in purpose, create an unmanageable machinery of government? In short, was this socialism in disguise? These questions, relentlessly insisted upon by the anti-New Dealers, were posed and answered, for the time being, by the election of 1952, but not as decisively as seemed at first. The great debate continues, and will long continue. It is the fundamental question in the history of politics, from the days of the Greeks until now.

2. *The Shadow of a Second World War*

Roosevelt was too shrewd a politician and too much preoccupied with his domestic problems to attempt to counter the national trend toward isolation in foreign affairs during the years in which the mounting forces of militarism drove relentlessly toward war in Asia and Europe. His only positive foreign policies were along familiar lines: the lessening of customs tariffs by the reciprocal trade treaties of Secretary of State Cordell Hull, a notable and long-needed reform, and the policy of "the good neighbor," resulting in multilateral treaties with Latin-American countries to prevent political and financial imperialism by a complete recasting of the Monroe Doctrine to joint guarantees of collective security for the Western Hemisphere. The Buenos Aires conference of 1936, in which these pledges were formulated with an eye upon the gathering storm in Europe, was followed by others during the war and after, culminating in that of Caracas in 1954, directed against the menace of communism. The historic distrust of the "colossus of the north" may still linger in the background, but it has apparently become more of a myth than a reality as the United States made good its promise of independence for the Philippines and ceased interference in Mexico and the Caribbean.

But on the vital issues of war and peace, Roosevelt did not risk coming to grips with a Congress and public opinion that was increasingly isolationist as the war clouds lowered across the Atlantic. If the countries of the Old World went to war, so the argument ran, it was their own affair, their own historical way of settling their disputes. We had been wrong, so it was claimed, in interfering in 1917; and moreover, our former allies wouldn't —or couldn't—pay the face value of their war debts (which they could not pay because of our tariffs).

A series of Neutrality Acts, from 1935 to 1937, forbade the shipment of arms or munitions to any nation at war— without regard to whether it was the innocent victim of an attack or the attacker. When charged that this was an utterly immoral law, its supporters insisted that there were no moral issues in international law, since the sovereign state was judge of its own actions. It has not been sufficiently realized to what depths of political anarchy the isolationist doctrine led. But Roosevelt was rudely made aware of it when, in a speech in Chicago in October 1937, aimed chiefly at Japan's undeclared war in China, he called for a "moral quarantine" against an aggressor, to check the "state of international anarchy," which like an epidemic was sweeping over peace-loving countries. The isolationists at once turned bitterly on the "warmongering" president, who then, like the experienced politician that he was, kept silent on this major issue, until Hitler actually began the preliminaries to World War II. Then again Roosevelt warned the American people that "when peace is broken anywhere, it is threatened everywhere." The tragedy of Europe had by this time reached the mind of America, as the radio carried the story of Nazi power and terror into homes in all parts of the country, and it began to be clear that the freedom in the New World might suffer eclipse if its light went out in Europe. The easy conquests by militarist Germany drove this thought home.

3. *Getting Rid of Neutrality*

In an address to Congress in January 1939, Roosevelt outlined the next stage of his policy. "There are many methods short of war, but stronger and more effective than mere words, of bringing home to aggressor governments the aggregate sentiments of our people." He then took the step beyond Wilson's neutrality by stating that he could not ask every American to remain neutral in thought as well as in action. "Even a neutral cannot be asked to close his mind or his conscience."

In the fateful year of 1940, as Hitler swept over western Europe, the danger to Great Britain was clearly seen to be a danger to the United States, if to German power on land and in the air were added command of the seas. In July twenty-one American republics met at Havana and, apprehensive of the German threat of aggression, resolved not to accept any transfer of sovereignty from an American to a non-American power. With Canada a joint defense board was set up, and in September Roosevelt transferred fifty destroyers to the British in exchange for ninety-nine-year leases on eight naval bases, stretching from Newfoundland to South America. By October, the first peacetime conscription in United States history had been put into operation, under which ultimately over thirty-one million men were registered and classified for military service, and more than seventeen million were drafted and examined for service in the armed forces. By

November Congress voted almost eighteen billion dollars for rearmament. The menace of war had now become so real that the country eagerly responded.

Another year was to pass before war came to the United States. Then it came, not from embattled Europe but from Asia, where, already in 1931, Japan had begun its aggression on the mainland of China by its occupation of Manchuria. In the undeclared war and truce with China which followed, Japan defied the efforts of the League of Nations for peaceful settlement and withdrew from the League. Its "peaceful penetration" ended in July 1937 in a ruthless attack on Shanghai, the conquest of the territory north of the Yangtze River and the commercial city of Canton on the south. The conscience of Americans was deeply troubled by the fact that much of the material for Japanese armaments came from the United States, under the conditions of neutrality. The sense of guilty partnership in Japan's war crimes in China was heightened by the mass murders in Nanking and in Christian colleges, for the missionary movement which supplies these schools and colleges had its roots in the churches everywhere. The country, therefore, began to react strongly against a neutrality which opened our ports to Japanese shipping, while China had almost no ships of her own. Pearl Harbor was but the last, fatal step on the path from which there was no turning as long as the militarism of Japan was engaged in the conquest of Asia.

CHAPTER XIX

---◆◆---

WORLD WAR II

The devastating march of the Great Depression struck Europe with full force in 1931, when, after the failure of the greatest bank in Austria, Great Britain finally went off the gold standard—which all the world had regarded for a century as the symbol of sound money. While this crisis was developing came the alarming news that Japanese troops had occupied Mukden, the capital of China's province of Manchuria. Thus the pathway from World War I reached, through its economic aftermath, to World War II; for in the undeclared war with China which followed, Japan's defiance of the League of Nations revealed the weakness of a body at cross-purposes because of the absence of the United States and the unwillingness of the European powers to assume all the responsibility for the maintenance of peace in Asia.

1. *The Issue: Nationalist Imperialism or World Peace*

Japan's unimpeded imperialist militarism was followed by Italy's equally unimpeded imperialism in Africa, which profited from the same arguments in Geneva, that no peace measures would be effective without United States support. The arguments may have been specious, but Mussolini moved on to the conquest of Ethiopia. Then came Hitler's chance. Testing the peace defenses of Lo-

carno around the German frontiers, on the Rhineland, in
Austria, and in Czechoslovakia, until the whole structure
created at Versailles crumbled at Munich, he launched
his legions against Poland and the West in World War II.

The issue was clear in both Europe and Asia. It was not
economics, though, that gave the timing. The European
aggressors had come through darker times some years
before, when Germany suffered its great bankruptcy as
a result of World War I and Italy was too poor to dream
of empire. But, while the new, incomplete structure of
peace remained unready, reluctant to act, and uncertain
of the forces at its command, the conspiracy against it of
nationalist imperialism armed and struck. As their armies
and navies swept from one success to another, their leaders, *Führer* and *Duce,* boasted like savage chiefs of the
new era of ruthless militarism which for a thousand years
would hold the nations in thrall. At first it seemed as if
their boasts would come true as German tanks and guns
broke through all defenses in "lightning war," and with
Poland defeated and the North Sea nations overrun,
France itself collapsed and all the Continent yielded to
the swastika. Italy, too, was making good its dream of a
new Roman Empire. Only Britain held out, in its most
glorious day of unflinching courage, the lone champion
of freedom in a world where all seemed lost. It was saved
by the "miracle of Dunkirk" when, by that kind of improvisation in which the British excel, almost four hundred thousand British troops were rescued from the
beaches by every kind of craft from British harbors under a thin but daring screen of aircraft protection.

Meanwhile Japan had, in 1937, begun its invasion of
China and, by the end of 1938, Prime Minister Konoye
boasted in a radio address to the nation that Japan held

"the key to the disposal of China" and was well on the way to establishing its "new order in Asia." The boast was never made good, however, for the poorly armed Chinese troops struck back at the invaders and prevented the occupation of more than the readily accessible sections of China; but by 1940 Japan set about the conquest of the tropical areas south of China, one of the richest regions in the world in material resources. The grandiose dream of a Japanese world empire seemed about to be realized, for its allies, Germany and Italy, were winning their wars in Europe and Africa, and the United States was tied by its Neutrality Acts. It is true that, alarmed by German victories, President Roosevelt had found the way to help Britain with ships and lend-lease so that it could hold the life line in the Atlantic, but the aggressors still held the upper hand.

All this was changed, however, when, on December 7, 1941, Japan attacked the United States at Pearl Harbor, Hawaii. Then it was suddenly clear that the whole Axis conspiracy against the peace was a challenge to all that America stood for, its treasured heritage of faith, courage, and the will to freedom. At once it met the challenge, not alone, but with the nations of the free world in America and Europe. Within a month after the United States had entered the war, the Western Powers joined in a solemn pact at Washington in a great coalition which was to bear a new name in history, the United Nations.

A long and bitter controversy has been waged both over the diplomacy in the months and years prior to Pearl Harbor and the military and naval responsibility for the failure to avert the catastrophe itself. The report of the Congressional Joint Commission on the investigation of the Pearl Harbor attack, together with its documentary exhibits, fills over forty volumes, and that does not include all of the official documentation which challenges the historian. In a scholarly and impartial survey of this source material, Walter Millis in *This is Pearl!* comes to the conclusion that "there can never be a final answer to the question of who was 'responsible' for the Pearl Harbor disaster. It was the end result of a highly complex chain of actions, reactions, good decisions and bad ones, in which human foresight and failure were inextricably mingled. . . . The record offers no support for the view that the Roosevelt Administration plotted to invite a Pacific War or even wished for one. There is, on the contrary, overwhelming evidence that the guiding thought was to stave off a war as long as possible. Yet it is true that Roosevelt and his advisers followed policies which, under all the circumstances, made the Japanese attack virtually inevitable. Why? The only valid answer must be sought in a consideration of the alternatives available at any given point in the process. To my mind, the Roosevelt Administration had no other choices than those which it successively took. Here, also, there is no doubt much room for disagreement. But sincere disagreement must demonstrate, not only that the courses followed eventuated in undesirable consequences, but that alternative courses would not have led to much worse ones. This is a canon of honest historical criticism which is not always observed."

2. *The Second Crusade*

The United States entered the war after its greatest defeat; but Pearl Harbor was not the full measure of its anxious concern. The Axis Powers seemed everywhere to be on the road to victory, and France, for the first time in its long history, was completely held down by the German invaders. Russia was still recoiling before their devastating armies, and the miracle of Stalingrad was yet to come. Only the British, beaten but unconquerable, had hammered shut the gates to Egypt and the Orient on the desert lines of El Alamein. Japan was mistress of the Pacific after Pearl Harbor and her victories over the British battleships off southeast Asia.

But the greatness of the crisis brought out once more, as in 1917, the true spirit of the nation, undaunted, almost unconscious of danger, confident in its strength and eager for action. With the nation united as never before, factory and farm mobilized at home while new ships and new armies went overseas. Their achievements are too many and too great be listed here, but on the pages of history they will shine forever, both as witness to the inherent strength of a free people and as a warning to future aggressors.

There were times when the world held its breath, as in the invasion of Normandy—the greatest amphibian invasion of all time and the most hazardous. Far-off coral islands like Tarawa, the jungles of Guadalcanal, and the caverned heights of Okinawa became inseparable parts of America, where its youth paid its "last full measure of devotion" on the long way back to avenge the death march of Corregidor, while an improvised navy and air force destroyed the sea power of Japan. In African battlefields, on the Anzio beaches, in the Apennines, the hitherto unbeaten Germans barred the road to Rome; and, after Italy and France were freed, Germany itself, the citadel of Europe, had to be taken. As the encircling invaders struck at its bastions, the Russians on the east and the British and Americans on the west, the Germans made one last desperate trial to break through in the Battle of the Bulge. But the Allies held, and the great invasion swept on over the Rhine, to link their forces on the Elbe. Germany paid in ruined cities and broken economy for the crime of war.

Japan still fought on and to prevent great loss of life in a seaborne invasion of its islands, Washington gave its sanction to the use of two atomic bombs, which the scientists had secretly prepared. At Hiroshima and Nagasaki, these weapons were first used, ushering in a new and most terrible kind of warfare. The tragedy is that they need not have been used, for we know now that the Emperor was already planning surrender. The devastation from American planes, burning the light frame-built cities, and the utter defeat of the navy which had been Japan's pride, were enough to bring the nation to its knees. On the deck of the battleship *Missouri*, it signed its surrender on September 2, 1945.

The greatest war in history was over. But the challenge of the peace had still to be met. If this could not be done the inescapable alternative would be a third world war, for wars between great powers are henceforth world wars. Science has seen to that. This newest thing in human society has already changed the arts of peace and is now revolutionizing the technique of war. The transformation thus begun is not a mere interlude in the history of mankind but, on the contrary, will go on with increasing power throughout all the future. From now on all war will be total war and therefore the preparation to meet it will also have to be total. This means that so long as the war system lasts it will not only denature the economic life of nations but will endanger all the freedoms within them. Isolation can no longer provide the safety it provided in the past. No single nation can adequately protect itself against a force which is bound more and more to conquer nature and thus change the whole basis of national security. To live well and prosperously in a world under constant threat of war waged under these conditions is simply impossible. On the other hand, the organization of peace is the most difficult task that has ever been envisaged by human intelligence. To this task we now turn and to the way in which its problems have been met by the United Nations.

CHAPTER XX

———◆———

THE UNITED NATIONS

We the people of the United Nations determined to save succeeding generations from the scourge of war, which twice in our lifetime has brought untold sorrow to mankind, and

To reaffirm faith in fundamental human rights, in the dignity and worth of the human person, in the equal rights of men and women of nations large and small, and

To establish conditions under which justice and respect for the obligations arising from treaties and other sources of international law can be maintained, and

To promote social progress and better standards of life in larger freedom, and for these ends

To practice tolerance and live together in peace with one another as good neighbors, and

To unite our strength to maintain international peace and security, and

To insure, by the acceptance of principles and the institution of methods, that armed force shall not be used, save in the common interest, and

To employ international machinery for the promotion of economic and social advancement of all peoples, have resolved to combine our efforts to accomplish these aims.

1. *The Charter*

These opening words of the Charter of the United Nations give eloquent and moving utterance to the fundamental purposes for which this second organization for world peace was founded. In varying terms these purposes are repeated and applied in the Charter itself, the text of which bears close resemblance to the Covenant of the League of Nations, that first great pioneering effort at world organization. Work upon the Charter was begun in Washington by a small committee called together by the State Department, and its draft, elaborated by the Dumbarton Oaks conference, became the blueprint for the San Francisco conference (April 25–June 26, 1945). Again, as in 1919, the structure of world peace had to be fitted into the confused outlines of history. It was not a constitution for the world such as idealists hoped might be achieved, but an instrument of practical politics.

Whatever the future of the United Nations, June 26, 1945, on which day fifty nations accepted the Charter, marks one of the most decisive events in history. By a strange coincidence, 730 years before almost to the day, on June 15, 1215, the first great charter of liberties was wrested from King John by the barons of England. Although the foundations had been laid for it in the laws and customs of earlier days, it built upon them a structure of freedom which was to become the proud heritage of the English-speaking peoples. For it gave lasting expression to the ideals of justice and equal rights within the law. In the San Francisco conference another charter was forged against a greater tyranny to establish institutions of peace and justice among nations.

The Charter covers three great fields of international relations: security—the maintenance of peace; welfare—the economic betterment of the nations; and international justice. The field upon which attention was concentrated was naturally security, the problem of peace and war. But no one could have foreseen that there would arise another conspiracy against the peace, equally as threatening to freedom as that of the Axis Powers against which World War II had just been fought. Although the Security Council was empowered to take whatever steps might be necessary "to maintain or restore international peace and security," the great principle of peace based upon freedom was sabotaged by Soviet Russia and the governments following its lead. Instead of one world there were two, and between them a "cold war" flared into battle on the hills of Korea. Thus the original purpose of the United Nations was violated; yet even the Communists insist that the purpose remains and that the path to world peace lies through the United Nations. This implies peaceful "co-existence" of communist and noncommunist peoples. To achieve this there must be a truce in the cold war; for there is no real peace where neither side trusts the other.

To meet this challenge, the United Nations itself must be given a new birth. Three important questions and many smaller ones await solution. First of all, the question of membership: shall the United Nations include all sovereign states which accept the conditions of the Charter, or shall the votes be weighted to express the sober, dominant opinion of the civilized world? Secondly, there is the great, unsolved problem of armaments and security. Thirdly, there is the constructive task of providing technical assistance and economic aid to backward countries.

In this last field much has already been done. While the chief task of the United Nations is the elimination of war and the threat of it, the Charter went beyond negative action to build a moral order by provisions for human welfare and international justice. Under the Assembly, or rather alongside it, the Economic and Social Council, created on the demand of mobilized American public opinion, performs services which in the course of time may be fully as important as those of the Security Council. It is composed of eighteen nations with varying terms of service and supported by nonpolitical agencies in economic and social fields, public welfare, and health. This is but a part of a vast scheme of international co-operation designed to substitute for war the more civilized methods of human intercourse. Never before has there been so great an effort to bring nations together for their common good and the realization of the moral law.

Finally we come to the question of international justice and the provision for an international court of justice as the supreme tribunal. With jurisdiction extending over so many diverse civilizations, it is destined to be the embodiment of an ever-developing international law, drawing upon the work of jurists, philosophers, and lawgivers of the past and the challenging demands of a new world order based upon justice.

Such, in outline, is the constitution of the United Nations, or at least a statement of its purposes. We have not touched upon some of its most novel features, such as the Commission on Human Rights and the United Nations Educational, Scientific and Cultural Organization (UNESCO). It is through instruments like these that the ideals of the present can be realized in the future. For that realization, however, the authors of the Charter will not be responsible. The best of instruments is useless unless there is the will to use it. What has been done is to create the opportunity and the means for accomplishing the greatest reform in the history of mankind—the elimination of war and the development of a world community under the moral order. This is the challenge of the great Charter of the United Nations.

2. *The United Nations in Action*

The opening years of the United Nations have been years of stress and storm beyond anything in peacetime history. The wreckage of disaster from the greatest of all wars had to be cleared away, not merely the devastation of cities and countryside but of the mind and spirit of the stricken nations. The frail structure of peace, raised amid hope and doubt after World War I, had been broken down by the great conspiracy of the Axis Powers, which had almost succeeded in the overthrow of freedom in Europe and the creation of an Asiatic empire of sheer militarism. Even before this danger to civilization was ended in World War II, the luster of the victories of the Allies was darkened by the menace of Soviet imperialism, intent upon a communist world empire.

Never has any other political creation had to overcome greater obstacles in its early years than those that confronted the United Nations. It might well be said of it, as was once said in another connection, that it was a triumph to have survived. But, to survive, the United Nations had to justify itself by its works. To see how it met this test, we must turn, hurriedly, to its history.

At the very first meeting of the Council, a threat of war was lifted when the Union of Soviet Socialist Republics withdrew its troops from a northern province of Iran, an achievement which should not be forgotten in view of the unsettled conditions in that part of Asia. The brilliant success of Dr. Ralph Bunche in stopping war in Palestine was one of the most notable episodes in the history of diplomacy. It was through the mediation of the United Nations that the war in Indonesia ended in the grant of independence by the Dutch to the seventy-six million people of that continent of islands, rich in its vast store of natural resources. War between India and Pakistan had already started when India appealed to the United Nations and, although no solution has yet been found for that hot dispute, the door to peaceful settlement, held open by the United Nations, is being used for negotiation. To these four cases of the stoppage of the threat of war and of war itself must be added some other eighty serious serious disputes submitted to the United Nations for mediation or settlement.

In 1949 the Assembly took over the settlement of disputes over the liquidation of Mussolini's short-lived African empire, and carried it out in spite of Soviet opposition.

Then came the supreme test of the United Nations, in Korea. On June 25, 1950, the North Korean communist army, armed by Russia and supported by China, opened war on South Korea, the ward of the United Nations, in a life-and-death challenge to it in Asia. But more than the fate of the United Nations was at stake in the terrible battles on the Korean hills—the fate of the free world. Thermopylae and Marathon were fought once more in the agelong struggle for freedom. In such a struggle, the United States had no choice but to lead the forces of the United Nations, and, through years of prodigious effort and heroic sacrifice, it held the ramparts against the first military crusade of communist imperialism. The supreme task of the future, both for the United States and the United Nations, is to find a defense of peace as sure and strong as that of war. The basis of that strategy lies in the United Nations.

3. *The Control of Atomic Energy and Armaments*

In August 1945, a new era had been begun in the history of war—and of civilization—when the first atomic bomb was dropped from an American plane on the Japanese city of Hiroshima, and a second one, three days later, on Nagasaki. Science, which had been increasingly taking over the technique of warfare, had at last achieved the absolute weapon, one with illimitable powers of destruction in the breaking down (fission) of the atom. The explosions in Japan, terrible as they were in the destruction of life and property, were not so important in themselves as in the far more terrible fact that such weapons could now be produced with ever-increasing power, to the point of endangering all life in the world. The most solemn warnings came from the greatest among the physicists whose research had made the bomb possible. They led public opinion in a universal demand to erect adequate controls to prevent its misuse, if not its total prohibition as an engine of war. This meant, first of all, the absolute control of developments of atomic energy within a country, and also—for the problem could not be limited by any frontier—of the international control on behalf of all nations.

The splitting of the atom had been the military secret of the United States, shared, up to the point of the firing of the bomb, with Canadian and British scientists. Russia had not been let in on it. That was impossible in the atmosphere of mistrust which, as we have seen, was consistently increased by Russia's own refusal to share its secrets with its allies. But, however justified this barring of the Soviet scientists from our laboratories, Moscow's sensibilities, always on edge, were deeply offended by it. The situation was rendered still more delicate by the fact that, before opening negotiations with Russia, President Truman invited the Prime Ministers of Great Britain and Canada to a conference in Washington in November 1945, as the first step in planning for international control of atomic energy. To clear the ground for control, the conference drew a line between the free exchange of scientific information for peaceful ends and "the spreading of the specialized information regarding the practical application of atomic energy, before it is possible to devise effective, reciprocal, and enforceable safeguards acceptable to all nations." This fundamental distinction was further developed in a series of recommendations to be made to the United Nations. The first of these called for a wide international "exchange of basic scientific information for peaceful ends." The second proposal, which naturally followed, was "for control of atomic energy to the extent necessary to ensure its use only for peaceful purposes." Then came the other half of the problem, the provision "for the elimination from national armaments of atomic weapons and all other major weapons adaptable to mass destruction." This preventive measure was followed by a demand for "effective safeguards by way of inspection and other means to protect complying states against the hazards of violations and evasions."

In January 1946, the United Nations turned these problems over to the Commission on Atomic Energy under the Security Council. But this commission was immediately confronted with two opposing plans: that of the United States and that of Soviet Russia. The United

States, having the secret of the bomb, and realizing its revolutionary effect as a weapon, proposed to turn it over to an international authority which would completely own and control the mining and processing of all atomic materials. This authority would have to be empowered to search anywhere for violations, which would mean having access to all of the secrets of heavy industry in other lands. This plan, however noble in outline, was utterly unacceptable to the Russians, who proposed to proceed in an entirely different way by outlawing the production and use of atomic weapons, and calling for the destruction of all existing bombs, yet with no adequate provision for international inspection. Although the American proposal received, time and again, the overwhelming endorsement of the General Assembly, the Soviet block remained adamant in opposition to it; while the United States was equally inflexible in its refusal to accept the Russian plan, because it would leave the Russians free to build up their armies and other weapons while denying the United States the possibility of using the bomb. Equally futile were the negotiations on the reduction of armaments in general, for no agreement could be reached as to how much each side should surrender or keep. Meanwhile, the U.S.S.R., through betrayal by American and British scientists, had acquired the secret of the bomb, and had begun its manufacture. The race in atomic weapons which followed reached its climax in successful experiments with the hydrogen bomb and thermonuclear energy.

Finally, in a striking effort to break this stalemate, President Eisenhower, in December 1953, in an address to the United Nations, proposed to concentrate upon the peacetime and beneficent uses of atomic energy and to build constructively along those lines. The underlying thought behind this new proposal was that a solution might perhaps be found in the strategy of peace instead of the strategy of war. The proposal went far. It was based on the idea that common interests in a common task might so engage the interests of all nations concerned as to lessen warlike tensions, and therefore create an atmosphere in which reason rather than either panic fear or militarism would prevail, with ultimate possibilities of armament agreements. In the President's words, it was a suggestion "to help us move out of the dark chamber of horrors into the light, to find a way by which the minds of men, the hopes of men, the souls of men everywhere, can move forward toward peace and happiness and well-being."

"Atoms for Peace" passed from a slogan to a program at the Geneva Conference on Atomic Energy of the United Nations of August 1955, described below.

The fact that atomic energy was first used in war may in time prove to be one of the greatest safeguards in connection with it. For its capacity for destruction was not left in the realm of theory. We had an object lesson which the world will never forget. Already, in a single day, the highest-powered artillery and the heaviest bombs of the preatomic age became antiques in the museum of war. Battleships and airplane carriers will yet for a while be the auxiliaries of this new force of destruction, just as the cavalry of the age of chivalry lasted down to World War I. But, just as the horsemen made way for artillery and tanks, the existing military equipment of all armies and navies in the world will have to yield to the inexorable forces in the atom. A thing too small for the eye to see has taken the mastery over all the gigantic machinery of war. The searing blast of millions of degrees Fahrenheit can now be directed to the destruction not only of cities but of nations and, if not controlled, to the destruction of the whole human race.

There is no more pressing need in all the world than that of the immediate control and direction of this new force. President Truman was right when he said that the atomic bomb is too dangerous to be let loose in a lawless world. A moment's thought shows that the problem of security takes on wholly new dimensions. Strategic frontiers are a thing of the past. This had already become true before the invention of the guided missile designed to travel through space to anywhere on earth, and it must be remembered that both rocket and nuclear bomb are only in their infancy, and that atomic-powered submarines can cross oceans without refueling. The capacity for destruction which so startles and alarms the world today is probably no nearer its final stage than the early uses of gunpowder compared with the explosions of today. Already the atomic weapons of 1945 are themselves antique, as the scientists have gone from the breaking of the uranium atom to the infinitely more terrible power and poisoning of thermonuclear weapons capable of ending all life everywhere.

The problem of the control of atomic energy is therefore not yet before us in final terms. Thermonuclear processes are still in their infancy and their future development will not depend wholly upon the discoveries of the scientists, but also upon the capacity of the engineer to keep pace with these discoveries. The fundamental principle of atomic fission, the breaking up of the atom, and the fusion process which is the basis of the hydrogen bomb, have already been largely explored and developed by the scientists, but the control of these vast new reservoirs of power is basically an engineering problem. In this regard, there is a certain parallel with the history of the first great scientific revolution in industry, when steam power took over the world's work. The early engines of Watt and Boulton broke down constantly owing to the imperfect nature of the iron in the boilers and cylinders. There were frequent explosions, so that these engines of the early days were relatively weak.

This backward look is not without a bearing on the problem of the control of atomic energy because, while analogies are often misleading, there seems to be no reason to doubt that some such development is ahead of us in the development of atomic power. In fact, it seems already to have begun in that the process of thermonuclear development is cheapening. The developers of atomic energy do not need any more such vast expenditures of money as were necessary in the building of Oak Ridge and Hanford, the pioneering manufacturing plants of the atomic age. This fact is fully as important as the increase of the amount of power, for it means that the Great Powers will no longer have a monopoly of it. This in turn means a revolution in the power structure of nations. It is not necessary to have a vast output of such new weapons to be able to threaten neighboring nations, or for them to make demands enforced by the new power which would secure for them a partnership in the development of atomic energy for peace. What we are therefore faced with is not merely a slow step forward in disarmament, but the development of an international community of nations aware of the absolute necessity of abolishing war itself. Until now this has been the dream of altruists.

4. *The Strategy of Peace*

Nuclear energy for the uses of destruction will somehow be outlawed, for war has become too dangerous an enterprise for any civilized nation to risk its existence by the use of such great and incalculable forces. In its indiscriminate destruction there are no victors left, only survivors —if any—in a ruined world. Both General Marshall and General Eisenhower had said this about World War II in Europe even without atomic bombs. But the very immensity of so great a danger makes the need for escape from it so much more real and pressing. Moreover, if these dangers are exorcised, there will be an ever-increasing, illimitable horizon for the development of its peace-time uses. The direction and control of these beneficent operations will have to be as definitely international as the controls for the prevention of war. Science, which was slowly making the world interdependent—although we thought the pace was fast enough—has now suddenly made isolation wholly impossible. The interplay of industry, agriculture, and commerce throughout the world will be necessary for the prosperity of any one part of it, and the location and capacity of the productive centers in which nuclear energy will be used is a matter of concern to all the world.

If the way to peace, or, rather, the way to the preservation of mankind lies in planning for peace instead of in a race in armaments, the situation of the free world is doubly fortunate. For the challenge to intelligence rather than to force should find the free nations possessed of a greater, more effective power in the strategy of peace than that of the rigid-minded communist leaders. In the long reach of the era of science which we are now entering, the solution of the greatest problem will be found only by minds adjustable to an ever-changing world—in other words, free minds. It is in this light that western Europe is now seeking the way to peace in that historic arena of national wars. The solution is not easy and we should not expect it too soon. But we must not allow the Communists to make it harder by keeping our attention narrowly upon policies of containment, with no apparent escape from them. It goes without saying that we must maintain adequate defenses on a world-wide scale. But in times of crisis, courageous, farsighted thinking is the best defense, indeed the only salvation.

How soon the chance may come for using it in practical diplomacy will not wholly depend on us; but in the United Nations there is always the possibility of such surprises as that at its first meeting, when the U.S.S.R. withdrew from the threat of aggression in Iran, or that revolution in membership which took place in the closing days of 1955, when sixteen nations were added to United Nations membership in one historic session of the Assembly. Although Japan was still barred by Soviet veto, the principle of universal membership was established, instead of the selective principle of the San Francisco Conference, which had limited membership to the powers that had been victorious in World War II and "all other peace-loving states, which accept the obligations contained in the present Charter and in the judgment of the Organization are able and willing to carry out these obligations." It could be argued—although no one did so—that the phrase "peace-loving states" was defined in the phrase which followed and that therefore the applicant for membership, by its very acceptance of the obligations of the Charter, rated itself as peace-loving. But such quibbling

was beside the point; the principle of universal membership put the accent on collective security, leaving no nation in the world free to avoid the two obligations of
peaceful settlement of its own disputes and aid in preventing war between others. In this regard the enlargement of
the United Nations membership by one fourth was an
adjustment to the enlargement of the possibilities of
atomic warfare described above. A universal danger is, in
theory at least, countered by a universal defense. But this
only opens up the supreme challenge to statesmanship, to
put something in place of war or the threat of it. The
whole future of the United Nations depends on how well
it can meet this test, one which the revolution of December 1955 will inevitably bring to the fore. For, in propor-
tion as the United Nations succeeds in lessening the
chances of war, it will turn from the negative action of
potential policing to the positive work of creating and
strengthening a world community.

Beyond the preservation of peace, the United Nations
is pledged to promote higher standards of living, economic and social justice, and international understanding.
By its system of trusteeships, it protects non-self-govern-
ing peoples. It initiated and operates technical assistance
to help underdeveloped peoples, an activity which the
United States has led under President Truman's Point
Four Program. In 1955 there were 880 projects in 82
countries under 1700 experts and some 1400 assistants.
Then, under the Economic and Social Council, there are
three regional commissions to deal with economic and
trade problems in Europe, Asia, and Latin America, and
one on human rights that looks beyond the material to
the spiritual well-being of mankind.

Finally, there are the specialized agencies, nongovernmental, consultative organizations like those on food and agriculture, world health, the children's fund, the United Nations Educational, Scientific and Cultural Organization (UNESCO), and the International Labor Organization.

These and a half dozen other parallel bodies have been building a world community for the long reaches of the future. The United Nations, as their sovereign unit, thus lays the foundation in justice and freedom, for a lasting peace.

CHAPTER XXI

THE MARSHALL PLAN

It is logical that the United States should do whatever it is able to do to assist in the return of normal economic health in the world, without which there can be no political stability and no assured peace. Our policy is directed not against any country or doctrine but against hunger, poverty, desperation and chaos. Its purpose should be the revival of a working economy in the world so as to permit the emergence of political and social conditions in which free institutions can exist. Such assistance, I am convinced, must not be on a piecemeal basis as various crises develop. Any assistance that this Government may render in the future should provide a cure rather than a palliative. Any government that is willing to assist in the task of recovery will find full cooperation, I am sure, on the part of the United States Government. Any government which maneuvers to block the recovery of other countries cannot expect help from us. Furthermore, governments, political parties or groups which seek to perpetuate human misery in order to profit therefrom politically or otherwise will encounter the opposition of the United States.

—General George C. Marshall, Secretary of State, in an address at Harvard University, June 5, 1947

1. *Recovery and Rehabilitation*

When in May 1945 the guns were silenced in Europe, the silence seemed more like that of the death it had so narrowly escaped than of the quiet gathering of strength to begin life anew. Cities were desolate; trade and industry lacked goods and capital. The treasure house of history lay in ruins. After November 1943 the most urgent needs of the war-torn countries had been met by the contribution of the United Nations Relief and Rehabilitation Administration (UNRRA) in a humanitarian effort unparalleled in history. In the months following the close of the war, United States shipments of relief supplies to the liberated and war-torn countries of Europe reached the incredible sum of four billion dollars, over two billions of which went to UNRRA. By the end of June 1947, the United States had shipped over eighteen million long tons of food to the European nations, including the Soviet Union, and to China, the Philippines, India, the Netherlands East Indies, and to Latin America.

Vast as were these contributions, they were mostly absorbed in immediate temporary relief, and little had been done in basic reconstruction. The task of statesmanship was to make this unprecedented generosity an investment in the upbuilding of a future international economy with a richer promise than could have been fulfilled in the narrow state system of the past with its rivalries and wars. This was the prospect which was opened by Secretary Marshall's address at Harvard University, quoted above. But of equal importance with the generous proposal of continued economic support from the United States was the condition attached to it, that the United States would not deal with each European nation separately, but they had to organize among themselves and present a joint program to the United States. This condition was clearly stated by Secretary Marshall in the Harvard address:

It is already evident that, before the United States Government can proceed much further in its efforts to alleviate the situation and help start the European world on its way to recovery, there must be some agreement among the countries of Europe as to the requirements of the situation and the part those countries themselves will take in order to give proper effect to whatever action might be undertaken by this Government. It would be neither fitting nor efficacious for this Government to undertake to draw up unilaterally a program designed to place Europe on its feet economically. This is the business of the Europeans. The initiative, I think, must come from Europe. The role of this country should consist of friendly aid in the drafting of a European program and of later support of such a program as far as it may be practical for us to do so. The program should be a joint one, agreed to by a number, if not all, European nations.

The Secretary of State correctly interpreted public opinion in the United States in insisting that American aid to Europe should not be parceled out in Washington, with the inevitable result of sharp and embarrassing rivalries, which would be left to Washington to settle. The result in Europe was the creation of an organization new to history, the Organization for European Economic Cooperation (OEEC). It took some three months for the Europeans to reach agreement, for the calculations involved many unknown factors, and there were no precedents to build upon, but finally agreements were reached, and in the course of seven years, 1948 to 1955, United States aid reached over twenty billion dollars. The exact amount can never be precisely set forth, for, as in all such calculations of long-term national spending, the value of the money changes so that the dollar of one

year is not the same as that of the preceding years. But in
this case the sums are so vast that the margin of difference amounts to relatively little. More important is the
fact that the costs of World War II were also for the defense of freedom—against another threat of world tyranny—and should not be left out of the calculations of
America's contribution in the defense of freedom. Then,
it must be borne in mind that Asia was being helped as
well as Europe.

The original "Marshall Plan" and other plans for foreign aid was finally fitted into a comprehensive Mutual
Security Program and taken over by a single agency, the
Foreign Operations Administration. There is nothing in
all history to match this peacetime strategy for international co-operation, either in the boldness of its conception or the extent of its actions. All in all, in the period
from 1940 through March 1955, counting expenditures in
the war, United States aid to foreign governments ag-
gregated the sum of over ninety billion dollars. But if the
investment in peace and freedom was great, it was justified by its success. Already, by 1950, the hard-stricken
Marshall Plan countries of Europe had so far recovered
from the greatest war in history that their industrial index
reached an all-time high, 38 per cent higher than in 1938.
Making due allowance for postwar booms, this is an incredible page in the history of economics.

2. *The Cominform and the Struggle for Germany*

Hardly more than a fortnight after the Harvard speech,
the three foreign ministers, Bevin, Bidault, and Molotov,
met in conference at Paris to consider the reaction of their
governments to the Marshall offer. Molotov had brought

to Paris a large staff of technical experts, which created the impression that Moscow was ready to co-operate to the full. But on receipt of a sealed envelope delivered during one of the sessions, Molotov suddenly launched into a bitter attack on the whole American plan, charging that it was capitalist imperialism extending control over Europe through credits which it would later collect. Without any further explanation, he suddenly left for Moscow, taking his experts with him, and it was evident that instead of lessening the tension of the cold war, the Marshall Plan had increased it. Well-organized French and Italian Communists were quite as violent as Moscow in their denunciations of what they called American economic imperialism. Strikes and disorders in both Italy and France continued throughout the rest of the year, but ended without a revolutionary outbreak.

It was especially in eastern Europe, however, that the reaction to the Marshall Plan ran its full course. A new organ for communist international action, known as the Communist Information Bureau (Cominform), was created at a conference in Warsaw as a direct answer to what was called "The American Plan for the Enthrallment of Europe." In a manifesto calling upon all Communists to join in a holy war on the Marshall Plan, Zhdanov, organizer of the Cominform, charged that the "imperialist and anti-democratic" camp of the free nations was organizing for the violent overthrow of communism everywhere. The perversity and utter falseness of this manifesto did not prevent its acceptance in all the countries under communist rule, and the communist nations joined together under the Council for Economic Mutual Assistance to organize eastern Europe against possible infiltration by the Western Powers.

On the central fringe of this communist world lay Germany, divided into four sections by the occupying powers. The Russians, who had suffered most from German invasion, were demanding more reparations than Germany could pay without being reduced to the status of a "congested slum in the center of Europe." The Western Powers, therefore, watched with suspicion and alarm the way in which the Russians began to organize eastern Germany so that it could deal more effectively with its own economic matters.

The final rift between the Allies came over the question of a new German currency. The Soviet reaction to the announcement of the currency reform was violent. All traffic from the West to Berlin was stopped and held under a tight blockade. A city of two and one-half million people had to be supplied, not only with food, but with all the other necessities of domestic, industrial, and commercial life. The answer of the West was an airlift, an unprecedented saga of technical skill, co-ordination, and power. For 323 days and nights American and British planes built an air bridge from beyond the Rhine to West Berlin, and in flights that measured about a hundred thousand miles, delivered over a million and a half tons of goods, much of which had first to be flown from the United States.

This incredible achievement gave an object lesson to Europe. It caught and stirred the imagination of Europeans and reassured the doubters of the ultimate outcome of the struggle for Germany. But fully as important was the manner in which it was settled. At the United Nations the American representative, Philip Jessup, and the Soviet representative, Jacob Malik, met in informal and confidential talks which involved no diplomatic face-saving, and by the end of June the blockade was lifted. The Western Powers had won a victory in this first great test of interference by the U.S.S.R. And the strategy of peace had also won its quiet but equally important gain.

The trade war between East and West had, however, a more sinister aspect than the mere blocking of economic intercourse. On both sides of the iron curtain hostility mounted at each new frustration, and the cold war time and again seemed to be preparing for the outbreak of hostilities which threatened a new world war. For the cold war was not a passing incident in history; it was a development rooted in history as well as in current disagreements and antagonisms. A glance at this background may help, not only to clarify the conflict itself, but to lessen anxiety as to the outcome, for it helps to explain why these things happened as they did.

CHAPTER XXII

THE COLD WAR

The challenge in the Charter of the United Nations did
not mean the same in Moscow as it did in Washington,
London, or Paris. The U.S.S.R. had no thought of renounc-
ing the right of revolution to disrupt the established order
and menace the peace of nations. To the Communists there
could be no lasting peace until the existing national state
system was overthrown. The realistic masters of the Kremlin were willing to subscribe to the high principles of the
Charter by interpreting it in this communist sense, as pro-
hibiting wars of "imperialist aggression," but not interfering
with the spread of communism by conspiracy or force.
Although there were times when Stalin as the bolshevist
dictator spoke of the possibility and advantage of peaceful
relations with the West, upon the whole the Communists
were brutally frank in their persistence in what has come
to be known as "the cold war," damaging and destroying
as far as possible the life-giving activities of the worlds of
economic welfare and international understanding.

1. *Moscow's Pledges, Given and Broken*

On November 11, 1943, it seemed as though a new dawn
had broken over the world, when, in the first political
conference with the foreign ministers of the United
States and Great Britain, Molotov, the most recalcitrant
of Communists, agreed that the U.S.S.R. would join in

a declaration proposed by Secretary of State Cordell Hull in which their nations bound themselves to estalish "a general international organization, based on the principle of the sovereign equality of all peace-loving nations, and open to membership by all such nations, large and small, for the maintenance of international peace and security." After the termination of hostilities they would not "employ their military forces within the territory of other states except for the purposes envisaged in the declaration and after joint consultation." The Moscow declaration was warmly acclaimed in both the British Parliament and the United States Congress in joint session. It seemed too good to be true; and it was.

The Moscow conference was followed a few weeks later by the Teheran conference, in which the three war leaders, Roosevelt, Churchill, and Stalin, meeting for the first time, planned the great strategy of the war, then at its most critical stage. As for the peace after the war, the declaration of the three powers was vague but reassuring: "We recognize fully the supreme responsibility resting upon us and all the United Nations to make a peace which will command the good will of the overwhelming mass of peoples of the world and banish the scourge and terror of war for many generations." *Pravda*, speaking for the U.S.S.R., commented: "Only a short time separates us from the Moscow Conference . . . but what a tremendous step has been taken along the path" of loyal cooperation in the postwar world.

Fourteen months passed before the leaders of the great alliance met again, at Yalta in the Crimea, months of the most momentous military events in history. On the western front the Germans had been driven from France, but the Rhine had yet to be crossed. In the East the Soviet armies by an incredible feat of arms had turned the German invasion into a disastrous retreat and were pursuing the beaten but still powerful foe with continuing and irresistible strength. But on the threshold of victory, the Kremlin began to show imperialist designs of conquest, as it planned to turn "liberated" Poland over to a communist government. To hold the Russians in check at the Yalta conference, Churchill and Roosevelt got from Stalin another pledge in a "Declaration on Liberated Europe," to establish in the territories won back from the Nazis "free elections of governments responsive to the will of the people, and to facilitate when necessary the holding of such elections." Had the shining promises of this pledge been kept by the U.S.S.R., there would have been no cold war in Europe.

Both Roosevelt and Churchill reported in Congress and Parliament that the Yalta conference had cleared the way for the final terms of peace. But even while they were speaking, Russia was already sabotaging the work so hopefully begun. While the Soviet army was occupying Rumania, Stalin's envoy Vishinsky gave its young king three hours in which to dismiss his prime minister and turn the government over to Moscow's nominees. Bulgaria was next to follow Rumania's fate; Hungary was soon overrun, and, when in 1948 Czechoslovakia succumbed, these nations, with Poland on the north, formed a ring of satellite communist states which brought Russian power into the heart of Europe.

In May 1945, the Nazis finally surrendered. In the meantime the shadow of communist imperialism had lengthened and darkened. It was time for a new conference and it met at Potsdam in July. At Yalta, it had been agreed that "the final delineation of the western frontier

of Poland should await the peace conference," but the
U.S.S.R. installed a communist administration for all
northeastern Germany, including sixty thousand square
miles of German soil. Neither at Potsdam nor in conferences held in the months which followed were any real
concessions made to the American and British protests.
President Truman and Secretary of State James Byrnes
at times seemed to hold their own in the long, weary
game of diplomacy, but a warning of the realities rang
out in Churchill's "iron curtain" speech at a college in
Fulton, Missouri, in March 1946:

> From Stettin in the Baltic to Trieste in the Adriatic, an
> iron curtain has descended across the Continent. . . . Police
> governments are pervading from Moscow. Athens alone,
> with its immortal glories, is free to decide under British,
> American and French observation. . . . [At the close of
> World War II] there were high hopes and unbounded con-
> fidence that the wars were over . . . I do not see or feel that
> same confidence or even the same hopes in the haggard
> world at the present time.

Reluctantly American public opinion accepted the inevitable conclusion that diplomacy was, in Soviet eyes, only
a new kind of warfare, to which Churchill applied a new
name, "the cold war."

Critics of American diplomacy at the Yalta and Potsdam conferences have charged it with naïveté in having
failed to fathom Soviet diplomacy, and there is something
in the criticism. But it seems also clear that the Russians,
like most Europeans, equally misread the American mind.
The speedy withdrawal of our troops from overseas no
longer meant what it meant in Wilson's day, a lack of
interest in the establishment of permanent peace in Eu-

rope—or, for that matter, in Asia. It was partly due to the fact that the American army, unlike those of the European continent, was an improvisation to meet an emergency, and had always been so considered. Sound instincts of democratic freedom lay behind the long-established tradition, best illustrated by the historic conversation of Grant with Lee at Appomattox, when the soldiers of the Confederacy were left free to keep their horses and mules for the spring plowing. In Europe only England shared this idea of soldiering. The Continental nations had a more realistic sense of military power behind policies of state. However, no one was keener to apply the lesson of Clausewitz—that war is an instrument of politics—than Churchill when he urged, unsuccessfully, that the war be waged through the Balkans to prevent the forward march of Russia.

From the standpoint of sophisticated diplomacy, such as Russia's, our failure to back up our policy in central and eastern Europe did, undoubtedly, seem naïve. But the Soviets, with equal naïveté, drew the wrong conclusion, that they could impose on us with impunity. No greater blunder could be made about Americans. There is a native shrewdness in reaching a decision and a readiness to back it up, which foreigners find puzzling, but which is the very breath of freedom. In 1947, two years after the fighting had stopped in Europe, the American people became reluctantly aware of innate Soviet hostility to all that the history of the United States stands for, and they reacted to it with militant unanimity in support of what became known as the Truman Doctrine.

2. *The Doctrine of Containment*

On March 12, 1947, in a message read to both houses of Congress, President Truman met the challenge of communist imperialism by a counterchallenge destined to realize the vision of Woodrow Wilson in the creation of a "Monroe Doctrine for the world," extending the guarantee of freedom to all peoples. The incident which led to this action was not the least incredible part of it, support for the royal government of Greece. There had long been open criticism in American anti-imperialist circles of British support of what was regarded as the reactionary government of King George II. But when in February 1947, the British Ambassador in Washington said that his government could not afford to continue defending Greece against communist attacks fed by its northern neighbors, both Congress and public opinion in the United States gave overwhelming support to President Truman when he proposed to take over the very task for which Great Britain had been so severely criticized. It took Congress only ten days to translate the message into law. Immediately American military and civilian personnel left for Greece and Turkey, and the long, hard task of pacification and reconstruction was carried through, although it took two years before peace was finally restored in Greece.

There was a touch of drama in the defense of the land of Thermopylae and Marathon against an invasion more dangerous because more insidious than that of ancient Persia. In his message to Congress, President Truman verged upon this parallel without mentioning it; for the enemy which the United States was confronting, and which, if unchecked, would endanger its peace and security, was not an economic theory but a despotism in government. The issue was clearly stated in the following terms:

> One of the primary objectives of the foreign policy of the United States is the creation of conditions in which we and other nations will be able to work out a way of life free from coercion. This was a fundamental issue in the war with Germany and Japan. Our victory was won over countries which sought to impose their will, and their way of life upon other nations. . . .
>
> The peoples of a number of countries of the world have recently had totalitarian regimes forced upon them against their will. The government of the United States has made frequent protests against coercion and intimidation, in violation of the Yalta Agreement, in Poland, Rumania and Bulgaria. I must also state that in a number of other countries there have been similar developments.
>
> At the present moment in world history every nation must choose between alternative ways of life. The choice is too often not a free one.
>
> One way of life is based upon the will of the majority, and is distinguished by free institutions, representative government, free elections, guarantees of individual liberty, freedom of speech and religion, and freedom from political oppression.
>
> The second way of life is based upon the will of a minority forcibly imposed upon the majority. It relies upon terror and oppression, a controlled press and radio, fixed elections, and the suppression of personal freedom.
>
> I believe that it must be the policy of the United States to support free people who are resisting attempted subjugation by armed minorities or by outside pressures.
>
> I believe that we must assist free peoples to work out their own destinies in their own way.

To the American people the principles embodied in this declaration of policy were familiar and accepted as fundamental truths. They seemed like voices from history, only blown on the winds of freedom to all corners of the earth. But they really marked a new era in history. For they committed the United States to a world-wide mission as the champion of freedom. That was something new—so new and so great a commitment that it constituted a revolution in both American and world affairs.

While the Marshall Plan and its successors dealt with the economic recovery of western Europe, the accent in the Truman Doctrine had been placed upon the military aspects of the defense against the encroachments of Soviet imperialism. It was natural, therefore, that the problems of recovery, vast and challenging as they proved to be, were less in the public mind than the danger of the outbreak of war itself. Therefore, throughout the early months of 1948, the United States and Great Britain led in forming a military association of the Western nations, a momentous step which resulted in the creation of the North Atlantic Treaty Organization (NATO). Woodrow Wilson's proposal in 1919 of a guarantee treaty with France against future aggression by Germany had been opposed on all sides, both in Washington and throughout the country, although now, looking back through the tragedy of World War II, it is recognized that it would have been the one essential step in the upbuilding of European peace at that time. The nationwide demand for speedy withdrawal from Europe in 1945 had played into the hands of Moscow, which moved the frontiers of the communist empire into the heart of Europe. Its final coup in taking over Czechoslovakia in 1948 and its threat to dominate the rest of Eu-

rope were responsible for the revolutionary change in
American policy which resulted in the United States acceptance of the alliance with European countries.

3. *The Brussels Pact and NATO*

The defense of the West had become the dominant concern of United States politics. Owing to the menace of
Soviet armaments, it was chiefly conceived in military
terms, with the atomic weapon holding a perilous balance
of power. Fortunately, the communist coup in Czechoslovakia in the early spring of 1948 stirred western Europe to a new sense of danger, and on March 17, 1948, a
week after the Truman message, five western nations,
Great Britain, France, Belgium, the Netherlands, and
Luxembourg, signed a treaty of collective defense, which
was destined, four years later, to be made the cornerstone
of the structure of European freedom. The treaty, which
was to last for fifty years, was to secure "the principles
of democracy, personal freedom and political liberty, the
constitutional traditions and the rule of law which are
their common heritage." Provision was made for co-
ordinating economic policies and for closer cultural co-
operation. Above all, it was a military alliance, all the signatories pledging "all military and other aid and assistance
in their power" to any one if attacked in Europe. All
questions arising under the treaty should go to a permanent consultative council composed of the five foreign
ministers, meeting on terms of equality, at least every
three months. This was the Brussels Pact, which Great
Britain, its chief architect, readjusted in 1954 at a conference in Paris to serve as a basis for Western European
unity.

Meanwhile, however, the movement for the defense of the West took on larger outlines in the North Atlantic Treaty Organization (NATO). The name is self-explanatory. The two nations west of the Atlantic, the United States and Canada, were to add their guarantees of peace and freedom to that of the European powers in the Brussels Pact. For the United States there was no other choice than to join in this new defense of freedom, although it involved an absolute break with the former trend toward isolation. Ultimately, the United States not only accepted membership in NATO but took the leadership in it. So great a decision, however, could not be reached at once, and it was not until a year later, on April 4, 1949, that the North Atlantic Treaty was signed at Washington by twelve nations: Belgium, Canada, Denmark, France, Iceland, Italy, Luxembourg, the Netherlands, Norway, Portugal, the United Kingdom, and the United States. The treaty was ratified by the United States Senate on July 21, without reservation.

Although a departure from tradition, this epochal act was not a departure from the central theme of United States history. The frontiers of freedom were no longer in the United States, but in the old world of Europe and the still older world of Asia. In the North Atlantic alliance the countries which had been the battlefields of two world wars were to be shielded against a third one; in Asia the organization of peace had still to await the issue of other ordeals in Korea and Indochina. But with equally firm decision, America faced both dangers and in the succeeding years assumed a new place among the nations, that of the champion of their freedom as well as its own.

In presenting the North Atlantic Treaty Organization

to Congress, President Truman invoked history as well as the present danger:

> The nations signing this treaty share a common heritage of democracy, individual liberty and rule of law. The American members of the North Atlantic Community stem directly from the European members in tradition and in love of freedom. We have joined together in the progressive development of free institutions, and we have shared our moral and material strength in the present task of rebuilding from the devastation of war. . . .

The North Atlantic Treaty Organization has as its head the North Atlantic Council, composed for the most part of ministers of foreign affairs, defense, and finance; but the most important organ is the military executive: Supreme Headquarters, Allied Powers, Europe (SHAPE), presided over by the Supreme Allied Commander in Europe. For this high office, unique in history, the unanimous choice of the nations was General Eisenhower (followed by Generals Ridgeway and Gruenther).

Under General Eisenhower's inspiring leadership, and with the backing of the signatory states, NATO overcame all the initial obstacles of doubt as to its competence to serve as a rallying point for the defense of the West. Its very success, however, aroused apprehension in certain quarters for fear that Russia might make a sudden attack to anticipate the further developments of the military arm that was growing under the energetic direction of SHAPE. Moscow, however, chose to use a peace offensive in a barrage of propaganda designed to discourage the build-up of NATO by nations which could ill afford such a costly diversion of their economic resources for military expenses. Instead of following up its aggressions in Europe, such as the support of the communist coup in Prague and the blockade of Berlin, it apparently was turning to an Asian policy in linking up with China, conniving and assisting in the communist attack on Korea. This trend of Soviet policy evidenced by the swing to the Far East was doubly effective in that the United States was forced to take on the heavy commitment of war in Korea, and the apprehension of danger was lessened in western Europe as little was happening there at the time except the constant stream of propaganda from Moscow and the satellite countries.

Designed at first as an emergency measure of the nations along the Atlantic, NATO responded to these new communist pressures in Asia by enlarging its scope and reaching out through Turkey and over Iran to Pakistan to link up with a new alliance of the five nations on the shores of the South Pacific. In this way the Truman Doctrine and the defense of the West became one. Only the geography was changed; the purpose remained the same.

From the standpoint of purely military history NATO has undoubtedly been a success, but it is a success measured in terms of military strategy, and the upbuilding of Western unity calls for a strategy of peace fully as adequate as a strategy of war. No one has ever brought this fact out more clearly than General Eisenhower himself on the occasion of the fourth anniversary of the signing of the NATO treaty when he said:

> The 200,000,000 people of the NATO nations are in the deepest sense bound together by a unity more profound than any pact. They are skilled in work, courageous in spirit and tenacious in their love of freedom. They—their

spirit and strength and resources—are indispensable to the defense of freedom everywhere. If they and their resources ever were captured and exploited by an aggressor, there would be no corner of safety anywhere in the world. But so long as these people and these resources are joined with those of the United States in our common cause, no aggressor can be blind to the folly of attack.

In other words, it is not only the armaments of NATO but the sense of a common interest among the peoples of the free world which is the bulwark of its safety. But, as the Canadian delegate, Lester Pearson, pointed out at an Ottawa meeting of the NATO Council, this sense of common interests rests on an economic basis which would have to stand an added strain by an increase in armaments. Therefore, although NATO itself was not designed to deal with economic international relations, it favored the growth of other organs of European unity. None of this hopeful development would have been possible, however, without the life-giving force of the Marshall Plan and the organizations to carry out its purpose in the recovery and development of postwar Europe.

The share of the United States in this movement toward European union has been gratefully recognized by European statesmen. Without the Marshall Plan, devastated Europe would have long remained impoverished and weakened, held to the discouraging task of recovery instead of moving forward. Without NATO the nations now beginning to aspire to European unity would have fallen back into the old anarchy of a national state system which recognized war as the final instrument of policy. But while recognizing that these initial contributions have been essential and fundamental in the upbuilding of a lasting peace, the European nations rightly feel that the architectural and engineering work on the upbuilding of the political structure of tomorrow is primarily their task, with the United States taking the position of a friendly neighbor, helping but not attempting to take the direction of their effort.

4. The Task for Statesmanship

The cold war was prevented from becoming a world war, not by the solemn pledge of the U.S.S.R. to the Charter of the United Nations, but by the changed nature of war itself. This major fact of our times comes to the fore in almost all the history that follows. The same scientific and industrial revolution which had produced communism by the machinery for mass production in the arts of peace has now taken over the science of warfare, so that even the militarism of the Soviet pauses on the rim of the abyss of a third world war. To make that pause endure is the supreme task of statesmanship and the test of the United Nations as the guarantor of peace. The terms of the problem are clear: the mistrust that hides in conspiratorial secrecy must yield to openhanded dealings. But all history shows, and never more conclusively than in the history of these last years, that the way for statesmen to break down the barriers of suspicion between nations is not by direct attack upon those policies on which they believe their safety or their way of life depends. This is an iron law of diplomacy. It holds even if the nation's safety does not really depend upon the policy in question, so long as that is believed to be the case. For security is a state of mind—one which politicians can communicate to those whose fate is in their hands.

The negotiations on the control of atomic energy illustrate this point. The Baruch Plan to place it in an international authority, which would take ownership and management out of the hands of national governments, and on which the Communists would be in a hopeless minority, was linked in their minds with the fact that there were Wall Street personalities advising Bernard Baruch, who, himself, had had Wall Street connections. It was, therefore, stated in Russia that the whole scheme was a plot to take out of Soviet hands the greatest of all sources of power. The truth or falsity of such an interpretation was beside the mark. No preliminary diplomatic effort had been made to clear away suspicion natural in the circumstances, and doubly so to the Russians trained to think in terms of conspiracy. But the suspicion was two-edged. The Soviet counterproposal, to abolish atomic weapons by international agreement, relying on the good faith of nations to carry it out, looked like a mere propaganda slogan, especially deceptive in view of the absence of any acceptable measure of disarmament in conventional weapons and man power.

With such a roadblock of mutual distrust on the path of negotiation, it was natural that agreement could not be reached; for in dealings between sovereign powers there must be a willingness to compromise, otherwise the nation that yields anything feels aggrieved and will not carry out loyally a commitment which seems contrary to its vital interests. Unfortunately it is in the field of security that compromise is most difficult, for the issue of national defense is that of life or death for a nation. Therefore it tends to harden its case, fearful that concession may mean the kind of appeasement that goes by the name of "Munich." To escape such a disaster and yet to lessen the danger of the cold war becoming a hot war—a new name for war itself—is only possible by the growing recognition of new, overriding interests on both sides. There are two ways for this to happen: one is by a shift from doctrinaire generalities to practical policies of restricted scope; the other is by the changed nature of war. Policies of economic or political expediency are as common in Soviet history as in our own. The outlook today for such partial approaches through trade or travel is not bright, but it will never get brighter if we draw down our own iron curtain alongside that of the U.S.S.R. History is full of surprises, and the dynamics of science are already increasing their number. The free world is certain to have its chance to work out this problem in the years to come; it cannot solve it without working at it. But the really compelling force for breaking down obstacles to understanding is the force which created them by the upbuilding of the diverse civilizations of today, a force greater than any statesman or soldier ever wielded—science. The conflict in ideologies between the communist and non-communist world is, in the last resort, a disagreement over the control of this new power.

The issue is not new, and history can already throw light on the probable outcome. For, in the first era of the Industrial Revolution, in the early nineteenth century, capital was as firmly convinced of the doctrine of *laissez faire* as communism is of its present collectivist doctrine under rigid state controls. So deeply convinced were the upper and middle classes of the iron law of wages that to interfere with it seemed like defying Providence. Yet the nation that stood out most strongly against government interference in business—England—is now the most highly developed "welfare state" in Europe, and has progressed step by step, without revolution. While analogies from history are often more alluring than justified, there seems no reason to doubt that the adjustments to reality will be any more lacking in the communist world than they were in that which the Duke of Wellington was convinced "would never be so happy and prosperous again." The rigid communist ideologist of today may be as mistaken in his view as the Duke of Wellington was.

One last word: how does this fit in with the maxim that in dealing with the Communists we must "deal in strength?" Certainly, nothing is gained by weakness. But strength in the central policy of security is not a barrier to adjustment in the day-to-day run of international affairs. The two should not conflict; if they do, the diplomacy is at fault.

CHAPTER XXIII

A PROGRAM FOR TOMORROW

The economic and political battlefields of the cold war have been chiefly in Europe. Elsewhere, as in Asia, the skirmishing lines have run into actual, desperate fighting; but in this titanic struggle between communist imperialism and freedom, the strategy of peace has been equally decisive. The United States had been unconsciously preparing to take its part in this ever since the movement of reform at the turn of the century had awakened its conscience to the unfinished tasks of democracy at home. History has yet to do justice to those who led in this moral crusade, who made politics a battleground for vital issues and lifted the vision of America to the shining goal of social and economic justice. As has so often been the case, most progress is made in times of adversity, when the structure of society is tested and the nation must stop and think about itself and the world. Then when the crisis passes and new problems arise, the nation can confront them with clearer vision and greater confidence.

1. *The Fundamental Freedoms*

Whatever the form of things to come, there is one eternal principle professed alike by the Communists and the free nations: the principle of justice in all human affairs. We meant this in the revolutionary ideal, "life, liberty, and the pursuit of happiness." The Communists profess as their ultimate goal the sharing of a better and happier life. The conflict lies in the conviction held by each that the method of the other is a betrayal of the principle itself; and so strong is this conviction that it obscures the fundamental purpose, just as in the era of the Protestant Reformation the war of creeds obscured the common Christianity. The only escape from this dilemma is to rise above it, as was the case in the history of religion. For the free world, that means the elimination of exploitation and colonial imperialism, and free trade among nations. Whether communism co-operates or not, the free world would be both freer and stronger.

This is the program for tomorrow. It was indicated in the Charter of the United Nations, which went far beyond the Covenant of the League in creating machinery to provide universal respect for, and observance of, "human rights and fundamental freedoms for all without distinction as to race, sex, language or religion." The League had pioneered in these fields, but had no such sweeping mandates as that of the Economic and Social Council of the United Nations. The advance made by the Charter over the Covenant was the measure of advance in American public opinion since Wilson's day, for it was the United States which insisted that "peaceful and friendly relations between nations" are based on "higher standards of living" and "solutions of international economic, social, health and related problems, and international cultural and educational cooperation." The history of the United Nations at first seemed to justify the criticism of those who thought that this emphasis on economic and social problems was too strong, for the political issues of peace and security took precedence in the troubled postwar period. The United States carried out its greatest international economic activities outside the United Nations, in the Marshall Plan and other generous measures of relief and rehabilitation. But, although questions of war and peace—including the control of atomic weapons—were more pressing than those of welfare, an international citizenship was developed in the common interest in world health, food and agriculture, finance, education, and the problems of labor, for each of which the proper organization was provided. But these "specialized agencies," as they were termed, left untouched the one most sensitive international grievance of backward or handicapped nations, their exploitation by the powerful and more advanced. The old colonial system, which had kept more than half of the world in subjection, had been outwardly destroyed in most of Asia, but resentment over past wrongs colored the new freedom. It has made peace insecure, for it bred a belligerent nationalism against all kinds of Western intrusion.

It was at this point that the United Nations opened the way to the only solution. It was prepared to offer "technical assistance" to backward, poverty-stricken peoples, to help them develop their own natural resources. The United Nations took this up and carried it on as far as it could in the face of communist opposition. Fortunately, the United States saw the vast importance of such a policy and made it its own.

2. President Truman's Point Four Program

In President Truman's Inaugural in January 1949, one of the great state papers of our history, he set forth in simple outline the four main points of foreign policy: support for the United Nations; co-operation in world recovery; protection against aggression; and the famous "Point Four," a "bold new program for making the benefits of our scientific advances and industrial progress available for the improvement and growth of underdeveloped areas." President Truman continued:

> More than half the people of the world are living in conditions approaching slavery. . . . Their economic life is primitive and stagnant. Their poverty is a handicap and a threat to themselves and to more prosperous areas. For the first time in history, humanity possesses the knowledge and skill to relieve the sufferings of these people. . . . We should make available to peace-loving people the benefits of our store of technical knowledge in order to help them realize their aspirations for a better life. And, in cooperation with other nations, we should foster capital investment in areas needing development. . . . We invite other countries to pool their technical resources in this undertaking. . . . The old imperialism—exploitation for foreign profit—has no place in our plans. . . . Democracy alone can supply the vitalizing force to stir the peoples of the world into triumphant action, not only against their human oppressors, but also against their ancient enemies—hunger, misery and despair.

This "bold, new program" was not wholly new. As we have already seen, the United States had already spent many billion dollars in foreign aid, both during the war and after, and it was a part of the peacetime strategy of the cold war. But it marked the vast distance traveled by the United States from the sheltered continent of isolation, as it saw that its peace and security depended on the good will of nations it hardly knew existed in the era of self-contained economy, now gone forever. The wartime aim of "one world" eloquently voiced by the leader of the political opposition, Wendell Willkie, proved to be a delusion, but the obstacles raised against it by the Kremlin were now being made steppingstones to further advance by a different road, through that half of the world which had been left behind in the march of progress. It has not been an easy road, and we lose our way if we try to travel it alone. The nations we would help and defend must help and defend themselves against all exploitation, including that by their own people. In short, the aim is to make the world safe for democracy in the only way it can be made safe—permanently.

Point Four will always stand out in history as a noble program both for the United States and the United Nations. Out of the cold war a great constructive movement was begun, which would substitute for the colonial exploitation so long practiced by the Western Powers, policies of support and co-operation. If it could succeed it might even build a bridge across a divided world. But the obstacles are many and great. It must not be a passing episode leaving in its wake only disillusionment and resentment. It must be based on long-term planning, for it reaches into the lives of peoples unused to change in ancient folkways. It must stimulate in them self-help instead of weakening the moral fiber by mere philanthropy. It must also repay the investment of good will by increased security and welfare for all. In these terms, and designed to meet these imperatives, it was the blueprint of the world of tomorrow. In so far as it succeeds, civilization, so long preparing, acquires new meaning.

3. *The Awakening of Asia*

Already Asia is awakening to this new day. Africa will follow. But Asia, the oldest and vastest of the homes of men, is already stirring with the awareness of a new destiny. The weight of the unchanging past is still heavy upon it; the temple bells from Rangoon to Kyoto still sound in the quiet air of religious contemplation, and the muezzin's call greets the dawn from the islands of the eastern seas to the shores of the Mediterranean. But through the busy days come the disturbing noises of the machine age, with its promise of economic and social change and its challenge to outworn social systems.

Because the political systems of Asia have been despotic, the social structure took over most of what is politics in the West. The supreme question, therefore, for Asia and the world is whether, in the changes introduced by the Industrial Revolution, the West can offer a guidance to a more acceptable way of life under freedom than the rigid political controls of communism, which brings politics into the homelife of the common man. To solve this question in terms of freedom, no better way could be found than in the practical demonstrations of Point Four, which are already at work in the social and economic spheres in those parts of Asia not behind the iron curtain. Too much must not be expected too soon. The awakening of Asia is, like science itself, a never-ending process. A new world is coming into existence in the ancient centers of civilization. Although the forces creating it are like those which have been transforming the West, it will always keep the essentials of oriental culture and will inevitably cherish the contributions which it has made in art, philosophy, and the understanding of life.

It is in this perspective that we must view the impact of communism upon the peoples of the Orient. Although its revolutionary movement may for a while exercise relentless power in the overthrow of age-old social structures, it cannot fasten permanently upon China, any more than upon the West, the iron fetters of an unchanging system of economics or government, for it is the expression of a dynamic force and not, as the Kremlin imagines, a monolithic, unyielding, final, and inevitable framework of society. Its crusade against the evils of exploitation is carried out, like all crusades, under a military system, with a commander and a general staff, to whom opposition is treason. All history shows that this is the most effective organization for waging war, but history shows equally clearly that it is not the best form of government for peoples at peace. Militarism, and that is what it is, either breaks down, as in Rome, or leads to catastrophe, as in Germany.

In China another way was found. As dynasty followed dynasty, the political structure was left less powerful, less the expression of the Chinese way of life than the social structure, based largely on the precepts of Confucius. Sooner or later the hidden power of this moral code should reassert itself. Communism cannot obliterate the Confucian version of the Golden Rule: "Do not do unto others what ye would not they do unto you." Thus, if it remains true to its ideals, China will ultimately arrive by a different path at the same goal as the West, in the search for justice under freedom. The communist masters of China are aware of this possibility and are concentrating their efforts to meet it by educating the youth of the country to rebel against the social even more than the political structure of the Confucian teaching. The fate of Asia will depend largely upon the issue in this great conflict of two ways of life.

The United Nations, created, like the League of Nations before it, to build a world community of peaceful

nations, has been forced to stand the test of its capacity in
Asia even more than in the Western world, for which it
was primarily designed. On the hills of Korea its contact
with the Orient has been by way of war; but in other
parts of the Orient it has worked with courage and devotion on such problems as those of Pakistan and India, and
has also had dramatic success in southeastern Asia. Moreover, alongside these efforts to establish and maintain
peace, it has been carrying out a unique and important
program in agriculture and industry. The fundamental
problem, however, still remains the elimination of war.

4. *The Gateway of Trade*

It is not in the temper of the American people to count
the cost of a great enterprise if it is necessary. Point Four
was a heavy and unfamiliar burden, costing millions an-
nually; but, under the pressure of the cold war, the new
administration which came to power in 1953 kept it still
going, with only slightly lessened support. But then the
second half of the program comes to the fore: where and
how could the nations whom we helped to produce goods
find sale for them if the markets of the world were closed
to them? Were we to repeat the terrible blunders of the
years after World War I, when we helped to restore the
crippled industries of Europe but then, by raising Chinese
walls of tariff against them, helped to bring on the economic catastrophe which was the prelude to World War
II? The modest but sound reciprocal trade policies of
Cordell Hull—the one statesman of his day who really
knew his Adam Smith—have remained so far a bulwark
against a repetition of the blindness of the 1920's, when
American money went abroad in vast amounts to invest

in foreign productive enterprises while we closed our markets to their goods. But the world is now more inter-dependent and the free world can only exist as a community of nations, linked by common interests. The gateways of trade must be kept open. The Communists claim that this is impossible for a capitalistic society, because the competitive economy of capitalism leads inevitably to conflict. The history of commerce gives the lie to this. From the days of the freebooters of the sixteenth century and the mercantile system of closed markets and the commercial wars in the era that followed, trade, though still greatly hampered, lessened its rivalries to peacetime strategies. Progress was slow, often blocked and turned back, but the body of world trade continued to grow in spite of obstacles. The vital part it plays in the world today is best seen in the anxiety of the communist governments to recover the East-West trade, so heavily hit by the cold war. World trade opens the pathway to world peace.

5. Coexistence

Running through the whole fabric of the history of these last years, the red thread of communism has been woven into almost everything depicted in these pages: the control of atomic energy, European and Asian affairs, the cold war, NATO, and the movement for European union. Everywhere, hostility has glowed beneath the ashes of disappointed hopes or flared in the open. Yet all along there have been reassuring statements of pacific intent mingled with recriminations. Each side has had its formula; the Communists denouncing capitalist imperialism, and the West calling for "deeds not words" to prove the genuineness of Soviet policy. Behind it all was a lack of confidence in the good faith of each by each. With the death of Stalin Moscow seemed to be feeling its way toward an *entente*, at least that was the impression in liberal circles in Europe, and British Labor, which has a strong following on the Continent, decided to investigate both in Moscow and Peking. The conclusions of Attlee and his colleagues were not far removed from those of Churchill and Eden, that the doors in the iron curtain should be kept open as far as possible. Yet both agreed with Eisenhower and Dulles that the only way to negotiate with the Communists was "from a position of strength."

This proviso has a different meaning in Europe from that current in the United States. Here it frankly means military strength; in Europe it means economic advantage as well. Our trade with eastern Europe has never been important; to most of western and middle Europe it is not only valuable but essential, and the defense of each country against the growth of communism lies in the soundness of its own economy. Reactionary politicians in Washington who talk of "co-existence" as a treasonable surrender to Moscow, have no understanding of the strength that lies in moderation. It is possible, of course, that communism, being a revolutionary cult, will not deal with the capitalist world on terms that it can accept; but the fact that it may refuse to do so now does not mean it will refuse forever. Revolutionary doctrines play their part in human affairs and then fit into the eternal pattern of things. What that eternal pattern will be for this strangely unpatterned world of ours none of us can say. But, in the flux of things which makes up the processes of history, it is for us to meet others on the terms we expect from them.

If coexistence is, in its lowest terms, a truce in the cold

war, at its best it is real economic and political peace. Time will show which it is; and there will be plenty of time—provided only that it endures. For the adjustment of the two worlds, the free and the communist, to each other, will involve more issues than those with which we grapple today, difficult and often frustrating as they are. But surely we may share the optimism of Eisenhower, Churchill, Schuman, and Adenauer in their belief that the chances of success are at present outrunning those for failure.

It is in this setting that we may find the solution for the final and most baffling problem, that of disarmament. It has never been possible to get agreement so long as the question came up as between two potential enemies, nor will it be possible on such terms in the future. For the surrender of armaments by nations that suspect others of hostile designs seems always to be a surrender of their national safety. But now we have a different approach, when the nations of the West, either under NATO or under the Paris agreement based on the Brussels Pact, accept international limitation and inspections of their armaments. Once this method of co-operation in the pacific use of armaments planned for defense only is well under way, or perhaps even before that, the U.S.S.R. may very well find its interest in the acceptance of similar arrangements or even come into the whole new European military system to justify its pacific protestations to its own people. This is, frankly, a strain on the imagination; yet stranger things have happened.

Unfortunately, military thinking, not only by soldiers but by civilians as well, tends to be rigid and impervious both to the lessons of history and to the changing conditions of today. So far as history is concerned, the spy sys-

tem of modern armies—which includes counterspying—
has often been misleading, as was sufficiently shown in the
military intelligence reports in World War II, in China
and Germany. As for the spying of scientific secrets, we
have ample proof of the ineffectiveness of its detection in
the field of atomic energy. Nevertheless, although the
system is inadequate, it will be resorted to unless other
methods of lessening apprehended dangers can be worked
out.

To deal with this central question of world affairs, the
United Nations, which had practically ceased active work
on the international control of atomic armament after the
U.S.S.R. challenged the West by its nuclear explosions,
and after the hydrogen bomb had immeasurably added to
the perils of nuclear war, took up once more the inescapable task in the spring and summer of 1954. Profiting from
past failures, it changed its technique of negotiation. Instead of public debate on this most delicate subject, in
which every change in position by a national delegate was
watched with suspicion in his own country, the conferees
held confidential sessions to get at the heart of the matter.
There is a real place still in the United Nations for the old
technique of diplomacy, as had already been shown in the
personal contact of Jessup and Malik, which brought the
end of the Berlin blockade. Indeed, although the public
sessions of Assembly and Council are necessary to prevent secret intrigue, yet in both the League of Nations
and the United Nations personal contacts of delegates
never lost importance. While the London conference of
experts in May 1954 did not reach final agreement, it did
open the door to a future *modus vivendi* as the United
States revealed a willingness to consider some "alternative
plan" or adjustment of the Baruch plan for the interna-

tional ownership of fissionable operations. Moscow did not move rapidly to meet this gesture, parleying with words; but six months later it was in a more adjustable mood, and the leverage which moved it was the offer of the United States to allocate to a "bank" of fissionable materials for peacetime use 250 pounds of fissionable material, and Great Britain 44 pounds, for use by other countries for experimental purposes for human betterment. As the U.S.S.R. declined at first to enter the bank, the United States went ahead with eight nations as members. Moscow, however, withdrew its objections and finally Vishinsky worked out with Lodge, the United States delegate, a compromise resolution supporting the eight-nations plan and calling for a scientific conference to create an international atomic agency to supervise exchange of atomic information and materials. The relation of the agency to the United Nations was to be settled later.

As a commentator in London put it, the Eisenhower offer is a repetition of the Marshall Plan in the field of productive power. The U.S.S.R. held off from the first great constructive act of American statesmanship, and lost the chance to share in its achievement. This time Moscow did not make the mistake of holding aloof from the planning. In a notable *démarche*, it linked the control of atomic energy with a general peace settlement and took an active part in the scientific preparation for the conference at Geneva in August 1955.

Science moves fast. Already the problem of the control of nuclear power has changed almost completely from what it was when first it was brought before the United Nations in 1946. The idea of a small international directorate controlling the whole output of atomic energy to prevent any of the powers from making it on its own is now utterly unrealistic. For science has not only vastly extended the field of nuclear operations, it has cheapened and simplified the process so that instead of enormous plants and prodigious outlay—open only to a great power —smaller and smaller plants for thermonuclear power can, with relatively little supply of raw material, change the nature of warfare by acquiring sufficient capacity for defense to reshape the alignment of nations. Indeed it is changed already, as far as military planning is concerned, for the distinction between "conventional armaments" and "weapons of mass destruction" disappears when armaments, nuclear or worse, determine the whole strategy of war. No "high authority" over atomic production can deal with this situation, which science is sure to change with each new discovery or invention.

This is not a discouraging conclusion; it is only a reminder that we are on the wrong path if we rely on spy work to take the place of positive measures to promote peace. When the danger of destruction becomes universal and the capacity for inflicting it practically unlimited, as it certainly will be in the future, the real issue is not the mathematical parity of weapons but the elimination of war itself. This has been the conclusion of every responsible soldier and statesman who has studied the problem. To reach and apply it is the supreme task of the United Nations, however long the path, whatever the obstacles, whatever the temporary failures on the way.

But more important than this revolution in warfare itself are its political implications. For the progressive cheapening and simplification of the process means that the great powers will lose their monopoly of power as smaller nations acquire the equivalent of large armies or heavy cannon. The great powers will continue to be able to afford more and larger weapons, but the menace of death and destruction in a few hydrogen weapons is sufficient to change not only the old politics of the balance of power, but also the alignment in the cold war. There is danger as well as hope in the democratizing of war: irresponsible Hitlers may use the threat of the new position of the small powers as blackmail instead of as a means of furthering peace. The solution calls for two lines of action: the upbuilding of enterprises for the peaceful use of atomic and thermonuclear energy, and the concentration of the United Nations on support for this co-operative effort by appropriate political agreements. This dual action was already under way in the United Nations studies in connection with the international conference in Geneva in August 1955. Through such studies the iron curtain should progressively disappear, as the new knowledge becomes a tool for general welfare instead of a weapon for universal destruction.

The program for tomorrow, therefore, is the most inspiring challenge to human intelligence since intelligence began. But behind the revolutionary forces of nuclear power lies the whole development of science. In our hurried survey of the great drama of politics we have not paused to give it its proper place in history. But in this fateful hour of decision, mankind has struck its tents for a trek into a world as rich in promise as it is fraught with danger. We are at the last frontier, the only one that has no limits in time or space. As the future beckons, however, we must pause to consider the meaning of it all. And in the mood of wonder and reverence, we close our notes on this long journey.

CHAPTER XXIV

THE LAST FRONTIER

The greatest event in the world today is not the awakening
of Asia nor the rise of communism—vast and portentous
as those events are. It is the advent of a new way of living,
due to science, a change in the conditions of work and in
the structure of society which began not so very long ago
in the West and is now reaching out over all mankind.

Long before the Ice Age, men chipped flint hatchets and
spearheads, but made little progress because the tools they
made had no power behind them but the brawn and muscle
of the arm. They never escaped from the fixed routine of
the seasons, and life repeated itself with little change. When
molten rock began to take shape under the blacksmith's
hammer, civilization widened and man began to assert his
supremacy over the crude forces of nature. But still, power
was lacking except for the winds in the sails of ships or the
running streams turning the water wheel.

Science changed all this when the machine began to take
the place of the all-important hand and a new order of
society was born.

The last frontier had been reached, that in which time
and space were to be reduced and overcome by the creative
mind.

1. *Invention*

The inventions which have remade the work of the world
are the gift of no one nation. The steam engine, the loco-

motive, the steamboat, the electric motor, the telephone, the telegraph, and radio, all come from the work of many minds in different countries, exploring and experimenting until some more fortunate genius hits upon a final solution or puts together the results of those who had worked before him. The world of science is a vast republic which offers the rights of citizenship to all earnest minds engaged upon serious study. English and French, German and Russian, Christian, Mohammedan and Jew, all have left us their heritage.

In the United States the opportunity was greatest and the rewards richest of any country in the world, and the American scientists would have doubly failed if with their varied backgrounds they had not stormed the citadels of the future with the broad confidence that is theirs.

2. *Million-handed Industry*

It was in England that machines began and only about the time of the American Revolution. As England lost its American colonies, it extended its economic conquest over the fields of cotton and the mines.

The spinning jenny took the place of the distaff and the power loom that of the hand weaver. New England managed to take over these machines, and the invention of the cotton gin spread the empire of "King Cotton" in the South and brought textile factories to the North. The time was soon to come, when in a single day—or hour— more thread was spun from the iron spindles of the textile mills than was twisted by skilled fingers in a thousand years.

A pump, to raise water from the mines, took on a wheel and became a steam engine; then it ate into the iron hills and drove the shafts still deeper to reach the goal that gives it power.

The age of iron and steel thus began to exhaust the source of its strength. Then chemistry created new substitutes for metal and discovered how to break power out of matter.

The history of mankind took on new contours and new meaning. Instead of repeating the past, it became endlessly, forever new. Life in town and country changed steadily, relentlessly. While cities rose to house the workers of the mills, the machine reached out to the farm, plowed the fields, and harvested the grain. The McCormick reaper, patented in 1834, had, by Civil War time, released an army of farmers to join the armies of the North. The local market then was no longer enough; for there were no bounds to what the earth could produce when the output was no longer limited by the strength of man but by the forces of nature yielding to his control.

3. *Welding the Nation*

It was not the Civil War but the arts of peace which made the United States one. War prevented division, but the nation was drawn together by its common interest in the peaceful exploitation of its natural heritage. As the lure of freedom, of self-owned homes, and of gold carried the adventuring pioneers over the prairies and mountains to the Pacific, and invention gave the farmers the modern plow for turning the soil and the reaper for harvesting, railroads pressed upon the ox-drawn wagons and the pony express, and bound far-flung settlements together. It was the worker and the thinker who made the nation one, after the soldier had cleared away the obstacles in their path.

Apart from the mountain barriers, the chief obstacle to unity was distance. Its only measurement was the time needed to go from one place to another, and in Washington's day it took as long to go from Boston to Mount Vernon as it now takes to go from New York to India. In Jefferson's day, it took Lewis and Clark two years to reach the Pacific at Oregon and return. In time measurement, the country was immeasurably large when the horseback trails pushed through the wilderness and the stage coaches jostled on the unpaved roads. But already, the surveyors, of whom Washington was one, were mapping farm lands and the roads linking the back country with the market towns. A few trunk lines, with roadside inns, were kept in better repair as post roads, and along them came the lumbering Conestoga wagons with their covered tops, like those that, years later, formed the caravans to the Middle West and beyond. But the country roads remained for a century little better than they were in Washington's day.

The river routes were different. Through all history they had been the avenues of inland trade, and the American river system was unrivaled in the world. The earliest ports were along the tidal reaches from the sea, but sailing ships beat their slow way against the current of the inland streams. Then came Robert Fulton's invention—or experiment—of the steamboat (1807) and soon the great rivers were filled with traffic, not only the coastal rivers, but the Ohio and Mississippi and the Great Lakes. As commerce grew, canals were dug to join the rivers. Although the canalboats were drawn by horses, the loads were many times greater than those of the wagons; and the great moment came in 1825 when the Erie Canal linked the Great Lakes with the Hudson River. Five years later (1830) came the first railroad, the few miles of the Baltimore and Ohio, pioneering in the revolution that, a generation later, was to bind the nation together with its iron network.

The conquest of distance brought the invasion of ideas. The interests of market town and countryside grew with the advent of news. In the early days communication was mostly by word of mouth, in school or church or public meeting. The town meeting of New England was like the agora of ancient Athens. Handwriting kept to its slow and stately style. But the printing press had begun to publish books and pamphlets, although there were no daily newspapers in Colonial days. It was Benjamin Franklin who popularized the printed word through *Poor Richard's Almanack* and the other output of his press. From these early beginnings was developed the vast organization of modern journalism, stripping the forests of the North for its hundreds of tons of paper for daily distribution, with a delicately adjusted news system responsive to the nerve centers of the world and recording indifferently history, gossip, and scandal for the casual or curious reader.

From the post chaise of Colonial days, with its memories of the English countryside, to the mail coach of the Wild West, racing past ambush on the frontier, the news came only as fast as the horses could bring it. Postriders and the pony express increased the speed and braved new dangers, but at best weeks passed between the exchange of letters from the different sections of the country. All this was changed as the railroads spanned the continent.

At the turn of the century, steam power, which had ruled the world of the Industrial Revolution, was forced to yield part of its empire to the internal-combustion engine; and, as the automobile pushed its web of roadways over the continent, the "horse and buggy days" became the symbol of something almost as remote as the Middle Ages, and filled with romance of half-remembered things. But in the invention of the airplane, the romance lay in the dream of future achievement. Few who, in December 1903, read of the launching of the frail craft of the Wright brothers on the bleak sands of Kitty Hawk, North Carolina, could imagine that its successors would one day outrace the sun around the world. But, for that matter, there is no reason to suppose that we who have watched for over half a century this prodigious achievement have any conception of what it will produce in the long stretches of the future.

The harnessing of the lightning had an even farther reach. From Franklin's kite to the wire of Morse's telegraph, the scientist and inventor pointed the way to telephone and radio, until electricity, that enveloping mystery, serves for sound and speech for all mankind. Voices follow the wires to register instantaneously in the farthest corners of the world, and the silent air can be tapped to bring floods of music into every home, as the masters of art produce radio programs to quicken the intellectual life of a listening nation.

Then sunlight flashed on the inner cell of the camera and registered the world outside. But life is motion and the picture, too, must move. From a flickering toy, science and art combined to create a mirror of the world and of life itself, enduring and universal. This miracle took on color and sound and thus combined within itself the elements of all the arts, and in so doing created a new one, swift as the changing scene itself, recording the lives of nations in moving flashes of thought and action, exultant in triumph, poignant in tragedy, and touched with all that subtle sympathy for the common man, which, more than politics, makes the world one. Then the miracle grew as television made the humblest home a portal to the universe. What if the chatter on the wireless waves is so often childish and meaningless, when the greatest minds can also be heard, or if most of the music is beneath contempt, when the master musicians can also break the silence of distant places? This is the dawn of civilization, when all life can stir to new inspiration in a world whose shadowy stage had long been waiting for the drama of life to reveal its full power and meaning.

4. *The Atomic Age*

The supreme achievement of science—the release of atomic energy—came, as we have seen, as a war measure. Work on it began in the darkest days of peril in World War II, when the disasters on land and sea were threatening the very life of freedom. Never was thought more powerfully mobilized to meet national danger than when America drew on the work of scientists of every land, who had been exploring radio activity, to break open the atom. It was a mobilization which, although carried out in secrecy—as they then thought—will go down in history to match in magnificence the moral leadership of Winston Churchill and his England in England's "finest hour," when it faced defeat with defiance and its airpower alone made good Churchill's challenge. Compared with that call upon an almost unarmed people to fight in the streets, if

necessary, against a completely armed invader, the vision
of the scientists who built the vast atomic munition plants
at Oak Ridge and Hanford was much more real. But the
glory of a great achievement will always be shadowed by
a doubt. Was it really necessary to drop the bomb on the
crowded cities of Hiroshima and Nagasaki? Could it not
have been an effective omen of defeat to Japan if it had
been dropped in the waters by a seaport like Yokohama?
We know now that American military intelligence was
mistaken in its estimate of Japan's will to continue the war
and that the terribly costly invasion of the main island—
which was the justification of the bomb—might not have
been necessary to end the war. However, Secretary of
War Stimson and his advisers felt justified by military necessity—the same kind of necessity as that which burned
the tinderbox houses of Tokyo and bombed the heart of
London and Berlin. The crime is war itself and the crimi-
nals those who resort to it for their own or their nation's
ends. And yet the conscience of America was troubled.
This gave an added sense of urgency to the search for
both the prevention of aggressive war and the peaceful
uses of atomic energy.

On the sixth of August 1945, the day the bomb was
dropped on Hiroshima, President Truman, in announcing
that revolutionary event in the history of warfare, called
attention to its long-range implications:

> The fact that we can release atomic energy ushers in a
> new era in man's understanding of nature's forces. Atomic
> energy may, in the future, supplement the power that
> comes from coal, oil and falling water, but at present it can-
> not be produced on a basis to compete with them commer-
> cially. Before that comes there must be a long period of in-
> tense research.

The intense research of the following years has already remade our conception of the universe, pushing the frontiers of knowledge ever farther away from the limited confines of the world of everyday experiences. Familiar things like light, heat and electrical currents can be explained only by the incredible fact that matter is also energy. We cannot turn back here to retrace all the important steps taken by the pioneers in this major exploration of reality, but to get our bearings at the start we need at least to recall the achievements of the great leaders.

The conception of matter as composed of infinitely small particles is as old as Indian philosophy and was taught by Greek philosophers some four centuries before the Christian era. Its most eloquent exponent was the Roman poet Lucretius, and it was again brought to light by Newton and Boyle in the seventeenth century. But it was only at the opening of the nineteenth century that John Dalton, chemist and physicist, applied the atomic theory to explain the differences between the "elements" of matter such as hydrogen, oxygen, nitrogen and a hundred other elements. The late arrival of modern science in the age-long evolution of civilization was chiefly due to the fact that even the most thoughtful and penetrating minds were handicapped in their observations of nature by not having adequate instruments to supplement or correct the impressions of the senses. The slowness of the process of scientific history was also due to the tendency to accept as doctrine the teachings of the past. Thus, from the days of the Greeks until the close of the eighteenth century, it was believed that the four elements out of which everything is composed were earth, air, fire and water. This belief not only blocked research, but it gave it a false turn in the theory that fire produces "phlogiston," a substance without color, odor, taste or weight. Modern chemistry began when Lavoisier attacked this belief, weighed the results of combustion and gave to "dephlogisticated air" (previously discovered by Priestley) the name of oxygen. The explanation of "inflammable air"—hydrogen—followed. But equally important with these discoveries was the method employed by Lavoisier and his successors, the use of laboratory scales in listing the elements by weight. A few years later, at the opening of the nineteenth century, John Dalton explained the different atomic weights of the elements by applying to them the atomic theory with its different weighted atoms.

This structural concept of matter was matched some thirty years later by another discovery of equal importance, when Michael Faraday opened up the vast field of electrical development. The next great step was taken at the end of the nineteenth century when it had become apparent to chemists that atoms were not simple but very complex compounds. The ways in which they reached these conclusions are too complicated to be described here. The existence of "rays," beginning with X rays to which Roentgen called attention in 1895, was one of the most important discoveries. The X ray readily passes through substances which are opaque to light rays. Then, two years later, Professor and Madame Curie discovered radium and found that certain "elements" heavy with atoms, like uranium, emitted rays or particles which were not atoms but small parts of atoms, and that in spite of the enormous energy thus released, a gram of radium would not be lessened by more than one half in two thousand years. Then, in 1906, Professor Einstein proved by theoretical calculation that the energy released from matter would be equal to the mass of the matter discharged multiplied by the square of the velocity of light, which is 186,000 miles per second. In other words, one pound of matter would equal the energy of ten billion kilowatt hours.

The third great new chapter in this history came in 1919, when Professor Ernest Rutherford succeeded in smashing the atom by firing a powerful "artillery" at it, using the particles shot off from radium. The target, the nucleus of the atom, was 100,000 times less in diameter than the invisible atom itself. Yet the "alpha" particle, as it was called from the first letter of the Greek alphabet, knocked hydrogen out of nitrogen and many of the lighter elements, thus changing them into different elements. From this and other experiments, the structure of the atom began to be better understood. It was found to be like a miniature solar system, with a central body, the nucleus around which revolve satellites called electrons moving like the moon or planets around the sun. The electrons are negative charges of electricity attracted and held in their orbits by a positively charged nucleus composed of protons (positively charged heavy bodies) and neutrons (uncharged heavy bodies). The hydrogen atom, the simplest and lightest, has but one electron, as the earth has but one moon. The uranium atom, the heaviest known of all, has at least ninety-two electrons, and is so complicated that some of the electrons break away from time to time, as is the case with the very heavy and insecure radium atom. So small is the nucleus of the hydrogen atom that the orbit of an electron around it is, in relation to its size, as far from it as the earth's orbit is from the sun; but the electron whizzes about its orbit at the rate of something like fourteen hundred miles per second, whereas the earth trundles around the sun at only eighteen miles per second. The atom, therefore, is mostly space with electrons at the outside and a nucleus at the center.

The energy of the atom—the force which holds the world together and balances the galaxies of the universe—is brought under human control by two different processes: the fission, or splitting, process for a heavy element like uranium; and the fusion process for such a light element as hydrogen. The uranium atom releases great energy when bombarded from the outside by small particles like neutrons, breaking its nucleus into two lighter nuclei. But that is only the beginning of the process, for some of the neutrons released from the original atom escape and go on striking other uranium atoms, thus setting off what is called "chain reaction." The fusion process works in the opposite way. It builds up atoms instead of splitting them, which seems to be the way the sun gets its boundless energy. The scientists calculate that four atoms of the lightest element, hydrogen, are fused together to make helium, the next lightest element, and when this takes place some of the mass is converted into energy, since the helium does not absorb all of the hydrogen. What is left over is energy. Since hydrogen is plentiful, fusion offers practically unlimited power—if it can be effectively controlled.

The heat from the splitting (fission) of uranium is so intense that it can trigger the fusion of hydrogen atoms in what has, therefore, been called the hydrogen bomb, the one used in the Bikini test. But the process did not stop there; the hydrogen fusion was followed by another fission, of uranium 238, and it was this third stage of the explosion which accounted for most of the energy released by the "hydrogen" bomb. The whole complicated, threefold action, depending as it does on the heat of the detonator, is termed thermonuclear, instead of merely atomic, activity. The poisonous radiations in the "fall out" of dust blown into the atmosphere spread out over thousands of miles. Scientists estimate that a ten-megaton bomb —equivalent in one blast to a force of ten million tons of TNT and five hundred times the power of the Hiroshima bomb, and yet only a little larger than the Bikini bomb— could spread radioactive dust over an area of more than a hundred thousand square miles instead of the seven thousand square miles mentioned in the Bikini report. Moreover, the poisonous rays not only kill if sufficiently intense; they spread disease of slowly fatal consequences. Strontium 90, produced in relatively large quantities in the uranium bomb, remains dangerously active for nearly thirty years and probably longer in the plants which animals eat. Finally, there is the long-term biological effect of radioactive material in human heredity, by changing the very basis of life, the genes which normally remain with little change from generation to generation. Radioactivity cuts in on the slow, stable process which is the guarantee of our continuance as human beings. Perhaps the most sinister aspect of this terrible possibility is the fact that such biological effects may not be known by the victims until long after they have been contaminated.

Fortunately scientists refusing to be muzzled by government censorship have spoken out clearly on these dangers, and in the first week in August 1955, just prior to the Geneva Conference on Atomic Energy, over a hundred of them from fourteen countries met in London to draft a report on the chief categories of potential nuclear dangers, both of immediate destruction and of the devastation which future generations would forever have to pay through disease, malformation or mental disability.

The rapporteur of the conference, Professor Rotblat of England, summarized the situation in the following terms:

> There is something particularly sinister about a bomb which is so designed as to poison the whole world with radioactivity. We have heard a great deal about the cobalt bomb, but we all believed that it would never be used. If our guess is correct, the hydrogen-uranium bomb is a kind of cobalt bomb; in fact, in some respects, it is even worse.*

The most awful weapon in the world has become too terrible to use, and war has ceased to be war. A civilization that has used it as the final argument of kings and nations has to find a new basis for politics. In short, history has to begin over again. Such are the long-range implications of thermonuclear power; but the world was not ready for them, and in the anxious interval ahead the most that could be devised was a truce between those in possession of the bombs, especially the two great powers, the U.S.S.R. and the United States. This was what President Eisenhower offered in the "Big Four" heads-of-state meeting in July 1955. As inspection to detect atomic armaments has been proven an inadequate safeguard, the American proposal concentrated on inspection by aerial reconnaissance of suspicious movements in apparent preparation for launching an attack. This proposal still stands on the agenda of the United Nations, in spite of Soviet opposition to it. We are therefore at an impasse still, with no clear promise of solution.

So much for the dangers of atomic energy. Against them there is and can be no absolute safety. The only hope for the future lies in the sharing of this power for pur-

* Bulletin of the Atomic Scientists, May 1955.

poses of peace. The proposal to do this, made by President
Eisenhower in his historic address at the United Nations,
seemed at first to have awakened only limited support. But
in the months that followed, eager and healthy rivalry began to develop in the building of atomic reactors for
peaceful uses, not only in the Western nations, but in the
U.S.S.R. as well; and when, in August 1955, just ten years
after the bomb was dropped on Hiroshima, the first international exhibition of atomic energy was held in Geneva
under the auspices of the United Nations, the result was a
most inspiring episode in the history of international co-
operation. For the thousand or more scientists from some
sixty-six countries the iron barriers of secrecy were let
down in all but the purely military field. The program
covered all the wide field of the peaceful use of atomic
energy, in medicine, in agriculture and in scientific research. But the chief interest was in its uses in industry,
for "atoms for peace" was also "atoms for power."

It is impossible here to enter more into this new world
of science and engineering. Although its exploration has
hardly more than begun, it is already threatening to
change the basis of economic life, and therefore of politics and our whole conception of the world and the conditions of human life. Compared with its potentialities,
those of the nineteenth-century industrial revolution,
which by steam and electricity remade the society of the
Western world, are quite secondary. For nations which,
like Britain, have almost exhausted the coal that fed their
furnaces, the new breeders give promise of renewed vigor,
while for the nations of Asia, like India and China which
have never had such power, there is the promise of a
wholly new era. Fortunately, the doubt as to the supply of
raw materials, which haunted the scientists at first, now is

being dissipated as new sources of uranium and thorium are opening up, and new techniques have been devised for extracting them from ordinary granite. Even if only a quarter of their amount in the rock is "leachable," still one ton of granite would produce energy equivalent to ten to fifteen tons of coal, and granite is only one of the rocks now being treated to discover new uranium supplies. It must be remembered that sea water is also a reservoir of metals.

But the new horizon reaches far beyond these promises of the future if the fusion process of the other bomb, that of the hydrogen atom, is harnessed as the fission process of uranium has already been set to work. In his opening address to the Geneva Conference, its president, Dr. Bhaba of India, challenged the scientific world with the prediction that within twenty years it would be possible to derive energy from the controlled fusion of heavy hydrogen nuclei. While others did not risk setting so early a date for the greatest of all conquests of power, there was wide agreement that nuclear science was already on the way to that far goal, and that it will play the dominant role in the future progress of civilization.

5. The Last Frontier

The caravan of civilization, moving with ever-increasing pace in spite of heavier loads, is approaching a great divide in the continent of experience. The world of primitive men which we are leaving behind is still around us, with ancient servitudes and haunting things beyond control. The Ice Age mind is still in seats of power. But we have struck our tents for a trek that opens vistas of a newer world than that which lured Europe out of the

Middle Ages and offered a "second chance" to our ancestors for livelihood and freedom. We are at the last frontier, the last because it has no limits in space or time, or at least none that mankind can ever reach. We have found by exploring the atom that matter is power in equipoise and that we can tap and use that ultimate power.

This is the culmination of that age-long history of intelligence which began before the Ice Age when the animal mind reached out beyond its animal equipment of claw and fang to master its world by tool or weapon. The strategy of life took on new dimensions as the problems of war or the chase were solved by the use of implements, for the path of advance was opened up by improving the tools. Their use was a constant challenge to ingenuity, giving a stimulus to the faculty of reasoning which finally marked man off from the animals. This, of course, is not all the story, but it is the part that connects with the era of science. Now, having supplemented the chipped stone and sharpened stick of primitive man by the vast industrial system of today and having explored the universe by instruments which far outreach the senses, we have finally come to the point where we can undo the process of creation itself, releasing from matter the original element, power. It is true that science has always reversed the process of nature, for that is what analysis, on which it is based, amounts to; but to undo the atom itself is a revolution which gives mankind a new place in the universe.

There is no way to measure the extent of the revolution of nuclear science, for we are only on the outer threshold of the new era which it has inaugurated. We are the cave men of the world of the future, fumbling our way amid dangers of our own creation, but the forces we have unleashed, which have power to remake the material world, can also be—and must be—the forces which remake the human world. Having tapped ultimate power we must master and control it. This necessity is now in the forefront of our thinking, as the menace of destruction darkens the world of today and our hopes of tomorrow. Yet the solution is implicit in what has already been done. It is the application of the Einstein equation to the mind, translating the rigid material of self-centered prejudice or greed into the dynamic force of justice.

This is no mere figure of speech nor the invoking of a worn-out slogan. The rights of man are the nuclei of all stable societies. The supreme fact in the history of our times is that we are now dealing with them directly, uncovering them with clearer vision and surer knowledge than ever before. The social and economic evils that were taken for granted in the past, as the inevitable incidents of an imperfect world, are now being analyzed and faced up to in every society that regards itself as civilized, although in greatly varying degrees, and not always honestly. But over against this general recognition of justice as the basis of a healthy society, we find the utmost disagreement as to its political and economic embodiment; until finally, the world is divided into the two great coalitions, communist and free.

Here again, however, science, as we have seen in the last two chapters, comes to the fore, preventing the bitter disputes from developing into World War III by the very terror of atomic weapons and other weapons of mass destruction. The scientific revolution in warfare, begun just before World War I, has now reached the point, in thermonuclear energy, where the weapons science can produce are no longer usable, at least not by truly civilized nations. The terror of their known possession is, or should be, a mutually preventive fact, holding the controversies of nations back from the abyss of war.

This does not necessarily mean that war between civilized nations is in fact the anachronism which it is in the light of reason, and it does not cover under its broad generalization such wars as those in Korea or in the jungles of southeast Asia. The frontiers of science will someday be those of peace, for that is the promise which lies in its capacity for good or ill, good that increases if shared in an interdependent world, and ill that destroys victor and victim alike. As yet, however, we are only on the threshold of that new era, and the watchers on the ramparts of peace and freedom must be vigilant and strong, and the defense must enlist every nation that appreciates what freedom means. Merely to stand guard, however, is not enough; nor is it enough to blow the trumpets from the wall, proclaiming freedom to a world that has had little share in the benefits of science, in its peacetime industries and in its war against disease. The sharing of these ultimate gifts of science with a world that has hardly yet begun to be civilized, constitutes the pacific strategy of offense, which, if resolutely carried out by the United Nations, may someday end—in any case it will lessen—the menace of the war that would end everything.

If this should happen, what would be left of the problem of communism? It would still be there, but limited in its propaganda appeal and its power to strike the all-out blow for world revolution. Left to itself, deprived of the inspiration of aggressive action, it would have to undergo the test of its capacity to make good its promises to its own people. Other nations, our own included, could look on, disturbed over only minor matters in international relations. There might even be—though this is questionable—some advantage in having two rival systems, challenging each other to make good, each in its own way, its promise of social justice.

But whatever happens to the communist countries, it is in the land of the pioneer, our own America, that science has reached furthest in its transformation of the conditions of life; and yet, in spite of this revolution in environment, the mind of the nation remains true to its inheritance of democracy and freedom. The only question that arises is whether it remains too deeply rooted in tradition to adjust itself to such prodigious changes as those of today. Yet this was answered, as we have seen, in the history of the twentieth century, taken as a whole. That history, we repeat at the close, should be a guarantee that the nation which took as its guide to thought and action "life, liberty, and the pursuit of happiness" will face the last frontier in the proud confidence of its enduring strength.

━━━◆━━━

CHAPTER XXV

THE MEANING OF IT ALL

The mind that has ranged the universe must now itself
    control,
For the force of the mighty atom is less than the human
    soul;
And simpler than any equation are the words forever true:
Do ye unto others as ye would they do by you.
This is the missing fulcrum for Archimedes' pry
To lift the weight of ancient hate, so the peoples that
    pass by
May reach together the shining goal that none can reach
    alone,
Helping each other along the way that each may make
    his own,
By joint consent surrendering the ancient right of war,
Alert to thwart betrayal, aware where dangers are
That lie in differing loyalties, where bickering conflicts run,
But offering charity to all, with malice toward none.
Then undismayed by the powers we wield, steady we stand
    and strong,
As the harp of the world keeps measure to life's triumphant
    song.*

                          J. T. S.

In the world crisis of today the question which haunts
thoughtful minds is: what is the meaning of it all? This is

* "The Way," in *Poems* by James T. Shotwell, Simon and Schuster,
1953; the text which follows is but slightly changed from that of an
article in *Think*, September 1953.

a very different question from that which confronts the governments engaged in a conflict of power, in which the issue is one of victory or defeat. It reaches beyond the tactics of action to the understanding of the fundamental issues involved. This at once carries it into the realm of history, for the forces engaged are as much those of the past as of the present and future. Nothing in human affairs can escape history, not even the revolution which attempts to defy it; for the despotism of the Kremlin is more Asiatic than communistic, and the final issue is the oldest and most constant one, that of freedom.

It goes without saying that this is not the way the Communists view the conflict, for those who have never lived under the regime of freedom cannot understand it. Some of the peoples of eastern Europe and Asia have never known what self-government meant, never having shared in that great experiment which from the days of ancient Greece challenged despotism in the West. We therefore cannot expect them to know what we mean when we present as an ideal of government the principles of the Declaration of Independence or the Gettysburg Address or even the Atlantic Charter.

But, more serious still, we ourselves are not wholly clear about this heritage of ours, won for us by the sacrifice and faith, the creative energy and tireless devotion of our forefathers. What is the harvest of their sowing, garnered into the rich storehouse of the Republic?

This is the supreme question of our time as we confront a future which represents new challenges to the intelligence and courage of men no longer finding either safety or welfare in the static world of habit and repetition. Still, although the scenes of the conditions of life are changing, even too rapidly for thought to follow, the human actors remain the same, limited by the same needs, responsive to the same desires as in the past. The mind that controls the atom is never wholly in control of itself. It responds to the instincts of primitive life as well as to the disciplines of reason.

Therefore, as we stand on the horizon of the future, we need to keep our bearings by tracing the pathway of civilization to our country and our own lives. For the crisis of today is part of that vast and tragic drama which kept throughout the ages—and still keeps—the undertone of primitive savagery, but which also rises to the highest themes of human thought, justice and mercy. As this short survey of an age-old theme makes clear, we are the inheritors of every gain made in the history of justice from the days of Hammurabi to those of the welding of Roman and English law, of the ideals of freedom from ancient Greece to Puritan England and revolutionary France, and of all the creative thought nourished by the arts of peace in every land. But this is only half the story, for the gifts of the Old World were fully matched by those of the New World, as the continent opened new paths of freedom and challenged mankind to rise above the past by making its own the greatest of these achievements, the quiet, long-delayed conquest of peace itself.

To no other land and to no other people has this supreme issue of the welding of the past and the future come with such compelling force. The heritage of other peoples, which becomes ours by right of their choice in coming here, is reinforced by the kind of life they have had to live, concentrating with steadfast purpose upon the conquest not of man but nature in the winning of a continent, intractable but kindly, spacious, and magnificent. Then, just when the New World was won from sea to sea, another new world was opened up by the discoveries of science, remaking time and space and recasting human relationships. Once again we are pioneers; but this time the pioneering will never stop; it will go on for ever. For it is a test, not merely of steadfastness and endurance, but of that final attribute of man: intelligence.

It is this new, new world which holds the promise of the future. The promise is by no means clear in the dawn's early light, nor in the red glare which gleams so menacingly on the ramparts of freedom. But one thing is clear: the cause of freedom, justice, and peace will ultimately prevail, for otherwise there is no future for mankind. Science has already seen to that by forging weapons of destruction that leave no hope either for victim or victor, making war—the supreme instrument of politics in the upbuilding of nations—an international crime that brings its own punishment.

The drama of history is still enacted on the ill-lighted stage where the animal in man has so long stalked its prey. But even while brute force acquires the most deadly power of mass destruction, the theme of the conflict is changing to the realm of the spirit. The principles of secular society, which each nation accepted for itself but denied in its relations with others, are now being forged in the white heat of controversy into universal concepts of right and wrong, applying everywhere, to everyone. The ultimate ideal with which communism beguiles its devotees is that of a classless world of increased welfare for all; its crime against society is not in its insistence on this goal, but in its ruthless methods of persecution at home and conquest abroad, which substitute for the ideal of a co-operative commonwealth the oppressive might of imperialist despotism. The Communists justify this reliance on force and violence as part of the unfinished revolution by which their regime will be established and, therefore, as only a temporary phase of their policy. But this reasoning is based on the assumption that there can be only one outcome, the triumph of communism everywhere and the submission of everyone to the despotism of those who would wield universal, unquestioned authority in the application of their doctrine. Until that day of triumph, communism accepts war as the instrument of its policy. Its propaganda for peace must be understood in the light of these conditions, which not only deny the validity of the peace movements among noncommunist nations, but distort the ultimate ideal of a world of economic justice by making that justice the synonym for rigid, bureaucratic despotism.

What, then, is the way to meet this challenge to the free world? Both history and the events of these last years of crisis point in a single direction: peace based upon freedom and justice. At last these great ideals must be made real. For too many centuries they have been professed in morals and religion but denied in the practical affairs of daily life and the politics of nations. As long as that hypocrisy mocks our ideals, the enemy has a case. We have, of course, a ready rejoinder in the fact that the Communists themselves have excelled as hypocrites in their dealings with other nations, but that is too easy and cheap an argument for a debate so serious as this should be. The real contrast lies in the fact that the Bolsheviki undertook to change society by a single movement, and that the noncommunist nations held to the slow, evolutionary processes of history. They have been slow to realize or at least to apply the Golden Rule, which is the Einstein equation for the free world, turning the inert mass of self-centered nationalism into the dynamics of mutual aid and welfare; and they have been equally slow to deny the agelong legitimacy of war. Now, however, with the advance of science, the only lasting prosperity comes from a working membership in the world community, and the only lasting peace from a recognition that war has become an anachronism between civilized nations, because its mass destruction escapes all limits of control or direction.

The meaning of history is thus becoming clear in the crisis of today, which seems at first sight to darken and obscure it. The clue to it is to be found, not in the records of great eras in either war or peace, but in measuring the rate of the advance of intelligence in the direction of human affairs, from the Ice Age to today. By far the longest period lies the other side of Egypt and Babylonia, where, through untold millenniums, mankind made infinitely slow progress in applying the mind to meet the dangers and problems of life. Then, about five thousand years ago, the process began to speed up in favored sections of the earth, as civilization began to come to grips with its ancient enemies, superstition and war. The great ethical religions, especially in the West, attempted with varying success to get rid of the fears and evil practices of superstition, a process which, by its accent on belief, tended to block criticism, that basic element of reason, but by its controversies prepared the way for future inquiry. Then came science, and in the incredibly short period of two or three centuries, it created a new world for the mind and remade the terms of the problems of war and peace. War must now go the way of superstition. In neither case will the great reform be complete or universal in our time; but there can be no doubt of the ultimate goal. Peace is not merely a vacuum left by the ending of wars. It is, as we have seen throughout this survey, the embodiment of the two eternal principles of justice and freedom—justice as defined in the Golden Rule and freedom as set forth in the declaration of the rights of man, by England and France, by the United States and the United Nations. Some day these rights may be embodied in world law, but that day is still distant, for unless law is the expression of the common will it is worse than meaningless; it is an impediment to progress. But with a rapidity without parallel in history, the varied purposes of nations are being brought into line, the contrary methods of the Communists notwithstanding. For, underlying all conflicting ideologies, the final fact remains that the moral order of the world is at last a living issue in practical politics.

The world has just begun to be civilized. Within a single lifetime we are turning the corner on the long stretch of centuries that reaches from beyond the Ice Age.

There is no parallel to this in all the history of mankind. No wonder, therefore, that the pathway of progress is blocked by ignorance and the ideals of justice and liberty are at times dimmed.

Humanity is on the march, but the goal before it is one that can never be reached; for, as we "follow knowledge like a sinking star beyond the utmost bound of human thought," we shall forever find across our pathway the shadows of heights still to be scaled—of ideals still to be realized.

ABOUT THE AUTHOR

For over fifty years professor of history at Columbia University, Dr. James T. Shotwell was Chairman of the National Board of Historians in World War I and Chief of the Historical Division of the Delegation to Negotiate the Treaties of Peace at its close. He was then charged by the Carnegie Endowment for International Peace, of which he is now president emeritus, with planning and directing the history of the economic and social effects of the war, and, in co-operation with statesmen and specialists in twelve countries, completed the survey in 150 volumes.

In World War II he was a member of the committee of the State Department which drafted the first blueprint for the Charter of the United Nations, and became honorary president, with Sumner Welles, of the American Association for the United Nations. He holds honorary doctorates from a dozen universities and high decorations from five governments.

POCKET GUIDE to the OUTDOORS

JEAN CRAIGHEAD GEORGE

with *TWIG C. GEORGE*

JOHN C. GEORGE, *and* T. LUKE GEORGE

DUTTON CHILDREN'S BOOKS
an imprint of Penguin Group (USA) Inc.

DUTTON CHILDREN'S BOOKS
A division of Penguin Young Readers Group

Published by the Penguin Group
Penguin Group (USA) Inc., 375 Hudson Street, New York, New York 10014, U.S.A.

Penguin Group (Canada), 90 Eglinton Avenue East, Suite 700, Toronto, Ontario M4P 2Y3,
Canada (a division of Pearson Penguin Canada Inc.)

Penguin Books Ltd, 80 Strand, London WC2R 0RL, England

Penguin Ireland, 25 St Stephen's Green, Dublin 2, Ireland (a division of Penguin Books Ltd)

Penguin Group (Australia), 250 Camberwell Road, Camberwell, Victoria 3124,
Australia (a division of Pearson Australia Group Pty Ltd)

Penguin Books India Pvt Ltd, 11 Community Centre, Panchsheel Park, New Delhi - 110 017, India

Penguin Group (NZ), 67 Apollo Drive, Rosedale, North Shore 0632,
New Zealand (a division of Pearson New Zealand Ltd.)

Penguin Books (South Africa) (Pty) Ltd, 24 Sturdee Avenue,
Rosebank, Johannesburg 2196, South Africa

Penguin Books Ltd, Registered Offices: 80 Strand, London WC2R 0RL, England

Text and Sam's sketches copyright © 2009 by Jean Craighead George
Illustrations p. 19, 28, 65-66, 72, 78-80, 104-105, 118, 125 copyright © 2009 by Steve Sanford

CIP Data is available.

Published in the United States by Dutton Children's Books,
a division of Penguin Young Readers Group
345 Hudson Street, New York, New York 10014
www.penguin.com/youngreaders

Designed by Irene Vandervoort

Manufactured in China • First Edition

ISBN 978-0-525-42163-4

1 3 5 7 9 10 8 6 4 2

CONTENTS

A LETTER FROM SAM GRIBLEY

Long ago I left the city and ran away to live off the land. I've been keeping notes ever since and now have enough for a guide to the outdoors. You can use it in city parks, the wilderness, and public lands east and west. There are many outdoor things to make and do here.

What I can't put in these pages is the smell of the wet woods after a rain, the violin-sound of wind in the trees, or sunsets that ask you to sit and celebrate the end of the day with a blaze of color. The peace of mind that spills through you like a waterfall. The voices in nature, too, can't be found in a guide. The rustle of leaves telling you to stop and listen or the silence of frogs, saying you're too close.

Sure there's a lot in this book, but there's lots more out there to discover. You can add to this guide yourself. You can spend a lifetime at it.

I hope you do. These days we need people to understand and protect nature. For instance, when you're gathering native nuts or seeds, plant a few so we will always have them. On the other hand, pull up foreign weeds, like phragmites, kudzu, and knapweed. Join organizations that help save the environment.

And have fun. Nature's great.

—SAM GRIBLEY

This guide has been compiled to show you how to enjoy nature.

First there are instructions as to how to pick a campsite and build a shelter.

Gathering wood and making a fire follow, two challenges that are fun and mesmerizing at the same time. There is something wonderful about wood-gathering and fire-making. It must be the cavemen and women in us that make it so compelling.

You will learn how to find water, that necessity of life, and then to get food by fishing with your own forest-made rod and fishhooks. When you catch a fish there are instructions for cooking it. You'll also learn how to identify and cook wild plants.

Once the necessities of life are satisfied—shelter, fire, water, food—you will find out how to have fun in the great outdoors. There is a section on making musical instruments for your soul, or maps for your brain. You can follow and lay a trail, track animals, and tie useful knots.

There is also a section on poisonous plants and medicine plants. You ought to know them even when not in the wild.

You'll find some practical stuff like how to stave off bears and ticks. But the section we like best in this guide is how to recognize some common birdcalls even when you can't see the birds, which is most of the time.

Now when we hear the winsome call of the wood-pewee at predawn singing "pee-a-wee, peeeeee," without looking up, we know its name.

A newspaper publisher named Horace Greeley once advised, "Go West, young man, go West and grow up with the country." Now we write to you, "Go wild, young one, go wild and learn to honor the planet."

—THE GEORGE FAMILY

WHAT TO TAKE

Before you pack, think about where you are going and what you might need. Sunglasses are essential for a trip to the desert, while a change of dry clothes is important if there's a chance you might get wet.

Here are some good things to pack (*for day trips):

*Water, at least two quarts per person
    for a day of hiking
*A whistle, handy to blow in case you get lost
*A flashlight
*"Moleskin" for foot blisters
*Band-Aids for cuts and scratches
*Comfortable, broken-in sneakers or boots!
*Insect repellent and sunscreen
*A map
*A pocketknife
*Water purifier
*Sweater or jacket
*Dry socks
*A notebook to write in and a book to read
*Magnifying glass, binoculars
Waterproof matches
Sleeping bag
A tarp and cord

Hatchet or small saw

Cooking pot or Sierra cup, fork and spoon

Toothbrush and biodegradable soap

If you are taking a long trip, there is a tradition in the north called "the Hudson Bay start." Get everything ready. Start off, but only go a short way on your journey. Set up your campsite. If you find you've forgotten something you'll only have a short trip back to get it. It's no fun to get all the way into the wilderness and find you have forgotten your knife!

There is one more thing I'd recommend you bring along: an open state of mind and some toughness. Out in the wild it can be your best friend. You may get cold or wet or tired; but that is part of being in Nature, and you can learn to enjoy that, too.

Nature is never predictable. Remember to be safe, to be prepared, and to know your limits. That way, you'll always have fun.

Other things to do:

Check the weather before you leave.

Let someone at home know where you are going and for how long.

Clear your mind and get your heart into the wilds.

"I am running away from home, and this is just the kind of forest I have always dreamed I would run to. I think I'll camp here tonight." I hopped out of the cab.

"Well, now, ain't that sumpin'? You know, when I was your age, I did the same thing. Only thing was, I was a farm boy and ran to the city, and you're a city boy running to the woods. I was scared of the city—do you think you'll be scared of the woods?"

"Heck, no!" I shouted loudly.

—MY SIDE OF THE MOUNTAIN

There are many national forests, Bureau of Land Management areas, state parks, and private lands (with permission) where you can find beautiful campsites. National parks are wonderful places to camp, but you may not pick plants or build fires except in designated places. Take care of our parks. This is one gorgeous nation.

Good campsites vary depending on where you are—forest, desert, or mountains. But generally look for a high, dry spot that's flat and near water. A sensational view is nice, but having woods around you is my favorite.

National forests are multiple-use regions, which means you can catch game when in season and pick plants. Fires are permitted during fire-safe seasons.

Find the national forests and parks nearest you by searching the Web on your home, school, or local library computers. Some helpful Web sites include:

The U.S. Forest Service:

http://www.fs.fed.us/recreation/map/finder.shtml

The Public Lands Information Center:

http://www.publiclands.org and http://plicmapcenter.org

The National Park Service:

http://www.nps.gov

Each outdoor area and park has its own rules and regulations. Contact the area or park officials to find out more about it before you go.

And if you can't get out of town, try camping out in your own backyard.

SHELTERS

I decided to make a bed before I cooked. I cut off some boughs for a mattress, then I leaned some dead limbs against the boulder and covered them with hemlock boughs. This made a kind of tent. I crawled in, lay down, and felt alone and secret and very excited.

—MY SIDE OF THE MOUNTAIN

If you're outdoors overnight you will want to build a shelter. You can make your own or bring along a tent. Lean-tos are cozy and fun to make. Here are two you can try yourself.

Lean-to Made with Reeds

First gather about 50 phragmites stalks. Phragmites, which are an invasive weed, are tall, feather-headed reedlike plants that grow in marshy areas and along wet roadsides. Eight plants will make a sturdy pole when tied together with cord (or string you've made yourself! See p. 28). Make six poles and secure them with a clove hitch knot (pp. 77 and 80).

Prop two of the poles against a big fallen log, rock, steep cliff, or any prop tall enough to make a shelter that you can crawl under. Tie your four remaining reed poles or sticks horizontally across the two leaning poles.

reed lean-to

Use phragmites stems and leaves as a roof or peel bark off a fallen log. Keep the pieces as large as possible. Now place the bark on the frame like shingles on a roof: they shed water and shelter you from wind. Real cozy.

Lean-to Made with a Tarp

A tarp is a valuable item. Here's a handy tarp shelter.

Hammer two Y-shaped sticks into the ground, six feet apart. Put a long stick between the two Y's. Hang your tarp over it. Leave enough tarp to hang over the front about 12 inches. Fold the rest of the tarp underneath to keep you dry.

Pound three pegs in the ground behind the tarp and two on either side of the front flap. Put a small stone at the fold on the inside of the tarp. Grab it from the outside and wrap it with string at the base. Tie it off with a square knot (pp. 76 and 78), leaving enough string to reach the pegs. This makes a small "knob." Do this with a stone opposite each peg. Tie the strings to the pegs using a clove hitch (pp. 77 and 80). Stone ties are a good trick because they keep you from having to punch holes in your tarp.

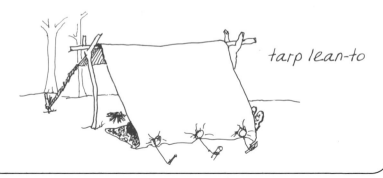

tarp lean-to

Bedding

Bedding can be made out of any dry material. Dry leaves, pine needles, and tree boughs will keep you warm and off the damp ground. Use what you can find.

The Tipi

A tipi is the best shelter ever, especially in a dry environment! It's warm in winter, cool in summer, practical all year round. A tipi is the most beautiful home you'll ever have and you can move it anywhere. Make one.

Get your dad or mom or your Boy or Girl Scout Troop to help you. It's also a great community project, although the Sioux Indian women constructed them all alone.

You can find the directions to make and furnish a tipi in *The Indian Tipi, Its History, Construction, and Use*, by Reginald and Gladys Laubin, 1957, University of Oklahoma Press.

The directions are clear and easy to follow.

tipi

FIRE

I must say this now about that first fire.
It was magic. Out of dead tinder and
grass and sticks came a live warm light.
It cracked and snapped and smoked
and filled the woods with brightness.
It lighted the trees and made them warm
and friendly. It stood tall and bright
and held back the night.

—MY SIDE OF THE MOUNTAIN

Fire can give you comfort, warmth, and hot food.

But fire can also quickly grow out of control and become dangerous. Keep in mind that you must always be alert to possible danger with fire. When used carefully it is a wonderful thing.

In areas at high risk for forest fires do not make a fire. If you are not sure whether or not it's safe to make one, check with an official in your area. Keep in mind that sparks from a fire can jump several feet and may drift even farther on a breeze. Clear the fire area of any material that might catch fire. A fire ring made of stones can help to keep a fire contained. To prevent forest fires, remember to:

DOUSE YOUR FIRE WITH WATER
BEFORE YOU LEAVE IT—
EVEN IF YOU THINK IT'S OUT!

Choose a Fire Location

First look for a spot that is out of the wind and relatively flat. Your fire should be a safe distance from your shelter, but close enough to warm you.

Try to place your fire in front of a natural heat reflector. Large boulders, stones piled up to make a wall, or a windbreak made of green branches will protect the fire from wind. It will also reflect heat back toward you. In cold weather a second "reflector" placed several feet behind you will make a warm area, and stop you from having to constantly turn around to keep "both sides" warm.

Make a Fire Pit

A fire pit will help to contain a fire. Dig a shallow dish in the dirt. Clear the area of leaves and debris at least six feet around the pit to create a safe area for sparks.

If the dirt is full of "peat" or decaying leaves and debris that can burn, then line the pit with stones. Do not use river or lake stones. Water in the river stones will heat up in the fire and can cause the stones to explode.

fire pit

Gather Fuel

Make sure you have a good and plentiful supply of fuel before you start a fire.

If the weather is fair, collect fuel from the ground. The fuel must be dry (dry wood will snap when broken). If it's been rainy, dead wood on standing trees will be the driest around.

You will need fast burning material to start your

fire. This is called *tinder*. Once the fire has been started, add larger and larger pieces of *kindling*. Kindling is made up of the dry twigs and branches that will catch fire easily from your tinder. Collect a range of sizes from the very smallest twigs to sticks the size of pencils and broom handles.

Finally you can add logs. These larger pieces of wood keep a good fire going and make coals, which are great for warmth and cooking. You can feed longer logs into the fire as they burn. Do this if you need a fire all night, but only if there's low risk for forest fire. Take shifts to tend your fire.

Make Tinder

Tinder is light airy material that will catch fire with just a spark. You need tinder to start your fire.

Good tinder can be made from the dry inner bark of most dead trees. The outer bark of birch trees is best. Dry reeds, grasses, thistle, and cattail down also make excellent tinder.

Pull, pound, and scrape your tinder to make it into a fine, light, airy ball.

More Tips for Starting a Fire

Make "fuzz sticks" by shaving curls of wood down the side of a stick. The shavings catch easily and help the fire to grow.

Gather hard chunks of pine pitch, the sap that hardens on pine trees. It burns hot and fast.

Build Your Fire

Once you have tinder, kindling, and wood gathered, you're ready to "build" your fire. Tipi fires and lean-to fires are my favorite methods. Here's how:

Prepare a Tipi Fire

Lean the tiniest twigs and sticks together to make a "tipi." Leave an opening so that your tinder ball can be placed in the center. If there is a breeze, place the opening toward the wind so that the small flame will be blown toward the "tipi." If the wind is too strong, put your body between the wind and your tinder.

Only make the fire as big as you honestly need it. Smaller fires are easier to control, use less firewood, and cook better.

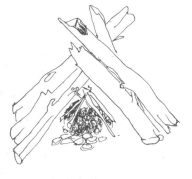

Prepare a Lean-to Fire

A simple way to start a fire is to lean small twigs and sticks against a short log. Place your tinder underneath the kindling and light.

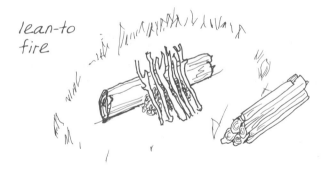

lean-to
fire

Lighting a Fire

If you don't have matches, starting a fire can be tough. But with practice you can do it. Then if you ever lose your matches or they get wet, you will always be able to start your own warm, cozy fire.

My favorite methods of starting a campfire are to use a bow drill, flint and steel, or a magnifying glass. Here's how.

The Bow Drill

The bow drill has been used to start fires for thousands of years. To make a bow drill you will need to make a bow, a spindle, a handhold, and a notched fire board. Success with this fire-maker requires practice and patience.

Wood for Handhold and Notched Fire Board: Except for the bow, which needs to bend, all of your wood should be dry. Cedar, willow, and sycamore are good to use. Hardwoods like oak and walnut are very difficult to work with, so avoid those. The drill and fire board should be made of the same type of wood, if possible.

The Bow: Use a stick about 2 to 3 feet long, preferably green. It should be strong but flexible and about ½ to 1 inch thick. Tie a cord, shoelace, or other string to one end. Pull the cord to make a slight bow and fasten the string to the other end. Make one knot tight (use a square knot, pages 76 and 78) and the other adjustable (use a clove hitch, pages 77 and 80) so that you can tighten the string as it stretches.

The Drill: Shave the bark off a nice straight stick that's hard and dry, about ¾ of an inch wide and 12 inches long. Carve both ends to a blunt point.

The Handhold: Either use a rock that fits in your hand and has a slight dent in the middle to hold the drill, or carve a pit in a small piece of wood that also fits your hand. This will allow the drill to turn and protect your hand at the same time.

The Fire Board: Use a dry wooden board, about ¾ inch thick and a foot long. In the center of the board, dig out a bit of wood to make a pit. Now cut a notch, almost, but not quite, to the pit. Make the notch the shape of a narrow piece of pie.

The Wrap: Wrap the bow's line around the drill.

Putting It All Together: Place the handhold on top of the drill and the point of the drill in the "pit" on the fire board.

STARTING A FIRE
WITH YOUR BOW DRILL

drill and fire board

using a bow drill

*transferring flame
to tipi kindling*

Hold the spindle in place by putting pressure on the handhold. Turn the spindle by pulling the bow back and forth.

Starting a Fire with Your Bow Drill

Remember to first gather fuel, prepare the tinder, and build a tipi or lean-to fire.

Put the fire board on a dry piece of bark. Place a bundle of tinder in the notch. Put the spindle in the pocket. Wrap the cord around the spindle and fasten to the end of the bow. Then place the handhold on the top of the spindle. Using a sawing motion with the bow, twirl the spindle until you see smoke. This will seem awkward, but with LOTS of practice you can get it. As the wood heats it will make a small pile of coals. Move them gently until they come into contact with the tinder in the fire board notch. A small flame should start. *Carefully* move the burning tinder on the piece of bark to the center of your tipi stack or lean-to.

Learning to use a bow drill takes work and a lot of practice. Just keep trying until you get it right.

Flint and Steel

Steel will create sparks when hit with any hard, sharp object such as flint. If you can make a fire with flint and steel, you'll never have to worry about running out of matches!

Flint is one type of quartz. It is a glassy, hard stone usually found in limestone. Other types of quartz can also be used and are milky white, pink, or gray. All are good for making sparks.

flint and steel with tinder

Place a bit of tinder on a dry piece of bark. Be sure you're near your kindling tipi or lean-to. Hold the rock close to the tinder. Using the back of your knife, or any steel object, hit the stone briskly. A spark should fly out. With practice you can get the spark to fly into the tinder. Transfer the flame to your tipi, blow, and your fire is started!

Magnifying Glass

If it's a sunny day you can use your magnifying glass to start a fire. The magnifying glass will concentrate the sun's rays into a point hot enough to start a fire. Hold the glass so that the sun's rays pass through it and are focused on a small bundle of tinder in the center of your tipi stack. First you'll see a point of bright, hot light on the tinder. The brighter and smaller this point of light is, the hotter it is—keep it hot to start a fire. Eventually your tinder will start to smoke. A fire needs oxygen to grow, so when you see embers, you can help the fire along by blowing lightly on them. A fire should start quickly after that.

**BE SURE TO DOUSE YOUR FIRE WITH WATER
WHEN YOU LEAVE YOUR CAMPSITE
EVEN IF YOU THINK IT'S OUT.**

I was coming back, circling wide, when I almost fell in it. Two sentinel boulders, dripping wet, decorated with flowers, ferns, moss, weeds—everything that loved water—guarded a bathtub-sized spring.

"You pretty thing," I said, flopped on my stomach, and pushed my face into it to drink. I opened my eyes. The water was like glass, and in it were little insects with oars. They rowed away from me.

—MY SIDE OF THE MOUNTAIN

Just like shelter and fire, you'll need to think about water before heading into the woods. You will only survive a few days without water, and can become dehydrated in just a few hours. Be sure to carry at least two quarts of water per person per day when off on a hike. In a pinch, here are some tips for finding good drinking water in nature:

Water from Plants

Vines yield pure water. Try them if you're real thirsty. Cut a notch in a thick vine as high as you can reach. Then, lower down, cut the vine all the way through. Hold the vine slightly above your mouth and drink. When the water stops, cut the notch deeper. Drink right out of the vine. No cup needed.

Vines like the kudzu, which grows in the South, give water that tastes better than tap water. Kudzus are weeds, so you can cut generously and drink well.

If you're in the Northeast try the wild grapevine, a woody vine with deeply veined, heart-shaped leaves. Cut the thick lower stems. Water drips slowly from them, but you should get a good drink if you are patient.

Wild grapevines are found in thickets and the edges of woods. If you feel like eating the grapes, go ahead! Ripe berries are purple to black and good—tart though.

WATCH OUT FOR POISON IVY! Poison ivy is a vine. Don't drink from or touch poison ivy vines. Find the common poisonous plants, including poison ivy, on pages 65 to 70, and learn to recognize them in the wild.

Condensation

To collect condensation tie a clean plastic bag around as many green leaves on a living tree as you can fit into the bag. Overnight the water from the leaves "breathing" will condense on the plastic, as leaves give off small amounts of water as they exchange carbon dioxide for oxygen. This is really pure water. Pour into a cup or turtle shell and drink.

Rainwater

Rainwater is a good drink and is usually pure.

Prop up a waterproof jacket, raincoat, or tarp slantwise on two sticks to catch lots of water. Funnel it down into a bucket. Boil three minutes to be safe.

Groundwater

Water from underground is called groundwater. It can be clean, but it's safest to purify groundwater before drinking. Drinking impure water can make you sick.

You have to dig for groundwater, so pick a low place where water-loving plants flourish: dig where you find skunk cabbages, reeds, willows, or mosses, and you'll hit water sooner.

It's a good idea to bring a little water purifier with you in a small bottle. If you are near civilization, use a few drops in the groundwater you've collected. Let it stand for several hours to give the purifier time to do its job.

If you are worried about the purity of the water, and don't have any water purifier, you can always boil the water to rid it of any harmful parasites. Boil for three minutes or more.

Salt Water

Never drink salt water; it can kill you. If you are on an ocean beach without access to freshwater, brackish water is better than salt water in an emergency. Brackish water is a mix of fresh and salt water often found near the shore. It may not taste very good and will make you sick if you drink too much of it. If you don't like the taste, you can improve it by pouring the brackish water through a sand-filled bag.

You can find pure water by digging far back from the ocean. Pigeons and mourning doves living along salt water shores fly to freshwater in the morning and late afternoon. Follow them.

This stream did not seem to have any calm water, and I must have walked a thousand miles before I found a pool by a deep undercut bank in the shade of overhanging branches. Actually, it wasn't that far, it just seemed that way because as I went looking and finding nothing, I was sure I was going to starve to death.

I squatted on this bank and dropped in my line. I did so want to catch a fish. One fish would set me upon my way.

—MY SIDE OF THE MOUNTAIN

After setting up shelter, making a fire, and ensuring you have enough water to drink, it's time to eat! Out in the woods there is nothing more fun than fishing. And what's more, fish taste better when you catch them with your own gear.

Making Fishing Gear

You should begin with the line. The best fibers are the inner bark of a dead limb off a basswood tree. Peel off the outer bark. The insides are stringy and tough. Tear into strips and braid together to make a strong fishing line.

Willow bark shreds into excellent fibers. Make the fibers as fine as you can. Braid and you'll have a tough fishing line. You can do this with oaks and other trees if basswood or willows can't be found. But they're not as good.

Dogbane stems also tear into strong fibers. Dogbane is a shrub with red stems and pale pink flowers. It grows 1 to 4 feet tall and is found in thickets along roadsides and also in abandoned fields. Swallowtail butterflies and iridescent blue green beetles, called dogbane beetles, love them. Look for the butterflies and beetles and you'll find the dogbane.

Palm leaves make good fishing line, too. Just pull off the fibers and braid them.

Making a Fishing Rod

Cut a sturdy willow branch or use any firm stick to make a fishing rod. Bamboo or dried phragmites make great

MAKING A FISHING LINE

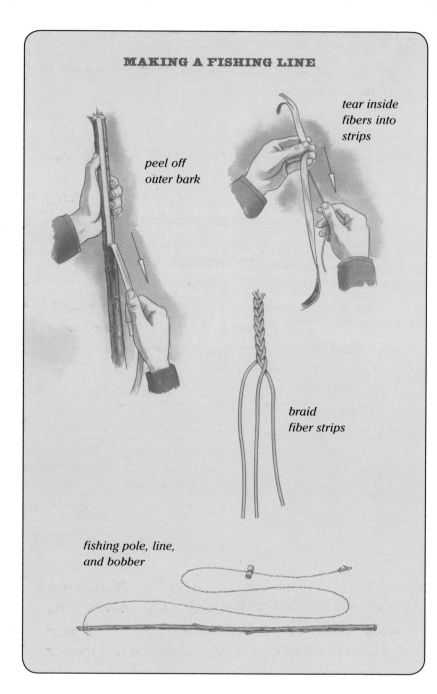

tear inside
fibers into
strips

peel off
outer bark

braid
fiber strips

fishing pole, line,
and bobber

rods. Tie your string to the end of your rod. Next make a bobber and a hook.

Making Fishhooks

Now you have to make a fishhook. Find a small stem with a twig at a 30-degree angle (see illustration *a* below). Cut off the stem and part of the twig so you have something that looks like a small fishhook. Sharpen the twig end and fasten the stem to your line. Tie a thorn or sharp sliver of wood at the top of the hook, pointing down so that it makes a latch. (See illustration *a*.)

You can also use a stem that has a thorn (see illustration *d*). Tie the stem to the line. If your hook floats, tie a small stone to the line just above the hook.

Safety pins or nails make good hooks, too.

various fishhooks

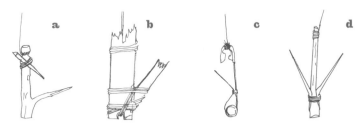

a   b   c   d

Bobbers

If you attach a bobber to your line it will show you when you have a bite by bobbing up and down. To place your bobber, drop your hook and line into the water until it hits bottom. Pull it up several inches and tie a piece of bark or dry wood that floats on the line at water level. (Use a square knot, pp. 76 and 78)

Cast into the water. When the bobber goes under, you have a bite—pull!

Bait

I like to use white grubs for bait. Grubs can be found in decaying logs. Fish love them.

Of course earthworms are good bait, too, as are grasshoppers or any insect that you can catch. Fish snap at movement, so keep your bait alive if you can.

various types of bait:

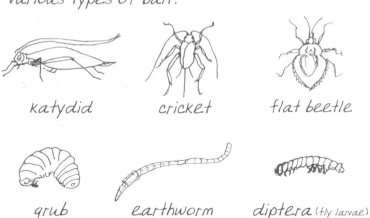

katydid   cricket   flat beetle

grub   earthworm   diptera (fly larvae)

Want to Get a Lot of Worms?

Worms live underground and so do the moles that eat them. Worms flee from moles and you can get worms to surface by sounding like a mole. Here's how: Drive a wooden stake into the ground and rub a piece of iron across it. Worms will surface in droves. Stop when you have enough for bait and the rest of the worms will go back underground. Amazing to see.

Fish Traps

Milk Jug Trap: If you have a plastic gallon milk jug you can make a swell fish trap. Cut off the neck of the bottle to make a hole about 2 inches wide. Cut off the top at the point where its sides become straight. Put a stone or two in the bottle. Bait the trap with insects or meat tied to one of the stones. Then invert the top and put inside the bottle. Sink the trap in a deep pool or behind sunken logs. The fish will swim in, but won't find their way out.

Dam trap: A dam trap is a clever way to catch fish. Build a dam of mud, wood, and stones. Extend the dam three-

milk jug trap

quarters of the way across a stream. This will divert the flow. Now build a circular trap below the dam with more stones. Leave the downstream end open about a foot or two. The fish swimming upstream will choose the slower water and will be trapped. A net across the swift flow on the other side will catch any fish going downstream. You'll have a great fish fry.

dam
trap

Spearing Fish

Indians sharpened sticks and speared fish. Split the shaft of a sturdy stick into three parts. Sharpen and then wedge them open with small bits of wood. You have to be both patient and quick to spear a fish!

Where and When to Fish

Fish like to rest behind logs, in the shadows of big stones, and under banks, so try casting in those areas. Fish the weeds also. Think like a fish and you'll find them.

If you have a boat and a big lake, go offshore a distance and let your line hit bottom. Then pull it up about one foot. Wait long enough and you'll catch a fish.

Evening and early in the morning are the best times to fish, because that's when fish are feeding. Just before it rains is also a good time, but stay away from water in a thunderstorm!

How to Clean a Fish

Before cooking and eating a fish, you must prepare it. Cut the belly from anus to head and lift out the innards. Rinse. Remove any scales by scraping them backward with a knife. If your fish is a catfish or eel, girdle the skin below the head and pull the skin off with pliers.

What Fish Is That?

What kind of fish have you caught? Here are some of the most common fish in North America.

Largemouth Bass live in warm freshwater, like ponds and lakes and some streams. They are a metallic green color with a spiny fin running up the back and a dark line running from eye to tail. Excellent eating. To get a big one use a mouse for bait.

Smallmouth Bass are bronze colored with vertical stripes and a small mouth. Usually found in lakes and streams with pebbly bottoms.

Common Carp are heavy-bodied fish with large scales. They have two *barbels*—they look like whiskers—on the upper jaw. Carp can grow to be 2 to 4 feet long.

Sunfish or Bluegills have round, flat bodies with dark spots on the back and back fin. They are "panfish," easily caught, cleaned, and fried whole in a pan. Delicious! Sunfish live in lakes, ponds, and slower parts of streams.

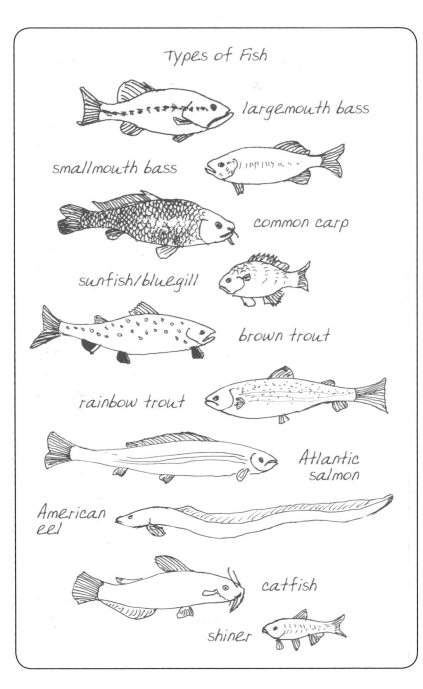

Types of Fish

largemouth bass

smallmouth bass

common carp

sunfish/bluegill

brown trout

rainbow trout

Atlantic
salmon

American
eel

catfish

shiner

Brown Trout is a pale olive-brown slender trout with large dark spots. It lives in cold streams and lakes.

Rainbow Trout is a speckled, colorful, long silvery fish. It has a pinkish red stripe along its sides and lives in cold lakes and streams. My favorite trout—it gets to be 3 feet long.

Atlantic Salmon are silvery salmon with small X-shaped spots. Juveniles have dark spots on their backs and red spots on their sides. They spawn in rivers north of Connecticut and otherwise live in the Atlantic Ocean. These fish are in trouble. Throw them back!

American Eel is a fish that looks like a snake. It lives in freshwater but breeds in salt water. The males stay in shallow brackish estuaries while the females migrate to freshwater.

Catfish have scaleless skin and slender barbels around their mouths. They live in lakes, ponds, and slow-moving streams. The channel catfish has a forked tail and can grow to 4 feet! There is also a dark blue catfish called a hardhead. Common fish and real good. Eat lots.

Shiners are the little fish or minnows abundant in freshwater streams. They are silvery with dark patches on their sides. The breeding males have big red fins. Eight inches is a big one.

Invertebrates

Crayfish are as delicious as lobsters. In the North, you can find them hiding under stones in shallow creeks. In the South, you can find them by the bushels in the bayous. Grab crayfish behind their pincers and cook in boiling water immediately. Make a crayfish feast.

Saltwater Mussels are abundant. They grow on rocks below high tide level, so hunt for mussels at low tide. Mussels are dark gray to black and usually found in clusters. Scrub clean and then cook your haul by boiling in a pot of water. Before you cook, discard any mussels that have cracked or opened shells. After you cook, discard any mussel shells that have not opened.

Freshwater Mussels are an edible but threatened species. Don't eat!

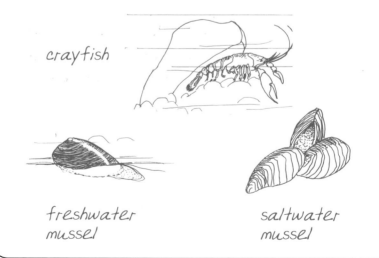

crayfish

freshwater
mussel

saltwater
mussel

Fresh Roadkill

Roadkill is excellent food if you get it right away. Check with your local conservation department for rules about collecting roadkill. A deer is a prize. Rabbits or squirrels can be excellent.

Bugs to Eat

Don't go "yuck." You eat bugs all the time. Those black bits in flour are flour beetles and weevils. The goodness in cider includes apple worms. Small grubs or tiny flies are often in fresh fruits and vegetables. Bugs are common in canned food, too.

Bugs are good for you. They are rich in protein and low in fat. Like fish, you should kill, clean, and cook insects before you eat them. To prepare, catch and then kill bugs in boiling water or in the freezer. Pull off wings, legs, and sometimes the head. Dip bugs in chocolate or eat them fried in butter or flour batter.

Some cultures consider crickets to be quite tasty. Skewer the crickets on sticks, hold them over the fire until they pop, then wolf them down. Crickets taste like popcorn but are much, much better for you.

cricket

And then the crop of crickets appeared and Frightful hopped all over the meadow snagging them in her great talons and eating them. I tried them, because I had heard they are good. I think it was another species of cricket that was meant. I think the field cricket would taste excellent if you were starving, so I preferred to listen to them. ·

—MY SIDE OF THE MOUNTAIN

Cooking outdoors makes everything taste better. When you get good at it you can cook almost anything out in the wild.

Coal Cooking

Roasting roots, potatoes, fish, and meat in the coals of a fire is an easy way to get a good hot meal. You must have a thick layer of coals. After the wood from your fire has burned down and the red coals are topped with a bit of gray ash, it is the perfect time to cook.

Dampen enough green tree or wild grape leaves to wrap several layers around the food you want to cook. Place the food in the center of the leaves. Add wild onions or garlic for a savory treat. Fold over the sides to make a neat package. Wrap with more layers of leaves.

Place your bundle in the coals, leave for 5 to 10 minutes. The outside leaves may blacken, but if the temperature and moisture is right the inside leaves will stay green and your food will not be burned.

Spit Cooking

A simple way to cook meat is to roast it on a spit above the coals. You can do this with a whole fish, too. Use a green stick. Tie the meat tightly onto it or push the skewer lengthwise through the meat so that it is firmly attached. Lean the spit up against a rock or lay it across two rocks. You may also suspend the spit between two

Y-shaped sticks. Turn the meat slowly as it roasts. It will smell and taste delicious.

Rock Boiling

"Rock boiling" cooking works well if you have a container such as a tin can, metal bucket, or a pot. The container can be as small as a cup, for tea, or larger for boiling tubers and meats.

Heat three to four rocks in a fire for about an hour. Then use leather gloves to pick up the hot stones, brush off the ash, and place them, one at a time, into the container. For a single cup, rocks about the size of a quarter can be used. For a larger pot use rocks the size of a softball. When one rock cools, put it back in the fire and put a hot one in the container. Keep repeating until your food is cooked.

REMEMBER NOT TO USE RIVER ROCKS AS THEY MIGHT EXPLODE!

Boiling Water in a Leaf

You really can boil water in a leaf. The water keeps the leaf from burning. You can boil water in a paper cup, too.

Use a mountain maple leaf or the biggest leaf you can find. Then gather several hair-thin stems to pin the leaf together so that it will hold water. Don't let the water drain out through holes the stems make. Place them high on the cupped leaf.

Now suspend the leaf-cup between two stones over a

small fire. Embers pulled from a larger fire are good. Use your leaf-pot to boil wild greens or eggs.

Pit Cooking

Pit cooking is so good that it is used in many places, like community fund-raisers and backyards, not just camping.

Dig a pit deep enough to hold your meal. Gather rocks and 16 inches of grass and greens.

Prepare any combination of vegetables, meat, or fish. Wrap the meal in leaves or tinfoil. Put to the side.

Line your pit with stones and build a good hot fire on top of them. Let the fire burn for about an hour to heat the rocks through and through.

When hot, remove coals with a shovel. Add a 6- to 8-inch layer of greens on top of the hot rocks, place your meal on top of them, and add another layer of greens about the same thickness. Cover with a large, flat stone, bark, logs, or soil—anything to keep the heat in.

The advantage to pit cooking is that you don't have to watch it, or worry about it burning. You can go fishing, collecting, or work on your camp while the meal cooks. When the stones are cool—in about an hour—the food is done. Cooking this way makes a tasty, moist meal.

Make a Solar Oven

If you want to use the sun to cook in the wild you will have to make this solar oven ahead of time. It is a nifty way to prepare a meal in a sunny climate. You can use it at home to help save electricity or firewood.

Take two cardboard boxes, one about an inch bigger than the other. If you can't find two boxes these sizes, cut one down to fit. Leave the four outside flaps on the larger of the two boxes. Cut them off the smaller box.

Make the lid for the smaller box: First, place the smaller box on a larger piece of cardboard. Trace the box in the center of the cardboard. Measure an edge about one inch deep around the outside of the small box outline. Score along outline of the small box and cut. Cut out corner squares, as in picture *a*, to make the lid.

solar oven lid (steps)

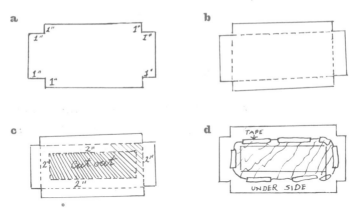

Cut out a window in the cardboard lid about 2 inches smaller than the small box outline. Cover the window with a piece of clear Reynolds Oven Cooking Bag (available in stores).

Now fold scored edges to make a snug-fitting lid. Secure in place with duct tape.

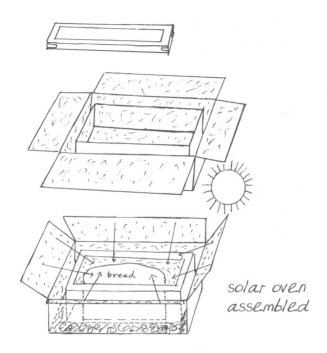

solar oven
assembled

The oven: Cover the insides of the two boxes and the flaps of the larger box with aluminum foil. Place the smaller box inside the larger one. Use wadded paper to center the smaller box in the middle of the larger one. Put food in the small box, cover with lid.

Place solar oven in the sun. Use flaps of outside box to direct heat toward the oven and to block any wind. It really works! You can even bake bread and biscuits.

Cooking on Your Car Engine

This may not be the most natural way to cook, but if you are driving somewhere, you might as well use the heat from your car's engine to cook while you ride. Make sure you put your food in a hot spot, but not near any moving car parts. You can tie the food in place with wire to be sure it won't fall off. Talk to an auto mechanic about the best places for cooking if you're unsure. Check the meal periodically to experiment with cooking times. Drive at least one hour to cook most things. (Note: Newer car models may not work!)

Some easy engine cooking recipes

Baked apples: Core apples and cut into slices. Take heavy-duty aluminum foil and put the apples in the middle. Sprinkle with sugar and cinnamon. Pour a bit of cider or water on the apples. Wrap the whole thing up tightly, pinching the seams to make sure there are no leaks.

Chicken: It takes a longer time to cook chicken, so plan this for a long trip. Cut chicken into small pieces, add a little salt, butter, or spicy flavoring to taste.

Dogs in a Blanket: Hot dogs wrapped in Bisquick make a tasty treat. Mix a batch of biscuit dough. Wrap it around the hot dogs. Grease and wrap aluminum foil around the "dogs in a blanket." A half-hour trip should do it.

"I'll have a salad type lunch," I said as I moved up the steep sides of the ravine. I discovered that as late as it was in the season, the spring beauties were still blooming in the cool pockets of the woods. They are all right raw, that is if you are as hungry as I was. They taste a little like lima beans. I ate these as I went on hunting food, feeling better and better, until I worked my way back to the meadow where the dandelion were blooming.

—MY SIDE OF THE MOUNTAIN

Edible plants are in the woods, marshes, fields, along roadsides—everywhere, even the desert. It's a good idea to have a naturalist show you edible plants before you go foraging. There are excellent botanists at nature centers.

Remember where the plants grow—in the woods, wetlands, or by the sea. You can find them more easily if you know their habitat. Some plants are common in one area and endangered in another. If you're unsure of a plant's status, check with your state Fish and Game agency before picking.

BERRIES

Blackberries and Raspberries • *Rubus allegheniensis*

Sunny thickets

Blackberries grow on thorny shrubs and vines with red or green stems. I try to beat the grouse, red foxes, and birds to them. Collect the berries in July and August. Eat right off the bush or use in jellies, salads, or desserts.

Red raspberries and blackberries are particularly good. Out west the tasty blackcap is one of several wild raspberry plants. You'll find them in meadows and burned over lands. Critters from mice to bears like raspberries. Get there early.

Salmonberries • *Rubus spectabilis*

Western, moist woods and shaded areas along streams

 These raspberry-type plants grow 6 to 12 feet high in California and the Northwest. The berries are yellow or red. They can be eaten as is or cooked and made into a dessert.

The wild things love them. So do I.

Cranberries • *Vaccinium macrocarpon*

Low mossy bogs

 Cranberry bushes are low, creeping shrubs with small, alternate evergreen leaves. They grow in Northern and Eastern bogs, like the Pine Barrens of New Jersey.

There are several kinds of cranberries, but all can be eaten raw (they taste better after an autumn frost). Best if boiled or dried and stored for Thanksgiving.

Highbush Cranberries • *Viburnum opulus*

Cool northern woods, thickets

 There is a bush called the tall bush cranberry out West and northward that is excellent. It is really not a cranberry but one of the *Viburnum* shrubs. The leaves have a maple leaf shape. The flower is white, the fruit a bright, translucent red. The berries hang on the shrub all winter. Deer love them.

They are great in pancakes and biscuits and make good jelly. Save some for the birds. They like them, too.

Blueberries • *Vaccinium spp.*

Barrens, tundra, moist woods, and bogs

 Blueberries are 3 or 4 foot tall bushes with sort of greenish zigzag twigs. Flowers are bell-like and the fruit is unmistakable—a blue berry with a starlike calyx on top. The foxes, opossums, raccoons, skunks, blue-birds, catbirds, orioles, phoebes, and robins will get them before you do if the deer don't. If you want any blueberries cover the bushes with netting.

Strawberries • *Fragaria virginiana*

Well-drained soil and rocky sunny areas

 Wild strawberries look like the kind you buy in the store, but are smaller and much more fla-vorful and sweet. There are also garden straw-berries that have gone wild. They are bigger but not as tasty as the truly wild ones.

Strawberries grow throughout North America and make a good dessert. If you don't get them first the quail and pheasants will. Songbirds like towhees and brown thrashers, small mammals like chipmunks and mice, and big ones like deer will also eat them.

GREENS

Dandelion • *Taraxacum officinale*

Open spaces, lawns

Everybody knows the dandelion. Native to Europe and Asia, it was brought to North America by colonists as a medicinal herb. Some say it is an ugly weed; I say it is beautiful—and good eating.

Cut the new leaves for a salad or cook them about ten minutes for a tangy, spinachlike treat. Make a coffeelike drink by baking the roots slowly until they are brown and brittle. Then grind and perk, like regular coffee, or dump in a pot of water and simmer like cowboy coffee. Doggone good. Dandelion flowers are excellent dipped in a batter such as Bisquick and fried.

Many wild animals eat dandelions, from mice, deer, and pocket gophers in the West, to chipmunks, cottontails, and lots of songbirds in the East.

Wild Potato or
Indian Breadroot • *Pediomelum esculentum*

Arid land, mostly in middle America

Wild potato, or Indian breadroot, is mainly found in the central prairies and dry lands. Five oval leaflets that whorl out from a furry central stem are a distinctive feature. The root looks like a turnip.

Settlers tried to cultivate the wild potato because it tastes like an Irish potato and is wholesome and nutritious. But, the wild potato wanted to be wild and they never were a success on farms. Plant them by scattering the seeds on an arid spot. Do not eat the seeds. They are no good.

Wild Rice • *Zizania aquatica*

Shallow water

Wild rice is a graceful grass. Yes, it's a grass that thrives in water, with light green stems that grow to be 3 to 6 feet tall. The rice itself is the seeds of the plant, which hang in drooping clusters when ripe, around August and September. The seeds are slender, encased in bristle-tipped husks, and need a little winnowing to get them out. The Native Americans harvested wild rice by knocking the stems over their canoes so that the rice fell inside. You can do the same.

Watch for waterfowl that feed on wild rice, like ducks, and songbirds like sparrows and bobolinks. Cook just like store-bought rice, by boiling in water. It is so good. Some species of wild rice are threatened in some states. Check with your state conservation department before harvesting. Save grains from your harvest and sow in shallow waters.

Wild Onion • *Allium canadense*

Rocky slopes, open woods, meadows

The wild onion is threatened or endangered in Vermont, New Hampshire, and Maine. Protect it there! Like all onions, it is a member of the lily family. These plants grow to a foot tall, have grasslike leaves, and are easily recognized by their ball of starlike pink or white flower heads, which appear from May to July.

Where it is common wild onion can be picked and eaten raw, though it tastes like sharp onions. Before the flowers appear, boil the tender leaf stalks and bulbs for a milder flavor. Rub on your skin to repel insects and protect from scorpion and lizard bites.

Plantain • *Plantago major*

Meadows, fields, lawns, roadsides

This weed shares its name with a banana-like fruit common in Latin America. But our plantain is very different. In the United States, *Plantago major* is common throughout the country. The leaves grow in a flat rosette, right on the ground. The flowers are white and atop a single, leafless stem.

Eat plantain leaves when they are very young, boiled or in salads. The leaves become stringy when they've grown older, so are best in spring. There's a seaside plantain that is also good to eat, but the weed in your yard is more common. Grouse and deer like plantain leaves. The seeds are eaten by cardinals, grasshopper sparrows, and small mammals like the cottontail rabbit and kangaroo rat.

Clover • *Trifolium spp.*

Open spaces, grassy lawns

Clovers are small, easy-to-recognize plants. They have three distinctive leaves and round flower heads. The white lawn clover is not the easiest to digest, but it has lots of protein in it and can be eaten in quantity if boiled for 5 to 10 minutes or soaked several hours in salty water.

There are 75 species of clover, so there is plenty to go around. Clover is found even in the city's vacant lots. The clean leaves are good cooked or just tossed in a salad.

Sharp-tailed grouse, quail, and pheasants like clover seeds. So do rabbits, antelopes, mule deer, and white-tailed deer. Bees especially love clover flowers. Find clover by following a bee.

Cattails • *Typha latifolia or Typha angustifolia*

Marshlands

Cattails are tall slender reeds with easy to recognize hot dog–shaped seedheads. They grow throughout the United States, particularly in marshes. Native Americans used cattails to make flour, baskets, and mattresses. They ate the early shoots like asparagus and the flower stalks like corn-on-the-cob.

When mature, the brown cigar-shaped seeds are soft and fluffy and make good pillow stuffing. Young shoots and stalks can be peeled and cooked. Young seedheads can be boiled and eaten like corn-on-the-cob with butter and salt. The yellow pollen found on top of the "hot dog" makes a protein-rich flour when mixed with wheat flour. Long tasty sprouts form at the end of the roots in fall. Boil once, pour off the water, and boil again for about ten minutes. Eat with butter and salt.

Today, cattails are being pushed out by another reedy plant called *phragmites.* Muskrats, who eat and build homes with cattails, are disappearing, too. Save these useful plants! Be sure to keep some of the seed fluff from each cattail you use. Scatter the fluff in wet places to help sow next year's crop.

Bracken Fern • *Pteridium aquilinum*

Roadside, sunny meadows, open spots among trees

 The Bracken fern is one of the most common and best-tasting ferns. It's large for a fern, growing between 2 and 6 feet high, and looks like a little tree topped with wide, lacy leaves that narrow to a point. The fronds are three-forked. The stems are woody. Harvest the young fiddleheads when 6 to 8 inches tall and run them through your hands to remove the outer fuzz. Boil like asparagus. They are wonderful. Do not eat mature ferns. They are bitter.

New York Fern • *Thelypteris noveboracensis*

Woods

Another good fern. People I know call it the New York fern because it tapers at the top and bottom—burning the candle at both ends. The fiddlehead is the coiled young frond of a fern. They are gathered when about six inches high, boiled 10 to 15 minutes, and savored.

Ferns are universal and abundant, yet wildlife doesn't eat them. Occasionally, in the winter, deer and rabbits will nibble them, also grouse. Maybe because these plants are so ancient—ferns are among the oldest plants on earth—they have had time to outwit their enemies. Take a hint, don't eat mature ferns.

Yellow Pond Lily • *Nuphar lutea*

Ponds and shallow lakes

The common yellow water lily grows throughout Northeastern and Central North America. It has curled petals and a large, flat leaf that's notched.

The large rootstalks are eaten either baked or boiled and mashed like potatoes. Change the boiling water once or twice if the taste is too strong. The large seeds can be popped like popcorn or baked and pounded into flour.

Daylily • *Hemerocallis spp.*

Waste ground, escaped from gardens

 Daylilies are very diverse, but all have large, colorful flowers. The buds and flowers from this common lily can be used raw on salads, cooked like asparagus, or fried like fritters. The underground tubers can be roasted like corn. Shoots are best in the early spring. In summer eat the buds and flowers.

Common Arrowhead or Duck Potato • *Sagittaria latifolia*

Shallow water and mud

 Spread throughout North America, though endangered in Illinois. Protect it there! The stalks grow in water, and they have flat, arrowhead-shaped leaves. Their white flowers bloom between July and October.

The edible tubers can be hauled from the water by pulling on the plant. The potatolike roots are at the end of long runners. They must be boiled and drained several times before eating. They are good mashed or fried, just like potatoes. American Indians thrived on them. Dry and save for a winter snack.

Pickerelweed • *Pontederia cordata*

Shallow water and mud

The pickerelweed (threatened in Kentucky) is similar to the common arrowhead: it grows throughout North America in water or mud. The flowers of the pickerelweed are blue and the leaves are rounder. It grows between 1 and 3½ feet tall.

The broad, glossy pickerel leaves can be used for salads or cooked. The early June leaves and flower spike can also be cooked or fried, and are surprisingly good. Raw pickerel leaves will make you itch, so only take a bite or two.

Wild Rose • *Rosa carolina*

Open areas from seaside to Western mountains

The wild rose, also known as the pasture rose, is found in Eastern and Midwestern North America. It has pink five-petaled flowers that bloom from May to July. In early fall the flowers become rose hips. These red seedpods, or "hips," are edible. They are somewhat mealy but tasty when cooked. You can make jam, tea, and candy from them. Eat rose hips raw by scraping off the tasty outer part of the "hip" with your teeth. Spit the seeds out onto the soil to help in sowing next year's crop. Rose hips are rich in vitamin C and iron and are used as an herbal remedy for many illnesses, from colds to arthritis.

ODDITIES

Giant Puffball • *Calvatia gigantea*
Woods, fields, lawns

You can't miss it. The giant puffball mushroom is a big, round, white ball with white insides. The biggest have grown to be over 4 feet wide, weighing 45 pounds! Most are smaller. Like all mushrooms, the giant puffball is a fungi, not a plant. It grows in woods and fields throughout North America and Europe. There are several kinds of puffballs, all good eating when the ball is white inside and out. ONLY eat when the inside is pure white—other, poisonous species of mushroom may resemble the puffball, but have colors or even fine lined silhouettes in the interior. If you're unsure, don't eat a wild mushroom.

If it's white and positively identified, eat the puffball raw or fry and serve as a tasty side for a meat dish. Black or dark insides even in puffballs are dangerous to eat. But you can stamp on them and they'll go "poof." It's fun and also spreads spores so that more will grow. Watch out for red squirrels. They love the giant puffball.

Edible Kelp • *Alaria esculenta*
Submerged rocks and shores, Northeast coast

The North Atlantic coast's edible kelp rang-es from red-purple brown to dark green with a satiny sheen. Not a plant but an algae, it grows from one to several feet long.

Dry in the sun, cook as a vegetable or soup, or eat as is. This bountiful seaweed is rich in calcium and vitamins A and B.

The Pacific Ocean kelp called kombu is also edible and is used in many Japanese dishes.

Prickly Pears • *Opuntia ficus-indica*
Rocky and dry sandy soil

Prickly pears grow throughout the West and Southwest of North America. Some species are endangered, so check with your conservation department before picking. The round, flat "leaves" of this cactus are called platyclades, or pads, and are tufted with sharp bristles. Watch out or wear gloves when harvesting this wild plant! The flowers are showy yellow and the small round fruit is a dull red.

The fruit, called cactus figs or tuna, are ripe from August through October. They can be eaten raw, right off the cactus. Cactus figs are good cooked like a vegetable, too. Best of all, take the green young pads, towel off the spiny, hairlike bristles, and fry in butter and salt. They are real good chopped with onions in an omelet.

ACORNS and NUTS

White Oak Acorns • *Quercus alba*

Eastern and Midwestern North America

 In fall, oak trees all over North America drop a harvest of nutritious, thimble-size acorns to the forest floor. Acorns, rich in protein, carbohydrates, and calcium, are a great source of food for wildlife and can be one for you, too.

The majestic white oak's acorns are some of the tastiest and easiest to prepare. This oak can live to be over 600 years old. You can find a picture of it on the back of the Connecticut quarter.

To beat the squirrels to the fall harvest, gather your nuts early. Some acorns are sweet enough to be peeled and eaten raw or roasted. Acorns contain tannin, some so much that they taste bitter. Tannin can cause an upset stomach, so it's best to get it out of the nuts. Peel the nuts out of their shells and boil them in a pot, dumping the water off a couple of times (or more!) until the liquid stays clear and the bitter tannin is gone. Now roast the nuts slowly until they are dry. Grind with a coffee grinder or mortar and pestle to make acorn flour.

Other good acorn-bearing trees are the chestnut oak, black oak, and live oak. Songbirds, like titmice, varied thrushes, and Carolina wrens, eat acorns. Woodpeckers, bears, turkeys, deer, and beaver love them, too.

Shagbark Hickory • *Carya ovata*

Rich soil, river bottoms, upland slopes east of Nebraska

There are several kinds of hickory trees in the eastern part of North America. Shagbark hickories have the best nuts. The shagbark is a tall tree with five leaflets on a stem. It has distinctive light bark that is very shaggy. The flavorful wood of a shagbark hickory can be used to smoke meat. It was also used by Indians in the Northeast to make the bows of their bows and arrows.

You can't miss the bark of the shagbark hickory or the pile of nuts that fall to the ground in September and October. Remove the husk. The nuts inside are egg-shaped with thick shells. You need a hammer or a stone to open them and a small pick to dig out the meat, but they're worth it. Shagbark hickory nuts taste wonderful and are nourishing, too. Super in muffins, pancakes, and cookies. You are competing with woodpeckers and squirrels for these, so harvest as soon as the crop is in.

Black Walnut or
American Walnut • *Juglans nigra*

Eastern deciduous woods

Black walnut trees often grow near water. These tall trees have large leaves featuring 7 to 17 toothed "leaflets." The walnuts should be gathered from the ground in October and November. When they first drop from the trees the nuts have thick green husks. Peel them off. The nuts inside can be very tough to open, so keep a hammer or stone handy. Once open, the nuts can be eaten on the spot or cooked. The nutmeat is sweet and delicious. Put them in muffins, pancakes, cakes, or salads. Be sure to plant a nut before you eat them all.

The green walnut husks will rapidly turn brown. They make a good dye or stain for tables and chairs and the like. Early American settlers used the dark brown dye to color their hair, while colonial children learned to write and draw using black walnut ink. You can make your own black walnut dye or ink by boiling the darkened husks in water. The husks will stain your hands, as well as any other material they touch. Wear gloves and old clothes. (See page 111, "Making Walnut Ink.")

American Beech • *Fagus grandifolia*

Eastern and Southern United States

 Beechnuts are a treat and all the wildlife thinks so, too. There used to be great forests of American beeches, and the nuts were an important food for the now extinct passenger pigeon. Beech leaves are serrated ovals and bright green in color. The smooth gray trunks of the tree are easy to recognize.

The small beechnut usually drops to the ground in the fall, after the first frost. The triangular nuts are enclosed in a spiny husk and hard shell. Peel, crack, and eat the nuts plain, or pound into flour. Roast and grind to make a fabulous coffeelike drink.

PINECONE NUTS

You can get the nuts from pinecones with a little work. Any pinecone nut is good and all are edible. Two of my favorites are the Eastern white pine and the Piñon pine.

Eastern White Pine • *Pinus strobus*

Eastern North America

The Eastern white pine is a useful tree. Native Americans used the pitch of this pine to waterproof baskets and canoes, and to treat wounds and illnesses. As the tallest trees in Eastern North America they can reach over 200 feet in height.

The pine nuts, found nestled in the slender pinecone, are the tastiest part of the Eastern white pine. The best way to identify this tree is the green needles, which grow in bundles of five. Eat the seeds from the cones raw or roasted. You can also make a swell tea out of the needles, which are high in vitamin C—just boil in clean water.

Piñon Pine • *Pinus edulis*

Southwestern United States and Northern Mexico

Wonderful nuts can be found in the cones of this small, beautiful pine tree, which usually grows to only 20 to 40 feet. Identify the trees by the needles that grow in bundles of two. Piñon nuts are a staple of Native Americans, eaten raw, roasted, or ground into flour. Pueblo and Hopi Indians use the sticky sap to waterproof baskets and as a glue to make jewelry or repair pottery. The nuts are so good that they are harvested and sold in grocery stores. Piñon jays, squirrels, black bears, and mule deer also enjoy this pine nut.

With pockets and good tough pants I was willing to pack home many more new foods to try. Daisies, the bark of a poplar tree that I saw a squirrel eating, and puffballs. They are mushrooms, the only ones I felt were safe to eat, and even at that, I kept waiting to die the first night I ate them. I didn't, so I enjoyed them from that night on. They are wonderful. Mushrooms are dangerous and I would not suggest that one eat them from the forest. The mushroom expert at the Botanical Gardens told me that. He said even he didn't eat wild ones.

—MY SIDE OF THE MOUNTAIN

POISONOUS TO TOUCH

Poison Ivy
Toxicodendron radicans

Poison Sumac
Toxicodendron vernix

**Atlantic Poison
Oak**
Toxicodendron pubescens

**Western Poison
Oak**
Toxicodendron diversilobum

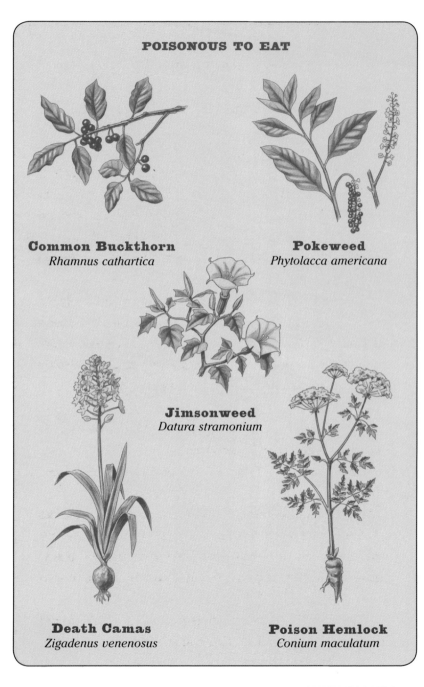

POISONOUS TO EAT

Common Buckthorn
Rhamnus cathartica

Pokeweed
Phytolacca americana

Jimsonweed
Datura stramonium

Death Camas
Zigadenus venenosus

Poison Hemlock
Conium maculatum

Poison Ivy • *Toxicodendron radicans*

All over North America

Poison ivy has three shiny green leaflets at the top of a stalk, which turn red, orange, or yellow in fall. It can be a small shrub or a vine growing up a tree. The seeds are white and come in the fall. For those who are allergic to it (that's most of us) touching poison ivy makes a rash that itches like crazy. It can blister the skin and last several weeks. The rash is caused by an oil found in all parts of the plant, dead or alive. Learn to recognize poison ivy so that you can avoid it.

Wash exposed skin with soap and water and apply ice to soothe the itch. Wash clothing. Some people are dangerously allergic to poison ivy. If you have a severe reaction, accidentally eat poison ivy, or inhale smoke from burning poison ivy get to a hospital as soon as possible.

Atlantic Poison Oak • *Toxicodendron pubescens*

Southeastern and Central United States

Western Poison Oak • *Toxicodendron diversilobum*

Western United States

A shrub or vine with three small, glossy oaklike leaflets at the end of a stem. Leaves can yellow in summer and turn bright red in fall. In the East it is usually a low shrub. In the West the shrubs reach 10 feet and can also grow as vines.

Don't touch. Just like poison ivy, the oils found throughout these plants can cause severe blisters and itchiness. Treat like poison ivy. If you have a severe reaction, get to a hospital.

Poison Sumac • *Toxicodendron vernix*
Wooded swamps and boggy areas,
Eastern and Midwestern United States

Poison sumac grows as a straggly shrub up to 15 feet tall. Look for 7- to 13-inch smooth leaflets. The veins to the leaflets are red. Berries are a glossy pale yellow or cream colored.

Like poison ivy, poison sumac has an allergen that can make you itch if you touch it, but is even more toxic. No fun. Treat the itch as for poison ivy. If you have a severe reaction, get to a hospital as soon as possible.

Common Buckthorn • *Rhamnus cathartica*
Southern Canada, Eastern and Midwestern United States

You can recognize this shrub or small tree by the black berries growing right on the limbs.

The berries and bark are poisonous and will give you diarrhea. Don't eat. But it's okay to touch, and the thorns are good for making fishhooks.

Jimsonweed • *Datura stramonium*
Throughout North America

Jimsonweed grows 1 to 5 feet tall and has large, pointed oaklike leaves. When flowering it is easy to recognize and avoid because of its 3- to 4-inch trumpetlike white to purple flowers.

All parts of Jimsonweed are very poisonous if you eat them, so don't. It can cause seizures, coma, or death. Get to a hospital if you accidentally eat it.

Poison Hemlock • *Conium maculatum*

Throughout North America in waste places and marshes

This highly toxic plant, often mistaken for fennel, parsley, or wild carrot, grows 3 to 7 feet tall. Its smooth green stems are stout and hollow, marked with purple spots near the ground. Leaves are lacy and triangular in shape. The flower, a flat white bloom made of many tiny flowers, looks like Queen Anne's lace or wild carrot. Poison hemlock stems are hairless compared to the hairy stems of Queen Anne's lace. Crushed poison hemlock smells bad.

Long ago, the famous philosopher Socrates was sentenced to death by drinking a cup of poison hemlock. Even a small bite can cause paralysis and death. Get to a hospital right away if you've eaten it.

Pokeweed • *Phytolacca americana*

Throughout much of North America

A weedy plant growing from 1 to 10 feet tall, with large lance-like leaves and reddish stems. Flowers, on a long stalk, are greenish purple. The berries are purple-black and droop. Native Americans used dye from these berries to decorate horses. The United States Declaration of Independence was first written in fermented pokeberry ink, as were many letters written home by soldiers during the Civil War.

However, eating the leaves, berries, or roots can cause vomiting, tremors, and death. Go to the hospital if you have eaten mature pokeweed.

Death Camas • *Zigadenus venenosus*

Western North America

Death camas grows to 3 ½ feet tall and is found only in the Western states, usually in dry meadows and open grazing lands. Its slender leaves are spikey and look a lot like daylily leaves. White- and cream-colored flowers bloom in fluffy clusters from April through July. Don't confuse with the wild onion, which is easily mistaken for death camas. Wild onion has a round ball for a flower.

All parts of this plant are very dangerous if eaten. If you happen to eat death camas throw up by sticking your finger down your throat, or by any other means, and get to a hospital.

MEDICINE PLANTS

Sometimes I eat turtle soup, and I know how to make acorn pancakes. I keep my supplies in the wall of the tree in wooden pockets that I chopped myself. Every time I have looked at those pockets during the last two days, I have felt just like a squirrel, which reminds me: I didn't see a squirrel one whole day before that storm began. I guess they are holed up and eating their stored nuts, too.

—MY SIDE OF THE MOUNTAIN

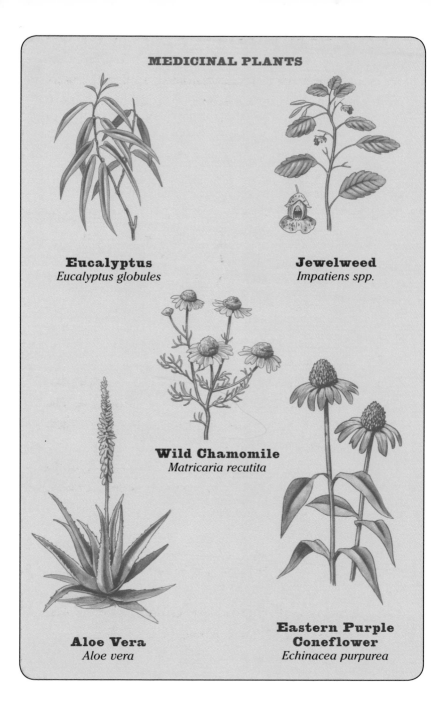

MEDICINAL PLANTS

Eucalyptus
Eucalyptus globules

Jewelweed
Impatiens spp.

Wild Chamomile
Matricaria recutita

Aloe Vera
Aloe vera

**Eastern Purple
Coneflower**
Echinacea purpurea

Most medicines in drugstores originally came from plants in the wild. These useful plants are still out there. Here are a few that are easy to recognize.

Aloe • *Aloe vera*
Southwestern and Western United States

The aloe plant has fleshy lance-shaped leaves that grow in a swirl. Flowers are red or yellow on a long stem.

For the relief of burns and to heal small cuts and scrapes, squeeze the clear gel from the leaf of the aloe plant and apply to the skin. Good plant.

Eucalyptus • *Eucalyptus globules*
Western and Southwestern United States

The eucalyptus tree grows 15 to 200 feet tall, with peeling bark and gray-green leaves that are lancelike. The eucalyptus tree is originally from Australia but now grows in the Western states.

The twigs can be chewed to help a sore throat, and a tea made from the fresh leaves is good for coughs, colds, and sore throats.

Jewelweed • *Impatiens spp.*
Wet, shady places, Canada to Georgia, Eastern two-thirds of North America

This plant has watery stems and hanging orange blossoms. Leaves look silvery when held under water.

If you have an insect bite or brush against poison ivy, rub the sap from Jewelweed stems on the bite or exposed places to help prevent a rash. Also wash skin and clothing with soap when you get home.

Eastern Purple Coneflower • *Echinacea purpurea*

Fields and road edges, Eastern and Central United States

Grows 2 to 4 feet tall with light green feathery leaves. Flowers have purplish petals surrounding a red-orange coned center. Some species are endangered. Check the status in your area before you pick!

If you feel like you're getting a cold try making a tea from the roots, leaves, and stems of the purple coneflower. Some people swear by it, others not so much. Make fresh, or dry some cuttings to keep on hand.

Wild Chamomile • *Matricaria recutita*

Road edges, waste places, and fields

Wild chamomile is a slender-stemmed plant with small daisylike white flowers and yellow centers.

Dry the flowers to make a pale golden tea that helps you sleep better, particularly on a lumpy bed. It's also good for stomachaches.

USEFUL KNOTS

I built the fire and was cooking the fish and making pancakes when Dad shot out of bed.

"Wild boy!" he shouted. "What a sanguine smell. What a purposeful fire. Breakfast in a tree. Son, I toil from sunup to sundown, and never have I lived so well!"

—MY SIDE OF THE MOUNTAIN

Knots are important to learn for camping, boating, and even at home. Here are a few to get you started.

Square Knot

The most useful knot I know is the square knot, or as sailors call it, the reef knot. It is good for everything from tying your dog's leash to keeping up your pants. It's not so good with cords of two different sizes or with nylon cord because the knot will slip.

See the illustration on page 78 to learn the square knot. The movements are right over left, left over right. Just remember that and you will always be able to make a square knot.

Fisherman's Knot

Useful for tying two ropes together. Use this knot to tie the leader on a fishhook to the fishing line. Also use it to make a long rope when you only have two or more short ones. Follow the instructions on page 79 to learn the fisherman's knot.

Bowline

The bowline makes a loop that is easy to tie and untie at the end of a rope. It's especially handy for boating. An easy way to remember the steps to making a bowline knot is: "The rabbit comes out of the hole (loop), goes around the tree (rope), and back in the hole again."

Practice the knot with this phrase as you follow the drawing on page 78.

Harness Hitch

This is a good knot to be made anywhere on a cord or rope because it doesn't need an end. It's useful for harnessing people together to haul or lift heavy objects. The harness hitch also makes a good climbing rope if you make the loops large enough to get your hands and feet into them.

First make a loop in the rope. Lay the left side of the loop across the rope.

Next twist the bottom of the loop to make a smaller loop within the larger loop.

Now pass the little loop over the left part of the rope and under the upper part of original loop.

Pull the knot gently into place, tighten and test it. Follow the illustration on page 80 to help you learn the harness hitch.

Clove Hitch

You can use this knot for many projects, such as attaching a tarp to anchoring pegs when making a lean-to. Study the illustration on page 80 to learn the handy clove hitch.

USEFUL KNOTS

Square Knot

Pass right line over the left,

then underneath.

The left line goes over the right and under it.

Tighten.

Bowline

Make a loop about twenty-four inches up the cord.

Bring the end up through the loop, around the line, and back down through the loop.

Pull on the long end to tighten.

USEFUL KNOTS

Fisherman's Knot

*Lay two lines beside each other
with the ends in opposite directions.*

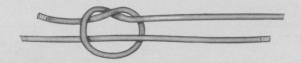

*Now take the end of one line and make a simple
overhand knot around the other line.*

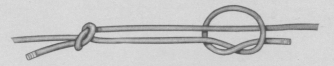

Do the same with the other end.

*Pull knots together by pulling lines
in opposite directions. Tighten.*

USEFUL KNOTS

Clove Hitch

Wrap short end around stake one-and-a-half times from front to back.

Bring end over line and around behind itself two times.

Pull tight.

Harness Hitch

Make a loop in the rope. Lay the line across left side of loop.

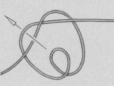

Twist the bottom of the loop to make a smaller loop.

Pass the smaller loop over the line on the left side and under the original loop.

Pull knot gently to tighten.

ANIMAL TRACKING

I was singing and chopping and playing a game with a raccoon I had come to know. From time to time I would tap on his tree with my ax. He would hang his sleepy head out, snarl at me, close his eyes, and slide out of sight.

The third time I did this, I knew something was happening in the forest. Instead of closing his eyes, he pricked up his ears and his face became drawn and tense. His eyes were focused on something down the mountain. I stood up and looked. I could see nothing.

"Now what's got you all excited?" I said, and tried once more to see what he had seen.

—MY SIDE OF THE MOUNTAIN

When the snow is on the land you can track many animals. By studying their tracks you can learn about their winter homes and feeding spots. Tracking is best when the snow is ½ to 1 inch deep. In summertime, you can track in mud along streambeds or lakes.

White-Tailed Deer

The hoofprints of the white-tailed deer of the East are easy to recognize. With each step a deer makes a cloven-pointed, or split-hooved print. Some say it's heart-shaped.

In soft ground, or if the deer was moving quickly, the print may have two impressions behind it, made by two toes called dewclaws that deer have on each foot.

The points of the hooves are in the direction that the deer was moving. In deep snow deer will make "drags" between steps from not lifting their legs high enough.

If there are deer around you will probably spot deer droppings. They look like little piles of plump raisins.

If you are close enough you might hear a deer snort or whistle sharply. They make this noise when curious or alarmed: *"whiew whiew ew ew."*

A white flash disappearing into the woods is the underside of a white-tailed deer's tail. The white flash is an alarm for other deer, letting them know that danger is near.

If a forest's foliage is chewed up to a six-foot level it means there are too many white-tailed deer in the area.

Mule Deer

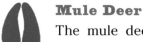

The mule deer of the West has large "mule ears" and a tail tipped with black. These deer are Westerners and don't come any farther east than the northwestern tip of Minnesota.

The hoofprints of white-tailed and mule deer look very much alike. But unlike the white-tailed, who runs with one foot after the other, the mule deer has a distinctive bounding gait in which all four feet come down together. He bounces.

The mule deer's droppings look like coffee beans.

Gray Squirrel

The clever gray squirrel is the most abundant of wild creatures. Squirrels live happily among people and will figure out how to get into your bird feeder no matter how you try to outwit them. In the wild, squirrels gather nuts and seeds to eat. Gray squirrels are great tree climbers and jumpers and are easy to spot by their big bushy tails. They use their tails for balance and to wrap themselves up in bad weather.

Gray squirrels draw their hind feet up in front of their front feet when they run. Follow the big footmarks, because they point the way.

Cottontail Rabbit

The cottontail rabbit gets its name from its short fluffy tail, which looks just like a white cotton ball. When a predator is close by, the rabbit will often "freeze," trying to avoid being spotted. Sometimes you can get pretty close to a "frozen" rabbit. When it does run, the cottontail puts his hind feet in front of his front feet—just like the squirrel. But you can recognize rabbit tracks because the hind feet of a cottontail are wider than the squirrel's and fuzzier. When following a set of tracks, also remember that cottontails can't climb trees. So if the tracks you're following end at a tree, the animal is probably a squirrel.

It's handy to know that cottontails tend to run in a zigzag manner and usually hide in the cuplike "forms" beneath bushes. Squirrels run for the trees.

 ### Dog and House Cat
Dog and cat prints are distinctive from those of other animals because their paws are padded and have only four toes.

 A dog puts its paws down in a zigzag pattern. Its claws are always extended.

A cat, on the other hand, puts down its feet in a fairly straight line. Cats have retractable claws.

Dogs generally have bigger prints, but because dogs come in all sizes and their prints can range from as big as a wolf's to smaller than a cat's, it is hard to tell a dog print just by measuring its size. Sometimes, to judge whether tracks are a cat's or a dog's, you have to consider each animal's habitat—where the prints have been found can offer clues to identifying the tracks. For example, the small, four-toed print of a toy dog isn't likely to be found in the wilds. So, if you see a small four-toed print in the wilderness, it's more likely to be the track of a feral house cat.

In town, a house cat is likely to hover around bird feeders and the foundations of houses. A dog often takes to the sidewalks, where there are fire hydrants with messages from other dogs.

Coyote

Coyote tracks are seen in the East now as well as the West. Their tracks follow the zigzag pattern of the dog and wolf, the coyote's relatives. Just like the dogs and wolves, a single coyote paw print shows one large pad behind the four smaller, pointed pads.

The front feet of wolves, dogs, and coyotes are a little bit larger than the hind feet. The front feet of the coyote are about 2 ¼ inches long (from tip to heel pad bottom), the hind about 2 inches long. The front paws of the wolf, on the other hand, are much larger. They measure about 4 to 5 inches long and 3 ¾ to over 5 inches wide, depending on the spread of the toes in soft mud or wet snow. You can't misidentify those huge wolf prints!

Skunk

Skunks are found from New England to the Pacific. They're most famous for their smelly spray, which they use as a last resort for protection against predators. Never provoke a skunk! If you've been sprayed, bathe as soon as possible to keep the odor from lingering. Add a little vinegar to soap or bathwater to help dissolve the oily skunk spray.

Skunks do not exactly hibernate, but they aren't very active in winter, either. So you're more likely to find skunk tracks in summertime mud than in wintertime snow. In warm weather the nocturnal skunk may trek around at night, slow and unafraid. His thick fur armor and smelly spray make him confident. Skunks are one of the few animals that will hunt and eat bees. Skunk fur is thick enough to protect them from bee stings.

A skunk print has five toes and five claws, which they use for digging and fighting. Skunk tracks usually end up in the den or hollow where the skunk lives, which may or may not smell skunky.

Raccoon

Raccoons have black fur around their eyes that makes them look like bandits. You can find raccoons almost everywhere, from the wild forest to the big city. They are nocturnal, often hunting for food at night, but will appear by day. Raccoons, like skunks, are omnivorous—they eat plants as well as small animals and insects.

Raccoon prints have five long toes and look like tiny human handprints. Their hind feet are longer and a little narrower than their front feet. Raccoons use their long fingers to "wash" food. You'll often find raccoon tracks in soft mud along streams.

When it is cold, raccoons are seldom out making tracks because they go into a winter sleep. It is not called "hibernation" because raccoons can awaken when it gets warm or when they are threatened. Real hibernators, like the groundhog or marmot, won't wake until spring.

Common Rat

The common rat usually lives around people, where it is guaranteed to find lots of food. Rats can make tracks that are pretty and starlike. Rodent tracks, including rats and mice, usually show a four-toe front footprint and a five-toe back footprint. Sometimes you can see the impression of a tail dragging along between the tracks.

Rat tracks usually lead to Dumpsters or garbage cans. Rats and other rodents make runways through grasses and plants. Sometimes you can spot these "rodent highways" in country fields and vacant lots.

Moles

The mole is a common resident of fields and suburbs. Like rodents, moles have five-toed clawed feet. Their front digging feet are broad and their back feet narrow. Moles spend most of their time digging for roots, insects, and worms underground. Moles make tunnels that you see on the surface of the ground as long mounds of pushed-up dirt. Dirt rolling away from a messy central mound is a nest.

The star-nosed mole doesn't leave runways on the surface of the ground, only eruptions here and there that look like little volcanoes. Most of the time moles are underground and it's hard to find mole tracks above ground. You are a good detective if you can find a mole footprint!

dog   bear   raccoon   rat   mole

Whether you live in the East or the West you can find these animals to track.

BIRDSONGS

The following morning I stood up, stretched, and looked about me. Birds were dripping from the trees, little birds, singing and flying and pouring over the limbs.

"This must be the warbler migration," I said, and I laughed because there were so many birds. I had never seen so many. My big voice rolled through the woods, and their little voices seemed to rise and answer me.

—MY SIDE OF THE MOUNTAIN

When you are busy at camp you often hear birds, but rarely see them. You can identify a bird by the sound of its song. Some birds seem to be saying English words. Here are some of the words and sounds they seem to say:

"Cheer, cheer, cheer, cheer"

Northern Cardinal

Eastern and Southern United States, Southern Canada, and Latin America

The male northern cardinal is bright red with a black mask. He's easy to spot. The female is a beautiful olive brown, with a gray mask and an orange beak.

"Old Sam Peabody, Peabody, Peabody"

White-throated Sparrow

Breeds in Canada or New England, migrates to the Eastern and Southern United States

The white-throated sparrow is small and has a brown and black striped back, gray chest, and white patch on the throat.

"Maids, maids, maids, put on the tea kettlelelelelelele"

Song Sparrow

Found across most of North America

The song sparrow is small, with a brown and gray streaked head and back. It often has a white chin and light-colored belly with prominent brown spots.

"Cheerily, cheer-up, cheerio"

American Robin

Found throughout North America

The American robin is most easily recognized by its red breast. It has a dark head and brown or gray back.

"Caw, caw, caw, caw" (harsh and noisy)

American Crow

Throughout North America

This crow is entirely black and often forages or roosts in large, noisy groups. Hard to miss!

"Peter, Peter, Peter" (shrill and loud)

Tufted Titmouse

Eastern United States and Mexico

The tufted titmouse is a small gray bird with a pale underbelly and a sharp tuft on top of its head.

"Teacher, teacher, teacher" (loud)

Ovenbird

Breeds in the Eastern United States and Canada and migrates to Southeastern states and Mexico for the winter

The ovenbird is small, with a white spotted breast and olive brown back. It has a thin white ring around each eye.

"Kra-a-a" (long and drawn out)

Clark's Nutcracker

Western North America, especially at higher altitudes

This relatively large songbird has a gray body and head with black and white wings that flash when they fly.

"Hew-li. Hew-li, hew-le, hew-li, hew-li"
(and other melodic notes)

Baltimore Oriole

Breeds in Canada, Eastern and Midwest United States; winters in Southeast United States and South America.

The male oriole is the easiest to recognize. He has a black head, brilliant orange-colored chest, and snazzy white wing bars.

"Mew" (scolding) and slow melodic phrases all day

Red-eyed Vireo

Eastern and Northern United States as well as Canada in the summer; migrates to South America for the winter

This small bird has an olive green back, pale belly, black streak through its red eyes, and a gray crown on its head.

"Chick-a-dee-dee-dee"

Black-capped Chickadee

Throughout the Northern United States and Midwest, and Canada

The black-capped chickadee is a small bird with a black head and throat, white cheeks, and a white belly.

"Jay, jay, jay" (piercing) and *"weedle-eedle"* (musical)

Blue Jay

Eastern and Central United States and into Canada

The blue jay has a blue crest on top of its head and bright blue, black, and gray feathers.

Flutelike sounds of three to five phrases ending with complex trill. Beautiful distinctive song, don't miss it.

Wood Thrush

Mostly in the Eastern United States for the summer, migrates south to Latin America for the winter

About the size of the American robin. The wood thrush has a brown back and black-spotted white breast and throat.

"Bob-o-link"

Bobolink

Fields throughout the Northern United States and Southern Canada, migrating to South America for the winter

Males at mating time are easiest to spot, with black faces and bellies, black and white backs, and a yellow patch on the back of the head. Females and males throughout the rest of the year are yellow-brown, with dark streaks on the head and back. Medium-sized.

FALCONRY

Almost where my hand had been sat three fuzzy whitish gray birds. Their wide-open mouths gave them a startled look.

"Oh, hello, hello," I said. "You are cute." With sudden nerve, I stood up, stepped forward, and picked up the biggest of the nestlings. The females are bigger than the males. They are the "falcons." They are the pride of kings.

—MY SIDE OF THE MOUNTAIN

What is falconry? It is training a falcon, or "bird of prey," to hunt small game, including rabbits, squirrels, and ducks, and then to return to you. Falconers cast or throw trained hunting birds from their hands. The bird climbs into the sky and circles high. When the falconer scares up game on the ground, the trained bird streaks to earth like a shooting star and grabs the prey with its talons.

Falconry is an ancient art. It came to Europe from China in the Medieval Age (500-1500 CE) and was very popular. Ownership was restricted according to class or birthright. Traditionally, only kings could fly an eagle or a gyrfalcon. An earl was allowed a peregrine, a yeoman a goshawk, a priest a kestrel. A lady could fly a merlin. Breaking these rules was punishable by paying a fine. Today, anyone with the patience and the desire to learn can be a falconer.

So, you want to be a falconer? I don't blame you. Falcons are awesome. They're even good for the environment, because it is important to have predators in the wild. Birds of prey help to control rodent populations and preserve the balance of nature in many other ways. When peregrine falcons were placed on the endangered species list in 1970, falconers helped these beautiful and important birds to make a comeback.

Some states will let kids of fourteen years or older become assistant falconers. Here's what to do: call your state conservation department and ask them to send you information on the rules, as well as instructions on how to become a falconer in your state. Then find a master falconer in your area (the state usually has a list) and volunteer to help him or her with the joy of keeping a falcon. The falconer will train you in handling, hooding, jessing, and protecting a bird. Falconry is a commitment. You must attend to your bird every day of its life.

The best book on falconry is Fredrick the Great's beautiful *The Art of Falconry*, written around 1250. All you want to know about falconry is in it. You can also try *North American Falconry & Hunting Hawks* by Frank Lyman Beebe and Harold Melvin Webster. Frank and John Craighead's *Hawks in the Hand* will give you a wonderful introduction to falconry. Your local library should be able to help you find these books, and more, on falcons.

peregrine
falcon

At the top of the meadow was a fringe of white birch. There were maples and oaks to the west, and a hemlock forest to the right that pulled me right across the sweet grasses, into it.

Never, never have I seen such trees. These were giants. Old, old giants. They must have begun when the world began.

—MY SIDE OF THE MOUNTAIN

Trail Blazes

A universal trail-marking system is used on hiking trails throughout the United States. These markings consist of "blazes": rectangles of paint about 5 inches long. Blazes are usually found on trees at eye level. If there are no trees, look for blazes on rocks, posts, or any other permanent landmark.

If two blazes on the same tree are two different colors, then you are on two trails at once. While you are going down an unfamiliar trail, be sure to keep watching the trees for blazes. If you do not see any, you might have wandered off the trail. Go back the way you came until you find a blaze.

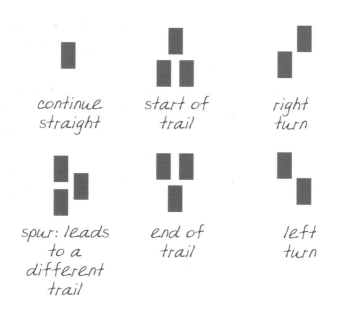

continue straight

start of trail

right turn

spur: leads to a different trail

end of trail

left turn

Lay a Trail

You can lay a trail to help friends find your path. Use this system in fields, city streets, wilderness areas, a town park, or anywhere.

Below are tips on how to lay a trail in the wild, be it woods or desert. Use your imagination to adapt these methods and be able to lay a trail in any environment.

Three stones and a pointer stone will tell your friends where your trail starts, or where you are turning off the well-trod path to begin your own trail.

A little way into your trail, pile up three stones with no pointer: it reads: "This is the trail." If you run out of stones, you can break the branch of a shrub to show the direction you are going.

Drop leaves in a regular pattern, three, two, three, two, etc., when you go across areas that are difficult to mark with stones or vegetation.

If you want to be sure your follower isn't going in the wrong direction, make an *X* of two sticks, which means "not this way." Put it across any paths your own trail crosses to be sure your friend doesn't go down the wrong trail.

Beside the *X* put a forked or Y-shaped branch on the ground. Turn the *Y* upside down and point it in the direction of your trail.

Tie rooted grass tops or weeds in a knot, with the heads pointing the way to go.

I wandered back to Great-grandfather's farm and began to explore. Most of the acreage was maple and beech, some pine, dogwoods, ash; and here and there a glorious hickory. I made a sketch of the farm on my road map, and put x's where the hickories were. They were gold trees to me. I would have hickory nuts in the fall.

—MY SIDE OF THE MOUNTAIN

Maps and Orienteering

Before you hike or camp in an unfamiliar area, go to an outdoor sports store and purchase a topographic map of the region. These maps are intensely accurate.

The brown contour lines of a topographic map show elevation. Lines that are close together mean the terrain there is steep. Lines farther apart mean the ground is more flat. Streams, railroads, cities, towns, woodlands, and swamps will each be represented on the map with a different symbol. Study the key to decode the symbols and keep the map handy as you explore.

A compass or GPS (global positioning system) are both powerful tools, but can be lost or broken. Learn the basics! With a good map and the basics of orienteering, you'll never be lost.

Finding North

A good orienteering skill is the ability to find north. Once you are facing north, you know that the opposite direction is south, to your right is east, and to your left west.

Make your way to any landmark by consulting your map and determining which direction you need to go to reach your goal, whether north, south, east, or west. As you move, frequently check your heading—north, south, east, or west—to be sure you are going in the right direction.

We all know that the sun rises in the east and sets in the west. Here are some more ways to orient yourself, without a compass.

Make Your Own Compass to Find North

Any magnetized object will point to Earth's magnetic north pole. Stroke a needle (or piece of wire) with silk. Stroke many times in one direction so that the needle becomes magnetized. Balance the magnetized needle by dangling it from a thread, or float it on water. The needle will point north. It really works!

Use the Sun to Find North

On a sunny day, drive the end of a three-foot stake into the ground. Put a stone at the end of the stake's shadow. Wait a couple of hours. The stake's shadow will move.

Put a different looking stone at the end of the new shadow. Draw a line between the two stones. This is the east-west line. The first stone that you placed is west.

Intersect the east-west line with a perpendicular line to form a cross (like this +). This second line runs north-south.

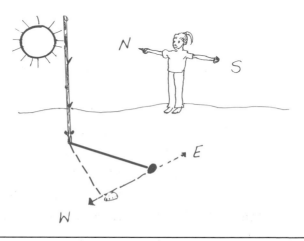

Remember, in the Northern Hemisphere the sun is to the south. It reaches its highest point around noon. Always keep this in mind when finding your way.

Moon Directions

If the moon rises before the sun has set, the lighted side of the moon will be on the west.

If the moon rises after midnight, the lighted side of the moon will be on the east. If the moon is full or new—break out your compass, read the stars, or go back to sleep!

Stars as Pointers to the North

On a clear night you can orient yourself quickly by reading the stars. If you can find the North Star, or *Polaris*, you can find north. Find the North Star by locating the Big Dipper. The two outer stars of the cup of the Big Dipper point to the North Star. The North Star is also the last star in the handle of the Little Dipper.

While stars appear to move through the sky all night, the North Star stays fixed. For this reason, the

Locating the North Star and Milky Way

BIG DIPPER

LITTLE DIPPER

NORTH STAR

North Star has been used for thousands of years to navigate by land and sea. It usually takes a bit of practice to be able to reliably recognize the Dippers and the North Star, but it's worth it!

Find more about the stars and good star maps at:

http://skymaps.com/downloads.html

http://home.comcast.net/~erniew/astro/plani.html

Bando taught me how to make willow whistles today. He and I went to the stream and cut two fat twigs about eight inches long. He slipped the bark on them. That means he pulled the wood out of the bark, leaving a tube. He made a mouthpiece at one end, cut a hole beneath it, and used the wood to slide up and down like a trombone.

We played music until the moon came up. Bando could even play jazz on the willow whistles. They are wonderful instruments, sounding much like the wind in the top of the hemlocks. Sad tunes are best suited to willow whistles. When we played "The Young Voyager" tears came to our eyes, it was so sad.

—MY SIDE OF THE MOUNTAIN

Climb a Tree

I love to climb trees and look around. The world looks different from way up there and it is very private in a tree. No one can find you. Hemlock and fir trees have lots of branches. You can use those branches to climb a tree like a ladder. Test each branch to be sure it is sturdy before you put your weight on it.

Tree trunks without branches, or with no branches close enough to the ground to reach, are tough to climb. You can use a rope to pull a limb down to you. Just throw one end of the rope over the branch, then pull. Only do that if the branch is sturdy.

Another way to climb a tree that has no branches, or none close to the ground, is to shinny up it. Hug the trunk with your arms and legs and push up by alternating them. You'll need to practice to get good at shinnying—stay close to the ground until you become skilled.

Tips on climbing trees:

1. When on a limb, stay as close to the trunk as possible—that's where limbs are strongest.

2. Only go as high as you feel comfortable going—remember you'll need to find a route back down.

3. Make sure a limb is not too weak to support your weight. Test each limb before you step on it. Dead limbs are not as strong as healthy ones.

4. Try going barefoot to get a good grip on the tree.

5. Wear long pants to avoid scratches.

6. Don't use spiked shoes on trees. Spikes damage soft wood tissues under the bark.

Making Your Own Map

Here's how to make your own map if you are going into the woods, or across the prairie or desert. Your own map can be a fun souvenir and useful on a trip.

First, find and label North, South, East, and West. Place North at the top of the map.

Mark your starting point, a road or trailhead at the beginning of your trip, then pick a distinctive landmark within sight of the starting point and count the paces to it. Mark the paces and the landmarks as you go. Landmarks can be old trees, notable rocks, a cliff—any easily recognizable, permanent part of the landscape. Pace on to the next memorable object, then the next.

If there is a good climbing tree or hill, climb it and draw the areas you see. Fields, lakes, swamps, different kinds of forests, or the direction of ridges are good elements to add to your map. See the illustration on page 110 for some examples.

Keeping Notes

It's fun and useful to record your adventures in a note-book. Jot down what you did and the date.

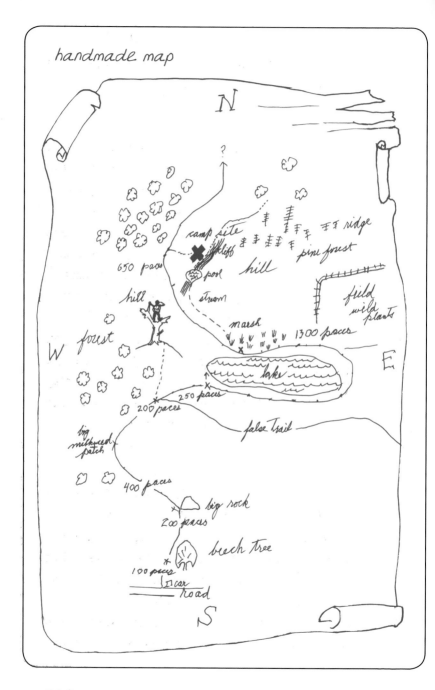

handmade map

N

?

camp site

cliff

650 paces

pool

stream

hill

ridge

pine forest

hill

field
wild
plants

hill

forest

marsh

1300 paces

W

E

lake

200 paces

250 paces

false Trail

big
milkweed
patch

400 paces

big rock

200 paces

beech tree

100 paces

1 car

road

S

I would choose a notebook of recycled paper. You can even make your own ink and pen.

Making Walnut Ink

Since the Middle Ages, scribes and artists have made ink and dye from the husks of ripe walnuts. On the tree, the husks start out green, fall, and soon turn black. Gather the darkened husks of about a dozen nuts and place in an old pot or can. Cover the husks with water and boil until half the water is gone. Stir and scrape the husks while they boil. Once the liquid is a dark brown-black and thick, allow it to cool. Strain it to remove the bits of husk. Store in a dark, cool place to prevent molding.

Make your own pen from a pencil-size twig. Sharpen the tip, then slice the tip in quarters lengthwise so that it will hold the ink. It works like a quill pen—ink will stay in the thin slices you have made until the tip is held to paper, then it will flow out onto the page.

Make a Returning Boomerang

Boomerangs have been used for thousands of years for hunting and fun. Here's how to make your own.

Find a tree branch that has a 135-degree angle in it (see illustration). It's best to use hardwood trees like oak, hickory, or dogwood in the East. In the West use sitka spruce, juniper, cedar, or mesquite.

Be sure to measure off a twenty-seven-inch piece in total, leaving about thirteen straight inches on each side of the kink. It's best to find a dead branch on the ground, because dry wood won't crack. Now carve the stick into a flat 3/8-inch thickness. Taper the edges. The boomerang should be light, weighing about 12 ounces.

Throw your boomerang underhand. Good ones can go about 100 yards and come back. Very cool.

boomerang

Make a Slingshot

I make two kinds of slingshots. Y-shaped slingshots are cut from a fork in a tree and equipped with thick rubber bands or strips of rubber that can be cut from the inner tube of a tire. A piece of leather tied between the two bands holds the "missile"—usually a stone.

The other kind of slingshot is like the one that David used to slay Goliath in the Bible story. I use this kind to hunt for food, including rabbits and squirrels.

To make a David and Goliath slingshot, put two holes in a small (about 4-inch) diamond-shaped piece of leather or heavy canvas, as in the illustration. Thread a piece of cord 6 feet long through each hole, loop back to the holes and tie. Use a square knot (pages 76 and 78).

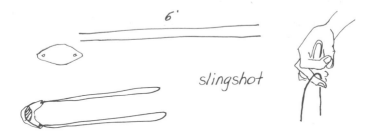

slingshot

Put your middle finger through the one loop and hold the other in the fist of the same hand. Now put a stone in the leather and whirl the whole slingshot around your head. The stone will stay put due to centrifugal force. When the slingshot has gathered speed, let go of the loop around your finger and—whiz, the stone shoots out. Careful of your aim! Slingshots are dangerous! Use a tree or a rock for target practice, but first make sure any bystanders are well out of range.

SNAP

RELEASE

slingshot launched

Making Clay Pots

Making your own clay pots is fun and useful, too. First you have to find a source of clay. The best place to look is along a stream. Once you find the clay dig it up and test a small piece. Make a roll about the size of a pencil and try to tie it in a knot. If it doesn't crack or break it's "good" clay.

Next, clean your clay if needed: put it in a container and mix the clay with water so that it is almost like soup. Then let it sit. After the clay has settled, skim off the twigs and grass that rise to the top. Pour off the extra water, remove the clay, and scrape off the stones and grit that have fallen to the bottom. Repeat if needed.

When the clay is clean you're ready to make your pots. You can form a small cup or bowl by rolling the clay into a coil and then curling the coil into a coil pot.

Another method is to form a ball of clay, then push your thumbs into the center and pinch outward until the bowl or cup is the right size and thickness.

Let the pots dry for several days.

When they feel dry to the touch, make a fire. Place the pots near the fire and gently turn them until they are bone dry. Once dry, remove the larger logs from the center of the fire and place the pots in the middle. Build a fire around the pottery and increase the size of the fire as the pots warm. Once the pots are hot, build the fire over them. Keep the pots in the fire until they glow red. When you see the red glow the pots are done. Let the fire die down and wait until the pots are cool. Rinse the ashes off of your pots and they're ready to use!

MAKING YOUR OWN UTENSILS

Gourd Spoons

To make your own spoon or dipper, grow some gourds in a sunny patch of ground or in a window box. To make little spoons, pick the gourds before they have grown too big. Cut them in half, scoop out the flesh, and dry.

For a water carrier, let the gourds grow bigger. Cut a hole through the neck to make a handle. Then remove the seeds, scrape the insides well, and dry.

Forks

To make a fork, you can cut and sharpen the ends of a split or forked twig.

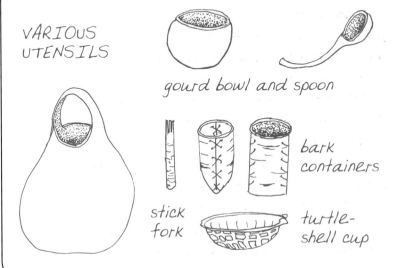

VARIOUS UTENSILS

gourd bowl and spoon

stick fork

bark containers

turtle-shell cup

A NATURAL ORCHESTRA

Pan Flute

People have made pan flutes from natural materials for thousands of years. Music piped from a pan flute is sweet enough to make you cry, and mysterious as the wind.

To make a decent pan flute you really have to have bamboo, although I know a man who can make them from horsetails, ancient plants that grow in swamps. Get the bamboo from a florist or Asian market if you don't live in the South where bamboo grows.

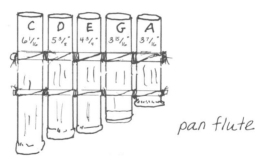

pan flute

Cut the bamboo into shorter and shorter tubes, each one having nodes at the bottom end if possible. Each tube should have a definite length, as marked in the illustration. Clean out the fuzz from the inside of the tubes. Each should be $5/8$ of an inch wide on the inside. Clean out the nodes from the tubes, except those nodes that make the bottom. Seal off any open bottoms with a penny and duct tape, or candle or paraffin wax. Try the tubes for pitch by putting each one against your lips and blowing into it, as into a bottle. To get the notes right shorten the length of the tube. When they sound good, tie the tubes to a flat stick with a square knot (pages 76 and 78) in descending order. If necessary, tie to a second stick to make the pan flute more rigid. You should have at least five tubes, eight if you get good.

When done you can play songs. Practice makes you an artist or at least a lot better. I should know.

Make a Willow Whistle

Willow whistles work a bit like trombones and sound like the wind in the woods. In early spring when the sap is running cut a 7- or 8-inch section of a willow or maple limb. It should be about as big around as an adult's thumb, straight as possible and without branches. Use a good sharp knife.

1. Now cut a slanting piece off one end of the willow, as in the drawing on the following page.
2. Cut a notch an inch and one half below the tip, as in the illustration. This is the top side of the whistle.
3. Now girdle (cut a ring) through the bark 3 or 4 inches below the notch, as illustrated.
4. Gently slip off the bark above and below the ring. Do this by first wetting the whole stick in water, then tapping it gently with the end of your knife, or rolling it carefully over another stick. Tap, roll and wet, tap, roll and wet.

WILLOW WHISTLE

1.

2.

3.

4.

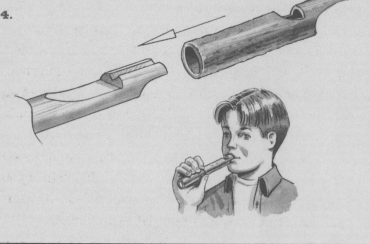

5. Eventually, as you twist and gently pull, the bark should slide off in two pieces. Be careful not to split the bark. Put it aside.

6. As in drawing 3, cut a flat swath in the stick, about an inch long, away from the notch. Cut a groove, as in illustration 4, from the notch to the end of the mouthpiece. Replace the bark for this section.

7. Slip the other piece of bark back over the lower part of the barkless stick. It should fit tightly. Blow through the mouthpiece and slide the lower piece of bark up and down. Whee, music!

Note: *In order for all willow whistles to keep working and not dry out, soak them in water.*

Flute

In spring when the sap is flowing, cut a straight section of willow or maple branch about 14 inches long and the thickness of an adult's thumb. Tap, twist, and gently turn until the whole piece of wood slips out of the bark. You should have a hollow piece of bark and a solid stick.

Now cut off an inch from the end of the wooden stick. Plug it into the end of the bark tube or use a penny, duct tape, or paraffin to seal the end. Cut an oblong hole an inch from the sealed end of the bark tube for a mouthpiece. The hole should be about half an inch long and one quarter inch wide. Now carefully cut five small holes on the top side of the flute. Blow across the oblong hole you have cut. Cover and uncover the small holes with your fingers to play a tune. Fill the woods with music.

NATURAL PERCUSSION

Pumpkins

There are a lot of natural percussion instruments out there in the fields and woods. Hollowed-out pumpkins are one. They make a rich deep sound when drummed with the hands. Get a friend to play a different sized pumpkin for a different sound.

Make "clops-clops," as bands call them, with coconut shells. "Hickory sticks" can be made with fallen branches of real hickory trees. Cut lots of lengths. When banged together they make different sounds depending on the thickness and the length of the stick. You can use other wood, too.

Grass Whistle

Don't forget to blow on a grass blade held between your thumbs. A great sound any maestro would want! The more kids playing grass blades the merrier.

Conch Shell

If you're near the ocean, find an empty conch shell and cut the closed end of it with a saw, leaving a hole about an inch wide. Blow like a trumpeter with pursed lips.

It's a strong note and shouldn't be sounded often. Maybe it's best used to call your gang together to make music.

Strike up the band far away from civilization. Only the trees will love this music until you perfect it!

Owl Music

Want to talk to the owls? Get a 6-ounce metal juice can, a 4-inch piece of ½-inch metal pipe and some duct tape. Pull the tab and drink the juice. Make a half-inch hole in the side of the can opposite the tab, about ¾ inch below the rim.

Flatten the bottom ¼ inch of the metal pipe and fasten it above the hole with the tape so it sticks up above the can. Wind the tape generously around the can to hold the pipe, then blow. Out comes the sound of an owl.

½ hole

Mournful Owl Sound

Imitate the "hooting" owls of the East and West at night. They will answer back and come over to you to see if you are a mate or an owl intruding on private owl property. Here are some owl calls to help you identify your neighbors. Use them sparingly:

"Hoo, who-whoooo, hoo, hoo"
Great Horned Owl

"Hoohoo-hoohoo, hoohoohoohooaw"
Barred Owl

"Whoo-hoo-hoo" (deep and booming)
Western Great Gray Owl

"Hooooo" (low and moaning)
Western Long-eared Owl

This can-caller is too low for screech owls. To lure in an Eastern screech owl, gargle a sad high note in a long wavering cry. In the West, whistle an accelerating series of low, soft notes to call the Western screech owl.

I was self sufficient, I could travel the world over, never needing a penny, never asking anything of anyone. I could cross to Asia in a canoe via the Bering Strait. I could raft to an island. I could go around the world on the fruits of the land.

—MY SIDE OF THE MOUNTAIN

Ticks

A tick is an eight-legged spiderlike creature. Some common ticks, including deer ticks, are the size of a pinhead. Others, such as dog ticks, are as big as a peppercorn. Ticks drink blood, like mosquitoes. However, unlike mosquitoes, a tick might feed on you or its host for several days before it drops off or is noticed. Ticks don't fly, but crawl up tall grasses or shrubs and wait for a warm body to come by. The tick senses a mammal by the heat it throws off and then drops onto its fur, skin, or clothing. The important thing to remember about ticks is that they carry some serious diseases, including Lyme disease and Rocky Mountain spotted fever.

Ticks live in forests and grassy areas throughout the world, and are often found around deer or horse trails. If you're going outside use insect repellant, wear pants and long-sleeved shirts, and tuck your pants into your socks.

When you come home, take off your clothes and hang them up. Ticks will climb up to the top of clothing and can be easily spotted and removed.

If you've spent time in a tick area, check your armpits, belt line, the places where your clothes were tight, and your hair. Comb it thoroughly. If you find a tick and it is embedded in your skin, remove it right away. Use a little Vaseline to cover the insect. Smothered by Vaseline, the tick will let go of you. Remove with a tissue or tweezers. Keep the tick in a plastic bag and take it to your doctor, where it can be checked for disease.

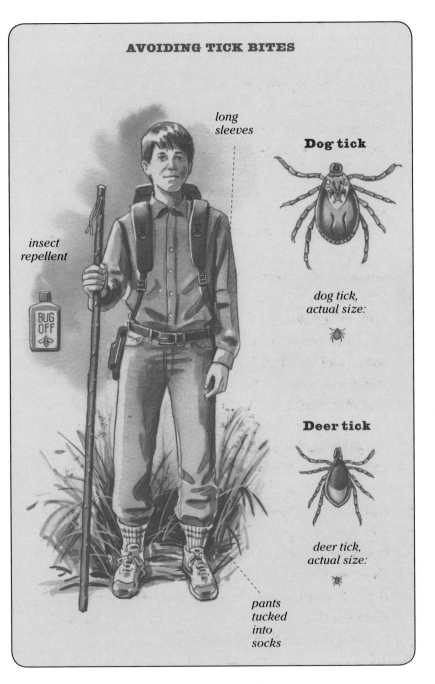

AVOIDING TICK BITES

long sleeves

Dog tick

dog tick, actual size:

insect repellent

BUG OFF

Deer tick

deer tick, actual size:

pants tucked into socks

Painful joints, rash or fever, or a red spot on your skin with a white bull's-eye in it are symptoms of Lyme disease. See your doctor immediately if you develop these symptoms.

What to Do in Bear Country

Bears, and all wild animals, can be dangerous. But you don't have to be afraid of bears if you respect them and observe a few simple rules when in bear country.

1. At night or when you leave camp for the day, store your food and anything aromatic away from camp and in bear-proof storage bins. Or, hang your goods from the branch of a tree. Make sure your bundle is at least 15 feet, preferably 20, off the ground.

2. Look for bear signs—scat and footprints—and be wary of dense berry-luscious vegetation. Avoid these bear hangouts.

3. Make some noise, particularly when you are hiking, to let the bears know you are in the area. Clap or sing and give the bears a chance to run away. Most will want to avoid you.

4. Stay at least 200 yards away from any bear you sight and back away if you are too close. If you want a closer look use binoculars or a telephoto lens.

5. Carry bear pepper spray and learn how to use it.

In an encounter, pepper spray repels 92 percent of grizzlies and black bears. Don't be one of the 8 percent! Learn to use that spray.

RECIPES

Sassafras tea is about as good as anything you want to drink. Pennyroyal makes another good drink. I dried great bunches of this, and hung them from the roof of the tree room together with the leaves of winterberry. All these fragrant plants I also used in cooking to give a new taste to some not-so-good foods.

The room in the tree smelled of smoke and mint. It was the best-smelling tree in the Catskill Mountains.

—MY SIDE OF THE MOUNTAIN

Following are some great recipes for the outdoors. Check the Edible Plants section of this guide for tips on how to find the main ingredients out in the wild. Most of these recipes are easiest to make back home in the kitchen, so gather out and cook in.

Acorn Pancakes

A breakfast treat

First make the acorn flour: prepare acorns, preferably white-oak acorns, by boiling in several changes of water or until the water runs clear, to rid the acorns of tannin. Cool and peel off hard outer coats. Roast in a 200° F oven until nutlike and brittle. Put dry acorns through a clean coffee grinder or pound to make acorn flour.

Now make the pancakes.

INGREDIENTS:

1 egg, well beaten
1 cup acorn flour
⅓ cup white flour
½ cup sugar or honey
2½ teaspoons baking powder
1¼ cups milk
3 tablespoons softened butter
¾ teaspoon salt
butter and maple syrup

In a bowl mix acorn flour, white flour, baking powder, sugar, and salt. In another bowl mix the egg, milk, and softened butter. Pour milk mixture into dry ingredients and mix just enough to moisten—don't stir too much. Spoon onto greased hot grill or frying pan. Flip over once. Serve with butter and maple syrup.

Lemon Daylilies

For lunch or dinner

2 dozen daylily buds and flowers
4 cups water
¾ cups sugar
½ cup white vinegar
juice and grated rind of 1 lemon
1 tablespoon of cornstarch
2 tablespoons of water
1 cup canned chicken broth
2 cups of cooked rice

Boil daylilies in 4 cups water for 5 minutes. Drain and set aside. Pour sugar and vinegar into a saucepan and heat until sugar is dissolved. Add chicken broth and stir. Add lemon juice and grated rind. Simmer for 15 minutes. Dissolve cornstarch in 2 tablespoons of water and add to sauce. Stir until cornstarch clears and sauce is thickened. Add daylilies to sauce and serve over rice.

Sourdough Starter

Everyone ought to have a sourdough starter. It traveled on chuck wagons heading West and with dog teams in Alaska. You can make your own in just sixty seconds. Put two cups of regular flour in a bean pot, mason jar, or bowl with a lid. Add 2½ cups of lukewarm water, stir, and set in a warm place. That's it. In four or five days you will have your own personal yeast factory, slowly bubbling like a Yellowstone wonder and filling the air with a heady fragrance.

Sourdough Pancakes

With your starter you can make sourdough pancakes. Put one cup of the starter in a mixing bowl and add:

1 cup flour
1 egg
2 tablespoons of cooking oil
½ cup milk
Blend in 1 teaspoon salt
1 teaspoon baking soda
and 2 tablespoons of sugar

Drop batter on a hot griddle with a large spoon. Serve with butter and maple syrup. Replace the batter you took out of the starter crock with 1 cup flour and ½ cup water. Leave out for the night and it will be ready to use the next day. Refrigerate your starter when not in use.

Dandelion Fritters

A savory summer treat

> 1 cup biscuit mix
> 1 cup milk
> 1 tablespoon of sugar or honey
> 4 cups of dandelion flowers
> ¼ inch of oil in skillet

Mix together the biscuit mix, milk, and sugar or honey. Heat oil in skillet until it sizzles when a bit of batter is dropped into it. Dip dandelion flowers into batter and drop into hot oil headfirst. Fry until golden. Turn with tongs and brown other side. Drain on paper towel and serve hot or cold.

Berry Leather

A sweet, easy snack that's great for hikes. Make this treat with any combination of berries.

Mash a heap of berries and strain them through a sieve to remove any seeds. Spread on a cookie sheet and dry in the sun or in an oven at very low heat. When dry, sprinkle with powdered sugar and roll or cut into strips.

In 1959, my book *My Side of the Mountain* was published. In 1960, it was awarded an American Library Association Newbery Honor Medal. The main character is Sam Gribley.

Sam Gribley is the voice of our family, a voice from the nights we camped by waterfalls, from the days we made lean-tos in the woods and fire with flint-and-steel.

Sam Gribley is my father taking me out in the fields to learn the flowers and edible plants, and into the woods to know the animals. He taught me to canoe the Potomac River rapids and build boats. My father held a PhD in entomology, the study of insects, and taught the younger generation to eat crickets. He made the outdoors fun and adventurous, and I was diverted from idleness into the busy drama of nature.

My brothers, John and Frank, are Sam Gribley. They wrote the amazing manual *How to Survive on Land and Sea* for the Navy. My brothers flew falcons behind our home when very few Americans were falconers.

John and Frank taught themselves and their friends this ancient art from a book called *The Art of Falconry* by Fredrick II of Hohenstaufen. They are the Sam Gribley who ran the rivers of the West and helped pass a law to protect our nation's rivers. My brothers studied and radio-collared grizzlies so that we might know more about these great bears and how to save them.

My son Craig traveled to the arctic to study the bowhead whale on the wilderness of sea ice. He learned from the Inupiat Eskimos the names of the arctic wildlife and habitats of the animals, how to build snow houses (some people call them igloos), and eat whale blubber. He is Sam Gribley.

And so is my youngest son, Luke, a PhD in ornithology, the study of birds. He camped in a tall dim forest in California and listened to the call of the marbled murrelet, an endangered seabird that nests in old-growth forests. Now he studies the bird's predators in hopes of reversing its decline.

Sam Gribley is Twig, my daughter, who now writes children's books about nature. Sam Gribley is Twig picking high bush cranberries along the Brooks River in Alaska while a wolf pack howls hauntingly and grizzly bears rustle the willows. She will put the berries into the morning "sourdough biscuits" that she will bake over a campfire.

And my granddaughters Rebecca and Caity, and my nephew, Kyle, are Sam Gribley, paddling twelve miles a day around alligators and frogs in the Okeefenokee Swamp in Georgia.

Luke II and Sam, my grandsons, are Sam Gribley, asleep in their snow house in the arctic where they live, while the wind howls and temperatures drop to 30° below.

Hunter and Ai Li, also my grandchildren, are Sam Gribley as they release salmon hatchlings they raised in their classrooms into the wild rivers.

My nephews and nieces, Karen, Lance, Charlie, Derek, Jana, and Johnny, and their families who study, weave, film, and protect the wilderness, are also Sam. In fact, Sam Gribley is four generations of our family.

Sam Gribley is not just our family's passion, but a love deeply rooted in all Americans—a love of the land to which we all came—the wilderness.

—JEAN CRAIGHEAD GEORGE

Christopher, Leahy W. *Peterson First Field Guide to the Insects of North America.* N.p.: Houghton Mifflin Harcourt, 1998.

Craighead Jr., Frank, and John Craighead. *How to Survive on Land and Sea.* Annapolis, MD: US Naval Institute Press, 1984.

Foster, David and Angier, Bradford. *Field Guide to Edible Wild Plants.* Stackpole Books, 2008.

George, Jean Craighead. *Acorn Pancakes, Dandelion Salad and 38 Other Wild Recipes.* HarperCollins Children's Books, 1995.

Laubin, Reginald, and Gladys Laubin. *The Indian Tipi, Its History, Construction and Use.* N.p.: University of Oklahoma Press, 1989.

Murie, Olaus J.; Elbroch, Mark; Roger T. Peterson. *Peterson Field Guide to Animal Tracks.*: Houghton Mifflin, 2005.

Peterson, Roger Tory. *Field Guide to Birds of North America.*: Houghton Mifflin, 2008.

Reid, Fiona. *A Field Guide to Mammals of North America.* N.p.: Houghton Mifflin, 2006.

Rushforth, Keith. *Field Guide to the Trees of North America.* N.p.: National Geographic, 2006.

Smith, Lavett C. *National Audubon Society First Field Guide. Fishes.* N.p.: Scholastic, Inc., 2000.

Wescott, David. Editor. *Primitive Technology: A Book of Earth Skills from the Society of Primitive Technology.* Layton, UT Gibbs-Smith Publisher, 1999; *Primitive Technology II: Ancestral Skills from the Society of Primitive Technology.* Layton, UT: Gibbs-Smith Publisher, 2001.

Wiseman, John. *SAS Survival Handbook: How to Survive in the Wild in Any Climate.* N.p.: HarperCollins Publishers, 2004.

INDEX

Page numbers in *italics* refer to illustrations.

The publisher gratefully acknowledges the generous contribution to this book provided by the George Gund Foundation.

PEARL'S SECRET

Pearl's Secret

A BLACK MAN'S SEARCH
FOR HIS WHITE FAMILY

Neil Henry

UNIVERSITY OF
CALIFORNIA PRESS
Berkeley Los Angeles London

University of California Press
Berkeley and Los Angeles, California

University of California Press, Ltd.
London, England

Library of Congress Cataloging-in-Publication Data

Henry, Neil, 1954–
    Pearl's secret : a black man's search for his white family /
Neil Henry.
        p.   cm.—(The George Gund Foundation imprint in
    African American studies)
        ISBN 0-520-22257-1 (cloth : alk. paper)
        1. Henry, Neil, 1954–   2. Afro-Americans—
    Biography.   3. Afro-Americans—Race identity.
    4. Beaumont family.   5. Henry family.   6. Miscegenation—
    United States—History.   7. United States—Race
    relations.   8. Racism—United States—Psychological
    aspects.   9. Seattle (Wash.)—Biography.   10. Saint
    Joseph (La.)—Biography.   I. Title.   II. Series.
    E185.97.H46 H46 2001
    973'.0496073'0092—dc21   00-053211

Printed in the United States of America
09 08 07 06 05 04 03 02 01
10 9 8 7 6 5 4 3 2 1

The paper used in this publication meets the minimum re-
quirements of American National Standard for Information
Sciences—Permanence of Paper for Printed Library
Materials, ANSI Z39.48–1992 (R 1997) (Permanence of Paper).

For Letitia and Zoë

Contents

Prelude

My great-great-grandfather was an Englishman named Arthur John Beaumont, who left his home in Kent when he was seventeen years old to sail for America, one of 200,436 immigrants who arrived in this country in 1856. A thin, pale-looking fellow with wispy dark hair and soft, penetrating eyes, he was called "A.J." for short by his friends and family. Like many young immigrants, he apparently came here with little in his pockets but with a heart overflowing with dreams of fortune and happiness.

To a large extent A.J. seemed to find what he was looking for, though it took a while, from what I initially gleaned about his life. Indeed, I knew relatively little about him when I started the research that culminated in this story of the dual racial legacy he left and my relationship as a black man to it. This much I did know: Soon after his arrival in America, the young man settled in a small town called St. Joseph on the Mississippi River in northeastern Louisiana, where he found work as an overseer on a cotton plantation.

A few years later, when the Civil War broke out, he proved his devotion to his new home by joining the Confederate Army and fighting as a lieutenant in an artillery brigade. Military service was something of a tradition in the Beaumont family, his father and grandfather having fought for king and queen against Napoleon at Waterloo, according to family lore. So Beaumont's own service in defense of Louisiana must have seemed a perfectly natural, worthy, and honorable fate. His unit was the 4th Battery of Louisiana Artillery, led by Captain Archibald J. Cameron, which saw action in numerous engagements ranging from Vicksburg to Red River over the course of the war, surrendering only when Robert E. Lee himself did, in April 1865.

After the war the English immigrant's dreams gradually came true. He returned to his beloved adopted town of St. Joseph, and over the last quarter of the nineteenth century, from Reconstruction into the Jim Crow era, he became a respected and admired figure in Tensas Parish as a plantation owner, merchant, town father, and civic leader. Indeed, his life story reads like the classic nineteenth-century American tale of the European immigrant who arrived young and destitute but died a natural death decades later in comparative prosperity as an old man.

I knew these details about my white great-great-grandfather's life largely by way of a yellowed newspaper clipping that had been passed down in my family for nearly a century, since its publication in the weekly *Tensas Gazette* on May 3, 1901. That was the year Beaumont died at sixty-two. The clipping, a very fragile thing about eight column inches in length, was his obituary and had been inherited and preserved by my mother in the top drawer of a bureau in her clothes closet with other family keepsakes.

But what had always fascinated me most about that brittle strip of newsprint was the story it didn't tell about A.J. Beaumont's life, a story I knew far more intimately through my family's oral history. This was his legacy as the inadvertent progenitor of an unusual black family—my family—that has endured proudly and exceptionally well over the century since his death. We were the ones, as my mother's brother, Uncle Sonny, sometimes said with telltale gruff irony when I was a child, who were "born on the wrong side of the blanket" long ago—descendants of Beaumont's post–Civil War sexual relationship with a freed slave in Louisiana, Laura Brumley, who became our ancestral matriarch.

I knew the details of our family's black history much better than those of its white history. Beaumont was always something of a mystery figure in our family's story—a white man remembered only vaguely and somewhat reluctantly through a faded old photograph and a newspaper clipping. By contrast, his longtime lover was a beloved and memorable figure, truly of flesh and blood. Laura's brilliant 1890 portrait and that of her beautiful mixed-race daughter, Pearl, my great-grandmother, hung proudly in the entryway of my house throughout my boyhood in Seattle in the 1960s.

These three people—A.J. Beaumont, Laura Brumley, and their daughter, Pearl—were perched near the top branches of my black American family tree as I knew it. And ultimately they were the inspiration for the story in the pages that follow, a personal history and narrative about my quest, 140 years after Beaumont's arrival in this country, to piece together the murky details about my family's racial past in the United States, a mixed ancestry with hidden branches not unlike that of millions upon millions of African Americans.

It is a story centered on a genealogy that was bifurcated from its start, rooted as it was in this nation's racist soil. While no obituary was ever published about Laura's life, it arguably was as fascinating and noteworthy as Beaumont's. In 1850, when Beaumont was about to enter adolescence in England, Laura was born on a cotton plantation just outside St. Joseph. The mulatto daughter of a slave born in Africa and a white physician who lived on a neighboring farm, she was the fruit of a taboo interracial relationship that was far more common in our history than we as a society have been willing to recognize.

The contemporary debate among historians over the significance of Thomas Jefferson's longtime romantic relationship with his slave Sally Hemings and recent DNA evidence proving that he fathered black descendants point to the ongoing volatility of this issue in American society. For many black Americans, however, what's perhaps most astonishing is how long it has taken for the interracial lineage of many African Americans to be considered a subject for serious public discussion and academic examination. Jefferson's family story, after all, is far from unique, as evidenced by a growing body of scholarly works devoted to black-white lineage, such as Edward Ball's *Slaves in the Family* and Henry Wiencek's *The Hairstons: An American Family in Black and White*. Certainly one reason the mixed-race history of many black Americans has not been seriously examined has been racism. Both blacks and whites have shown uneasiness about this history. For black Americans, miscegenation traditionally has connoted the stigma and shame of the slavery era. For whites, the discussion has been even more muted, and not only because race mixing was viewed as a cultural taboo. Were white society to publicly admit the obvious—that many blacks carry white blood—it would also have to accept their rights to fully equal citizenship—rights that the power structure could not allow. Nearly 225 years after the Republic's founding, we have yet to reach a point of equal acceptance of all Americans.

In the mid–nineteenth century, of course, there was little equality for a mulatto like Laura Brumley. Her mother worked as a cook in the kitchen of the plantation, and Laura grew up as a house slave, scrubbing floors, washing dishes, and changing bed-sheets. However, she was very much adored, according to family legend, by Sarah Tullis, the wife of the plantation's owner. A New Englander by birth, with firm moral principles rooted in the Bible, Sarah despised slavery, though she had married into a southern family that believed in it fervently. Her way of fighting the system was to educate Laura as best she could. And so the time-honored story of education providing a way out of oppres-sion began to be written in our family. Using her family Bible as a textbook, the white woman defied southern laws by secretly teaching the mixed-raced child to read and write. She also trained Laura in a number of household skills, including sewing. By the time the Civil War ended, fifteen-year-old Laura, with her radiant brown face and dark curly hair, was a literate young woman who had experience as a seamstress—a trade that has often served as the first step on the ladder to improvement for generations of impoverished American immigrants. She seemed set to endure the challenges her people faced at the end of slav-ery, the only system they had ever known.

Sometime during this period immediately after the war, my great-great-grandmother Laura met and fell in love with the English immigrant and Confederate war veteran A.J. Beaumont.

It was the beginning of a long affair described as respectful and loving by those who remembered Laura, one that resulted in Pearl's birth in 1877.

This child—my great-grandmother—grew up looking very much like her namesake jewel, a pretty quadroon girl with brilliant alabaster skin, straight dark hair, and a fiery disposition. But she also was cursed to be born in an era and a place in which she was denied a meaningful connection to her father, a white man who was central to her life and her mother's, yet who existed, on the other side of the color bar, in a world where black people of all hues were forbidden.

This may have been part of the reason—no one in my family knows for sure—that in about 1890 Laura decided to move away from St. Joseph, her past, and everything she had ever known. She took Pearl and steamed north to St. Louis, where she eventually opened a boardinghouse for black travelers and laborers that she operated into the World War I era. It was there that Pearl grew into a woman, fell in love, and married a dashing black man named Frank Hall—a rake and reprobate who had an unfortunate fondness for ragtime honky-tonks and gambling. In 1896, at the age of nineteen, Pearl gave birth to their daughter, my grandmother Fredda.

My black family's last known connection to the white branch of the family tree occurred shortly after this period, when Pearl's tempestuous marriage fell apart in 1899. Pearl turned to her white father for support that year, sending him a letter to tell him about her life in St. Louis and about her baby—his granddaughter—and enclosing a photograph of herself holding the child. A month passed, as Pearl waited for a reply from Beaumont. Then a year. Nothing but silence.

Then one spring day nearly two years later, she received a letter from her white father, written by hand on stationery bearing the letterhead of his flourishing mercantile business in St. Joseph. This letter, like Beaumont's obituary, has been passed from one generation to the next in my family. Now yellow and brittle with age, preserved in its original envelope with its two-cent George Washington stamp and St. Joseph postmark, it reads simply:

April 25, 1901

My Dear Pearl:
In looking over my papers in my safe I came across your picture, also your daughter's, and your letter to me dated May 3, 1899. I must acknowledge that you are my daughter and I feel that I have done you a great injustice in not acknowledging the receipt of your letter. If this reaches you, write to me.

Your affectionate father,
A. J. Beaumont

Along with the letter Beaumont sent a photograph of himself, also still in my family. It shows the well-dressed figure of a content and prosperous southern gentleman with warm eyes, a soft smile, and an impressive French imperial beard.

It's likely that Pearl felt elated by the letter and photograph, for her white father finally seemed to be reaching out to her, after so many years. But then, without warning, another letter arrived in her mailbox. Inside, a friend in Louisiana had enclosed a clipping from the *Tensas Gazette*—the obituary announcing Beaumont's death.

The white man's letter essentially amounted to a deathbed confession to his illegitimate black daughter, the kind of last-gasp cleansing effort a guilty soul makes before entering eternity. Unfortunately, as often happens, the accompanying burden of regret was passed on to the living—to Pearl, according to my mother, who adored her. The stunned and saddened woman, then twenty-three, was left with the bitter realization that the love, reconciliation, and recognition she had always desired from her white father would now be impossible to obtain.

Beaumont's death was also painful for Laura, who, despite the passage of so many years, the distance in miles, and society's racial barrier, had never stopped loving him. When he died, people in my family recalled, a part of her died as well. Still, the former slave lived a proud, courageous, and independent life and became known throughout black St. Louis for many distinctive qualities. She was an expert equestrian who proudly rode her horse with an almost regal bearing; she was a devout Baptist fond of singing Negro spirituals around her boardinghouse; and she was a chaste, proper, and God-fearing soul who forbade her tenants to play the hot sound of ragtime or jazz, then in vogue, on the piano in her parlor, calling it the devil's music.

When Laura died in 1932 at the age of eighty-one, so many years and miles removed from the Louisiana plantation where she had learned to read and write under the guidance of the kind white woman whose family owned her, she was loved and respected in her adopted city. And those closest to her swore that after A.J. Beaumont she never took another lover, white or black.

Pearl's heartbreak lasted for the rest of her life.

My mother once told me of a rumor that the fiery Pearl had boarded a Mississippi River steamboat and traveled back to St. Joseph to try to claim an inheritance from her father's estate in

Louisiana, but that she was turned away by Beaumont's furious white widow. No one knew if that part of the family story was really true or even if A.J. Beaumont had ever married. But there is no doubt that Pearl held on to her father's letter, the obituary clipping, the yearly Christmas cards sent by the plantation mistress, Sarah Tullis, to Laura in St. Louis, and the old photographs, preserving them almost as if they were holy relics.

When Pearl died in 1944, these keepsakes were passed on to her daughter, Fredda, who had married in 1916. Fredda and her black husband, Edward Clifford Turner, lived a long and very happy life together in St. Louis, where they raised three children. She, too, cared deeply about holding on to these artifacts, for she always felt that one of the cruelest parts of being a descendant of slavery was feeling bereft of a sense of personal history and identity.

Before Fredda died in 1982, many of the old relics were passed on to her second daughter, Mary, my mother. Mary had settled in Seattle in 1956 with my father, John Robert Henry, a pioneering black surgeon who hailed from North Carolina. They raised me, my two older brothers, and my younger sister there.

Today A.J. Beaumont's photograph, his obituary, and his 1901 letter to Pearl still rest in my mother's desk drawer amid a host of other mementos passed down over the past 150 years—keepsakes that have both fascinated and perplexed me since I was a boy.

It was in Seattle, as a middle-class black kid growing up among white people during the era of racial integration in the 1960s, that I first came to wonder about the strange incongruity of my white ancestry. My mother and her family loved to talk about the characters in our family's past during regular get-togethers, so I grew up knowing quite a bit about our proud and colorful black history as it unfolded in places as far-flung as Mississippi, Louisiana, North Carolina, Missouri, and Washington State.

But for a long time I was also intrigued by the history no one seemed to know much about, especially the story of A.J. Beaumont. The white man's name was rarely mentioned in our house when I was growing up, and when he was referred to, my mother and her family would lower their voices, as if they were telling a secret too sensitive or perhaps even shameful for outsiders or youngsters to hear. I thus came to know him only vaguely as the "Englishman" in our black family album—the plantation owner, Confederate officer, and descendant of Waterloo veterans whose white blood was somehow mixed up with ours. (And mixed up with that of other whites who, unlike Beaumont, were nameless and largely unrecalled, their blood ties to us undocumented and untraceable across the color line.) How, I sometimes wondered as a youngster, could this prototypical white southern patrician in the photograph, this very personification in my mind of America's racist past, a past we despised so much as a people, be a part of us inside?

When I grew up, I became a journalist, and the unanswered questions I carried with me about A.J. Beaumont's life and legacy took deeper root somewhere in the recesses of my adult mind, fertilized to no small degree by my experiences with racism as a young black man coming of age in America. My profession had trained me to ask myself questions and to find ways of getting answers. So whenever I reflected about Beaumont, about the traces of white blood coursing through my veins, and especially about race in America—a subject nearly every black person in this

country must think about quite often—my mind brimmed with questions, almost to the point of obsession.

Did Beaumont really marry and raise a white family in Louisiana not long after his relationship with Laura ended in the 1870s, as was rumored in my family?

Did he produce other children besides Pearl?

If so, what became of them?

Were there white descendants of A.J. Beaumont, cousins of mine, living in America today?

Where was this white family?

What stories did they have to tell about race in America from their "legitimate" branch of our shared ancestral tree?

How had their lives and experiences during the twentieth century differed from ours?

And, if these white relatives existed, could I find them, meet them?

As I imagined this white family, I naturally thought more and more about what it means to be black.

My family's experiences, like those of most black people in America, have mirrored the stresses and strains of our nation's racial history, from slavery through Jim Crow to the integration of the 1960s and on into the complex world of multiculturalism that seems to define the present. We have struggled through adversity, battled racial discrimination, loved, raised children, and pursued our dreams in many places around the country.

But, unlike many black families, mine has been comparatively privileged, favored by good fortune. From the 1850s, when Laura was a little girl on the Tullis plantation, to the present, we have been an upwardly mobile family, valuing education above all other gifts, seeing it as the only reliable avenue to security and freedom in a society often hostile to us because of our skin color. My grandfather—Fredda's husband—worked all his life as a postal clerk in St. Louis, and he felt the sting of witnessing less worthy men regularly promoted over him because they were white, yet he endured the pain of this discrimination stoically, never losing his deep religious faith. He did this not only because a government job was prestigious and rare work for a black man at the time, but also to ensure that his children received the loving home and education he knew they would need to survive in America.

My hardworking, strict, and ambitious father went to medical school to become a surgeon in the 1950s and eventually migrated to Seattle to raise his family because it was one of the few places in America then where hospitals would allow a black surgeon to practice. Growing up in the Pacific Northwest, my two brothers, my sister, and I were the first generation in our family to become friendly with white Americans, to live with them as equals in the same neighborhood, to understand and be allowed to compete with them in their own element. And to a large extent, as products of racial integration, we have succeeded in their world, at least according to their measures of success. My brother Wayne received an Ivy League education and became a lawyer. My other siblings, Bobby and Sharon, both carried on a family tradition and took up teaching in Seattle, Bobby in a private middle school and Sharon in the same public elementary school where she and I were among the first few black kids in the 1960s. I became a writer for the *Washington Post* after earning degrees at Princeton and Columbia in the 1970s, an educational and career progression unthinkable for most black people in America as recently as a generation ago. Our lives reflect the kind of unusual but significant progress made by advantaged black Americans over the generations since slavery, despite the hazards of racism and discrimination.

As I made my way in my career, traveling across America and to distant parts of the world to report for the *Post*, I sometimes thought about trying to find the white Beaumonts and comparing their family's story to my family's. I imagined one day writing a kind of flip side to Alex Haley's seminal adventure in *Roots*, where he traces his African forebears. But, within the frenetic pace of my newspaper career, I never seemed to find the time to pursue the search for my white kin.

Then in 1992 two things happened: I left daily journalism for a full-time teaching position at the Graduate School of Journalism at the University of California, Berkeley, and I became a father for the first time. Both events, occurring when I was thirty-eight, played a significant role in focusing my mind to re- search and write this book.

While the job change allowed me the freedom and time to investigate the project, fatherhood gave me a fresh sense of purpose in getting it done. Put simply, I wanted to be able to offer my daughter someday a better understanding of my family's racial history than I had had when I was coming of age and a clearer picture of the dynamic complexity of race and prejudice as they are woven into the fabric of America.

Little did I know when I started out on this journey that I would have to navigate some rough emotional and psychological terrain before gaining a far greater appreciation and understanding of my very blackness than I had ever realized was possible.

Nor did I know that by the end of the search I would find, like bits of gold at the rainbow's end, sparkling pieces of historical evidence—indeed, gifts bestowed on me from an unlikely source—that gave a deeper and richer context to our story as a family and a people in America.

But that is getting a bit ahead of things.

What follows, from its beginning, is a memoir of my search and the story I discovered on the other side of the tree.

BEGINNING FAMILY TREE

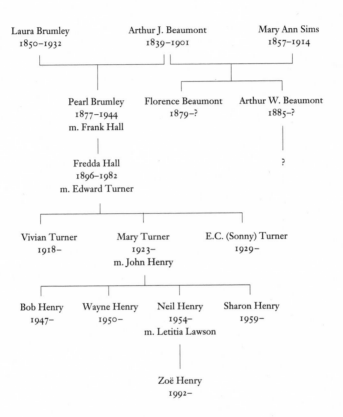

Laura Brumley
1850–1932

Arthur J. Beaumont
1839–1901

Mary Ann Sims
1857–1914

Pearl Brumley
1877–1944
m. Frank Hall

Florence Beaumont
1879–?

Arthur W. Beaumont
1885–?

Fredda Hall
1896–1982
m. Edward Turner

?

Vivian Turner
1918–

Mary Turner
1923–
m. John Henry

E.C. (Sonny) Turner
1929–

Bob Henry
1947–

Wayne Henry
1950–

Neil Henry
1954–
m. Letitia Lawson

Sharon Henry
1959–

Zoë Henry
1992–

PART ONE

Search

CHAPTER ONE

Clues in Microfilm

How do you find the descendants of a white man who was born in England in 1839 and died quietly in a small town in Louisiana nearly a century ago? How can you discover if this man even left white descendants?

When I started my project years ago, I didn't know if the Beaumont family still existed, largely because it was my under-standing that the fragile link my black family had to the white family before the turn of the last century was severed when A.J. Beaumont died. For all I knew, the Beaumont branch of my ex-tended family tree ended sometime after the century's turn with Arthur's death and later that of his white widow, whose name I didn't even know.

My great-grandmother Pearl, the quadroon daughter Beau-mont fathered with the freed slave Laura Brumley during the Reconstruction era, apparently tried to contact her white family in Louisiana sometime after her father's death in 1901 but was rebuffed. Anyway, that's what my mother vaguely remembered from stories she heard in her childhood in St. Louis. But even my mother didn't know for sure.

The whole Beaumont story was shrouded in mystery, a chapter in our distant past that no one in the family talked about very much when I was growing up, or wanted to talk about. I think this was largely because the real gist of that story—our blood link to racist white people who essentially had cast our ancestors aside as inferior and illegitimate long ago, during the plantation era— was certainly nothing to be proud of. And we were a family that, by contrast, had been blessed with many extraordinary black forebears to inspire us and accomplishments to celebrate.

I didn't have a lot of leads for my search, apart from Beaumont's old photograph, the brittle newspaper clipping that announced his death and noted his familial ties to Great Britain, and the fragile, yellowing letter the old man had written by hand on his personal stationery to Pearl shortly before his death, in which he guiltily acknowledged that he was her father. What I had were our family's oral stories and loving memories of Laura and Pearl, chiefly those of my mother and her younger brother, Uncle Sonny. They remembered Pearl from their childhood in St. Louis in the 1920s and 1930s and could recall the confusion and lonely torment she felt until the day she died, at sixty-seven in 1944, over her mixed racial background and the rejection she had suffered from her white father.

For about a decade, when time permitted, I dug into every resource I could find in search of the white Beaumonts—census records, court files, old microfilms of southern newspapers. At one point I even got some research help from both the British Imperial War Museum and the British National Army Museum, which I first contacted in June 1989 while on a two-day layover in London. I was en route to Kenya that summer, about to spend three years covering Africa for the *Washington Post* as a foreign correspondent based in Nairobi. I recalled that A.J. Beaumont's obituary stated that his father and grandfather had both served heroically as British Army officers during the Battle of Waterloo in 1815. So I contacted the military museum, seeking clues to the whereabouts of Beaumont's family in England. Perhaps they would know how to contact their American cousins—if they had any American cousins.

I pursued my unusual hobby in a number of crazy ways. I sought out genealogical societies on the Internet when I became computer literate in the 1990s, and I corresponded with numerous historical societies and libraries, from Kent in England to Natchez in Mississippi. I researched Social Security, immigration, and U.S. military records on CD-ROM and microfiche at various temples of the Church of Jesus Christ of Latter-Day Saints, which is headquartered in Salt Lake City and home to one of the finest libraries for genealogical research in America. At one point I even mailed letters to every Beaumont I could find in every telephone directory in Louisiana and Mississippi—thirty-five households in all. I got fascinating responses from people in many of those white homes, though none were able to provide a verifiable link to the genealogical history I sought.

But that wasn't the hardest part of my work. I now realize that one of the biggest obstacles in my restless searching was not a lack of resources or tools at my disposal or even places to hunt. It was the strange fear and unsettling ambivalence I often felt about what I was struggling to do. Essentially, I was trying to fashion a bridge over a chasm between white and black people that our nation's racial history and separatist customs had created. The difficulty of this struggle often played itself out in an internal emotional war over my feelings about race, about white and black people, and about the story I was attempting to uncover—feelings that went back to my growing up as a black kid in white middle-class Seattle in the 1960s.

I had little luck in my periodic search for a number of years. No luck in London. No luck in the historical archives in Louisiana. No luck with those letters I sent to all those households in the South.

But then one hot Thursday afternoon, on August 7, 1997, I finally happened upon an important clue.

During my summer break from teaching journalism classes at Berkeley in 1997, I decided to spend nearly all my time in a last concerted effort to find answers to the Beaumont puzzle. Nearly every day that summer I went to work at a microfilm reader in the public library near my home in Davis, California. The Yolo County Public Library in California's Sacramento Valley might seem an unlikely place to hunt for elusive clues to a family story buried long ago in the Deep South, but it turned out to be perfect for what I needed to do. Located just ten minutes from my house, the one-story building on the edge of the city's Community Park possessed two newspaper microfilm readers in good working order in its reference area, and it was these readers that were key to my search.

Day after day I flew back in time, my eyes peering closely at the reader as I scrolled from week to week in the years 1901 to 1916. I was hunting for clues to the whereabouts of A.J. Beaumont's white survivors in a newspaper called the *Tensas Gazette*, one of a number of old southern small-town newspapers copied on reels of microfilm that I had procured through my university library at Berkeley. The *Gazette* was Laura's and Beaumont's hometown weekly. It was started in the early 1800s and remains today one of the oldest continuously published newspapers in Louisiana. Printed in the old levee town of St. Joseph, the county seat of Tensas Parish, hard on the banks of the Mississippi River in northeastern Louisiana, it contained news from throughout the region.

In truth, as the summer was drawing to a close, I was starting to feel depressed by my lack of progress. For weeks I had been working on a set of six *Gazette* microfilms, on interlibrary loan from Louisiana State University, and I had a sinking sense that I might never find what I was looking for. When I began this latest tack in my research, I thought for certain I'd find a clue somewhere in time, some old footprint in the snow of history to tell me what happened to Beaumont's white survivors after he died in 1901.

Did they take over his business and cotton-growing interests in Louisiana? I wondered. Were they as prominent and successful after the turn of the century as he appears to have been in the 1880s and 1890s? Did they move on and settle somewhere else in America after his death?

St. Joseph numbered no more than 720 residents (and Tensas Parish, 19,070) at the turn of the last century, most of them engaged in cotton growing and related river work, and the local pages of the *Gazette* between 1890 and 1914 often read like notes from a church social. Almost everybody in St. Joseph's white society and that of the surrounding parish seemed to know everybody else, from Mayor Bondurant and Sheriff Hughes to society belles like Mrs. B.F. Bonney and Miss Inez Losey to Dreyfus, the druggist; Kershaw, the tool dealer; and Collins, the kindly old "colored" man who worked as a bailiff at the parish jail. Members of the Tullis family were frequently mentioned, including the *Gazette*'s publisher and editor Hugh Tullis, a lawyer who would go on to a distinguished career as a state judge. This was the same Tullis family that had once enslaved my great-great-grandmother Laura Brumley and many others on their plantation in St. Joseph and who remained prominent social and political leaders in the parish for many years after the Emancipation Proclamation. It was the same Tullis family whose matriarch, Sarah Tullis, had educated Laura, in defiance of the law. The old newspaper was filled with events and scenes from the lives of white people in the Delta region before and after 1900. The people who toiled to support their way of life, my black ancestors, provided little more than an anonymous and faceless backdrop to the stories.

Entire columns in the *Gazette* were given over to breathless descriptions of the most arcane happenings, and I ineluctably found myself swallowed up in the rhythms of the small town's life as I journeyed through the years.

A Negro man living on Buckhorn plantation was kicked by a mule on Tuesday of last week and after extreme suffering died on Friday.

We desire to return thanks to the officers of the steamboat Goldman for highly appreciated courtesies on her trip down last Monday and up Thursday.

A large buck was run into town last Tuesday by some hunters, and after a hot chase was finally killed in the duck pond field.

There were weekly write-ups about family visitors from neighboring villages and towns, like Rodney, Natchez, Hard Times,
and Waterproof, about Mississippi River fishing derbies and
moonlight hayrides, about baseball games between rival city
clubs, and about mint julep soirees on Tensas Parish's finest
plantations. Even the smallest changes in weather in St. Joseph
were noted in fascinating detail in the *Gazette:*

> The weather for the past week could not have been improved
> for the purposes of the cotton planter, and under the rays of a
> summer sun cotton is growing rapidly.

But it was the weddings, illnesses, and death remembrances in
the small town's comfortable white society that received the most
consistent and devoted attention, and I studied each of these
news items for clues about the Beaumonts:

> Mr. Guy N. Hunter paid a beautiful tribute to Mrs. Guice's
> memory when he said she was a sweet, unselfish Christian gen-
> tlewoman, who never thought of self, whose greatest happiness
> was in giving pleasure to others. She was ever ready to comfort
> the sick and distressed, and the world was made better by her
> influence and gentle ministrations to others.

It seemed a reasonable hunch that I would find the name
Beaumont in those pages somewhere, some year, some month or
day, after the turn of the century. After all, A.J. Beaumont had
lived in St. Joseph for more than forty years after his arrival in
Louisiana in the late 1850s and had become a well-known figure
there before he died nearly a half century later. From my research a year earlier, using the same microfilm readers in the

Davis public library, I already knew that Beaumont was something of a town leader, frequently mentioned in the *Gazette* between 1870 and 1900. His obituary in 1901 took up eight column
inches on the local page.

This English immigrant, I had learned, served on the city
council for a short period in the 1880s; he was also a school board
official, a private investor in civic improvement projects (including a lucrative wooden plank toll road on the city's levee), a saloon and billiard hall owner who specialized in fine cigars and
German brews, a cotton grower, and a prosperous dealer in plantation supplies, whose store occupied a central place on the
town's main thoroughfare, Plank Road, not far from the Tensas
Parish Court House. Indeed, Beaumont frequently advertised for
business in the *Gazette*, especially in the weeks when the Tensas
Parish Circuit Court was in session and St. Joseph filled with
lawyers, jurors, and others on business from throughout the
state. His name appeared in listings of liquor license applications;
it could also be found among the faithful attendees of Tensas
Parish Democratic Party meetings during Reconstruction and
the rise of Jim Crow.

Each detail I had mined about Beaumont's life in St. Joseph
during my earlier research fascinated me. On the paper's society
pages, for example, I had discovered:

> Mr. A J Beaumont will open his billiard and pool room early
> next week, the entire room has been refitted, the pool and
> billiard tables recovered, and everything put in first class condi-
> tion. This room is the prettiest and most comfortable of any in
> the State, outside of New Orleans, and well supplied with every-
> thing that can contribute to the comfort and pleasure of his
> guests. (November 21, 1885)

A J Beaumont invites lawyers, clients, witnesses and jurors to call
at his palatial saloon and billiard rooms during court. . . . Everything imaginable for the comfort of the inner man can be found
at Beaumont's. (April 30, 1886)

We return thanks to Mr. A J Beaumont for a pitcher of mint
juleps kindly sent to this office. (May 7, 1886)

At other times I had found Beaumont's name hidden amid the
dark lines of type in local news stories about events large and
small:

Fire was discovered in the house in the rear of the saloon of Mr.
A J Beaumont on Monday night about 11 o'clock. The alarm
was given and the blaze was soon extinguished, doing little harm
to the buildings. The fire was evidently the work of an incendi-
ary, as the building caught from the outside. The house was
occupied by the barber, Wm. Thomas. (July 6, 1894)

There is a herd of unbroken ponies that grazes around St. Joseph
and every evening about sundown goes to the lake in front of
town to water, and then dashes across the levee and down the
road through town like onto a charge of cavalry. This is a great
source of danger to people who are driving their wagons and to
children whose nurses take them walking about that hour. Quite
recently this cavalcade of horses going at full speed startled a
team of mules hitched to a wagon in front of Mr. A J Beaumont's
store and caused a run-away. Had it been a carriage with ladies in
it the danger to life and limb would have been great. We do not
know of any way to correct this evil and would be glad for someone to suggest one, short of killing the ponies. (August 21, 1896)

Some items in the newspapers before the century's turn had offered intriguing glimpses into Beaumont's prosperity in business:

Mr. A J Beaumont is having his store beautifully painted and decorated. Mr. Sam W. Hazlip is doing the work and this in itself is a guarantee that the job will be well done. . . . Mr. Beaumont also has fitted up a room in his store next to his office for the accommodation of customers. Comfortable chairs and tables are there, and the strictest privacy can be obtained by those desiring it. (September 18, 1896)

Other lines had provided a passing glance at the mundane details of his life:

FOR SALE A good large iron safe. Very cheap. Apply to: A J Beaumont, St. Joseph. (June 4, 1897)

Indeed, I had spent the previous summer, in 1996, combing through the years before Beaumont's death, meticulously collecting each of these items, finding in their accumulation a slightly more detailed portrait of my great-great-grandfather and his white family, one that added color and context to my search. From all the information I had gathered, it seemed clear to me that Beaumont had been a beloved and respected member of the white landed gentry and merchant class in St. Joseph, a quintessential nineteenth-century immigrant who saw his dream of prosperity and freedom in America come true.

With each morsel of information I obtained, I grew convinced that Beaumont's name must have lived on in St. Joseph after his death, through his white survivors. But, so far, no matter how closely I searched the microfilms, I couldn't find the clues I needed. The surname Beaumont seemed to largely disappear from the life of St. Joseph after 1901.

By the time I got to the year 1914 in early August, I didn't know if I could carry on much longer. My research had already turned from a hobby into something of an obsession and had pervaded slices of my personal and professional life in one form or another for nearly a decade. Yet deep down I felt torn about this project, tantalized by my discoveries but frustrated by the obstacles. Often, during that sweltering summer, I returned home to my wife and daughter feeling distracted and moody. I agonized, knowing there had to be an answer somewhere—but where? At the same time I loved the hunt and felt immense excitement over even the tiniest historical discovery. Like the electrifying moment more than a decade earlier when, sitting at a long wooden desk at the National Archives building in Washington, D.C., I discovered that A.J. Beaumont did indeed marry a white woman and have children with her after his long affair with my great-great-grandmother Laura.

I had been investigating 1880 and 1900 census records on black sheets of microfiche over a stretch of hours that summer afternoon. The Archives building on Pennsylvania Avenue, with the famous words "The Past Is Prologue" etched into a granite cornerstone near its ornate front door, was filled with hundreds of people that day, all searching for clues to their origins and ancestors among the library's many historical files and databases. Most of these people were not professional researchers, just ordinary Americans looking for personal meaning and identity in the details of our shared national history. Some were excitedly hunting through the manifests of the hundreds of passenger ships that arrived at New York's Ellis Island before and after the turn of the last century, hoping to uncover parents' or grandparents' names and the exact name of the ship they arrived on and its date of arrival. Others were scanning the state-by-state records of

Union and Confederate muster ranks, hoping to find their ancestors' names and priceless evidence of their small marks on our national history. Still others, like me, were searching copies of the original handwritten notes in our nation's census records for bits of information about their people, their blood kin.

Throughout the 1980s, spurred in no small measure by Alex Haley's exploration of his family's black heritage in the 1976 bestseller *Roots*, the nation's libraries and archives of genealogical materials experienced heightened use by Americans searching for clues to their past. Before then, genealogical research in this country was not nearly so popular. It was usually the hobby of people seeking validation of Old World nobility or royalty in their bloodlines. But after the enormous success of *Roots*, both in print and as a television miniseries, many Americans, white and black, began searching enthusiastically for even mundane details of their ancestors' lives, as a way of connecting personally to history and their racial and ethnic identity.

I was just one among many curious people in the Archives that day in 1986, my hunt for the footprints of my white forebears just another among many searches through time. My search, though, represented perhaps a new twist in the usual process. Whereas once the interracial heritage many Americans share was largely off-limits to public discussion or even research, the explosion of interest in genealogy in the 1980s helped shatter the taboo. Haley himself, in an interview in the *Washington Post* shortly before his death in 1990, pointed to the mixed-race heritage of many black Americans as the next frontier he hoped to explore in his sociological research.

As I was looking through census records on microfilm and microfiche that afternoon in Washington, I suddenly came upon Beaumont's name and household. It was startling. There in fine cursive writing penned by the 1880 census taker were Beaumont's full name and that of his wife, Mary Ann, whom he had married in St. Joseph in 1878. The marriage came one year after Laura gave birth to Beaumont's mixed-raced daughter, Pearl. I also found in the Archives' census microfiches the names of the white children Beaumont subsequently produced with his wife— Florence, born in 1879, and Arthur W., born in 1885, both in St. Joseph.

I scribbled this information down on a piece of scratch paper and later filed it away in my desk drawer at home, elated by the discovery but not knowing what, if anything, to do with it. Still, this tiny proof that Beaumont had indeed had children with his white wife intrigued me and formed the germ of my search. Perhaps Beaumont's children had had children of their own who were living somewhere in America today, distant cousins of mine.

When I found more time to pursue the chase in the 1990s, I discovered wonderful material in the newspaper microfilms, including details about the historical context of Beaumont's life in the late nineteenth century in St. Joseph. This information riveted me. For example, while relationships between white men and black women in the Old South were certainly not uncommon during and after slavery, one story I found in the *Gazette* pointed up unusual demographic imbalances in St. Joseph that may have contributed to an even greater number of such relationships. In February 1873, during the period Beaumont and Laura were meeting in St. Joseph, the newspaper published the following note about city life, which, while written in humor, nonetheless illustrated a reality about life for young white men laboring in a small, rural, out-of-the-way river town 150 miles north of New Orleans:

> The most serious topic in St. Joseph seems to be the scarcity of young ladies.
>
> Our little town has 15 promising young men, including lawyers, merchants, preachers, steamboatmen and planters, all anxious to get married and there is not a single young lady, not promised, in town. We understand that these young men have had several meetings recently, to consider what steps could be taken for their relief. The last proposition we have heard suggested is to start General Stephen Routh out with full power of attorney to act for the unfortunate young men who are unable to leave their business—each one binding himself to accept the selection made by General Steve. Two have volunteered to accept widows not older than forty.
>
> Poor boys!

Uncovering such slices of a bygone life fascinated me intellectually, but I was troubled by my growing obsession. I often felt a vague uneasiness and inexplicable hurt deep inside the more I worked on this project and sometimes wondered if, in the end, my search was pointless or, worse, harmful in some way—if, indeed, I was doing something vaguely disloyal to my own people by devoting so much time and mental energy to trying to find a different sort of "roots" in the white family of a man whose good life seemed dependent on the very system of injustice and inequality under which black people had suffered for so long.

A.J. Beaumont and I were distantly linked by blood and DNA, but the differences between us could not have been starker. I was a forty-three-year-old black man, a husband and father living at the dawn of the twenty-first century in a postindustrial America that was contending with new challenges of ethnic and racial "diversity" and sharpening disparities between the rich and the poor, the informed and the ignorant.

The contradictions of my America were staggering. It was a time of seemingly boundless opportunity and sickening hopelessness and alienation, an age of unsurpassed economic riches when children gunned down children in schoolyards. The wealthiest society the world had ever known, we nevertheless seemed unable to guarantee that young people graduated from high school knowing how to read and write. Still, we were witnesses to stupendous wonders nearly every day. Scientists sent robots to Mars to test for life and made genetic copies of sheep and other living creatures, while ordinary people could find information about practically anything within the blink of an eye by the mere touch of a finger on a computer keyboard.

On the one hand, African American men like me had an 81 percent chance of being either dead, jobless, or in jail by the time they were twenty-one. On the other hand, it was an age in which black Americans had rocketed to outer space in proud, patriotic service to their country, pronounced landmark judgments on the U.S. Supreme Court, headed the nation's Joint Chiefs of Staff in wartime, and led public opinion polls for president of the United States.

A.J. Beaumont was a white man from a far different age, a poor immigrant who, like millions of others, came to this country in the nineteenth century in search of a dream. He benefited tremendously from his adopted nation's racist way of life in Louisiana, becoming a proud and successful member of the landed white southern gentry. And by all family accounts he, like so many other white men of his age, did not feel any meaningful moral responsibility for his mixed-race offspring, my great-grandmother Pearl.

I looked at Beaumont's old photograph countless times during my quest, the one he had sent to Pearl in 1901 as an expression of his regret over his failures as a father to her, the one that had been handed down from Pearl to Fredda to my mother. Cradling it in my hands, I often wondered what his life and times must have been like.

He lived between 1839 and 1901, a period that saw the full flowering of the Industrial Revolution in England and the rise and greatest glory of the Victorian Empire. He lived during the time of the potato famine in Ireland and the Opium Wars in China. The invention of the telegraph and Morse code and the heyday of the railroad age occurred during his lifetime, which ended at the dawn of the internal combustion engine and the age of flight. His contemporaries were giants like Darwin, Hugo, Marx, and Lincoln; Tchaikovsky, Monet, Whitman, and Edison. And he lived during the times that had always fascinated me most, not the least because of their lasting effects on my racial and family identities—the eras of slavery, Civil War, Reconstruction, and the rise of Jim Crow in the American South. It was an extraordinary period in human history, and I found it infinitely interesting to study.

But at times I found myself seething with an almost atavistic resentment at Beaumont's photograph as I worked at my computer and in the library, frustrated by my failure to locate his white heirs and growing embittered by the Gilded Age prosperity and smugness I saw reflected in his unchangingly pale and silent face. I couldn't help seeing in his portrait the face of every white man I had ever come to despise in my life and every white man whose racism, arrogance, and privilege had translated into oppression, injustice, and untold pain for so many. I saw in it all the obscenities of slavery and all the evils of the plantation era, when white men like him whipped and tortured my ancestors and took black women like Laura for their pleasure whenever they liked. I saw the degradation my mother had suffered in the 1940s whenever she had to travel on squalid Jim Crow railcars to attend her segregated library school. I saw all the cowardly white administrators who, terrified by the idea of a black physician ministering to white patients, said no and shut hospital doors in my father's face when he sought to establish his career as a talented young surgeon in the 1950s. And I saw in Beaumont's face the faces of white strangers in Seattle whose ignorant prejudice marked my coming of age during the era of racial integration in the 1960s.

Indeed, it was in that decade of my childhood that my family first got to know what white people were like, on their own turf. In many ways, I realize in hindsight, the genesis of my search for the Beaumonts lay in that era.

Up until the 1960s all generations of my family lived in a racially segregated America—in St. Louis, Winston-Salem, and Nashville. Even in Seattle, where my parents migrated in 1956, after my father finished his surgical training in the Deep South, the neighborhoods and schools were segregated by local custom if not by Jim Crow law. The city's black residents were largely confined to a several-mile-square patch of real estate in the inner city called the Central Area, where the public schools were predominantly black and abysmally staffed and supported, compared with schools in white areas.

Infused by the ideals of equal rights and opportunity that galvanized their generation of black professionals, and buttressed by legal advances of the civil rights movement elsewhere in America, my mother and father decided in 1960 to test Seattle's de facto system of racial segregation. Unable to buy a house outside the Central Area because of their race—and thereby unable to gain access to premium public schools for their children—my parents secretly commissioned a white middleman named Franz Brodine to purchase a piece of property for them in the city's south end, in a middle-class subdivision called the Uplands, where the public schools were good. For many years, under a 1920s-era racial covenant governing the subdivision, blacks and Asians—unless they were working as domestics—had been barred from residence in this pleasant neighborhood on the shore of Lake Washington.

Although such racial covenants governing neighborhoods and housing were ruled unconstitutional by the U.S. Supreme Court in 1948, the restrictions were still observed in practice in many American cities. My parents' clandestine method of purchasing property in a white neighborhood was typical of the sleight-of-hand upwardly mobile black people in northern cities had to resort to in order to better themselves, to secure equal educational opportunities for their children, and to force the nation to honor its constitutional guarantees. It was one thing for the courts to decide that racial segregation was illegal, as they did throughout the 1950s and 1960s, but it was up to individual black people like my parents to test those decrees, to force the change, and to deal with the personal consequences.

It was on a beautiful street lined with lush, vase-shaped elm trees and tall, elegant pines, amid rows of stately homes overlooking the lake, that my mother and father decided to build a house. After Brodine signed the property deed over to my parents, they commissioned the city's only black architect, Benjamin McAdoo, to design and build the house. A relatively new arrival in Seattle, with a growing reputation for his work, McAdoo took special care with our house, in part because he wanted to make sure our historic move went smoothly. He had already designed and built several other houses for white families in the neighborhood and was well aware that he couldn't live in any of them because he was black. Our victory would be his as well.

For months, as our house was being constructed, the white neighbors were unaware of who owned it. Then, shortly before we moved in that December, they found out the new arrivals were a black family. Terrified of us and distressed over an assumed deflation of their property values, our prospective white neighbors convened emergency block meetings to cobble together strategies to thwart us. When the city's mayor, Gordon Clinton, got wind of the controversy, he urged civic mediators to quell it somehow. But the white neighbors persisted. They sent petitions from house to house throughout Seattle's south end to gain wider support for their efforts and pooled their money to offer my father a buyout at 200 percent of his purchase price. Anything to stop us.

But my parents were determined. We moved into our new house at 6261 Lake Shore Drive South a few weeks before Christmas 1960, the first black family in Seattle's uplands subdivision. From that day, my life changed forever. I was six years old, the product of a proud and loving black world, embarking on a new childhood in a world where my family and I were clearly alien and unwanted.

My closest friends, my teachers, my neighbors, the first kid I ever fought with my fists, the first girl I ever kissed on the lips—practically everyone who populated the universe of my school-age childhood—was white. I was the quintessential poster child of the era of racial integration, a drop of color on a field of snow. I was the first and only black kid in my class from first to seventh grades. I was the only black kid on my Little League teams, in my Cub Scout troop, and at swimming school. I learned to read, write, and enunciate English with perfect diction and grammar, to use a protractor and slide rule expertly, and to sing first tenor in classical ensembles in the school choir.

Indeed, I outdid most of my white classmates in practically every school subject and was popular enough to be elected president of the student body in junior high school by a landslide. At the height of the Vietnam War in 1968, when I was fourteen, I was awarded a prestigious American Legion medal by local war veterans for civic leadership and academic achievement. I was, in their eyes, the ideal young citizen, a model American.

But I was also hopelessly mixed up.

For the incongruities that defined my childhood were profound and difficult to comprehend. From early on, I felt a weight attached to my childhood on Lake Shore Drive. I knew that, as a black kid, I was in some way carrying a flag for my race and must never let it touch the ground in disgrace. My mother especially taught me to be proud of being black, repeatedly explaining that living amid the white middle class in Seattle was a pioneering and noble venture. Not many black people got the chances my siblings and I had, and we should make the most of them, both for ourselves and for other black people who might come behind us. My parents made it clear that failure—in school, in our behavior, in life—was not acceptable, a lesson my father used his leather belt to reinforce.

So I definitely knew I was black. It was precisely because I was black that I had to make excellent marks in school, that I had to prove I was as good as any of the privileged white kids. No matter that my skin was a light brown color, I knew that, in the eyes of most white people, I was as black as any African American boy in this country. Throughout the civil rights struggle in the 1960s, as my family, from our distant vantage point in the Northwest, followed events in the South through the newspapers or on television, I certainly knew what was at stake and whose side I was on. I knew that when Martin Luther King, Jr., and Medgar Evers led boycotts, sit-ins, and marches, they were fighting for me, not just the striking sanitation workers in faraway Memphis or the brave voting rights workers in Mississippi. The fire hoses, police dogs, and bloody nightsticks I saw to my horror on the *Huntley-Brinkley Evening News* could just as easily have been trained on me or anyone else in my family, had we been living in Selma instead of Seattle.

At the same time I became aware of the subtle paradox that black people are not all alike, that as a race we have recognized and fostered divisions and pecking orders among ourselves based on the very sorts of physical differences in skin tone and hair texture that have fed white racism. My hair was what my mother, her family, and her friends in Seattle's small but close-knit black bourgeois society called "good hair" because it wasn't rough and nappy, like that of most dark-skinned black people, but curly, comparatively straight, and soft, like the hair of whites. My skin, in their eyes, was a pretty "tan" or "yellow" or "red" color, not dark "as the ace of spades." I was said to be fortunate because I didn't have "liver" lips or kinky, unkempt hair that looked like "dust on a jug." While my mother instilled in me a deep sense of pride in our race and our history of struggle as a people in America, she also made it plain that black families like ours were somehow different and more blessed within our own society precisely because we had fairer skin and were closer to being perceived as "white."

When my mother was growing up in her bourgeois family in St. Louis, her dark-skinned father often used to say half-jokingly that America's race problems never would have festered so long had Abraham Lincoln not freed the slaves. With all the interracial children produced under slavery, America would have become fully racially mixed in time and the system of slavery and human inequality would simply have "withered away." "You must try to improve the race," Grandpa from time to time instructed my mother during her adolescent years in the 1930s, encouraging his daughter to choose a light-skinned man as her mate. Light was simply better than dark, and the more white in us, the better.

Even as a child in Seattle, in my deep unconscious I was never able to reconcile such an appalling contradiction. How could we feel truly proud of being black inside if the less black—the whiter—we appeared seemingly made us "better," more favored in society and among our own people? If being black was indeed something to be proud of, why did we have to leave black people behind in so many ways in our endeavor to live with and model ourselves after whites? How could such outward racial pride and traces of inner self-loathing coexist?

I remember feeling shame the first time I read *Nigger*, Dick Gregory's searing 1964 memoir about his impoverished child-hood in the 1940s in St. Louis. He wrote bitterly about the racism that he, with his dark skin, encountered from the black bourgeoisie, who generally had lighter skin. Although this big-otry stemmed in part from the animosity of many established black St. Louisians toward poor, backward black sharecroppers who, like Gregory's family, had migrated north during and after the war, it was also based on skin color. Gregory was constantly made to feel as if he were little more than an ignorant, dirty, shiftless "nigger"—not by whites, but by the snobbish blacks who occupied a higher social station based not just on livelihood and income but also on lighter skin color, straighter hair, and other physical features. Their bigotry was just as malicious and crippling as any he ever felt from white people, Gregory wrote. That he grew up in St. Louis in the same era as my mother, in the same neighborhood, yet came away deeply wounded by the very classist and racist pathology she had been conditioned to believe in, confused me as a teenager and left me despairing whenever I tried to figure racism out. How was the racism of my loving fam-ily any different from the white racism we all loathed?

"Good" hair. "Light" skin. "Thin" lips. "Proper" articulation. Such were the subtle messages and code words about race that filtered into my unconscious mind as the child of a black profes-sional family. "You come from good stock," my mother used to say to me with pride, an expression that was somewhat meaning-less to me as a little kid but became infinitely fascinating and richly ambiguous by the time I entered adolescence. *Good stock.* What did that mean? "You've got good blood," she would reply, usually after an impatient sigh over my obtuseness. "You come from good ingredients, like a good soup." Still, the phrase would flit around my brain like a firefly in the dark, intriguing and yet not quite reachable or knowable. I knew the expression must have something to do with race, with black and white, as did so many things in my life. In time I came to an understanding of my mother's pet phrase that somehow satisfied me both emotionally and intellectually. "Good stock" suggested I had the best qualities of both races in me. But more important to me, the expression seemed to connote such human qualities as strength, rootedness, intelligence, devotion, and identity, admirable qualities that many in our black family line epitomized. That had to be it. "Good stock" must encompass both character and color. Such was the truce I eventually made with my mother's expression.

For the longest time when I was a kid, I had no idea where my family's lighter features and relatively straight hair came from. I rarely thought about it, actually. My parents always made it clear that the overriding reality we needed to understand, for the sake of identity and survival—despite all the contradictions and nuances of race as they manifested themselves in our family—was that we were black in a racist society dominated by white people.

Still, as a small child I used to gaze at our family's photographs in albums and on the living room walls in Seattle and admire not only how handsome and beautiful many of our black relatives and ancestors were but also how breathtakingly varied they were in skin color and physical appearance. Our family album was a living, breathing testament that "black" people in America come in all shapes, sizes, and colors, ranging in skin tone from my grandfather Clifford's rich chocolate brown to my sister Sharon's creamy ivory. Yet we were all one family, each of us definitively "colored," "Negro," "black."

It wasn't until I was about twelve that I began to put a few things together about our family's mixed racial past, almost by accident. My grandmother Fredda—Pearl's daughter and the granddaughter of A.J. Beaumont—was visiting us in Seattle from St. Louis with her husband, my grandfather Clifford. How I loved it whenever they visited, bringing with them their soft Missouri drawl, which filled our house in the distant Northwest with loving echoes of our southern heritage. One warm summer evening I was standing at Grandma's side while she played Scrabble with my mother and grandfather on our living room table. She asked me to help her craft a word with the tiles in her wooden holder, but as I snuggled next to her, my eyes kept falling on her gentle hands as they held the tile holder, hands mottled slightly by age spots but clearly white in color. They were as white as the hands of my white teacher, Miss St. Martin. My eyes traced a path from her hands to her bare white arms to her face, a kind, expressive face with warm hazel eyes and skin as white as that of any white woman in my neighborhood. It was as if I had never really *seen* my grandmother before that moment. I was stunned and slightly amused by the strange revelation that my beautiful black grandma was not "black" in appearance at all. I next noticed my dark-skinned grandpa at the table and then gazed at my mother, one of their three children, a perfect blend of the two, a woman with tan-colored skin and wavy dark hair. I realized there was something mixed up about us. We were probably not unlike the milk shakes my sister and I loved to make in the summertime, using chocolate and vanilla ice cream and mixing them with milk in a bowl to make a creamy brown. But where this mixture in us, as people, came from I hadn't a clue as a child. While the revelation stayed with me, inside my mind somewhere,

I rarely thought about it consciously in my childhood and never asked any questions, so busy was I with the fun of growing up.

In many critical ways my childhood *was* happy, so "integrated" with the lives of white people in the Uplands that it lent validation to the ideals of the age. We proved—in an isolated, microscopic fashion, at least—that a black family could live in a sea of white people of the same advantaged class, with shared values, if everybody could get over the initial fear and ignorance of each other. My childhood was not unlike *Leave It to Beaver*, with my siblings each cast as Wally, my parents as Ward and June, and me as the Beaver. Were it not for the color of our skin, we could have passed as just another family in our pleasant town, which resembled the Mayfield of the Cleavers. Decades later my memories of those days in Seattle remained filled with happy family summer vacations to Washington's pristine Olympic Peninsula, salmon-fishing charter trips with my father in the Pacific Ocean off Neah Bay, rafting escapes on Lake Washington, and endless pick-up baseball, basketball, and football games on lazy summer afternoons with my white neighborhood pals.

But amid the happy times were a number of cockeyed, wretched experiences that colored my awareness of the white world as a black child. Sometimes happiness seemed to come in tandem with hurt, precisely because of race. Once, when I was seven, I skipped up the block to visit a white school pal at his home for the first time, only to see his front door slammed in my face with a loud bang by his mother, who hadn't known Tommy's friend was black. In another incident, at nine, I visited another house up the street where two little white girls had invited me to play, only to have their grandfather chase me from the yard with a long wooden stick in hand, snarling, "You

black . . . !" And then there was the time, at ten, several schoolyard jerks encircled me as I headed to my classroom, taunting me
with shouts of "Chocolate! Chocolate!" Too scrawny to fight
back, I looked up at the bullies through my thick horn-rimmed
eyeglasses and repeatedly muttered the only thing that came to
mind: "Vanilla! Vanilla!" The crowd of white kids watching this
scene fortunately began to laugh uproariously at my rejoinder,
and I managed to slip into class without a bruise or a scrape. A
sharp wit, I learned, could be as useful in a schoolyard pinch as
the solid right cross my older brother Wayne preferred.

My mother and father explained that these racial episodes,
these occasional scrapes with white fears and ignorance, were not
my problem. I didn't cause these incidents and they were not my
fault, my parents told me. They were simply part of the complicated and challenging experience of being black in America. All
black people in all strata of society had similar encounters. My
parents said racism was *their* problem, those ignorant and hateful
white people's problem, and that the best thing we could do was
show our resilience in the face of the storm and continue pursuing our life goals. Get over it and deal with what matters most,
they insisted, things like school and family and friendships. Don't
let the occasional bigots defeat you or force you to lower yourself
to their level. Thus my method of coping with prejudice, like my
mother's and father's and that of so many other black Americans,
became to swallow the hurts, to stow them away in a little box inside my soul somewhere, and try to get on with my life without
allowing them to cripple me.

But, of course, the hurts accumulated. They festered over
time. And somehow, many years later, they seemed to be coming
to a head inside me during my search for my white kin. The old

photograph of A.J. Beaumont became a kind of key to a locked portal to my psyche, releasing all sorts of long-pent-up personal memories about race as I pursued the white branch of my family tree.

Taken and developed sometime in the 1880s in a studio called Washburn's on Canal Street in New Orleans (according to the label on its border), Beaumont's portrait, which for posterity had been mounted onto a sturdy slice of cardboard, seemed fairly typical of studio portraits of that era. Pictured against a grayish backdrop, he posed very formally for the camera, apparently seated, wearing what appeared to be a dark tweed jacket and a satiny floral tie. His head was facing slightly to the left, his hair neatly combed with a crisp part, his French imperial beard classically trimmed. It seemed the unmistakable image of a proud, middle-aged Confederate veteran, a man obviously very comfortable with his civilian life some twenty years after the conflict.

Now, more than a century later, the photograph had become a kind of symbol of so many racial incidents in my own life. It was Beaumont's image that came to mind whenever I recalled the white administrator who headed the Princeton-in-Asia office on campus, which sponsored students spending semesters abroad for academic credit. One day during my junior year in 1975, I visited the office to inquire about spending a year in Taiwan or Japan, since I was majoring in political science with Asia as a focus. I took a seat and, after an exchange of small talk, the administrator looked me up and down nervously for a moment and cleared his throat. Then he confessed that the program had never sent a black student to Asia before and that he felt many alumni and host families would object to my participation. "It's not that I object," the white man said as he squirmed in his chair. "It's just . . . I'm sure you understand."

I also saw Beaumont's image clearly in my mind whenever I recalled a newsroom confrontation I had as a young journalist in 1982 with Larry Kramer, an editor at the *Washington Post*. I had just written a feature article about cockfighting in the Maryland countryside, a story so colorful and newsworthy it was scheduled by the paper's top editors to be published on the front page the following day. Now, though, Kramer was worried. One year after the scandal of Janet Cooke, a talented young black writer who had fabricated a sensational story about an eight-year-old heroin addict, the pudgy white editor was questioning whether I, too, a young black writer, had fabricated my story. After all, weren't we all alike?

I wanted to strangle the editor, just as surely as I wanted to murder the Princeton administrator. I wanted to pound the white bastards with two-by-fours and grind them into the floorboards under my feet. But instead I swallowed my emotions, told myself to work harder, and stowed away the hurt and resentment for the sake of moving on.

"Thanks for your time," I told the white Princeton official before shoving my books under my arms and trudging back to my dormitory room, seething with anger and sadness.

"No, Larry, it's true," I told my white editor, struggling to contain my emotions. "I didn't make it up. It's a great story."

Maddeningly, as I reflected on my past, I saw the face of A.J. Beaumont as an all-purpose emblem of white racism. Yet it was this very white man, this seemingly archetypal plantation-era figure whose life during Reconstruction seemed to represent all that my people despised and feared, whose blood was a part of mine. I began to hate the thought of him as much as I hated the warped, ugly pathology of racism at the heart of American culture, the system that ranked people according to their place in the wide spectrum of human skin tone and hair texture, lending grudging favor to black people like me whose looks were marginally closer to the white ideal while unfairly classifying darker people as ugly, undesirable, or unintelligent. I hated this insidious injustice, which ran directly counter to the ideal of human equality that gave direction and powerful meaning to my black ancestors' lives and, by extension, my own. And I hated the thought that it was only by a quirk of ancestral fate that I had been born "lucky" in this regard, that I was somehow more blessed in my culture because Beaumont's blood and the blood of other white people in our ancestral tree coursed with the black in my veins.

But most of all I hated this: the thought that I, too, had ineluctably internalized this racist pathology as the product of a privileged class. After all, didn't I prefer lighter-skinned women when I became a man, just as my society and family background conditioned me to? Didn't I often think they were prettier than darker women and that straight hair was finer than kinky? When I was feeling especially insecure about my abilities, in school and later in my careers in journalism and teaching, didn't I feel vaguely inferior to white peers because of my blackness? Indeed, didn't the sickness of my culture manage to seep its way through the gate to my soul, teaching me to distrust myself because of the black in me?

There was an old street saying about racism that my brothers and I sometimes cynically recited as we made our way to school in the rain and wind in Seattle—"If you're white, you're all right;

if you're yellow, you're mellow; if you're brown, you stick around; if you're black, you go back." It seemed as true when I was an adult as it did when I was a child. Was it, then, at least partially true that my family and I had endured comparatively well in America precisely because we had drops of white blood mixing with the black? Was that was our most telling advantage in the end?

Since leaving Seattle, I had been a journalist for twenty years—exciting, deeply challenging years that had seen me pursue news stories around the world for the *Washington Post*, from the cotton fields of Mississippi and the tough streets of Washington, D.C., to the embattled countrysides of Nicaragua, Liberia, and Ethiopia. But in very few of those hundreds upon hundreds of reporting projects had I felt the level of unsettling rage and anxiety that my search for my white cousins brought out. I often felt in my research as if I were peeling back the pulpy layers of some forbidden fruit—inexorably, almost involuntarily—and I was deeply troubled about the truths I might find at the core.

It had all seemed so simple that night in 1981 when my search essentially began. I had been a professional journalist living in Washington, D.C., for five years and was visiting Seattle on vacation. My mother and I, as we often did, were chatting about our family history over beer, and I was laughing with her as she recalled stories from her childhood about her grandmother Pearl, who she said was whiter in complexion than even my grandma Fredda. Mom regaled me with stories about Pearl's mother, Laura, the freed slave who was the offspring of a slave born in Africa and a white physician living on a neighboring plantation in Louisiana. There was also white blood on my father's side, Mom told me, in the form of a nineteenth-century

German-Jewish plantation owner in North Carolina named Lowenstein. Mostly, though, she talked glowingly about Laura's loving affair with the Englishman, which produced Pearl.

I had heard all these stories before, and I never got bored hearing her tell them. My mother was a wonderfully gifted storyteller who loved to punctuate her words with gales of laughter.

"We've got America in us," she told me that night. "We've got the story of America."

"But how do we really know all this is true?" I asked.

It was then that my mother rose from her chair, padded to her desk, opened a drawer, and almost nonchalantly pulled out the artifacts at the heart of my search: the photograph of A.J. Beaumont, his obituary, and the letter he had written by hand to his mixed-raced daughter, Pearl, shortly before he died. I gently held the fragile paper up to an overhead light and was startled by the clarity and beauty of the old man's penciled handwriting.

I had vaguely known such keepsakes existed somewhere in our family archive since I was a child. But now, as a working journalist, I suddenly began to recognize their remarkable value. It was as if in these artifacts I had stumbled upon an original work by Picasso or a long-lost manuscript by Langston Hughes.

One of my story editors at the *Washington Post* used to teach young reporters that stories had little value in journalism unless you collected a paper trail of evidence to back them up. "Make sure . . . you get . . . the documents," Bob Woodward would say in his telltale monotone voice, which made for mimicking behind his back in the newsroom.

Well, here, before me, on my mother's desk were documents of a sort, small threads of evidence that this old story from our family's past was true. And it was a story that must, I was sure, be filled with important lessons about race in America if I could fill it out.

Where did the white family go?

The key thing I needed to do was pinpoint where Beaumont's descendants went after his death so I could pick up a trail that might lead to the present day. I believed that if I found where his wife and children settled after leaving St. Joseph, assuming they had left, I could go to the county courthouse closest to their new home and research all kinds of property, probate, and tax records, which might provide clues to other places these descendants—if there were descendants—had resided over the subsequent decades.

I didn't know if the Beaumont surname had lived on. I didn't know if his children had children. All I knew from my research was that Beaumont's immediate survivors must have departed St. Joseph sometime after his death, because their names didn't appear in census or property records there after the turn of the century. There were no Beaumonts listed in any directory in Tensas Parish.

All I had to go on, really, were the newspaper microfilms, which offered fascinating clues to the family's comfortable way of life in St. Joseph society before A.J. died, like this snippet about the ninth birthday of his son, the white half brother of Pearl:

MASTER ARTHUR BEAUMONT entertained his young friends on Monday night at a charming birthday party, which was largely attended and highly enjoyed by the young folks. (November 2, 1894)

I happened upon just two mentions of his survivors' names

after Beaumont's death in 1901. One was this advertisement, published among dozens of others on the front page of the *Gazette:*

> FOR SALE CHEAP—One dump cart, practically new, and one dog-cart and jumper nearly as good as new. Either or both can be had at a bargain. Mrs. A J Beaumont, St. Joseph. (April 21, 1905)

The other item was a review on the society page of a musical concert in which Beaumont's widow performed:

> The St. Joseph Dramatic Troupe entertained their friends Tuesday evening at the Masonic Hall. A large and enthusiastic audience attended [showing] their appreciation with frequent applause. . . . Miss Eva Caldwell and Mrs. Arthur Beaumont delighted the audience with several rare musical selections including "Schubert's Serenade." (April 1906)

After that—nothing, literally nothing, for years and years on microfilm. Beaumont's survivors essentially disappeared without a trace after 1906, in an age when few records existed that would provide a paper trail for U.S. citizens as they moved from place to place.

And so on that hot August afternoon in 1997, I focused on the year 1914, studying the *Gazette* as I had for so many other, earlier years, searching it page by page, column inch by column inch, my eyes scanning the glass screen for any clue in the advertisements or news and society pages. I turned the knob of the microfilm reader, watching closely as the events of June 1914 glided slowly by. As I wandered from day to day, history came alive. I saw several stories and news items in those weeks about "coons" and "the Nigger problem" that attested to the racial crudities of the day in Louisiana:

A few days ago a darkey named Beverley went into Dreyfus' store and reaching over the counter gently drew from it a pocket book containing $100. Immediately, Dreyfus missed it and accused Beverley of taking it. . . . Beverley, finding himself cornered, quietly drew the pocketbook from the back of his neck. The darkey was last seen in the company of the sheriff and will be invited to spend the next few years with Major James at his "training band" at Baton Rouge.

I passed on.

On June 26, 1914, the big news was about the arrival of U.S. troops in Veracruz, Mexico, where they had been dispatched by President Woodrow Wilson in response to a crisis between the two countries. "Pathetic Scenes in Vera Cruz," cried a headline over photographs showing Mexican refugee children receiving food from American soldiers. On page 3 of the same day's *Gazette* a compelling photograph showed two men and two women, dressed all in black, picketing on a sidewalk in New York City. The headline read, "Mourners in Front of Rockefeller's Office." The story detailed a labor strike in a Colorado mine owned by the widely hated industrialist John D. Rockefeller and the nationwide protests over his use of violence to quash it.

Amid all the stories were fabulous old advertisements for "wonder" cures like Lydia E. Pinkham's alcohol-laced elixir for "feminine troubles," for a new refreshment called Coca-Cola, which promised "vim" and "vigor" to all who drank it, and for the Edison Phonograph, described as a revolutionary new "sound producing machine." I loved looking at the ads, which seemed like vintage Madison Avenue antiques coming to life before my eyes. But as fascinating as they were, the displays were a diversion from my true task, and I tried my best to ignore them. I wandered on, page after page, scanning each line of type in the old newspaper—not sure of what I was looking for exactly and not even sure it existed.

Then suddenly it happened.

Scrolling through the issue of June 26, 1914, I saw something strikingly familiar out of the corner of my eye. I turned the knob gently to reverse the film. I thought I had seen the letters "BEAU . . ." in a small headline on page 12 with the local news.

The words and letters were maddeningly tiny in the *Gazette*, and the paper was so old and brittle that the film image couldn't reproduce the entire page. I had to keep fiddling with the enlargement and focus knobs to find what I thought I saw amid the splotches and blemishes left in the newspaper by time.

There it was again. "BEAU . . ."

I enlarged the item so that it filled the entire screen and adjusted the focus. I wasn't mistaken.

DEATH OF MRS. A.J. BEAUMONT

Last week we inadvertently omitted mentioning the death of Mrs. Mary Ann Beaumont, relic of the late A.J. Beaumont, who was for so many years a resident of St. Joseph.

Mrs. Beaumont at the time of her death was living with her son, Mr. Arthur W. Beaumont, at Vicksburg.

Mrs. Beaumont was a good Christian lady who bore ill will to no one and was always a faithful, loving wife and affectionate mother. Together with her husband she lived in St. Joseph many years, including in her list of friends her every acquaintance in our town, and after the death of Mr. Beaumont in 1900 [*sic*] she made her home in Vicksburg, where her son had employment and has since continuously resided.

Mrs. Beaumont was a faithful and consistent member of the

Catholic Church and died in full communion with that Ancient Faith. Her remains were taken to Natchez for interment. The many friends in this parish extend her son deepest sympathy in his bereavement.

I read the article several times closely, then pressed the "copy" button to try to capture a printed image of the story. A moment later I pulled the warm sheet of paper out of the machine, the story somehow feeling more real and believable as I held it in my hands. I noted the mistake in the date of A.J.'s death and smiled inwardly at the article's stuffy Old World language, particularly the reference to Mrs. Beaumont as a "relic."

As I read the word "Natchez," so many memories about my search came to mind. I remembered receiving from the St. Joseph public library a few years earlier a listing of headstones in the historic Natchez City Cemetery and finding A.J.'s and Mary Ann's names in the lists. I remembered reading about the tradition in those days for white people to be buried in Natchez, about sixty miles south of St. Joseph, since the city was located high on a bluff and not prone to flooding from the Mississippi River like so many other Delta towns.

But it was another word in the small newspaper story that stood out as brightly as a beacon from all the rest. I heard myself read the word aloud, the sound soaring into my mind like a trumpet note, echoing over and over.

Vicksburg.

The family had moved to Vicksburg, the storied old city located just north and across the river from St. Joseph in Mississippi.

I felt a new surge of energy and returned to work. I looked at the screen some more to scan other stories and ads near Mary

Ann Beaumont's obituary, which was near the bottom of the page. One ad touted a surefire rheumatism cure called "rub-my-tism." It was next to an official Louisiana state notice of a forthcoming exam for teachers' certificates.

I enlarged the image on the glass screen to look at each page in quadrants. The story of Mrs. Beaumont's death was in the lower left quadrant of the local news page amid a host of other short social items.

> Mr. and Mrs. Carneal reached home Monday after spending several days visiting friends in New Orleans. . . .

> Mr. and Mrs. Salvador Baragoan are receiving congratulations on the coming of another baby-girl. This now gives Salvador five queens and one king. . . .

I scanned up and down the page before heading to a new page of local news and on to another. Then, almost instantly, my eyes were grabbed by an item on page 6. I saw the letters "Beau . . ." again and felt the same sudden jolt of excitement that had filled me just moments before. The item rested amid a series of local announcements, sandwiched between an ad for an anthrax vaccine and another announcing an upcoming St. Joseph school board meeting. It stated simply:

> Mr. and Mrs. Arthur Beaumont and little daughter are visitors to St. Joseph this week.

I read the sentence several times more, admiring each word as if it were a pearl in a long necklace. I finally had the piece of evidence, the illusive footprint in time that I had been searching for. In 1914 A.J. Beaumont's surviving son, also named Arthur, had a child. I had advanced the white family's story by a generation.

It was then that I realized that my odds of bringing Beaumont's white family story forward from his arrival in America in 1856 to today had increased from the nearly impossible to the feasible in the short span of several minutes. Perhaps I really could accomplish what I had wanted all along in my research, to compare my black family's history over the past 150 years with that of our white cousins.

I couldn't believe my luck. After a long spell of frustration I had picked up their trail.

A couple of hours later I packed up my notes, the photocopies, and the reels of microfilm and headed out to my car, my brain filling with questions, my heart still throbbing with excitement. I switched off the Giants baseball game on the radio as I merged with traffic on Covell Boulevard to travel home on the outskirts of Davis. I headed west in the direction of California's coastal range, which glowed purple and blue on the horizon in the radiant late afternoon sky.

Think, I told myself as I drove, feeling a nervousness in my fingertips as I held the steering wheel.

Think.

A.J. Beaumont's son was still a young man in 1914—just twenty-nine. What if he had had other children later, maybe even a son or two? They could certainly be alive somewhere in America today, I conjectured, and perhaps even the name Beaumont had lived on. Somewhere. Maybe.

If so, that would certainly make the search easier.

I made a left turn at the Circle K store onto Lake Boulevard, heading south toward my house, and soon a series of familiar imaginary scenes started playing in my head, the same fantasies that had both fueled and haunted my search from the start, the ones in which I envisioned myself meeting the living white descendants of A.J. Beaumont in the flesh.

The scenes invariably transported me from the here and now to some other reality, a different sort of consciousness. My body certainly was driving my old blue sports car that afternoon, but my mind was being swept far away, under a crazy momentum all its own.

These mental images were always the same. I saw myself calling a phone number I had gotten from a phone book or information operator in some town or city in America. I saw myself dialing it and feeling my stomach tighten as it rang.

"Hi," I would say, after a voice finally answered. "Is this the Beaumont residence?" I would introduce myself, then say, "You're not going to believe this, but . . ." And then I would tell the voice the long story about my work and the relationship between my family and his.

I would tell the voice I was a writer and now a teacher of journalism at the University of California, Berkeley. I would say that I was calling because I hoped to tell a story about America in the parallel lives of our families, to write a book about race relations, about how some things have changed and how other things have stayed the same through the long years our families have lived in our country.

The voice in these scenes would sound stunned, startled, nearly speechless. On my bad days I would imagine the Beaumont descendant not believing a word of what I had to say to him. But on my good days my imagination would be more forgiving and I would sense understanding, or at least intrigue, on the other end of the line. The voice would tell me "Sure" in my imagination, "of course" I could come visit his house to ask questions about his family, his ancestors, and their lives over the past century.

The next thing I knew I would find myself flying to some town or city in America. I would rent a car and find the house I was looking for by studying a city street map or asking strangers on street corners for directions, as I had done so often when hunting down news stories around the world.

I would park in front of the white family's house, walk up the path, and knock on the door. In my imagination the wooden door with its leaded glass window was eerily like so many front doors I remembered from all the houses in the white neighborhood I grew up in.

When the door opened, I would see the white Beaumont descendant in person, finally, after all the years of searching. I would smile, extend my hand, and shake his. Then I would be invited into the white stranger's house, as I had been invited into strangers' houses in many other places for my work. I would enter bearing copies of Arthur Beaumont's photo and Laura's and Pearl's, along with copies of his obituary, the letter he wrote to Pearl in 1901 before he died, and copies of other material I had acquired over the years. I would take a seat on a comfortable sofa and glance around the living room as the white Beaumont family members examined in amazement what I had brought.

The living room would be like any other in America on a weekend afternoon: a football game playing on a television set near a fireplace where several logs were burning. Above the mantle would hang family photographs of smiling husband and wife and three or four cheerful children. On another wall, near a picture window, I would spot other photographs, much older ones, brown with age, of Beaumont ancestors dating back more than a century.

At this part of my imaginary scene, I would rise from the sofa to get a closer look at a photo near the center of the collection. I would feel my heart race as I recognized it, the very same photograph of the English immigrant and Confederate war veteran that had lasted an entire century in my family, the one he mailed in 1901 to my great-grandmother in St. Louis. It would be the final bit of proof I needed.

The scene played on as I drove home that afternoon, my mind still racing at breakneck speed.

I would return to the sofa and take out my notebook and pen from my jacket pocket and get to work. I would start interviewing my subjects just as I had interviewed countless sources for my newspaper stories. I would try to make them feel at ease with me and wouldn't interrupt them as they spoke. But I would be persistent in my questioning as I gently guided the conversation.

"Did you know anything about this? Did anyone in the family ever talk about it? What did your ancestors remember about A.J. Beaumont?

"What do you do for a living? Where were you born? Who were your parents and what did they do? What did they dream? What kinds of lives did they want you to have? Which dreams did your ancestors realize in America and which were dashed?

"Yes, I would love to have some coffee, thanks."

I would get an array of answers:

"No, we never knew anything about this. Had no idea! It's amazing, simply fantastic! So this makes us related, I guess. . . ."

"Well, very distantly," I would say, feeling a vague uneasiness.

"Oh, we've been many things in our family over the twentieth century, Mr. Henry. Yes, we have. Steel fitter, prison inmate, Ku Klux Klan member, Communist, and priest; circuit court judge, baseball player, beauty queen, and vagrant; social worker, army veteran, schoolteacher, con artist. Methodist, Democrat, PTA member, Mason.

"We've wanted our kids to live better than we did. Don't all Americans believe in that? Our dreams are the same dreams the country over. . . ."

Eventually I would get around to the questions I cared about most, the ones about race and bigotry in America that had driven me all along in my research. And I would feel an old welter of emotions—rage, hurt, sorrow—begin to rise inside me.

Did you ever feel anything deep inside, as our family surely did, about the great events and seminal figures in our nation's racial and social history over all these years?

What did you white people think about the Scottsboro Boys and Paul Robeson, W.E.B. Du Bois, and Martin Luther King, Jr.? What did you feel about George Wallace and Malcolm X, about the integration of baseball and the army? Where did you stand on affirmative action? How did your ancestors feel about Plessy v Ferguson *and* Brown v the Board of Education?

While my family was struggling to make its way in America over these many decades in the face of racial prejudice and discrimination, from Nashville and St. Louis to Seattle in the far Northwest, where did you, our white cousins, stand?

Are you people any different today? Are you any different from the way I imagine your bigoted white ancestors were so long ago when Laura and Pearl left Louisiana to make a new life for themselves in St. Louis?

CHAPTER TWO

Road Maps

I pulled into my garage in Davis that afternoon and entered our house through the kitchen door, carrying my notebooks, artifacts, and microfilms in my black canvas shoulder bag, feeling enveloped by the harsh, penetrating heat of the desert evening. It was late when I stepped into the kitchen, nearly 6 P.M., so I immediately began to cook dinner for my wife, Letitia, and our five-year-old daughter, Zoë, filling a big iron pot with water to cook pasta, then chopping onions and garlic to go along with a few links of Italian sausage. I still felt exhilarated by my discovery in the *Tensas Gazette* a few hours earlier, but my excitement was now tempered with some uncertainty and anxiety as I pondered the possibilities. What if I did find this white family? Could I ever gather the nerve to meet them and talk to them?

I went outside to pick some tomatoes for salad from our small garden in the backyard, where we had also planted zucchini, watermelon, basil, parsley, and a variety of peppers. Amid them all was a stand of gorgeous yellow sunflowers, sturdy, straight, and tall, where my daughter loved to play hide-and-seek with her friends. The garden was a splendid sight, rich with life and glowing with color and greenery in the desert heat. I heard blue jays squawking and sparrows chirping near our rooftop, gazed at the white butterflies dancing amid the tomato plants pregnant with fruit, and I took a deep breath, longing to capture forever the magical moment in my mind's eye. Such beauty, such peace, I thought, right in my own backyard.

I loved Davis and the Sacramento Valley, especially at that time of year, and felt thankful that Letitia and I had decided to make the town of 54,905 our home. I even had grown to love the dry heat, which often soared above 100 degrees for days at a time in the summer. I had first moved to Davis late in 1991, after finishing my tour of duty in Nairobi, Kenya, as my newspaper's Africa Bureau chief. Letitia was then earning her Ph.D. in political science at the University of California's campus in Davis, and I joined her there after getting an appointment as a visiting lecturer for a semester at Berkeley's Graduate School of Journalism. I took a leave of absence from the newspaper, and when my Berkeley appointment turned into a full-time faculty position later that year, I quit the *Post* for good. It was time. I had put in fifteen years in daily journalism and needed to make a change for the sake of my personal life. I wanted to start a family and have the time to see it grow, a luxury I couldn't easily enjoy while chasing news stories around the world.

Letitia and I thought about moving closer to Berkeley, an hour's commute west on Interstate 80, but by then Davis had curiously grown on me. It had the comfortable size and feel of a small town, with an easy, gentle pace of life (fittingly, the official logo was a bicycle, a favored mode of transportation). It was the kind of town where smiling strangers said hello to each other on the sidewalks and jogging trails and where residents and grocery salesclerks knew each other by their first names. Davis was the first place I lived as an adult that remotely resembled the Seattle of my childhood in that way.

The city possessed a comparatively affluent, highly educated, and tolerant population whose professional lives centered around nearby Sacramento, the state capital, and the well-regarded local university. Their political attitudes were generally progressive. For many years the local representative from the Davis and Yolo County area was Democrat Vic Fazio, one of the most liberal members of Congress. It was indeed an eccentric little city, whose officials once proved their environmental sensitivity by authorizing $13,000 to build a special tunnel under a local highway to protect endangered toads and once enforced a local noise ordinance by citing a woman for snoring too loudly in her apartment. The city council at one point voted to change the name of a local street called Sutter Place, after being aroused to indignation by allegations that its namesake, California pioneer John A. Sutter, was an immoral "sexual predator" and enslaver of Indians. But the council eventually backed off, partly because it realized there were many other streets in town, such as Conquistador Drive, with similarly questionable origins, and that the expense and endless political arguments sure to follow such changes might not be worth the bother.

If there was any form of political feeling in town that might be considered extreme, it had to do with abuses committed against animals and vegetables rather than people. Animal rights groups, for example, regularly protested outside the UC Davis science research facilities, with the more radical groups sometimes expressing their outrage over the treatment of monkeys and rodents used in research by pouring blood and other debris on the driveways leading into the premises. The temporary mayhem and the police arrests that followed such acts were sort of an annual rite that citizens in Davis had grown used to. In the late 1990s, when stunning advances in biotechnology and agricultural engineering were made at research institutions like UC Davis, protestors found new reason for outrage, sensing conspiracies by scientists and multinational corporations to redo the planet's genetic makeup to the detriment of humanity and all flora and fauna. A group calling itself "Reclaim the Seeds" claimed responsibility for destroying a UC Davis research field full of genetically altered vegetables one night, pulling up each and every plant by its roots.

Such idealistic naïveté occasionally brought national attention to the town. Arch-conservative commentator Rush Limbaugh—who got his start in talk radio in nearby Sacramento in the late 1980s—sneeringly dubbed it "The People's Republic of Davis." Davis's population was about 4 percent black, 8 percent Latino, and 13 percent Asian, but the city's largely white heart was often in the right place when it came to issues like diversity and human rights. Admittedly, Davis suffered very little in the way of homelessness, violent crime, joblessness, and other ills plaguing bigger cities. People in Davis could afford to be proudly liberal by nature and tolerant of human differences largely because they didn't have very many significant differences to tolerate.

Still, I enjoyed Davis despite its provinciality and often precisely because of it. I enjoyed playing softball and golf and fishing with pals I had made in town. I enjoyed pedaling with Letitia and Zoë on the bike paths leading along Putah Creek toward Lake Berryessa to the west. And I loved jogging through the groves of olive trees and ancient valley oaks and the abundant tomato and corn fields that surrounded the city in the lazy summers. Davis was a tranquil place, where I didn't worry if I forgot to lock my door or left my windows open at night. It might seem plain, but it was conducive to reflection and raising my family. I found time and space there to think and to live.

After many years as a nomad, living in places from New York City to Nairobi, I was tired of packing up and moving every couple of years. The Sacramento Valley was where I landed at thirty-eight and finally decided to make a home, a place to call my own despite its flaws and quirks. The long commute to work was difficult but worthwhile for two chief reasons: housing in Davis was eminently more affordable than the depressingly overpriced Bay Area and—most important—the city's public school system was recognized as among the finest in the state. I realized that in putting our daughter's public school education first Letitia and I were making lifestyle trade-offs not unlike the difficult ones my parents made for similar reasons a generation earlier in Seattle.

Sometimes life's realities struck home in Davis, shattering my sense of calm and triggering a deep-seated rage over prejudice and racial ignorance that often scared me. One day a black father who lived in my neighborhood decided to teach his two teenaged children how to drive a stick-shift car in a large abandoned parking lot just outside town. The lot was located on the grounds of a hospital that had recently closed and relocated elsewhere, but inside the building several employees were still at work. One of them noticed the car and its black occupants driving awkwardly in the lot and telephoned the county police in fright, thinking the father and his children were going to rob the premises. Within minutes three squad cars sped to the scene. The white officers surrounded the car and at gunpoint ordered the occupants out. The father and children were badly shaken by the incident, which aroused great regret and breast-beating about injustice in the community. To me it confirmed what I and other blacks and Latinos in Davis had known all along: the reality behind that old acronym DWBOB—Driving While Black or Brown—was something the liberal, self-satisfied white community knew nothing about.

Many whites in Davis did not even realize the depth of their own ignorance or prejudice. To my never-ending anger and stupefaction, the local newspaper, the *Davis Enterprise*, occasionally confirmed this. One evening, for example, the newspaper prominently featured a news story about an attempted kidnapping downtown. The paper's crime reporter soberly wrote that the suspect in the case, who had fled the scene, was not "the typical suspicious-looking sort by usual police standards. He was a white male adult . . . [and] had no noticeable accent."

Here my small hometown newspaper was doing its naive and racially ignorant best to caution my comfortable white neighbors about the dangers presented by people who didn't "look" or "speak" like them, in an article that was deeply insulting to me and my family. The worst part was that the newspaper didn't realize the offense it was blithely committing, the racial prejudice it was condoning and perpetuating, until I and several other Davis readers angrily demanded an apology in writing.

At the same time deep down my anger was exacerbated, I knew, by the tormenting statistics that black people were in-

volved in crime—and suffered as victims of crime—at a higher
rate than any other group in America. My unspoken frustration
and outrage over black crime were almost as profound as my spoken anger over white stereotypes about us. It was easy for white
people to perpetuate a godawful stereotype, after all, when examples of black crime abounded. And I knew, to my inner guilt,
that one reason I had chosen to raise my family in Davis was that
the city was so tranquil and safe, unlike other urban areas I had
lived in previously, including the inner cities of Washington and
Baltimore. There life had never been completely secure, and I
often lived as if under siege, behind barred windows and triple-
locked doors and beneath the piercing nighttime glare of police
helicopter searchlights. On the one hand, I wanted my daughter
to grow up with an open mind about life and people and their
many wondrous varieties. On the other hand, I wanted her safe
from the world's many dangers, dangers that so many other black
children in America's inner cities had to face every day.

My love-hate relationship with my adopted hometown often
manifested itself so suddenly, without warning, that it was hard
to prepare myself for the occasional shock to my equilibrium. I
remember October 3, 1995, the day the Los Angeles County
Superior Court jury rendered its verdict in the O.J. Simpson
murder case. I watched the verdict that morning on television at
my house and was stunned by the predominantly black jury's not
guilty decision. Hadn't they seen the same mountain of evidence
that millions of others had seen in the televised trial—the bloody
footprints, the history of spousal abuse, and other incriminating
records against Simpson? Contrary to the view that the news
media frequently presented, that blacks in America were a mono-
lith of agreement that Simpson was innocent, some of us felt that

he was guilty and shared in the outrage that broke out across the land over a perceived miscarriage of justice. A few minutes after the verdict, however, I went with Zoë to a shopping center in Davis, to purchase a bag of doughnuts. It was there that I began to sense something else, something strange and unnerving in the wake of the verdict. I noticed it most clearly in the faces of the white strangers I ran across that morning, inside the doughnut shop and in the walkway outside. A small group of UC Davis students, an elderly couple, a trio of young women—all almost uniformly cast sharp, sudden glances my way before quickly averting their eyes, dismay and outrage at the verdict still etched on their faces. I felt as if I had stumbled into a gathering where I was obviously not welcome. Conversations seemed to cease or at least become much more muted in my presence. It was as if in me, the only black man in the vicinity, my white fellow citizens suddenly saw the living incarnation of the injustice they had witnessed only moments before on national television. It was as if a black jury member or O.J. Simpson himself were in the doughnut shop, not me. Because I was black, I must somehow have been a party to all that was horribly wrong in the Simpson saga.

Whether this was in fact how these white people felt, I cannot be sure. No words were spoken. But certainly there was a telltale tension in the air. And I knew that racism and bigotry often manifested themselves in public in the stony, awkward wordlessness of silence. It was a cold and eerie feeling, one that stayed with me during the emotional weeks that followed and soon tempered my outrage over the verdict itself. Indeed, after that experience in the doughnut shop with Zoë, a part of me naturally began to ponder the many godawful miscarriages of justice against black victims of white violence in our history, reflections that helped me conclude bitterly at times, "An eye for an eye . . ."

It was racism in Davis, and the city's continued reluctance to recognize its hallmarks, that prompted me to chat with a woman named Tansey Thomas, a black longtime Davisite who served on the city's human relations commission. We were discussing an incident that Letitia had witnessed in the city's community park one day, in which a group of seven-year-olds in a summer city program were playing a chase game. Two black boys were playing with about a half-dozen white girls in the game, in which the black boys were dubbed "monkey" and "gorilla" while chasing the squealing girls. The boys called themselves these names, and so did the girls. All of this happened under the supervision of white city recreation workers. Letitia was so outraged by the blatant racial overtones of the game that she wrote a letter to the newspaper to complain about it. Her letter soon triggered another angry letter to the paper, from one of the white girls' parents, who said Letitia didn't know what she was talking about, that the game wasn't racist at all, largely because the black boys "had created the game" themselves. This troubling aftermath reflected a breathtaking ignorance about race and racism on the part of the white parent as well as the city— which seemed perfectly willing to assume that two seven-year-old black boys had a better understanding of the rudiments of racism than adults of any color did. I was so disturbed that I brought the matter to the attention of the city council. It was then that Thomas contacted me.

"It's especially hard in a town like Davis for black boys," she said. "I raised a boy here. It's always like they're the ones who are the scary outsiders and 'bogeymen' in these children's games. It seems perfectly innocent at first, especially to white kids and white parents, but the repercussions can be pretty severe in the long run." Thomas told me about the problems her child had encountered in a Davis elementary school, where he was one of only a few black boys and often came home complaining about being called names, including "nigger."

Thomas said she had complained to teachers and administrators but was told that her son was too "sensitive" in his play with other children. Someone suggested that he should just ignore the name calling and the kids would eventually stop. "Besides, they're only words," this person added. Thomas told her son he could not hit others for calling him names, but he could use words to fight back. So her son did just that, using the one slur he hated most to hurt his tormentors back: nigger.

"Pretty soon he was calling everybody who bothered him nigger, unbeknownst to me," Thomas said, chuckling softly at the memory, "no matter what they looked like, no matter how white." A few weeks later Thomas heard a knock on her door. Opening it, she found a distraught white mother with her little boy, who pleaded with Thomas to tell her son to stop calling the white boy names.

"It was the most amazing thing that ever happened in my life," Thomas recalled. "Here on my doorstep was the mother of a blond, blue-eyed boy begging me to have my boy stop calling him nigger." She said her son had learned that white people were not that much different than he was, for they, too, hated to be called names. But, as Thomas pointed out, the incident also showed the extraordinary, sometimes ridiculous lengths to which you sometimes had to go in order to force a largely white, affluent, "progressive" community to wake up to its intolerance and prejudice.

Not surprisingly, my deepest fury erupted whenever such cases of mind-boggling racial ignorance involved my daughter, even remotely. She was born on a warm September night in 1992 in a small county hospital in the nearby town of Woodland. (Letitia and I named her Zoë because the name's classical meaning in Greek, "life," seemed so simple and joyous to us.) From that moment my existence became a whirlwind of bottle feedings, diaper changes, soccer games, ballet lessons, singing recitals—all the scenes and sideshows that make up the crazed theater of child-rearing. It was a joyous transformation of my life that I happily embraced.

But into this new life came episodes that confirmed with startling clarity the endurance of racial ignorance in America. I sometimes was driven to despair over the realization that my little girl would have to struggle with it as all of us had, in one way or another, from the beginning of slavery on this continent. Far from ending after one generation's long fight, such ignorance continued, festering like some kind of bacteria, from one generation to the next.

When my daughter was three, I remember, I called a local preschool, the Davis Parent Nursery School, to see about enrolling her because a few friends of ours had recommended it. One of the questions I asked the school official who answered the telephone had to do with the ethnic and racial diversity of the kids. She answered that the school was largely white, "unfortunately."

"We sure would like to have more black and Hispanic kids," she told me, "but it's hard. Our kids generally come from two-parent households, you know." For hours I darkly ruminated over her comment. What was she really saying? Obviously, she assumed that black and Hispanic families weren't normally blessed with both a mother and a father, like the white families in Davis. And this belief gave her a "reason" for saying it was difficult to mesh "different" cultures in one school. Whatever her nutty and uninformed point, I stewed over it in frustration and sadness.

Some months later, while Zoë was attending a different preschool, the white teacher asked the kids in her class, who were mostly white, to cut out magazine pictures that looked like their parents to make a collage of their families. It was an innocent enough project. But in the magazines the teacher chose to pass out there was not one black or Asian or Latino face. The minority children had to construct their families using all-white faces. The next morning, after hearing about the incident from Letitia, I stormed into the school to confront the teacher. I was probably more stunned than she was by the hot anger I heard in my voice.

There were, of course, mundane incidents with vaguely racial overtones that cropped up in our everyday life in Davis—just as they crop up in the lives of black people all over America. Like the morning Zoë and I went to a Blockbuster video store downtown. As soon as we entered the door, the white saleswoman made sure to ask for my book bag for security reasons. I glanced around the store and spotted a middle-aged white man in clear view of us, browsing freely with a big paper shopping bag in his hand. I pointed my finger at him, then heard myself curse at the store clerk and call her a bigot as I felt blood rush to my face in sudden rage. I was stunned at how unnerved I had become, instantly ashamed that I had sworn at the baffled white clerk.

Zoë, who was five then, had absolutely no idea why I was so livid. She had no idea why I grabbed her hand abruptly or why we left the store so briskly without getting the Bugs Bunny tape I had promised her. And I found I couldn't really explain it to her when I returned to the car. Or at least I didn't know how to begin, what words to use.

Even the most seemingly trivial incidents could drive me to distraction in those days. Once Letitia told me that a blond-haired girl in Zoë's class had informed Zoë, innocently enough, that she was black and would stay black "even when you're grown up." The girl's words didn't bother Zoë in the least, nor did they bother Letitia. But I dwelled on the incident for days, turning it over in my mind to look at it from every conceivable angle, wondering if there was some ulterior meaning and, if so, what the girl's parents had done to educate their child about the significance and meaning of skin color. I felt weak, powerless, no longer able to just accept some things and let them slide, as I had done so often in the past. It was as if in approaching middle age, as I continued with my search for the white family on the other side of my genealogical tree, a Pandora's box periodically opened up inside me, spilling out demons left and right.

I saw these race demons increasingly in my daily scanning of popular culture too, and wondered at times if I was losing my mind. Were the demons dancing only for me? In my obsession I began to keep a running tally of the number of times famous and accomplished black people were referred to by their first names in newspaper and magazine headlines and on television. Within weeks my list filled a small notebook.

Why were Steven Spielberg and George Lucas always "Spielberg" and "Lucas" in the press, I wondered, while Spike Lee was often simply "Spike"?

Was it mere happenstance that actors like Richard Gere, Tom Cruise, and Bruce Willis were always "Cruise," "Gere," and "Willis" and Denzel Washington nearly always "Denzel"?

Why did headline writers and television commentators often refer to white political figures such as Bob Dole, Jerry Falwell, and George Bush by their last names, yet feel perfectly free to refer to Jesse Jackson as "Jesse" and San Francisco's Mayor Willie Brown simply as "Willie"?

It was the sports world that presented the most glaring and frequent examples of such incongruity. The surnames of white superstars appeared in sports page headlines and on magazine covers, and television and radio announcers uttered their names reverently on the air—Marino, Gretzky, Clemens, Bird, and Elway, for example. Black star athletes were more likely to be mentioned informally by their given names or nicknames in print and on the air—Deion, Michael, Keyshawn, Reggie, Shaq, Magic, Rickey, Latrell, Ozzie, Charles, and Bo among them—as if little more identification were necessary or even pertinent or merited.

A sane mind, I figured, would be capable of accepting such evidently innocuous cultural conventions and move on, especially since such conventions seemed to bother so few others, including the black personalities themselves. Besides, these black celebrities, among them the women known to the multitudes simply as Oprah and Whoopi, were earning far more fame and money every year than most white people could dream of. What was the big deal?

But the more I thought about it and the longer my cultural

tallies grew each day (based chiefly on local papers like the abysmally provincial *San Francisco Chronicle* and local television news stations), the more despairing and obsessed I became. The not-so-subliminal message seemed to be that white Americans owned surnames worth respecting and honoring—sure evidence, in short, of roots, of identity, of a birthright and valued past. Black people, by contrast, no matter our level of achievement, could expect to be treated in a far more condescending and informal fashion in popular culture, as if our status were on a par with children, say, or household help—because by definition the last names of black Americans didn't really count, at least to white America.

Indeed, it wasn't much of a mental stretch to recognize in such modern cultural conventions a peculiarly enduring legacy of nineteenth-century antebellum America, when white slaveowners commonly forbade blacks their rights to surnames in order to discourage them from feeling connected as families and to facilitate their sale and separation. In this sense, demeaning first-name-only references in popular white American culture were not too far removed in spirit from the age of the plantation, of Aunt Jemima and Uncle Ben. At least that's how my tormented mind increasingly began to see it.

Sometimes late at night, when I couldn't sleep, I found myself wondering if my mother and father had felt the same things I did now when they were entering their own middle age in Seattle in the 1960s and reassessing their lives. Did they feel the same simultaneous sense of African Americans' progress and deep disappointment over lingering racism as I did? Did they ever wonder how many generations had to pass before such latent and blatant prejudice was finally wiped away? Why would my daughter likely have to contend with the same old hurt and struggle, the same maddening inexplicability of race?

I picked a handful of basil leaves from my backyard garden, taking a moment to inhale the herb's sweet odor as it mixed with the perfume of Letitia's climbing white roses. I then plucked a half-dozen plum tomatoes from a vine, cradling the produce gently in my hands, and returned to the kitchen screen door, which I opened with my foot. I re-entered the kitchen, placed the tomatoes on the countertop, and began to wash the basil. Letitia was getting a drink of cranberry juice from the fridge for Zoë, who was down the hall in the living room, lying on the floor on her stomach and cradling her head in her hands as she watched her *Pocahontas* video.

"Pasta okay?" I asked.

"Sure," Letitia said softly, swiping a lock of her dark brown hair from her forehead as she poured the juice in a cup. She looked tired and emotionally frazzled after a long, sweltering day of watching Zoë and obviously wasn't in the mood for talking. It was so unbearably hot and everyone was so tired.

But I just had to tell her what I had discovered in the library. I had to share my excitement over finally making progress in my work, which had been proceeding at such a glacial pace.

I rinsed the tomatoes in the kitchen sink, then took a sharp knife and began to cut the red fruit lengthwise on my cutting board, placing the sweet, juicy slices atop thin wafers of fresh mozzarella. On top of the salad I would sprinkle chopped basil, salt, and pepper, then olive oil. It was Letitia's favorite summer repast, and I loved making it for her.

"I think I had a little breakthrough," I said as I watched Letitia sip a drink of water.

My wife looked at me without speaking, an invitation to go on. A cool and exacting academic with expertise in political theory and African economic development, she was often befuddled by the emotional fits and starts that accompanied nearly everything I touched in my work. But to my never-ending amazement Letitia was never-failing in her emotional support. She listened to me with supreme patience and for some reason had as much innate faith in what I was trying to do as I did.

Until I met Letitia at thirty-five, my experiences with the opposite sex had been nothing short of a tangled mess, a tempestuous jumble of false starts and ill-fated choices, all in a lush variety of shapes and hues. I was certainly an "integrated" black man in that sense, for as the product of racial integration and the new cultural liberties of the 1960s, I had felt free to enjoy the company of women from many different races and backgrounds. In my coming of age I did not feel in the least restricted, partly because of my naive belief that race didn't really matter when it came to the ways of the heart and partly because most of the girls I was around when my adolescent hormones began belatedly to stir were white. I simply didn't know many girls who were my color.

Still, at seventeen my first choice in love turned out to be the beautiful black daughter of a surgeon who had trained with my father at Meharry Medical College, a historic black school in Nashville, and, like my father, migrated to Seattle in 1956. Southerners by heritage, she and I had both grown up in the virgin world of the Pacific Northwest, though in different neighborhoods, and I was certain our lives were destined to be linked forever. When she broke off our two-year relationship during my first year at Princeton, I was crushed. Soon afterward she became betrothed to a white student she met at the University of Washington.

A few years later I fell madly in love with a woman I met in graduate school in New York City. Like me, she dreamed of becoming a famous journalist, inspired by the heroic stands of the press during Watergate and over the Pentagon Papers. Both of us were also filled with youthful wanderlust, dreaming of international travel. Also like me, she was short and rather slender, with very curly dark hair, dark brown eyes, and light brown skin. But unlike me, she was an orthodox Jew from a first-generation Syrian immigrant family in Brooklyn. Her family detested me for being both black and a gentile, in their eyes a pagan. Still, she and I were idealistic enough to try to make the relationship work. Love could conquer all, my hopelessly romantic heart figured. Despite my receiving numerous late-night phone calls from her brother in Brooklyn, in which he vowed to drive down Interstate 95 to Washington and gun me down if I persisted in seeing her, she and I decided to elope a couple of years after we met. We were married in a civil ceremony at the old state courthouse in Annapolis, Maryland. In the three years that followed, she would sometimes awake late at night and weep over missing her family, who didn't want much to do with her after the terrible sin she had committed. Whether her family actually pronounced her dead and sat *shiva*, the Jewish ceremony of mourning, I wasn't sure, but the effect was pretty much the same. After a few years my first marriage collapsed from its own emotional weight, the victim of many pressures and deceptions, not the least of which

derived from the wide divergence in our family, racial, and religious backgrounds. That breakup, too, was devastating.

I was certain I was fated to fail miserably in love, partly because I was such a cultural oddity, evidently born to straddle the
very complicated worlds of black and white people. Indeed, the
inner turmoil spurred by the breakup of my marriage in 1986 led
me to examine many other aspects of my life and emotional history. In the months after the rupture I was propelled into psy-
chotherapy, finding in the Connecticut Avenue office of a kind,
Harvard-trained black psychiatrist named Dr. Henry Edwards a
badly needed sanctuary where I could vent my deepest pains and
sorrows twice a week—a wailing wall for all my anger and frustration, much of which derived from race. Unlike so many other
black men in America, especially those who were impoverished
and arguably had far greater and more urgent cause to feel alien-
ated and adrift, I was fortunate, as an employee of a rich American corporation, to enjoy generous medical insurance that paid
for my treatment. The many months of turbulent sessions with
my insightful and intelligent black doctor certainly helped
smooth the rough edges of my emotional upheaval.

I remember that year of the breakup, 1986, as one of intense
inner despair personally. But paradoxically, it was also a year of
growth and success professionally. I was the only black reporter
on the *Post*'s prestigious National Staff and traveled to the far
corners of America in pursuit of fascinating stories, from as-
tronomers' discoveries at Kitt Peak National Observatory in
Arizona to the heroic efforts of public health nurses in rural
Mississippi to reverse trends in infant mortality. And it was a year
of many women in my private life, women from differing backgrounds and walks of life. How I feasted at the table of delights

of the opposite sex that year, finding myself gravitating toward women who, like me, were somewhat outside the social and cultural norms. In the ashes of my first marriage I aimlessly (and often comedically) drifted from one relationship to another in Washington and elsewhere, like a sailor with a defective rudder.

Few of these relationships worked, but all the women were certainly fascinating for their sheer range of personality and ethnic diversity. One was a blue-eyed Swedish news broadcaster with long blond hair who once modeled blue jeans in Stockholm and cooked terrific meatballs and pasta. I met her on the subway coming home from work one rainy night and offered her the use of my umbrella when we disembarked at the Eastern Market station. In truth, I was simply dazzled by her beauty. But I broke up with her some months later when I realized we didn't have a great deal to talk about, her understanding of race and racism in America in particular being very limited. Another brief affair was with a fiery half-Chinese, half-Filipino woman from Manila, a legislative assistant I met at a party on Capitol Hill one night. Just one week later, on a whim, I found myself traveling to France with her for a vacation. That relationship ended almost as quickly as it began, like a Roman candle fizzling in air. I went out briefly with a pretty and very talented black jazz singer who specialized in crooning the blues in smoky clubs and at Smithsonian museum recitals. Later I dated an accomplished young black newswoman with whom I enjoyed talking late into the night about writing and reporting. But that relationship, too, quickly failed because her assertiveness, which had served her well in the daunting climb up the ranks of her magazine's newsroom, had a brashness I wasn't used to.

I found myself going in and out of quite a few such relationships, most fairly brief and fraught with weird disconnects, cultural divides, and communication gaps. A number were slapstick comedies like something out of a Marx Brothers movie. I was a very active and adventuresome (though somewhat reluctant) bachelor during those chaotic years after my first marriage and, in retrospect, a pretty hapless and lost one too, a bit out of my element and depth.

Then, one night in January 1989, I met Letitia. I was at a conference in Lusaka, Zambia, where I had traveled to prepare for my posting in Africa. There she was, standing in a long black dress with her arms folded in the middle of a cocktail party crowd. She was a tall woman with short dark hair and a pretty face. I was certain I had seen her somewhere before, but I wasn't sure where.

"We've met," I blurted out innocently enough as I strolled up to her, a pensive look on my face and a drink in my hand.

"Oh yeah?" she said somewhat skeptically. "Where?"

I was serious, but she thought my line was a come-on.

We both started laughing sheepishly over the cliché and later went for drinks, where I learned she was an Africa scholar working for a nonprofit agency in Washington, D.C., that informed Congress about African issues. Educated at Smith College and Columbia University, Letitia was extremely bright and knowledgeable about Africa. She cared about the continent with a passion that was infectious, and over the next few weeks, back in Washington, helped educate me about my upcoming assignment overseas. In a sense, I violated a cardinal rule of journalism: "Never ever get involved romantically with a source," I warn my students at Berkeley. But I fell in love with Letitia.

A child of poverty raised by a single mother, Letitia grew up understanding nearly as much, if not more, about the black experience in America as I did, an improbable circumstance, given that she was white, of Hungarian, Swedish, and other European ancestry. She spent part of her childhood in the 1960s as one of only a few white kids in the black, low-income Anacostia section of southeastern Washington, D.C. Indeed, her background was almost the mirror opposite of mine. Her teachers, neighbors, school pals—all were black. She was even baptized, at eight, in a pool of righteous water one Sunday morning at a black evangelical church.

Letitia knew about the sting of racism too, on a gut level that jibed closely with mine and helped cement our devotion to each other early on. While I understood prejudice from a black middle-class perspective, Letitia had experienced its more blatant, white working-class form when she was child.

Once, while traveling to visit relatives in West Virginia, her mother and a black male companion were stranded on a desolate rural road when their car broke down. Car after car sped by on the lonely highway without assisting them, as Letitia, then a little girl, stood nearby. One car driven by a white fellow did slow to help, but when he noticed the black man with Letitia and her mother he scowled and sped off. Hours later a kind, elderly black man in a dilapidated pickup truck finally stopped and rescued them.

"You remember this," Letitia's mother had told her, tears of shame and rage filling her eyes. "You remember who it was who didn't bother to help us and who it was who did."

Letitia despised racism and never forgot all the other episodes of petty cruelty and ugliness she experienced growing up with poor whites in West Virginia, blacks in Washington, D.C., and Latinos in south-central Los Angeles. Her intelligence awed me

as much as her sensitivity to and simple understanding of prejudice and the complexity of human existence. Still, she and I often
laughed over her first impression of me. Assessing my brown
skin, my mustache, and my curly hair that starry night in Zambia
when we met, she thought at first that I was Cuban, then Puerto
Rican. It was almost by a process of elimination that a day or two
later she deduced I was African American.

Her reaction was one I often got from strangers in my travels
in America and around the world, who at first glance would appear perplexed about my racial origins. In college a friend once
described me as a "universal ethnic," suggesting I could pass for
practically anything if I wanted to. It turned out to be oddly true,
often to my amusement. In Athens, Greeks asked me for directions on the street, thinking I was one of them. Same thing in
Mérida and Mexico City with Mexicans, and in Managua with
Nicaraguans. From Asmara to Kingston, I received similar
friendly responses from East Indians, Eritreans, Ethiopians, and
other darker-skinned people who thought I was one of them. But
in Uganda, in East Africa, the initial reaction of some strangers
was strikingly different. Because interracial relationships between
Africans and immigrants from India and Pakistan were traditionally reviled by Ugandans, who had killed and evicted thousands
of Asian immigrants under the reign of Idi Amin in the 1970s, I
was viewed quite contemptuously by strangers in Kampala who
thought I was a "half-half" before realizing I was an American. In
their eyes, a brown-skinned, curly-haired "half-half" like me was
little more than a mongrel, a half-breed sullying Ugandan national pride and ethnic identity.

In America when I met a white stranger for the first time, either socially or during interviews in my work, my appearance

would often spark a quizzical expression that would linger as the person struggled to identify me racially. A typical conversation would go something like this, with the stranger aiming mightily to identify me without actually broaching the touchy, discomfiting subject of race:

"Nice to meet you, Neil. Where are you from?"

"Seattle," I would say. "I grew up on the West Coast."

Hearing this, the stranger would nod, hoping I would go on to answer the question more fully so it would be possible to figure out what my blood origins were. But I usually remained quiet.

"So, your folks were from there?" the stranger would ask after the pause, taking a crack at the puzzle from another angle.

"No," I would answer. "They were from Missouri and North Carolina."

Another nod would be followed by another awkward pause, a more deeply furrowed brow, and then: "And they, uh, were also born in this country?"

I often had fun with that question too, explaining succinctly that yes, indeed, my people's roots went quite a ways back in America—"waaaaaaay back!"—long before the birth of the Republic, since slavery was certainly older than the United States itself. In time, though, I would relieve the white stranger's agony with a smile and say, "I'm black. I'm an African American with many other things mixed in."

The bond between Letitia and me was sealed during my time overseas between 1989 and late 1991, when I traveled across Africa to report on wars, famines, and the dynamic political change that broke out as the Cold War ended. I had been picked for the Africa beat by my white bosses at the *Post* not because I wanted the position and had applied for it. I hadn't, in fact, and

Arthur J. Beaumont (1839–1901), ca. 1880. The author's great-great-grandfather arrived in America from England when he was seventeen and found prosperity as a plantation owner and merchant in Louisiana, after fighting for the Confederacy during the Civil War. Photo courtesy Vivian DeShields Raspberry.

Laura Brumley (1850–1932) (left) and her daughter, Pearl (1877–1944), ca. 1890. Born into slavery in Louisiana, Laura was educated by the plantation mistress. She gave birth to Pearl after a long affair with A.J. Beaumont. Photo courtesy Mary Turner Henry.

Pearl Brumley Hall, ca. 1900. The quadroon daughter of A.J. Beaumont and Laura Brumley, Pearl was briefly married to Frank Hall, a black gambler, and gave birth to Fredda Hall, the author's grandmother, in 1896. Photo courtesy Mary Turner Henry.

Pearl Brumley Hall, ca. 1920. A fiery, passionate woman, Pearl longed for a relationship with her white father and his family but was rebuffed because of her race. Adored by her black family, she died in St. Louis at the age of sixty-seven. Photo courtesy Yvonne DeShields Days.

Fredda Hall Turner (1896–1982), ca. 1916. The daughter of Pearl, Fredda easily could have passed for white, but she felt that love was far more important. She married Edward Clifford Turner, a black postal clerk, and lived happily in St. Louis, raising three children there, including the author's mother. Photo courtesy Mary Turner Henry.

...Office of...

A. J. Beaumont

...Dealer in...

General Merchandise and Plantation Supplies

St. Joseph, Tensas Parish, La. *April 25* 1901

My Dear Pearl

In looking over my papers in my safe I came across your picture also your Daughters and letter to me dated May the 3d 99 I must acknowledge that you are my daughter and I feel that I have done you a great injustice in not acknowledging the receipt of your letter if this will you write to me

Your affecionate Father

A J Beaumont

A.J. Beaumont wrote this letter to Pearl shortly before his death in 1901, finally acknowledging her as his daughter. The letter and its envelope remained keepsakes of Pearl and her black descendants. Courtesy Mary Turner Henry.

A family reunion in 1958. Foreground: Neil at four (center, arms raised); brother Wayne (left); brother Bobby (right). Back row: John Robert Henry, Jr., the author's father (second from left); grandparents Fredda and Edward Clifford Turner (third and fourth from left); Mary Turner Henry, the author's mother (fourth from right); Edward Clifford Turner, Jr., Uncle Sonny (third from right). Photo courtesy Vivian DeShields Raspberry.

The author in 1968, at fourteen, receiving an American Legion award for exemplary scholarship and citizenship. Though popular, he felt "mixed up" racially during the era of integration in largely white Seattle. Photo courtesy the author.

At twenty-one the author found fulfillment in writing; here he is typing an article about African students he met during a trip to China in 1975. The piece was later published in *The Crisis.* Photo courtesy Mary Turner Henry.

The children of Dr. John and Mary Henry in 1977 in the backyard of the family home in Seattle, built in 1960 against the protests of their white neighbors. Left to right: Neil, Sharon, Wayne, Bobby. Photo courtesy Mary Turner Henry.

Dr. John Robert Henry, Jr., in 1945, as a young physician after graduating from Meharry Medical College in Nashville, a legendary institution that trained many generations of the nation's top black doctors. Photo courtesy the author.

The author's mother, Mary Louise Turner, at twenty-two, as head librarian at Bennett College in Greensboro, North Carolina, in 1945. She would marry Dr. John Robert Henry, Jr., the following year. Photo courtesy Mary Turner Henry.

Mary Turner Henry at thirty-one, as a young mother in 1954 on the porch of the family house in Nashville. Neil, as an infant, on her lap; Bobby, center; and Wayne, right. Photo courtesy the author.

The author's grand-parents Fredda and Edward Clifford Turner, ca. 1930, in St. Louis. Fredda, like her mother, Pearl, and her daughter Mary, felt that the cruelest part of being a descendant of slavery was feeling bereft of a sense of family history and identity. Photo courtesy E.C. Turner, Jr.

knew little about the continent when I was first approached by Mike Getler, the foreign editor. If there was any part of the world outside America I was keenly interested in covering, it was China, a country that had fascinated me since my college studies of Mao and Chou En-lai. But, from my previous reporting, my editors saw an unusual spirit of adventure in me, a spirit that certainly was needed to cover a difficult assignment like Africa. They knew me as a clear and concise writer, and my blackness was a critical plus in their eyes for covering a region that often was treated as an afterthought, if that, in the paper's coverage of the world. So I became the fifth black foreign correspondent in the paper's history, an assignment I accepted not so much because I had eagerly sought it, but because I was living in an era in which pioneering opportunities for black men in American professions were still too rare to be refused. It was important, in other words, to take on all challenges, to grasp all new opportunities, whether you sought them or not, if for no other reason than to set a benchmark, to plant the race's flag, for those coming behind you.

Letitia visited me in Nairobi numerous times, bringing welcome relief to the otherwise frenetic pace of my existence in Africa, which marched to the pounding rhythms of news in the thirty-five countries on my beat. Unlike some black Americans who travel to Africa in search of identity or elusive "roots," I entertained no such fantasies when I ventured there. I knew who I was and what I was in Africa to do. My job was to write about a continent in tragic turmoil, and that I did, counting rotting corpses of victims in the ethnic strife of Liberia and Somalia, traveling with heroic aid workers through rebel-held Ethiopia, witnessing unruly police gun down demonstrators protesting for democracy in Kenya. My work was both challenging and heart-breaking, and I grew to love and admire many of the people who struggled for liberty in the nations I visited. I felt enormous respect for their courage and their aspiration for political change. But as an African American I never felt I was "one" culturally with any of Africa's wondrously diverse millions, who despite breathtaking poverty, enjoyed a strong sense of place and ethnic identity, which I secretly envied and admired. Sometimes, in fact, I sensed that Africans looked at me somewhat sorrowfully, despite my wealthy American-ness, as a cultural orphan of sorts, a comparatively "rootless" being who, unlike them, didn't know where his ancestral village was. To many Africans there was no sadder fate than that.

The challenges in my work were all-consuming, and in many ways they brought me face to face for the first time with my own sense of mortality. With each month that passed and each danger I confronted on the continent, I grew more and more cognizant that I was living on borrowed time. Such is the feeling many Western correspondents in Africa face at some point, because the beat so often requires covering war. In the course of performing my job there, I survived the wreck of an ancient Kenya Airways 707 in Ethiopia, counted corpses shortly after their slaughter in Liberia, and had a submachine gun trained on me first by a crazed soldier in Sierra Leone and then by a cop in Kenya. With each incident I found my journalistic nerve, my inner youthfulness and sense of invulnerability in pursuing stories, become harder and harder to summon. I became somewhat wary in my assignments, a quality that I knew could only sap my practice of the craft. I had always prided myself on my intrepidness in searching for the complete story, whether it was about the destitute in the flophouses of Washington, D.C., the convicted killers in the prisons of Maryland, or the migrant workers earning slave wages in the tomato fields of North Carolina. But the raw truths and terrors of the Africa beat began, over time, to wear me down inside, to weaken my soul. My experiences left me feeling, for the first time, powerless as a journalist to convey adequately the sheer magnitude of the human stories I encountered—and to get my distant readers in America to care.

Part of my professional crisis, too, stemmed from my inner realization that Africa's many, and maddeningly inexplicable, fights were ultimately not my own. I didn't want to die covering a story I didn't have an intense personal stake in, and the longer I worked as a journalist in Africa, the more I felt there was a real chance I might have to die, and probably senselessly. That stark realization came to me perhaps most clearly one night in Somalia several days after the fall of the dictator Mohamed Siad Barre in 1991, as I watched hundreds of tracer bullets soar into the sky from celebrants' pistols and submachine guns, knowing that the same bullets would fall seconds later somewhere in the city, possibly wounding or killing people at utter and senseless random—as indeed happened to several people, I discovered the next day. I also grew increasingly convinced that the most meaningful story for me—the story I *was* willing to wage war over, the one simmering in the cauldrons of race—was located somewhere in America. And that it was that fight I needed somehow to rejoin, to examine again, to find answers about. America was the place I needed to return to before my time was finished, the locale of the story I needed to face, the source of the roots I needed to rediscover and somehow come to understand better.

Letitia was my link to sanity in those years in Africa in many ways, a wellspring of patience, devotion, and understanding. Despite the pressures of my job, she and I managed to find time to enjoy the splendors of the continent on our own terms. We hiked together in the beautiful rocky landscapes of Zimbabwe; enjoyed safaris in the wildlife preserves teeming with wildebeests, lions, and elephants in Kenya; drank libations with a village chief in Ghana, where Letitia's mother was serving in the Peace Corps; swam in the warm turquoise waters off the Seychelles in the Indian Ocean. By the time my work in Africa was coming to an end, Letitia and I realized we wanted to make a life together.

Now, six years later, she was my wife and a mother, somehow keeping our home and family together in Davis while continuing to research and write about Africa and teaching courses in African politics to top U.S. and African military officers at the Naval Postgraduate School in Monterey. She remained no less a marvel to me now as when I had first met her.

I stood over the stove, folded my arms, and looked into my wife's eyes as I waited for the pot of water to heat up. Letitia was the only person who truly understood what I was trying to do in my peculiar search, understood how even the most arcane discovery could nonetheless carry significant emotional repercussions for me. I told her about the *Tensas Gazette* microfilm I was working with and the year 1914. I told her I had found the obituary for A.J. Beaumont's wife. Not only that, but I had discovered that the white family moved to Vicksburg after Beaumont died.

The water began to boil. I snapped the spaghetti in half and tossed it in the pot.

"And the son had a daughter, Tish," I said. "That was in the microfilm too. He had a little girl in 1914, probably about Zoë's age."

"So maybe she's alive?"

"I don't know. Maybe. Or maybe the little girl had kids who could be alive somewhere today. Or maybe there was later a son or two who could be alive. The thing is I've brought the story forward by thirteen years."

A little light came to Letitia's dark green eyes then and she smiled. The child-care fatigue in her face seemed to lessen.

I went on: "I don't know what the hell to make of it, but I think I found them, at least where they were in 1914. I can't believe I found them."

She stood with her arms at her sides, hands folded before her, and her back against the kitchen counter. Then, lifting her arms and walking toward me, she asked, "Squeeze my back, will ya?" I folded my arms around her waist and held her tight, lifting her firmly to stretch her vertebrae into place. I heard the bones in her back crack into alignment. It was her regular therapy for fatigue, our regular kitchen hug.

"Vicksburg, is that in Tennessee?" she inquired.

"No, Mississippi," I said. It was the site of a famous Civil War battle, in the very heart of the South. "Remember the siege of Vicksburg? It was Grant's first big win, the battle that made his reputation," I explained, recalling all the Civil War books I had read voraciously years earlier as I tried to put Laura's and Beaumont's lives into context in my mind. "Vicksburg fell the same day the Union won at Gettysburg. On July 4, 1863. It helped turn the tide of history."

I felt myself growing excited talking about it.

"So you're going there, right?"

"I guess so," I said hesitantly after a pause, suddenly brought back to reality, feeling vaguely ambivalent once more about what

I was attempting to do. "But shit, Tish, you know—it's like finding a needle in a haystack. . . ."

She ignored my negativeness and asked me to show her Vicksburg on a map. We went to our bedroom on the other side of the kitchen, where all my files and Civil War and civil rights history books were cluttered in messy heaps next to our computer. I reached into a pile of papers atop a cardboard box near the desk and pulled out a dog-eared road map of Arkansas, Louisiana, and Mississippi, where I had marked the towns of St. Joseph and Natchez with little red dots. I sneezed from the dust.

"How do you find anything in this mess?"

I opened the map and spread it on our bed. I pointed out Vicksburg and circled it in blue with a pen.

"About forty miles from St. Joseph, see?"

"How far is all this from Atlanta? You're going to Atlanta again this semester, aren't you?"

I grunted in reply. Georgia was not on the map, so I reached into my pile of papers and pulled out a fold-up map of the United States. I opened it and placed it atop the other map on our bed. Here I had marked Seattle, St. Louis, and Winston-Salem, North Carolina, in red.

Letitia found Atlanta, then glanced at the distance legend at the bottom of the map. She used her left forefinger to measure the miles between Atlanta and Vicksburg. "Look, there's a major highway that goes right there," she said, pointing to the meandering blue and white line marked I-20. "Probably about four hundred miles."

She knew I was due to travel to Atlanta for two days in October to attend a professional and graduate school fair put on by the city's historically black colleges, Spelman, Morehouse, and

Clark Atlanta University. Every year scores of educators and administrators representing the nation's top professional and graduate school programs convened there to set up placards and booths on the floor of Atlanta's Omni Convention Center and try to recruit the city's top black undergraduates.

With affirmative action eliminated in California through the passage of Proposition 209, Berkeley and other schools in the state were under tremendous pressure to maintain minority enrollments. My journalism school decided to put money into a new recruiting initiative to attract black students. For many years the school had sat back on its reputation as a top institution of journalism education and presumed the best students of all backgrounds would find Berkeley without much work on its part. Now the school's administration realized that we needed to do much more—to go out and find *them*. It was not just a matter of believing in the educational benefits of "diversity" in the student body. It was also a question of economic imperative, for we had to keep the school competitive with other top programs, like those at Columbia and Northwestern.

At Berkeley we were in the difficult position of being legally forbidden from factoring in race or gender in our evaluation of applicants. We supposedly couldn't even discuss race or gender or ethnic background at our admissions committee deliberations. Yet at the same time we were under great pressure from representatives of American news media corporations who would baldly ask us every year at graduation who our top black and minority prospects were, having increasingly come to realize that a diverse news staff could result in a finer and more credible product. They wanted to hire them.

It was a kind of warped, Alice-in-Wonderland, Through-the-

Looking-Glass predicament in which we were attempting to hew to the letter of California's new anti–affirmative action law while at the same time doing our damnedest to get around it for the sake of education, the quality of the craft, and the future of journalism.

"Why don't we just go to the black schools in Atlanta to get some top people from there?" I had urged our school's administrators the year before, when faculty members were asked frantically for ideas. The next thing I knew, I was given money to fly to Atlanta to trumpet the benefits of a Berkeley journalism education to the city's gifted black college students. I believed in this cause with all the zeal of an insurrectionist and loved meeting the young adults. What's more, I felt a special, rare kind of inspiration and pride in Atlanta, a oneness with a generational, racial zeitgeist—believing that I was performing a small role in advancing an old cause of my people and, especially, my family.

For at its heart my family's story, and that of many other black families in America, has always been about education. Nothing else has been more important to black Americans' survival and fulfillment than that. *Education.* And getting *access* to education. Such critical opportunities were being limited, I felt, by the rollbacks in affirmative action, with possibly devastating results for the new generation I was charged with training. In my own time affirmative action had played a significant role not just in opening doors for people like me, doors that had long been barred to dark-skinned people, but also, and perhaps more important, in changing the culture of America's schools and workplaces. Changing the culture held the promise of improving American society, establishing a certain tolerance and acceptance of differences and a commitment to the principle that all people, regard-

less of race, background, or gender, should be allowed the chance
to prove themselves. I didn't know where the post–affirmative
action age would lead us, but I did know one thing: that without
access to opportunity, especially access to education, we were lost
as a people. Education was certainly the critical link in my family history, dating back to Laura's learning to read and write as a
child on the Tullis plantation in Louisiana. And education surely
was as profoundly important to my generation more than a century later. Without education we were at the mercy of whatever
hell white America wanted to foist on us. Education was our only
protection as a race, the greatest birthright and legacy we could
leave to those we loved.

When I was in Atlanta the previous year, trying to recruit
black students for our program at Berkeley, I thought often
about my mother, who attended a segregated, all-black Atlanta
University in the 1940s while earning a graduate degree in library science. I reflected on how her values about education had
been passed down to me during my childhood in white Seattle.
To my mother, education didn't mean just schoolwork, academic
achievement, or training for a livelihood. It meant education
about the world too, about the different kinds of people who in-
habit it, and it meant moral enlightenment, particularly when it
came to racial issues. In many ways she was the fire and spiritual
force behind our family's transition from the black world to the
white middle class in Seattle in 1960. Despite her own experiences with racism, she somehow maintained an abiding faith that
most white people, under their skin, would prove to be as decent
and caring as other people if they could get over their fears and
ignorance about us. My mother had always felt our biggest challenge as a family was to sustain this faith and not become so em-

bittered by our experiences with racism that we became blinded to the basic goodness of most white people. The worst thing I could do was hate white people back, she often told me. To hate in reaction to prejudice only served the ends of the racists, she felt. I somehow had to be better than that.

This spiritual framework of my mother's life, and by extension of my own, was erected early on in St. Louis, where she was born Mary Louise Turner in 1923. She was the second of three children of Edward Clifford Turner, a genial postal worker who was the son of a freed slave, and Fredda Turner, the shy daughter of Pearl and granddaughter of the English immigrant A.J. Beaumont. My mother grew up in a very stable and loving family centered in the Ville—short for Elleardsville—an admired St. Louis neighborhood known throughout the Midwest as a mecca of black culture and achievement in the first half of the twentieth century.

My mother always spoke lovingly about her childhood in the Ville, for it was a place where a black child, especially an advantaged black child, could grow up feeling proud of her color. The Ville in the 1920s and 1930s was to the black Midwest almost what Harlem was to the East during the Harlem Renaissance years, a source of rich culture and identity. The inner-city neighborhood was home to a thriving black middle class made up of steady government workers like my grandfather, as well as doctors, dentists, artists, undertakers, chauffeurs, and craftspeople. The Ville featured numerous movie and musical theaters and boasted elite black schools, including Charles Sumner High School, the first black public school built west of the Mississippi River, where my mother finished first in her class in 1940. As a child in Seattle, listening to her describe life during the heyday of the Ville, I felt the same sense of longing and loss that a white child born in America must feel listening to immigrant parents tell stories about the wonders and joys of Budapest or old Warsaw. The only world I knew was the world of white people. As a black child growing up so far removed from the lives of most of my own kind, I tried to imagine such a wondrous place made up entirely of black people, all my people, many of them very successful and accomplished, living, as she described it, like one big extended family that ate together, worked together, played together. It was magical to my child's mind.

An old adage about the Ville from my mother's youth held that a black child could be born, raised, and receive a fabulous education—from grade school at John Marshall Elementary, to Sumner High, to Harriet Beecher Stowe College, all the way to medical education at Homer G. Phillips Hospital—without ever having to leave the five square miles and forty-three blocks of her or his neighborhood. It was in the Ville that my mother was bred to be proud of her color and her advantaged class, despite the degradations of racial segregation, and to value learning.

As my mother told me, her own life choices as a black woman were made plain to her from the time she was little, when she accompanied her mother, Fredda, on trips downtown to pay the family bills. Fredda, the granddaughter Beaumont never met, informed her that of all the people in America, "colored" women had the hardest lives, and that if she wanted to have a happy life, she had to prepare early. One day in 1935, when my mother was twelve, Fredda made a point of taking her to Stix, Baer and Fuller, a bustling St. Louis department store, where Fredda wanted my mother to see the efficient and very attractive uniformed black girls, many of them light-skinned like my mother, working as stockers, elevator operators, and in other menial positions.

"Aren't they pretty?" Fredda asked her. My mother was indeed enchanted, she remembered, by the black girls' beauty and zest as they called out "First floor! Lingerie, perfume, hats!" and opened the elevator doors with a flourish.

"So pretty!" my mother replied.

"Now look down, Mary," my grandmother told her. "Don't just look at their faces and pretty hair. Make sure you see their feet."

My mother said she lowered her head and what she saw was clearly imprinted in her mind more than a half century later. Each of the beautiful young women wore shopworn, threadbare loafers beneath horrifically swollen ankles, testimony to their hard lives and the poor pay they received for their labor.

My mother and grandmother turned away.

"They didn't study, Mary. They didn't take their schooling seriously, do you hear?" Fredda said as they left the store. "And they're the lucky ones, because at least they have jobs. Such pretty, sad girls. They spend their lives on their feet and can't even afford shoes.

"Your father and I can't afford to send you to college," Fredda added. "You'll have to earn it on your own. But you remember these girls. . . ."

My mother finished at the top of her class at all-black Harriet Beecher Stowe College in the Ville and set her eyes on becoming a trained librarian, a profession that, in her day, was among the most prestigious a black woman could enter. In 1944, while studying for her degree in library science at Atlanta University, she met my father in Greensboro, North Carolina, during a semester working at a small black college library. After a few dates she fell in love with the handsome young medical student from North Carolina and soon realized she had two divergent paths before her: one leading to a doctoral degree in her field and perhaps the directorship of a university library someday if she worked hard enough; the other to a life with John Henry as wife and mother.

When their courtship stalled after a year and my father confessed to her that he probably wasn't ready to marry, my mother quit the South. She was accepted into a graduate program in library science at the University of Michigan in Ann Arbor, one of just a few black students in the program.

But one night my father phoned her from North Carolina to tell her how much he missed her. Then he wrote a love letter to her. Then he phoned her again and asked her to marry him. She said yes, quit school immediately, and happily hopped over to the other path. And on a beautiful snowy afternoon, Christmas Day 1946, she and my father were married at All Saints' Episcopal Church back home in St. Louis before scores of family and friends. She always said it was the happiest day of her life.

My parents dreamed a big dream that many other postwar, upwardly mobile black people shared in those days: that they could be the first generation of black people in America's long racist history to enjoy the same freedoms and access to good neighborhoods and public schools for their children as white people did. It was the guiding principle of their age. The time, they believed, was long past for America to honor its constitutional ideals by applying them to all its citizens. This was particularly imperative after a long, bloody world war in which millions, including many black American soldiers and sailors, had died to bring such freedoms to people in Europe and Asia. Some generations are lucky to be marked forever by an overriding passion or human ideal. For my parents' black generation it was equal opportunity and racial understanding.

Unlike my father, my mother possessed a strong religious faith to buttress her political convictions, and it, too, was a legacy of her upbringing in the Ville. She was raised in the Episcopal church, the denomination of choice of the city's black bourgeoisie. She believed that faith was as critical to a meaningful life as a good education and that in many ways the two went hand in hand. In Seattle years later, my mother was the driving force behind our attendance at a predominantly black but racially integrated Episcopal church, St. Clement's, each Sunday, where our Sunday school education complemented our grade school lessons. (This weekly ritual was not observed by my comparatively taciturn father, who was a pragmatist at heart and an atheist by nature. He pointed out to me on more than one occasion when I was a child that more wars had been fought in the name of God than any other power.)

Faith was perhaps most important to my mother when it came to grappling with racism. She felt that our family's inner strength, forbearance, and understanding of the racial obstacles we encountered in Seattle—our character—would somehow be rewarded in the end, much as Christians believed that God always redeemed the good and the just.

One of my mother's favorite prayers was the "Serenity Prayer," which was etched into a ceramic plaque that her mother had hung on the wall of her kitchen in St. Louis during the 1950s and that remained there long after her death in 1982. I often gazed at it as a child during our occasional summer visits to our ancestral home from Seattle in the 1960s, contemplating its meaning:

God grant me the serenity to accept the things I cannot change, the courage to change the things I can, and the wisdom to know the difference.

The prayer was most often associated with Alcoholics Anonymous, whose members used it to assist them spiritually toward recovery from addiction. For my mother and her mother the prayer offered support and comfort in the struggle not against booze but prejudice and racism. At the same time, while upholding the prayer's sentiments, my mother's beliefs were mixed with a sizable degree of gritty moral outrage and worldly skepticism, especially toward white prejudice.

Often when I was a kid in Seattle, my mother wrote letters home to her family in St. Louis, spilling out her deepest fears and dreams for us as we made our pioneering entrance into the world of white people during integration. This one, which I found in my mother's old house in St. Louis during a visit in the 1990s, was typical, filled with the passions of her age. Written by my mother several months before we moved, it was addressed to Fredda, who had feared our migration from Seattle's black neighborhood to a white one would be a terrible mistake. Fredda had preserved the typewritten letter in a plastic casing in a bureau drawer, knowing it would one day become a keepsake as precious as any.

Saturday afternoon
September 10, 1960

Dear Mama:
    The boys started [at the all-white] school Wednesday, and they are not at [the all-black school in the Central Area]—thank goodness! We made a trip down to the school board and got a special

transfer. Bobby's going to the junior high school in the district where we will move and Neilly and Wayne are going to elementary school in the new district. I drive them every morning and pick them up, 20 miles a day. I looked at my poor little children when I let them out that first morning and thought what a burden they had to bear because they were colored. If somebody had dumped me out like that I would have stood on the curb and jumped up and down and cried to go home. I took them to their school rooms and met their teachers and left them to swing it alone. The rest of the day I paced the living room and prayed. . . .

Now, with only 3 days in school Neil has learned how to read 4 sentences and is carried away. Wayne is delighted. I have never seen him so completely relaxed and sure of himself and so dedicated to learning. Every afternoon when I pick him up he stands by the flagpole, smiling that little secret smile he has with a twinkle in his eye and leaps in the car to tell me what happened that day. He and Neil are the only Negroes in the school and he knows the score and is quite mature about it—much more mature than a lot of adults would be, including his Ma. . . .

Yesterday I was sitting here meditating, trying to understand your bleak attitude about our move [into the white neighborhood] and getting the kids out of these all colored schools. Suddenly, it dawned on me that you don't understand the problems we face in Seattle. (It took me a long time, too, living here with the problem every day.) In the olden days when I was a little girl, growing up and going to school in the Ville, there were no problems for you, as such, because the St. Louis school system was one of the best in the country. And though the schools were segregated they were for all practical purposes equal to the whites' inasmuch as the teacher supply came from the two separated but supposedly equal city colleges.

At that time the teaching profession attracted the best Negro women who for the most part were dedicated and took pride in a

*job well done. . . . Here in Seattle the situation is entirely different
and mirrors the situation in all larger cities in the north and west.
The school the boys have been attending in the Central Area for the
past 4 years is now 99 percent Negro, which is quite alright if the
faculty were strong and sympathetic and dedicated.*

*But they are not. Over half of the kids come from illiterate,
underprivileged homes and discipline is nil. These schools have
a very high percentage of teacher turnover every year. I have
watched Wayne become increasingly handicapped year by year
by one weak, undedicated teacher after another.*

*After much haggling I finally managed to get him into a
colored teacher's room and he pulled himself up. Unfortunately,
the school board's policy is to disperse Negro teachers throughout
the system. I have worked with the PTA and the Urban League
and other organizations dedicated to raising the educational
standards and teacher qualifications of these Negro schools until
the city's segregated housing situation is relieved.*

But until then, what are we to do?

*Gradually it dawned on me that my boys were suffering and
being given an inferior education. Since a good education is the
best legacy John and I can endow them with we decided on the
move. Ponder that statement Rachel Robinson [Jackie Robinson's
wife] made not long ago—"What's wrong with our kids going
to an all-colored school? Nothing, if they're going to live in an all-
colored world."*

*So yes, we have sacrificed a 35-year-old home with an $11,000
mortgage in a cozy black neighborhood for a brand new home with
no view and a higher mortgage on a street of hostile whites for a
principle—and for what we believe will enhance our children's
future.*

*Who can say whether we are right or wrong? We take pride,
however, in having the courage of our convictions. And though we*

are harassed by these white people by day, we sleep the sleep of the
just at night and take comfort in the fact that we are not alone—
in Seattle, or throughout the country—because other Negroes,
though small in numbers, are taking the giant step.

Here's hoping that this next generation will be armed for battle
with good and equal educations, ready and willing and able to take
their rightful places in the integrated society their parents and
grandparents fought and raved and shouted for. . . .

A longtime librarian for the Seattle public schools, my mother
was full of zest when it came to practically everything in life—
reading, politics, the social whirl among other black wives in
Seattle's small but growing black bourgeoisie—and often her
perspective on my experiences growing up with white people
could be sharp and biting. Despite her religious convictions, she
wasn't above calling a white person a "racist bastard" or "poor
white trash" when the occasion suited and her ire was sufficiently
raised. But she didn't like saying such things out loud in front of
me. At some point in the mid-1960s she shortened the expletive
"poor white trash" to "PWT" and later to simply "Pee Dub" in
her vernacular, to use whenever she felt compelled to explain
why certain white people acted as crassly or maliciously or stu-
pidly toward us as they did.

As a kid, I considered my mother one of the prettiest women I
knew. I don't know exactly why. Maybe because I paid more attention to her than to any other woman I knew. She had high,
round cheeks; soft, curly black hair, which she often wore close
cropped and which turned an elegant gray as she grew older; and
expressive dark eyes that reflected rage and joy with equal fervor.
I often could tell exactly how she felt just by looking into her eyes.

I thought she was pretty not only because her face was so radiant and her eyes so full of life or because she had her hair clipped nicely by a hairdresser practically every week and often dressed in very fashionable clothes. Her prettiness, to me, went beyond her physical appearance. She carried herself with elegance and style, possessing a sureness and pride in her walk and bearing. Long after I became an adult, my friends and acquaintances would tell me that that was the first thing that came to mind on meeting my mother—that *this* was a woman with class. It was doubtless her background in the Ville that produced this quality.

Vivacious and highly opinionated, she was never sparing in pointing out the difference between right and wrong as she saw it in our everyday lives, often doing so with a sharpness that could deeply sting. Once when she was purchasing a lamp in an electric appliance store in Rainier Valley, an impertinent white shop-keeper made the mistake of calling my mother by her first name after seeing her full name, Mrs. Mary T. Henry, on her bank check. My mother—reminded of the demeaning manner in which white merchants and other strangers often addressed black women in the South, considering them little more than sub-servient "girlies" and "mammies" and "queenies" without last names—exploded.

"My name is Mrs. Henry, do you understand? You do not address me by my first name, *do you understand?*"

I was awed by her temper.

"Don't you ever let those people treat you like that," she said bitterly to me and my sister, Sharon, after we had returned to the car, her eyes filled with tears.

That was in 1968, the year Martin Luther King, Jr., was assassinated. I was fourteen, and the racial rage and violence that quickly broke out across America in the murder's aftermath made our home near Lake Washington seem the only shelter from trouble and fear. The Sunday after King's killing, my mother attended her racially integrated Episcopal church to hear words of spiritual consolation, guidance, and hope from the white clergy. She expected to hear something to help her deal with the pain she felt, something to commemorate all that King had struggled to do. But she returned home that afternoon enraged.

"The minister didn't mention Martin Luther King once, can you believe it?" she cried. "How can they go on and on about angels and archangels when the world is coming apart like this?"

She didn't attend church again for several years.

"You've been given advantages that a lot of people don't have," she told my older brother Wayne and me as we sat in our family room one windswept night that terrible spring, watching the news bulletins on television about the rioting in Washington. "You've gone to good schools, you've had clothes on your back and food in your stomach, and you've never had to want for anything. You've been lucky. But you can never afford to forget you're black in this country. Never, do you hear? And you should do what you can, you know, to help other folks come along, even if it's just a little."

Three decades later I was about to return to Atlanta to renew my own small initiative to help counter the effects of the end of affirmative action at my school in California. It was my modern-day battle in the old war for access to the American dream that my people had always fought, my way of doing "a little" to help the cause and to continue to honor the "giant step" my mother had written about so passionately in her letter to Fredda all those years before.

But could I also find a way during the same brief trip to find answers to our old family mystery? Could I follow up on the clues I had discovered in microfilm and piece together the white family story concealed somewhere on the other side of our ancestral tree?

It was going to be such a quick trip to Atlanta, and deep down I felt I would need weeks instead of hours or days to accomplish my task. I wondered if I would have time to squeeze in a visit to Vicksburg at all. I knew I would have only a few days in the South before I had to return to teach my classes at Berkeley.

"Of course you can," Letitia insisted, turning to me, her eyes peering into mine, her finger resting again on the map of Mississippi. "You're going to be in the South anyway. You've got to."

I knew she was right. So I thought quickly about everything I would need to do. There was so much. I would first rent a car and then make a rapid, hard charge in one day through Georgia, Alabama, all the way across Mississippi to Vicksburg. If I timed it right, I might be able to have a full day or perhaps even two full days there to research court records and historical documents, to see if the Beaumont family paper trail really existed and to determine how far I could follow it.

Vicksburg was the seat of Warren County in Mississippi. That meant that any civil, property, criminal, or probate judgments the Beaumont family might have been involved in would certainly be in the files there somewhere. With luck I would be able to find a copy of A.J. Beaumont's widow's will and perhaps the children's marriage certificates, if the family had resided in Vicksburg long enough.

I had a lot of preparing to do, I knew. A lot of phone calls and appointments to make.

Letitia called Zoë to the dinner table a few minutes later, and after I placed the pasta and salad before us, I said grace, as I usually did each night, using the same prayer my mother recited before meals in Seattle. It was funny, but I had spent my adult life in a profession, journalism, that valued earthly skepticism much more than spiritual faith. Yet somehow such faith remained rooted in me.

> Lord be our holy guest,
> Our morning joy, our evening rest;
> And with this daily bread impart,
> Thy loving peace to every heart.

We then ate the pasta, salad, and sausage as the sun set in the sultry evening air outside our open kitchen door, and afterward Zoë and I played tic-tac-toe as Letitia cleared the dishes from the table. I became so lost in thought that my daughter had to keep telling me, "Your turn, Daddy," and "Play, Daddy, play!" Still, my mind drifted again and again to Vicksburg, to Natchez and St. Joseph, and to the task ahead of me, to Laura, Pearl, and Arthur Beaumont.

All that time, all that searching.

Amazing, I thought.

I always knew I would travel somewhere, perhaps many places, in America when I started on the strange and vexing odyssey years earlier to find the white family whose blood my family shared. But deep down I guess I knew the truth all along, that the trail I sought, the clues I needed, and the answers I so badly wanted were ultimately buried somewhere in the South.

It had always been that way in my family.

Always, the South.

CHAPTER THREE

Natchez

I flew from Sacramento to Atlanta on Saturday, October 11, arriving in the Georgia capital late on a humid and drizzly night. The next morning I rented a compact car at a downtown agency near my hotel to begin the long drive west to Vicksburg. With my wrinkled old road maps on the seat beside me, I was on the move by 9:30 A.M., passing quietly through Atlanta's deserted Sunday-morning streets. I soon found an on-ramp to U.S. Interstate 20 and followed the freeway out of the city as it wound its way on a southwesterly 450-mile course through the pine forests of Georgia and Alabama and the kudzu of Mississippi toward the Mississippi River.

Fall semester at Berkeley was in full gear, and once again I was overwhelmed with course work and lectures back home. The focus of my attention was the eleven graduate students in Journalism 200, an intensive course in news reporting and writing that students were required to pass if they wanted to go on to specialized training in television and print journalism and eventual careers in the field. The course was a baptism of fire in the intricacies of the craft—much as anatomy is for medical students, perhaps, or torts for law students—and something close to hell for both me and them. I was teaching them how to gather information and interview sources and ordering them to write and rewrite staggering numbers of news and feature stories on deadline, all of which I had to edit. The assignments I issued each morning ranged from the mundane to the zany:

> The Berkeley City Council meets tonight. Cover the session. Write 500 words about the most newsworthy action, direct news lede. Deadline: midnight.

> Nudists are demonstrating at Sproul Plaza tomorrow as an expression of their First Amendment rights. Write 700 words. Interview at least one of the nudists in depth, and get reaction on the record from First Amendment experts on campus and onlookers. Deadline: 7 P.M.

> Find a vacant lot in Berkeley. Go to the county assessor's office with the lot's address and research its history as far back in time as you can go. Find out who owns it now. Contact the owner. Find out what he or she plans for the property, if anything. Write a memo about your research. 1,000 words. Deadline: Monday, 8 A.M.

The students were also invading the criminal courts in nearby Oakland to write about murder, armed robbery, and rape trials, and learning how to research civil and criminal court files and other public records critical to the work of journalism. One of my students, a twenty-seven-year-old black woman from Oakland, had taken my assignment to write a short profile about a figure in the judicial system and turned in a remarkable story about an old high school boyfriend who was doing time in Santa Rita State Prison for dealing drugs. I edited her piece closely, then fired off a quick note to her:

> Excellent work, Nandi. Here's what I'd like you to do now.
> Please make this a commentary. Tell the reader what you
> remember about going to school in Oakland and how you
> feel personally about the destruction of so many lives of people
> you knew, through drugs, crime, and alienation. Also provide
> more information about what life is like behind bars for your
> old boyfriend and what he foresees for his life when he gets out.
> Let's aim to get this piece published on a local op-ed page.

Another student, a thirty-one-year-old former schoolteacher from Oakland who had decided to change careers to become a journalist, was writing his master's thesis on the daily struggles of Eric Brooks, the lone black student in that year's entering class at the Boalt Hall School of Law on campus. The law school had seen a sharp drop in minority applicants in the wake of the anti–affirmative action Proposition 209. Many activist groups saw Brooks's lonely plight as a cautionary tale about the future of higher education in the state. My student's first draft of his thesis about Brooks was very rough but filled with potential. I ordered him to pursue the piece further:

> Rob: Wonderful job to get the access you have. You are the
> only member of the Bay Area or national press who has been
> able to get this story in the kind of depth it requires. But the
> key to making it work will be how well you are able to under-
> tand Brooks. Get to know him. Go to classes with him. Unwind

with him. He is an unusual man in a very unusual circumstance, and the better you are able to present him in flesh and blood as a human being, the better the reader will connect to the story and the important larger issues involved here.

But now I was in the South, taking a short breather from the fires of my daily life as an educator, putting my lectures and schoolwork aside for a few days to try to solve the old puzzle at the heart of my family's racial story while also trying to recruit a few more black students for our program from the black colleges in Atlanta.

It was a gray, still, and misty Sunday morning as I headed into the Georgia countryside, conditions that made the rolling farm-land and stands of tall pines passing silently by outside my car windows appear remarkably lush and timeless. As I flowed with the light traffic through the three states, alternately hearing preachers shout their sermons, church choirs sing soulful hymns, and broadcasters chatter play-by-play about a pro football game on my car's AM radio, I felt within me the sharp emotions I had harbored for the South since my childhood in Seattle.

Nearly every road sign I passed on the six-hour trip evoked a jarring memory of some racial or historic event that touched things deep in my soul. As I drove through Birmingham, I peered downtown, wondering where in this old brick- and rust-colored steel town was the small black church where four girls were killed by a white terrorist's bomb in 1963 as they prayed during a serv-ice. I could hear the words of George Wallace ringing in my mind's ear—"Segregation now, segregation tomorrow, segrega-tion forever!"—words the belligerent white governor had defi-antly shouted during his inaugural address in 1963. Six months later he mounted his "schoolhouse stand" to block two black students from enrolling at the University of Alabama in Montgomery.

I drove past a highway exit leading toward Philadelphia, Mississippi, the small town where three civil rights workers were gruesomely murdered in 1964 by white vigilantes out to stop black people from asserting their right to vote.

These places were key landmarks in the history of the struggle that I remembered vividly from my boyhood in Seattle. From our faraway vantage my brothers and sister and I had watched the civil rights movement in the South unfold in the 1960s on television and in the newspapers. The South was where bigotry had always been overt and brutal, in contrast to the sullen face of prejudice I had known when I came of age in Seattle, Princeton, and Washington, D.C.

But the South in my mind didn't just connote oppression and brutality. Like many of my attitudes about race and our family history, my feelings about the region were a complex mix, for the South was also deeply inspiring. It was the same region that saw black people in many of their finest moments in history, bravely joining the boycotts and marches for equal rights led by Martin Luther King, Jr., and Medgar Evers and showing supreme courage in individual acts of defiance, like that of Rosa Parks, the black woman in Montgomery, Alabama, who turned the world upside down by refusing to give up her seat on a bus to a white passenger.

As I drove on, my mind filled with King's words of April 3, 1968, the stormy night before he was killed, from a speech he delivered to a packed black church in Memphis. I remembered seeing King that night, in news clips on our television set in Seattle, as he passionately affirmed his belief in the civil rights struggle and racial integration while eerily expressing acceptance of his own mortality. In my mind I heard the fire in his voice, the crowd's ecstatic shouts and cries, and recalled feeling one with our history, even as a fourteen-year-old black boy so far away:

> We've got some difficult days ahead, but it really doesn't matter with me now. Because I have been to the mountain top. Like anybody I would like to live a long life. Longevity has its place. But I'm not concerned about that now. I just want to do God's will. And he's allowed me to go up the mountain top. And I've looked over. And I've seen the Promised Land. I may not get there with you. But I want you to know tonight that we as a people will get to the Promised Land. So I am happy tonight. I'm not worried about anything. I'm not fearing any man. My eyes have seen the glory of the coming of the Lord.

On toward the Mississippi River I traveled, toward the muddy, seemingly endless body of slow-moving brown water that inspired so many American writers, from Mark Twain and Edna Ferber to Langston Hughes. It was the same river Laura and Pearl had steamed northward along in the 1890s to begin their new life in St. Louis, leaving A.J. Beaumont and their native Louisiana behind. And I remembered one of my earlier visits to Mississippi more than a decade earlier, in 1986.

I was working then as a national correspondent for the *Washington Post* and came up with the idea of writing a long feature story about race relations at the University of Mississippi nearly a quarter of a century after its first black student, James Meredith, had been admitted under protection by federal troops amid a hail of gunfire from white racist protesters. I wanted to know how relations between blacks and whites had changed there over the years. Had ties improved? Or degenerated? Were there any real ties between the races at all?

Journalism had been a godsend to my life in that way, allowing me the chance to make a terrific living doing what I loved to do more than anything in life: satisfy my curiosity. Best of all, newspapering had offered a startling contrast to my college experience at Princeton, four years that were essentially a black hole in my life, which even now I recalled with anxiety and pain. But I couldn't help thinking about Princeton whenever I considered my fifteen-year career at the *Washington Post*, because the two experiences had such opposite but profoundly lasting effects on my life.

I went to Princeton in 1972 essentially because—encouraged by my older brother Wayne, who by then was enrolled at Brown— I had applied and been accepted. It was one of the best schools in America, and as a young black man whose ancestors had struggled hard to gain access to education, I felt honor-bound to take advantage of the opportunity, to push the walls of the racial envelope, to once again see how I measured up.

But from the moment I arrived on campus carrying my two suitcases, which had been marked "NH" in big letters by my diligent father with strips of masking tape, I was badly intimidated— by the prep school culture, by the aura of old wealth and alien traditions, by the strange political and scientific discourses of the era. One of the biggest controversies on campus during my years at Princeton was over a speaking invitation that a group of my white fellow students had extended in 1973 to solid-state physicist and Nobel Prize winner William Shockley. Shockley was a

Stanford professor who was far more noted nationally for his belief that black people were genetically inferior to whites than for
his work in physics. A predecessor of the contemporary conservative race and intelligence theorist Charles Murray, he also fervently believed that people of lower intelligence should be paid
money to be sterilized. That way, Shockley felt, the brighter
lights of the species, white people, could be protected from the
wasteful effects of miscegenation.

As I went through my daily routine of classes and studies,
often eating alone in the mammoth dining halls or retreating to
my dorm room, I couldn't help believing that Shockley was only
expressing aloud what most white people in America and on my
campus privately felt about black people already. And as much as
I hated his theory, I secretly wondered if Shockley—a supposedly brilliant scientist, after all—was correct in his beliefs, could
somehow prove black genetic inferiority, and I wondered in the
end what it said about me.

The controversy symbolized the tenor of my dismal years at
Princeton, along with my odd ways of coping with them. I was a
virtual recluse at college, someone whose picture you will not
find in any school yearbook and who participated in no campus
activities worth memorializing. I hung out with neither the rich
white preppies who favored weekend beer busts and Beach Boys
music nor the small band of black students who dined together,
lived together, sat together in lectures, smoked herb and danced
to the Ojays and Tower of Power together, and otherwise tried
to find security as a group in the midst of the white majority on
campus, much as conscripts might move en masse from bunker
to bunker in hostile territory.

I was something of a loner by nature and didn't trust companionship based solely on my skin color, mainly because it was so alien to my background, and Princeton's ivy and gray-stoned foreignness only made me even more aloof. Actually, by the time I went to college, I had become somewhat wary of other black people, thanks to some painful experiences with blacks of my own age, starting in junior high school. The curiously proper way I spoke, the unhip way I dressed, the excellent grades I earned, the white friends I hung out with from my neighborhood—to my black peers these were contemptible earmarks of my background growing up among whites. To the black kids, most of whom were poor and hailed from Seattle's inner city, I was something of a freak and quite ripe for ridicule, a black boy who couldn't dance, couldn't talk the dialect, strolled to class religiously with big tomes under his arm, always had money for lunch, and most suspicious of all, was well liked by the white teachers. For all these things I was, in the words of some, an "Uncle Tom." When several black toughs in my junior high first spat that expletive my way, my face burned hot with shame. But who was the real traitor and shame to our race, I wondered bitterly as I trudged home that day—the black person who tried to advance and change the white man's world or the one who never had the guts to try?

At Princeton I didn't feel a part of either the black or the white world really, and the people I counted as my friends on campus were similarly misfits of a sort—a secretly gay black art student from New Jersey, a lonely white physician's son from a small town in Iowa, and a poor Sephardic Jew from Seattle. My one pitiful attempt at hipness in college was to grow a huge Afro. At one point it encircled my head like an astronaut's helmet, with mounds and mounds of black curliness. But even in this effort my mixed racial ancestry proved inescapable. For whenever I put my head under the shower in my dorm, the big Afro melted, reconstituting itself into a thick, wet mass of limp, straight strings that hung down the back of my neck.

In general, I was so overwhelmed by the task of trying to succeed academically, shoulder to shoulder with what I presumed were the brightest young white minds in America, that my presence on campus amounted to little more than a spectral one. What kept me going was the fear of letting my family down, especially my mother. I often told myself that I simply couldn't fail because she had invested so much of her savings and hopes in my expensive education. And so I buried myself in books essentially from the time I arrived to the time I left, finding intellectual inspiration in the lives of Mao and Melville and Paul Robeson and relief from boredom in the marvelous movies from the 1930s and 1940s playing on New York City and Philadelphia television stations, which I often watched late at night on my rickety black-and-white set. I suspect I became just as knowledgeable about the works of John Ford, Frank Capra, and Howard Hawks as I was about Chinese political history, my submajor.

I graduated from Princeton with academic honors, but my thoughts and insecurities about race, prejudice, inferiority—and my elusive place in a society where there didn't seem to be too many people like me—haunted me during my isolating years there. To this day some of my fondest memories of college are the times late at night in my senior year when I freely roamed the campus in the tranquil darkness to scavenge for twigs, fallen branches, and other pieces of wood in order to make fires in the small brick fireplace in my single room at Dod Hall. I loved those late-night fires. In those moments I felt perfectly at peace in my aloneness, in control of my little world, and oddly content with my ascetic apartness from both whites and blacks. When my last class was finished that spring, 1977, I packed up and left Princeton for good, one week before commencement. I swore to myself that I would never return. In my class album there was no photograph of me nor any listing of activities. Only my major, political science, was mentioned. Otherwise, I was a faceless name in the records.

But life changed dramatically when I left. If nothing else, my college years had taught me that I could survive on my own in a forbidding environment if I had to, not unlike Natty Bumpo in the frontier wilderness, and that I could compete successfully with anyone if I put my mind to it. These qualities served me well when I was hired after graduation to be a summer intern reporter on the Metro Staff at the *Washington Post*, where I learned to write obituaries, cover the police beat, interview beauty queens, fire chiefs, strippers, derelicts—in short, learned all the ropes of life as a cub reporter. Inspired by the exploits of Bob Woodward and Carl Bernstein to take a shot at newspapering as a calling, I was one of fourteen interns that summer working in what clearly was a plum job for any young, ambitious writer, just three years after President Nixon's resignation and the *Post*'s journalistic triumphs during Watergate. In the *Post*'s eyes my internship application had displayed the "right" pedigree, beginning with my Ivy League education, which editor Ben Bradlee and the Graham family, who owned the paper, considered virtually essential for editorial hiring at the paper. The application had also included a couple of newspaper and magazine articles I had written about a three-week trip to China I had taken the previous summer with a group of writers and students—a temporary escape from

Princeton that proved exhilarating and certainly showed I had the kind of adventurous spirit on which journalism thrived.

But, I'm sure, most impressive to my employers was my race. It was just a decade after rioting had destroyed inner-city Washington in the wake of King's murder, and the *Post* remained eager to employ energetic, young black reporters who could help cover the largely black city and explain it in human terms to its largely white and very influential readership. Just nine years earlier President Johnson had convened a special panel to examine the causes of the inner-city riots in the 1960s. The National Advisory Commission on Civil Disorders, more commonly known as the Kerner Commission, warned in the conclusion of its 1968 report that America was moving still further, dangerously so, toward becoming two societies, black and white, separate and unequal, and it levied sharp criticism at the nation's white mainstream press for not reporting adequately or fairly on the problems of blacks and the poor. The commission urged American newspapers and broadcast media to employ more minorities to help convey to the public the full story behind the social and racial issues that had exploded so violently in the streets.

Racial integration, in short, was still a new phenomenon at America's newspapers, including the *Washington Post*, when I arrived in 1977, riding the wave of progress and transformation begun only a few years earlier. Indeed, in many ways the mid- and late 1970s set the stage for a golden era at the *Post*, giving rise to an extraordinarily gifted cadre of black journalists, all of whom I was proud to call my peers and contemporaries, all of us trained under fire in our idealistic youth in the crucible of the *Post* newsroom. How I admired the sharp wit and wisdom of columnist William Raspberry, the smarts and terrific writing style of New

Yorker Juan Williams, the folksy cool and streetwise city reporting of Louisiana-born Courtland Milloy.

It was a pioneering time that led later to seminal and provoca-
tive works by many of these black writers, books that richly
evoked the tenor, struggles, and victories of the age. Two works,
Jill Nelson's *Volunteer Slavery* and Nathan McCall's *Makes Me
Wanna Holler*, are bitter memoirs documenting their racial struggles within the very white corporate structure at the *Post* that embraced me and allowed me to flourish. A third autobiography,
Patrice Gaines's *Laughing in the Dark*, traces her remarkable rise
from poverty, drug use, and imprisonment to become an award-
winning feature writer on the big-city daily. Another black writer
whose skills were sharpened at the *Post* was James McBride, author of *The Color of Water*, a memoir tracing his relationship with
his white Jewish mother, his childhood in New York's housing
projects, and his family's unusual success. Still another personal
history, Keith B. Richburg's *Out of America*, recounts his experiences as my successor as the paper's Africa Bureau chief, a con-
troversial memoir whose damning and unmerciful rant against
African corruption and tribal wars aroused indignation among
many blacks in America. A sixth book, Eugene Robinson's *Coal to
Cream*, examines the differences in perceptions of race he encountered as a young black American coming of age in South
Carolina and later as the *Post*'s South America Bureau chief
based in Brazil. Another brilliant journalist trained on the *Post*'s
National Staff in the 1980s was Malcolm Gladwell, a biracial
Canadian with a flair for science writing who rose to be the
paper's New York correspondent before joining the *New Yorker*
and authoring *The Tipping Point*, a fascinating study of social epi-
demics. Still other volumes are groundbreaking works of jour-

nalism, including Leon Dash's *Rosa Lee: A Mother and Her Family in Urban America*, a Pulitzer Prize–winning series of stories about the hardships of a black woman's life in the South and Washington, D.C.'s ghetto, and two by Juan Williams—*Eyes on the Prize*, a history of the civil rights struggle, and *Thurgood Marshall: American Revolutionary*, his compelling biography of the black Supreme Court justice. Such books reflect not just the talent of the era's black journalists, but also the wide range of perspective among them.

My entrance into this journalistic brotherhood near its inception after the tumult of the late 1960s was a proud and exciting one, but it also was the source of my greatest secret at the *Post*, a secret I guarded closely when I was hired full-time in 1978 after earning a master's degree in journalism at Columbia University. This secret and all its irony made me smile inside, as if I were getting away with some monumental deception. I knew I had been hired partly because of my blackness, but the fact was that, as a product of white Seattle and Princeton, I likely comprehended little more about the lives of ordinary black people in America than the average young white reporter. In many ways I was as sheltered and ignorant as any of them. But I was certainly curious and hungry when I arrived. God, was I hungry to experience slices of American life that my wilderness years in Seattle and Princeton had told me little about. After four years in virtual hiding as a hermit behind Princeton's ivied walls, I sprang into the gritty world of urban America, much like a leopard freed from its cage, and eagerly used the *Washington Post*, just as the *Washington Post* certainly used me, to learn about life in a way that books and Princeton could never teach.

As a young reporter my intelligence, street smarts, and journalistic skill were tested often by my editors in the *Post* newsroom, a place that operated in a high-pressure style informally known as "creative tension." This phrase, coined by executive editor Ben Bradlee, described a method of newsroom management that essentially assumed that *Post* employees were at their most productive and creative if they were regularly made to feel somewhat tense or uneasy in their highly competitive jobs. Every day presented new tests for reporters and editors—new challenges to their security—and it was only the strongest and brightest, the top editors felt, who would thrive under such pressure and competition.

One day during my baptism of fire as an intern, in August 1977, Washington's brand-new subway system suffered a major breakdown after an underground flood. That afternoon I was immediately sent out to interview stranded commuters on Capitol Hill, and I returned hours later to write a feature story about their reactions. As I sat at my typewriter nervously pounding out a lead for my story, a cigarette dangling from my lips, I noticed my editor, Herbert Denton, stride back and forth between my desk and that of another summer intern reporter, a young man named Eduardo Cue. Denton, appointed just a couple of years earlier as the first black city editor in the *Post*'s history, stood silently behind me for several moments, eyeing my story as I typed it out, before inexplicably heading back to Eduardo's desk to do the same.

Finally, after about a half hour, Eduardo, a white Spaniard schooled in the United States, approached me with a crestfallen expression on his face: "Herb told me to fold my stuff into your story," Eduardo informed me. "He likes your piece better." Neither of us had known that Denton had sent us out separately to report and write the very same story that day. The test? To see whose reporting and writing skills measured up, whose story was best to print. It was my story that was published in full the next day, along with photos of the subway breakdown, with Eduardo's name second to mine in the joint byline. I thus passed, with flying colors, a typical but important test at the newspaper, proving my ability to report and write quickly and well—without even knowing I was being tested.

Although the system of "creative tension" at the *Post* often seemed little more than corporate cruelty, with each test of my journalistic promise, I somehow managed to survive and indeed to flourish. I truly enjoyed the frenzied pace and the constant intellectual stimulation my new profession offered, and most important, I saw myself increasingly as part of a larger moral and ethical enterprise that carried immense value in a democratic society.

I explored many sides of Washington in my early work as a journalist, from the daily travails of the black poor in the housing projects of Anacostia to the alienation of middle-class white youth in the Maryland suburbs. I soon found I was very good at asking questions, mainly because I was bursting with so many of them about practically everything: Why were so many people standing in unemployment lines every day? Where did they come from, and what were the stories of their lives? How did a family in such circumstances get by on so little each week? Where did a jobless derelict go for food by day and for shelter by night? How did a cop investigate a murder or a rape? How many victims were dying of gun violence in Washington each year, month, day, hour? Each question bred countless others, and with each answer I got and each compelling feature and news story I produced, I rose in the *Post* newsroom, gaining respect and admiration from my peers, local and national awards for my writing and reporting, and greater professional and personal confidence.

Fed up with feeling intimidated by white and black people as I had been in college, I found liberation and release in my new calling, blissfully throwing myself into a host of unusual investigative reporting projects with the full backing of my *Post* editors. They encouraged me to try to follow in the paths of Orwell, Kerouac, and Steinbeck, to use my curiosity to tell stories about the lives of ordinary people and the downtrodden. One winter I lived the life of a derelict in Baltimore and Washington, eating in soup kitchens, sleeping in flophouses, and panhandling for change with the down-and-out to write about the experiences of the homeless in a twelve-part front-page series. Another year I spent three months exploring Maryland's decrepit state prison system to write a long series of stories about inmate abuses and the need for institutional reform. Still another year I spent a summer month working undercover as a migrant tomato and cotton worker in the sweltering fields of North Carolina to expose corrupt practices in the rural labor system. How I loved exploring such worlds and ways of life so strange to me, loved the feeling of writing well about the stories I uncovered and the people I met, as if I were pinching the world on its fat behind to get its attention and shouting, "Take a look at this!" I loved seeing my byline printed above my discoveries, on the front page of the distinguished newspaper, to be read by millions. But perhaps most of all, I loved feeling the power of my words to do a little good in society, helping to spur reforms in rural labor in North Carolina, bringing new light to problems in the criminal justice system, and letting Americans see the plight of the faceless homeless in a way they perhaps hadn't considered before.

My assignments at the *Post* emboldened me, enabling me to transcend barriers within myself in many ways. If I had felt fearful, wary, and isolated as a student at Princeton, I felt fearless and engaged with the world as a reporter in Washington. A large part of the difference was that I found people at the *Post*, black and white, who believed in me—Herbert Denton, Charles Krause, Howard Simons, and David Maraniss chief among them—brilliant editors and writers who were generous in their teaching and guidance. And for the first time in my life I found a community of people like me (inside, at least)—young, eager, and ambitious reporters and writers, most of us bound as comrades not by our color or class background but by an overriding sense of shared professional mission, an integration of ideals and values. For some odd reason we believed in journalism and its power to inform and improve humanity. If I had wondered at Princeton what my place was in society as a cultural oddity, I found a powerful and creative one at the *Washington Post*. Apart from occasional incidents with racial overtones that I had to swallow for the sake of rising higher, like my confrontation with the small-minded editor who questioned my credibility on a story in the wake of the Janet Cooke scandal, I generally felt my racial unusualness was welcome at the *Post*, my talent encouraged, my potential greatly valued.

In time I was asked by top editors to join the National Staff, where I essentially was given free rein to travel the country in search of good stories. I especially loved writing about race relations in places as far-flung as Cairo, Illinois, and Rosebud, South Dakota, and about black coal miners in West Virginia, the homeless in Utah, and casino workers in Nevada. It was during that period of my career in the mid-1980s that I visited the University of Mississippi at Oxford, where I spent a week throwing myself into the life of the campus, interviewing teachers, administrators, and students of both races to gain an understanding of the progress of racial integration there. My long feature story about the university and the photographs I snapped there, which appeared on the front page of the *Post* about a week later, reflected the complex reality of race across America: while I was impressed by the progress of integration and the brilliant ambitions of the black students, I was also discouraged by the stark divisions between blacks and whites, from classroom to dining hall.

One of the most startling experiences during my visit occurred when a young journalist for the campus newspaper, the *Daily Mississippian*, phoned me in my hotel room to request an interview. He had heard that a *Washington Post* reporter was on campus to write about the university and its history, and he wanted to put together a short feature about my visit. I agreed to the interview and arranged to meet the student at a certain time and at a certain table in the cafeteria in the student union.

When I arrived at the appointed hour, I found the student at the table, his notepad at the ready. But as I took my seat and extended my hand, I noticed the young man, a freckle-faced sophomore with blond hair and blue eyes, slowly turn a bright crimson as he stared back at me. As he nervously proceeded to interview me, he stared closely at his pad and held his hand over his eyes like a visor, as if a searing light were shining in his face. The more he continued like that, stammering through his questions, the more obvious it became that he was shielding his eyes to avoid having to look at me.

Finally, after a few minutes, the student dropped his hand and said, "Look, I'm sorry. This is hard for me. I've never spoken to a black person like this."

I was surprised and for a minute thought he was kidding. But after a moment's silence I realized his torment was genuine, and I tried to put him at ease. "That's all right," I said. "Just talk to me like you'd talk to anybody else."

He was the son of a Hattiesburg, Mississippi, Cadillac car dealer, he told me. The only black people he had ever run across in his life were either domestics in his household or servants for his father. He had never spoken to a black person as an equal before—certainly not anyone who represented a superior station in life, as I did—and the experience was extraordinarily jarring for him. It was as if the only world he had ever known had been shattered right before his eyes in the cafeteria at Ole Miss.

As we continued the interview, I answered all the student's questions as plainly as I could, but inside I also experienced a strange epiphany of sorts. It's hard to describe it in words now, so many years later, but as I sat there I felt myself smiling inside, exulting over what seemed a private milestone in our long family history. "Attaway, Laura and Pearl," I heard myself saying inside my mind. "That one's for you."

For in a sense the incident signaled a small confirmation that we had indeed come a long way as a black family over the past century and a half since slavery and Reconstruction. And the fact that I found that affirmation in Mississippi, the heart of the South, the very region of America where it all had begun for us, was profoundly moving.

Mississippi. That state had represented so much to my family over the years. Mississippi was where my mother's paternal grandfather, Young Turner, was born a slave on a plantation near the town of Rodney. He fled north at the outbreak of the Civil War, served in a black Union Army regiment, and afterward settled in a small town called Lebanon in south-central Illinois, where he was taught to read and write by members of a sympathetic white family. In time Young Turner became not only a remarkably successful farmer and town leader but also one of the wealthiest men of any color in his region of the state. And like Laura, he valued education above all other gifts for his nine children, who included my grandfather Edward Clifford Turner. When the white leaders of Lebanon approached the successful former slave in 1892 to ask him to donate funds to help endow the local college, Young Turner replied that he would certainly do so, but for a price: that his second daughter be admitted to the racially segregated school. She was, and four years later, in 1896, after breaking the color barrier, Mamie Turner became the first black graduate of McKendree College and went on to a long career in teaching, like many other women in the Turner family.

Mississippi. The name alone evoked many memories and haunting visions as I continued to drive west that misty October day toward Vicksburg, for it was the source of some of the best and worst times in my family's past during segregation. Mississippi was where my father had sharpened his surgical skills in a rural black clinic in Mound Bayou in 1955 and 1956, a time that coincided with the some of the bloodiest struggles in the civil rights movement.

We were living then in Nashville, where my father was training in surgery at all-black Meharry Medical College. As part of this specialized training, each year's class of five or so young surgical students was required to provide care at Taborian Hospital in Mound Bayou, some 300 miles away. This twenty-bed clinic had been started in the 1930s with funding from a black fraternal organization. The small hospital in America's poorest Jim Crow state offered the only medical care available for black people within a 200-mile radius covering Mississippi and parts of Arkansas and northern Louisiana. Most of the patients were impoverished sharecropper families who were barred from the region's white hospitals.

The Mound Bayou program provided the Meharry surgical students with firsthand experience in the field. It had been started in 1947 by Matthew Walker, Meharry's dean of surgery, a legendary charismatic surgeon with bushy sideburns and a courtly manner, whom my father studied under and greatly admired. Dr. Walker's idea was to have his surgical residents spend six-month segments providing care at Mound Bayou.

So every few weeks during his six-month residency, my father kissed my mother good-bye on our front porch in Nashville after a two-day visit and made the five-hour drive south and west through Tennessee and the lush, lonely countryside of Mississippi in my family's Pontiac. Often he worried what he would do if he ever had a flat tire or ran out of gas and found himself at the mercy of the sullen, faceless, poor white men who drove the beat-up pickup trucks and ran the filling stations and deeply resented the push for black equality. In many ways Mississippi represented the front line of the battle over equal rights, a battle that was becoming increasingly bloody. Mississippi was where a black preacher, Gus Lee, had been killed in 1955 by suspected white gunmen angry over his attempts to register black sharecroppers to vote. It was where the state's NAACP leader, Medgar Evers, was similarly arousing passions among black people and drawing death threats from angry whites. And it was the state where fourteen-year-old Emmett Till had been murdered by white thugs in 1955 for the crime of winking and saying, "Thanks, baby," to a white female store clerk. As I drove through Mississippi, heading through the rolling green fields toward the Mississippi River, I tried to imagine my father's intense feelings more than forty years earlier as he made his regular journey through the state. He used to say he felt almost haunted on those trips, the feeling lifting only when he made it to Mound Bayou, a historically all-black town where he was on duty twenty-four hours a day, working and sleeping at the medical clinic and treating every surgical emergency that came his way.

He was on duty there the night of November 26, 1955, when a black civil rights activist named Gus Courts was rushed into the clinic at about 10:30 P.M., having suffered serious gunshot wounds to his stomach and left arm. A grocer in the central Mississippi town of Belzoni, eighty miles south of Mound Bayou, Courts headed the local NAACP chapter and was leading a drive to register blacks to vote. He had been standing with his wife at his cash register when a car with two white men stopped out front. Shots rang out from an open window of the car and struck him after shattering the store's front window. Friends immediately helped Courts into a car and rushed him as quickly as they could to my father's operating table, nearly two hours away and across two Mississippi counties. En route, as Courts bled profusely in the back seat, they passed two hospitals reserved for whites only.

My father was awakened from his bed in the clinic and immediately went to work. He realized that he would have to quickly and deftly open up the patient's stomach, find and extract the bits of metal, and begin patching the holes in the intestines if the patient were to survive. For more than four hours that night, into the predawn hours, he labored with his glistening instruments and gloved hands, cutting through the patient's insides all the way to the abdominal cavity, feeling for the shotgun pellets, then doing his best to repair the holes and stop the leaks of blood and other internal fluids. He did the same for the patient's arm, which had suffered extensive nerve damage. It wasn't until after my father had finished stitching the patient up, had satisfied himself that the man would not go into shock from the severe loss of blood, and was convinced that the victim would survive the shooting, that he found out who his patient was and the circumstances of the attack.

The next day Associated Press and *New York Times* reporters sped to Mound Bayou to interview my father about the operation and the shooting, which represented another milestone in the unfolding struggle over black rights. The story was carried in newspapers around America, as well as *Jet* magazine, which published a series of photos of Courts with my father in his hospital room.

In addition, my father was interviewed by FBI agents sent from Memphis to investigate the shooting. He showed them the shotgun pellets he had extracted from Courts's arm and stomach but was told to keep them. For weeks he kept the pellets in his wallet, expecting to hand them over to the authorities whenever they called for them. But they never did. And Courts's assailants, like those of so many other black martyrs in the South, were never captured.

Courts survived. He moved to Chicago with his family to make a new life far away from the horrors of his native Mississippi and two years later traveled to Washington, D.C., to give Congress one of the first firsthand accounts of the growing bloodshed in the South being suffered by civil rights workers. I found his testimony in a leather-bound edition of the *U.S. Congressional Record* for September 1957 in my library at Berkeley, two floors below the library office where I had procured the *Tensas Gazette* on microfilm. Part of it reads:

> I was born in Mississippi, my parents and grandparents before me. We helped to make Mississippi rich and prosperous. Now, just like those Hungarian refugees from Russian oppression, you see before you an American refugee from Mississippi terror. I have had to leave my grocery business, my trucking business, my home and everything. My wife and I and thousands of us Negroes have had to run away. . . . We are the American refugees from the terror in the South, all because we wanted to vote.

Journalist Carl Rowan once wrote that when he was covering the civil rights movement in the South, he asked Courts why he, an ordinary small-town grocer in rural Mississippi, elected to put himself in such terrible danger in the first place. Courts told him, "Young man, you wouldn't understand. I just wanted to be able to say that I voted once before I died."

My father told me that he tried to contact Courts while on a visit to Chicago some years after the shooting, but by then Courts had become somewhat reclusive in his exile from Mississippi and declined to see him. He said Courts died in the early 1960s, without having the satisfaction of seeing President Johnson sign into law the Voting Rights Act of 1965, guaranteeing the ballot to every citizen regardless of race.

As I drove through Mississippi that quiet Sunday morning, I tried to envision what life must have been like for my father and mother in the South during segregation, for I could remember them only as they were during the era of racial integration in faraway Seattle many years later. I was just over two years old when we left Nashville in 1956, and my only memories of racial segregation were very faint. I vaguely recalled traveling with my family in our two-door Pontiac on dusty southern roads and my mother keeping a big glass Mason jar on the floor between her feet in the front seat. Since we couldn't use public restrooms while traveling on the highways in the South because of Jim Crow, my big brothers, Bobby and Wayne, and I had to pee in the Mason jar, which once held pickles and still smelled like them. Pissing into an old pickle jar at fifty miles an hour over bumpy roads wasn't an easy trick, and sometimes, despite their best efforts, my brothers would miss and Mom and Dad would get sore. But that was about all I could remember about those days. I had a hazy impression of warm Dixie wind coursing through the car windows, of my father's strong brown hands grasping the steering wheel, of that infamous pickle jar. From my childhood vantage point in the Pacific Northwest, it seemed as if there had been a long, dark, nightmare period in my parents' past, one I couldn't remember and would never know, one my mother often summed up for people in Seattle by saying simply, "We wanted to get as far away from the South as we could back then, and we certainly did."

But it was more complex than that, certainly in my father's case. One of my fondest memories of growing up was of the many times I joined him on his house calls to visit his patients in Seattle, a regular occurrence in our first years there in the late 1950s and early 1960s, when he was working long hours to make himself known and to establish his general practice among the city's black residents. This was long before the days of managed health care, at a time when medicine truly was *personal*. It was in many ways the prime of my father's life, as he pushed himself to succeed as a young black physician in Seattle. He was the most dashing and highly skilled man I knew, and I was proud to be his son. I thought he would be young and strong forever.

Many evenings after dinner Dad would make house calls in Seattle's Central Area or stop at the various hospitals on the city's "Pill Hill" section downtown, overlooking Puget Sound, to look in on patients he had operated on. I remember sitting in the front seat of our car as we traveled around the rain-slicked streets of the hilly green city, my short legs hanging over the edge, hearing the clatter of the windshield wipers as I rubbed my hands across the mottled surface of my father's black leather medical bag resting on the seat between us. When we stopped at a stranger's house, I would remain in the car, filling in drawings in my coloring books or watching the rain splatter and pool and race in rivulets down the windshield. I never saw my father treat his patients, but I nevertheless felt like I was helping him out in some small way, even if just hanging out in the car.

In the early days house calls were the meat and potatoes of my father's practice. During his baptism in medicine in North Carolina, just after he finished medical school in 1944, he had often delivered babies at odd hours of the night in rundown sharecropper shacks in the tobacco town he grew up in, Winston-Salem. When he migrated to Seattle after finishing his surgical training in 1956, he continued offering this sort of personalized care. He was a compassionate physician, especially to the poorest of his clients. Once he called my mother from the office to say he had just visited an elderly cancer patient at her apartment in a rundown section of the Central Area and told her the freezing winter weather would kill her before the cancer did. "Go downtown and buy an electric blanket for her, will you?" he asked, giv-

ing my mother the address. And my mother did, immediately—
she often performed such deeds on a moment's notice in support
of my father's work.

As a child I knew little about what exactly my father did to
make people well, but I knew it was important work and that his
patients were always remarkably thankful for his visits and very
respectful to him. I watched these strangers shake my father's
hand reverently and look into his eyes with admiration and gratitude when they said good-bye to him on their front steps, often
walking him to the door of his car. I invariably felt delight whenever Dad finally hopped back into the car with his medical bag in
hand and said, "Okay, Neilly, let's go to the hospital now," or
"Okay, Neilly, back home."

He was born in 1920 and raised in the shadow of the tobacco
factories in Winston-Salem, the only son of a black physician also
named John Robert Henry. His father was a thin, light-skinned,
courtly man who, as a member of a very small stratum of black
professionals, was something of a town leader. My father thus
grew up around medicine. The brick family house on East Sixth
Street was three stories tall, with the upper floor reserved for living quarters and the downstairs used exclusively by my grandfather as a medical office. At nearly all hours of the day during my
father's childhood, the ground floor was filled with patients suffering everything from broken bones or the flu, to mumps,
measles, or chicken pox, to tuberculosis or cancer.

As a boy, my father cleaned the medical office, washed his father's instruments, and folded and stocked the linens. What he
didn't enjoy for long periods during his boyhood, though, was a
mother. Irma Neal Henry, my grandmother, was an adventurous
young woman, a liberated soul way ahead of her time, who left

her husband and family on many occasions to travel far and wide. She visited the Soviet Union in the 1920s to see firsthand what life was like in a revolutionary society where she had heard that all people, including black people, were recognized as equals. (According to my father, she returned later saying it wasn't true at all and that Russia was much too cold.)

Often, as a boy, my father would accompany John Sr. in a horse-and-buggy to make house calls on patients in the Carolina countryside—much as I accompanied Dad in the car on his house calls forty years later in Seattle. They would usually return home bearing wild game or fresh vegetables as payment for my grandfather's services.

John Sr. was admiringly known as "Cap" by my father, a shortening of the word "Captain," and as "Harry" to others in Winston-Salem who knew and worked closely with him. He loved to smoke Cuban cigars and recite poetry by Whitman and Poe, and he liked nothing better than to sit in a chair on his front porch on hot and humid summer evenings, with his legs propped up on a post, and watch the traffic go by on East Sixth Street. A devout Methodist, he believed in moderation in everything, especially politics and race relations in his conservative southern city, and was keenly aware of the tenuous nature of black existence under the ever-present heel of white oppression in the South. The aphorisms my grandfather often recited reflected his attitude toward provocation and conflict:

> Thoughts unexpressed may sometimes fall back dead,
> But God Himself can't help them once they are said.

> Boys flying kites haul in their white-winged birds.
> But you cannot do that when you're flying words.

While my father similarly believed in moderation and nonviolence when it came to race relations, he developed an edge to his beliefs as a young man to go along with his desire to push the limits imposed by racism. He came of age at a time in the first half of the twentieth century when there were not many opportunities for young black men. He could have become a Pullman porter or a waiter or a civil servant or some other kind of service worker, as did many other black men who desired something better than manual labor. But he preferred a recognized profession like dentistry or medicine, as his father had, largely because he wanted respect from people.

That was always the most important thing in his life. *Respect.* One summer during his college years he worked as a baggage handler at Chicago's Union Station, toting suitcases, footlockers, and hat boxes for crowds of white travelers. Loading baggage wasn't the hardest part of the job, he told me. The toughest part was the arrogant and imperious way white people often treated him. "Hey, boy!" they liked to shout. "This way, boy!" "Grab a bag, boy!" Far more than money or other earthly gain, my father wanted the respect of others. He became a doctor because he enjoyed it, to be sure. Saving patients' lives on his operating table with his two gloved hands was certainly a satisfying calling. But he also felt a priceless sense of personal dignity and racial pride whenever people, especially white people, had to address him as "Doctor."

Respect came in both big and small ways. I remember once when I was kid he went to great pains to show me the proper way of paying for things after seeing me toss a crumpled dollar bill on the counter of a drugstore, where I was buying some soda and candy. "Like this," he told me, handing over a dollar folded neatly down the center. "Don't ever crumple money like that. Shows you've got no upbringing, that you don't think much about the person you're giving it to. Show respect for people."

And he certainly felt it was equally important to demand respect back. Whenever my white school pals visited me to play in our house on Lake Shore Drive, I knew to remind them even before they entered the house that they should be sure to address my father as "Dr. Henry," not "Mister." (He would have let me know about it if they didn't.)

My father was meticulous about many things, a result, no doubt, of both his profession and his upbringing. The suits and ties he wore always appeared neatly pressed, his shirts fresh from the cleaners, his leather shoes shiny. Upon arriving at his office in the morning, he would take off his jacket and immediately replace it with a starched and pressed white physician's jacket with "Dr. Henry" stitched in red at the pocket. His grooming habits were just as neat, his hands and nails perfectly clean at all times. He combed his thin, curly hair straight back from his forehead and, to keep it in place, would often slick a special white lotion on it that my older brother Bobby used to laughingly call "Stay Back." Frequently on call for medical emergencies, my father carried an electronic beeper with him at all times. In his suit jacket pocket he kept a small black leather-bound notebook in which he would jot down daily reminders—"See Sikes," "Beer," "New office stationery." Over the years his little black notebook turned smooth and glossy from use.

My father's disciplined personality helped to give our family life a conservative tone, one that extended in many ways to his children, perhaps me especially. The rise of Muhammad Ali in the 1960s, for instance, presented me with a dilemma. While I admired Ali's skill in the ring, I had also been taught as a boy in my father's household to detest braggarts and the conceited and to esteem humility in all things. Quiet acts of excellence always meant more than mere empty words, I was told, even if one could back the words up. Jim Brown, Willie Mays, Elgin Baylor—those were my kind of heroes.

In the face of this personal dilemma over Ali's fiery rise, I managed to find a compromise: I rooted happily for the loudmouthed champ whenever he fought white guys, no matter how obnoxious and disgraceful his behavior out of the ring, because it was important in my mind, always, that black defeat white. But when Ali fought a black contender, I usually rooted hard for his opponent, who invariably showed much more humility in the face of struggle. I figure I was probably the only black kid in America pulling in vain for quiet and dignified black fighters like Floyd Patterson and Jimmy Ellis to knock the champ down to size.

Such conservatism also influenced our household outlook on political and social change. During the civil rights movement we were squarely in the nonviolent camp of Martin Luther King, Jr., Julian Bond, and Ralph Abernathy and wary of angry provocateurs like Stokely Carmichael, Malcolm X, and H. Rap Brown. The latter were hotheads and anarchists whose political style seemed to threaten to overturn with bullets and firebombs everything we valued, including the hard-won integrationist gains that our folks had struggled and fought for through so many generations. Our ancestors had worked for centuries to claim their share of the American dream, and we were not about to accept regression after finally joining the middle class. To white America our household may have seemed fairly radical. But to black

America we were comparatively conservative in our goals and outlook.

As a young man, my father was thin but tightly muscled. He loved to play tennis and had won a number of black amateur tennis tournaments in his native North Carolina. His skin and eyes were brown, and he wore a mustache throughout his adult life, which he liked to keep pencil thin across the top of his lip, as his favorite singer, Billy Eckstine, and the suave movie actor Errol Flynn did.

As his children, we had to be sure to answer the telephone at home with a clear, pleasant "Hello?" because, as my father often reminded us, we never knew who might be on the other end—a patient in distress, another physician, the hospital calling on an emergency. The greeting was critical, he said, if only to tell the caller that this was a house where the caller was welcome and the residents concerned. There simply was no room for moodiness or discourtesy on my father's telephone line.

Impressions were important, my father emphasized, but impressions meant nothing if they were not backed up by the substance of skills and deeds. That was critical. You had to *prove* yourself worthy of the respect you demanded from others.

At twenty-one, when he finished all-black St. Augustine's College in North Carolina in 1941, my father, with his father's backing, went off to Meharry Medical College in Nashville, an esteemed and renowned institution that had educated many decades of black physicians. If you were black and wanted to be a physician in the United States in the years before about 1950, Meharry was surely the place to be, a shining jewel in the crown of black education in America. In fact, Howard University's all-black medical school in Washington, D.C., and Meharry were almost the only places to learn medicine, since aspiring black physicians, with few exceptions, were not admitted to other U.S. medical schools before the advances of the civil rights movement. As late as 1976, fully half of all black physicians working in America had been educated at Meharry.

The school was named after five Irish brothers from Indiana who donated $30,000 to endow the school in 1875. The endowment represented the fulfillment of a promise one of the brothers, Samuel Meharry, had made after a kind black family had rescued him and given him shelter in 1826 when the salt cart he was traveling in tumbled off a country road in the Ohio Valley and became mired in a swamp. According to legend, Meharry vowed to do something one day for the race of the people who were so compassionate and generous to him. The medical school endowment was his gift.

My father finished on the dean's list in his 1944 class of fifty-nine at Meharry, and in short order he married my mother, the pretty daughter of an upstanding St. Louis family, and my older brothers, Bobby and Wayne, were born. But after returning to Winston-Salem to work with his father in the small-town practice, he soon stagnated and yearned to branch out on his own. Not only into his own practice but into a specialty—surgery, the most exciting and challenging branch of medicine in his era.

The Korean conflict provided my father with a fortuitous ticket out of North Carolina. Realizing he was about to be drafted anyway, my father volunteered for the military in 1951. After completing his training in Texas, he promptly went overseas to work as a U.S. Army physician in a Military Ambulance Service Hospital unit. He was posted not in Korea but in

Heidelberg, Germany, where my mother, Bobby, and Wayne accompanied him and where I was soon conceived. Afterward he returned to Meharry to study surgery in 1954, the year I was born.

It was during their two years in Nashville between 1954 and 1956 that my parents decided to make a break from the South. Their experiences in the newly integrated U.S. military, living and socializing with white service families and enjoying the comforts attached to my father's rank as captain, had exposed them to the benefits of equal opportunity for the first time in their lives. My father in particular was keenly aware of the limits of opportunity—and respect—he could ever find among white people in the South.

This bitter reality had been brought home to him in many ways under Jim Crow, and sometimes his joys and his inner rage were bound together precisely because of racism—in much the same way as I experienced in Seattle a generation later. For example, the night before he became a father for the first time in 1947, he had taken my mother and Fredda in his new car to a movie in Winston-Salem. Afterward, as they were getting into his long black Pontiac, a white woman in an adjacent car stuck her head out the window and exclaimed, "Boy, whose car is that you drivin'?"

My father was infuriated. "Mine," he muttered. "Whose car is that *you're* driving?"

But the damage was done, the insult swallowed. All the way home on what should have been one of the happiest nights of his life, my mother recalled, he fumed, trembling and cursing under his breath, enraged at the disrespect the white woman had shown him. Years later it wasn't my brother's birth he recalled so distinctly, but the earlier incident in the parking lot of the Carolina Theater, behind the Robert E. Lee Hotel.

My father knew racism imposed strict limits on his life and potential in the South and that no matter how skilled he became in medicine and surgery, no matter how great the deeds he accomplished, he would always be in the eyes of many suspicious white people just a black boy with a shiny car. But, after his military experience in Germany, he recognized that life could be much better elsewhere, that black people got a fairer shake in other places. He had visited big northern cities like New York and Philadelphia before and discovered that life in other parts of America wasn't as pervasively harsh for blacks as white people made it for our family in the South. Not that he ever felt the North was the Promised Land or anything close to it. It was just that he could do a little more as a black man in the North. He could ride streetcars and buses, for one thing, and sit wherever he damn well pleased. He could freely try on shoes and hats in department stores without having some white clerk point him to the door or call the cops on him. He could go to picture shows and museums and use whatever public men's room he wanted. And he could vote in elections, a right not granted to millions of blacks in the South.

When he completed his surgical training in Nashville in 1956, my father moved us to Seattle, largely because it was one of few cities in America at that time with hospitals willing to accept a black surgeon on staff. It was a bold move under any circumstance. My father was just thirty-six years old and had already accomplished a lot, to be sure, especially for a young black man in America's early postwar years. But it was our new house, the house he and my mother decided to build in 1960 right in the heart of an affluent white neighborhood to gain equal access to the best public schools for us, which turned out to be the most important achievement of all for him, he later told me. For it signified more than anything else his empowerment and progress as a man from the segregated, oppressive society he had always known to something else, something better and more just, something that had always been denied him before because of white racism.

It did not come easy. The costs he paid for the "giant leap" to the white middle class may have been hidden, but they were real. When our white neighbors on Lake Shore Drive banded together in the months before our move to offer us $100,000 not to move in—a huge sum of money in 1960—my mother suggested to him that if those white people were willing to go to such extremes to keep us out, they might also be willing to go to terrible extremes to make our lives hell once we moved in.

"Maybe this isn't so good for the kids, John," she remembered confessing to him in a moment of deep anxiety and doubt.

But my father simply answered, "It's principle. You don't bend on principle," no matter how much money the white man dangles in front of you. That was not the way to earn respect.

Instead, several nights after dinner in the weeks before our move from the black world to the white, my father got in our family car and drove out to the new neighborhood to visit a few of our prospective white neighbors in person, knocking on the front door of several stately houses on Lake Shore Drive to extend his hand, introduce himself, and try to allay their fears. A few of our new neighbors were Jewish, including a dentist and a physician, both of whom had joined in the opposition to us, a fact that especially troubled and disappointed my mother. Indeed, when my family was living in Germany in the mid-1950s, they

had visited the remains of Hitler's concentration camps and
sensed the horrors suffered by Europe's Jews during World War
II. If any people should know about prejudice and injustice and
be able to sympathize with the aspirations of minorities, my
mother felt, surely Jewish people should.

But my father got little satisfaction when he visited our white
neighbors on those cool autumn nights after dinner—only fear
and empty words about declining property values. Exasperated,
he went downtown to the head office of the John L. Scott Realty
Company, the biggest real estate brokerage in the city's south
end. John L. Scott himself had been very active in organizing our
neighbors' opposition to us, once he heard that black people had
somehow, by some trick, purchased property in his territory. My
father said he met Scott at his office to try to understand more
about him, to find out why he and all the white people were
against us. He remembered asking the white realtor, "Why are
you doing this? Do you even know any Negroes? How can you
do this when you don't even know us?"

"This is business. It's about what's best for us and what's best
for you in the long run," Scott replied. "And I do know Negroes,
Dr. Henry. I like Negroes a great deal. That fellow downstairs
shining shoes in the lobby. His name's Sam. He's one of my best
pals."

My father left Scott's office shortly afterward, knowing there
would be no getting through to any of them, no matter how hard
he tried, no matter how much he reasoned. We would simply
move in when our house was finished and take whatever came.

Years later as an adult, whenever I thought about my father's
experiences back then, I wondered how he ever managed to balance within himself all the conflict and torment he must have felt

about our move and about white people. He once told me that the rainy day we moved into our new house—December 1, 1960, less than three weeks before his fortieth birthday—was the proudest day of his life, far prouder even than his graduation from medical school or even his first day working as a surgeon on the medical staffs of the white hospitals in Seattle.

"Because of everything we went through," he explained to me. "Because of what it meant. Because it was bigger than us."

He meant, I think, that our move was historic and deeply symbolic of a new era in America in which capable black people everywhere were simply *expected* to make such stands for equality and racial progress. To make a stand for the next generation.

The house was my father's stand.

But, for that experience, he had to endure a great deal of hurt, just as he did so many times growing up in the South. And as with so many things about my father, I never understood exactly how he did it. How he overcame. How he dealt with all those hurts, fitted them inside his soul. He was a quiet, often moody, melancholic, and guarded sort of man. Certainly he carried himself with an outward sense of purpose, pride, style, and conviction, but he repressed many demons deep inside him. Beneath the skin he kept tightly contained a box of pain, sorrow, and rage whose depth none of us, even my mother, ever really knew. The strongest emotion we ever saw my father express was anger, which erupted most harshly during the times he beat me or my brothers in our basement. The punishments were fairly regularly inflicted on our bare buttocks for transgressions large and small.

"Get my belt," he'd snap in a seething tone, quickly concluding all discussion about the boyhood wrong I had committed. Whereupon I would have to trudge to the clothes closet in his bedroom, select a leather belt from its door rack, and meet him downstairs. Wordlessly I would hand the belt over to him, lower my pants and underwear, and bend away from him at the waist. The basement would erupt then with the sounds of his furious voice, the slap of leather on flesh, and my shrieks of pain.

Don't you ever talk back to your mother that way!

Whap!

I won't, Daddy, I won't!

Whap!

Do you hear me?

Yes, Daddy, yes, Daddy, yes!

Whap!

Ever!

The beatings were excruciating, the pain sometimes lasting into the next day and the emotional repercussions lingering far longer. Bobby suffered his last beating at Dad's hand at age sixteen and afterward reflected for hours, amid angry tears, on how much those lashings told him about what slavery must have been like, when masters whipped slaves like mules.

But even in those terrible moments my father's rage was remarkably brief and tightly controlled. Swiftly he returned his inner fire to its box inside his soul, almost as soon as he unleashed the final lash. Today experts on child development consider corporal punishment of all forms abusive, and they may not be far wrong. But such punishment was the only way my father knew how to correct our behavior, and at that time it certainly was not an uncommon method in many homes, black or white.

My father concealed his hurts and sadnesses just as completely as his anger. My mother once told me that the only time she ever saw him weep was late one night in their first year of marriage, in 1947, when they were living in Winston-Salem, and he learned that one of his patients had died. He had worked so hard to save the patient, she recalled, and he was absolutely inconsolable with grief as he lay in bed beside her.

Now, many years later, with Mississippi's history flashing through my mind and its lush scenery flowing by my car windows in a blur of greens and browns, I was traveling due west through the state toward the Warren County Court House. I hoped to find clues to our old family puzzle there, to find the white Beaumonts whose blood we shared from so long ago. But remarkably, as I traveled, I realized my ruminations were focusing not on the white branch of our family tree, but on the black.

It was shortly after 3 p.m. when I arrived on the outskirts of Vicksburg, where I had appointments with courthouse officials and researchers scheduled for early the next morning, a Monday. Realizing that I had a couple of hours of Sunday afternoon daylight left, I immediately decided to press farther on in my journey. I turned at Vicksburg and headed due south through a forest of green hanging kudzu vines on a sleepy two-lane highway called the Natchez Trace, near the Mississippi River, to the city of Natchez, fifty miles away.

It was a fairly quick trip, for I found myself approaching the city about an hour later. Located high on a grassy bluff overlooking the Mississippi River, Natchez was a storied old town noted for its cool summer breezes and antebellum mansions. It also possessed a historic cemetery in a prime, majestic location high above the river. Throughout the nineteenth century this cemetery had provided an eternal resting place for the genteel white residents of Delta towns for miles around. I knew that A.J.

Beaumont and his widow, Mary Ann, were among them. I
wanted to find their graves.

I slowed to enter the city. Amid a clumsy collection of jarring
road signs directing visitors to the city's gaming casinos jammed
on the riverfront (Natchez is now known far more for its gambling enterprises than its antebellum gentility), I spotted a small
white sign with a historic landmark symbol informing me that
the city cemetery was just north along the river. I traveled along
a city street lined with beautiful mansions shaded by majestic
magnolia trees, some of the houses featuring grand whitewashed
porticos and tall poles flying Mississippi's red, white, and blue
state flag. The street soon wound its way into a far less prosperous neighborhood dotted with ramshackle and abandoned
houses. A little beyond this neighborhood, I found the cemetery
on the right-hand side of the road, on a beautiful plateau opposite the river to the west.

Framed by low stone walls and iron fencing, the cemetery was
a rolling expanse of trim green grass dotted with trees and sprinkled with what seemed like thousands of headstones. It was divided into numerous sections, and I drove slowly through the
first section on the right-hand side nearest the front gate, trying
to glimpse the dates of death and last names engraved on the
headstones, hoping to find a date somewhere near 1901, when
Arthur Beaumont died, or a preponderance of surnames beginning with B. Of course, as I quickly realized, to my private embarrassment, people don't die in chronological or alphabetical
order. I would have to hike on foot through those many confusing sections of headstones to locate the area with the graves from
Beaumont's time.

I parked my car and set out through the magnolias, my sandaled feet making crunching sounds in the twigs and grass. The afternoon air had turned muggy and misty, and within a few minutes beads of sweat began to collect on my brow and neck as I walked slowly amid the dead. I was alone in the cemetery save for the cicadas buzzing in the closely trimmed grass, the songbirds chirping in the treetops, and a half dozen or so dark-clad attendants at a burial on a far edge of the graveyard, seemingly a mile way.

Several of the cemetery's sections featured truly ornate iron fencing turned brown and rust-red by age. I spent more than a half hour roaming in one of those sections. Dating to the mid-nineteenth century, it presented a vast tableau of marble headstones and granite markers, some of them massive monuments topped by beautifully sculpted angels and Virgin Marys.

I continued wandering through the groves of magnolias from one old section to another. I found an old, small Jewish section and a Roman Catholic one. Scattered throughout the graveyard were numerous headstones featuring the engraved weather-worn letters "CSA," denoting that the interred was a Confederate veteran of the Civil War. Repeatedly, I ran across headstones engraved with surnames—Watson, Bondurant, Garrett, Newell—I recognized from my hours and hours of microfilm research in the old *Tensas Gazette* newspapers. These were Arthur Beaumont's friends and contemporaries during his life in St. Joseph, and their names were mentioned alongside his in numerous articles about the town's white society in the late nineteenth century.

As I rambled up and down the graveyard's knolls, I came across the cemetery office, a small two-room building with leaded-glass windows perched on the edge of a single-lane road coursing through the property. Near the door a sign read "1914 Shelter House." The building was closed, its windows and door locked tight. But near the door was a big metal bell with a long cord attached. "Ring for Superintendent" read the small hand-printed sign beside it.

I pulled hard on the cord several times, and the loud clangs of the bell echoed through the graveyard in the warm, muggy, early evening air. I waited. I took a seat on a granite wall to gather my breath, suddenly thinking for a moment what a wickedly fine assignment a graveyard search might make for my journalism students at Berkeley some day.

> You need to locate one grave out of thousands in an old cemetery. You have the name of the deceased and the dates of birth and death, but that's all. You have no other guide or reference to assist you. Find it. Deadline: 5 P.M.

I laughed softly to myself.

Several more minutes passed. No one came.

I had only a few minutes left before it would be too dark to continue, and I felt tired and sore from all the hiking, climbing, and searching after a long day's drive. Perhaps I should come back another day, I thought.

I rose and began to walk slowly to the other side of the cemetery office, where I found a pleasant little hollow near the front gate. It seemed the most tranquil section in the entire cemetery, a level expanse of green about two hundred yards square in a prime location close to the river, bordered by an old wrought-iron fence. A dark metal sign and historical marker near the fence described the section as "1st Zurhellen Addition," one of the oldest in the cemetery. Another sign close by read:

> Natchez City Cemetery—Established in 1822 on a 10-acre tract, the cemetery grew into a park notable for its variety of

19th century iron and marble work. People from all walks of life are buried in the cemetery.

I decided to wander through that section of the graveyard on the way back to my car. I strolled slowly between the rows of headstones, my eyes glancing at the names etched into each one. Many of the graves dated back to before the turn of the century. I came across one reading "MCGEE" in big letters amid the graves of a dozen or so family members—Nathan, Irene, Sarah. Among these but slightly apart, I spotted a small headstone reading, "Mammy—Henrietta Clark—1820–1908."

I walked on.

Then, on a monument barely ten feet beyond that one, I saw the letters "BEAU . . ." out of the corner of one eye. I stopped in my tracks, instantly feeling a familiar tingle in my spine, the same sensation of alert I had felt whenever I ran across those letters during my microfilm research in Davis and Berkeley.

I stepped closer and read all the letters in bold uppercase: "BEAUMONT."

The name was engraved near the top of a six-foot-tall marble obelisk. My eyes wandered to other words engraved higher on the obelisk in a half circle above the surname. "On Thy Cross I Lean," they read.

I lowered my eyes to a level beneath the name "Beaumont" and found these words:

In Memory of My Beloved Husband, Arthur J. Beaumont, Died
    April 30, 1901, Aged 62 years.
As a Husband Devoted
As a Father Affectionate
As a Friend Ever Kind and True.

I jotted the words down in my notebook and tried to capture the headstone's appearance in a line drawing. The monument seemed impressive, slightly taller than me, not as grand or elaborate as some in the graveyard, but certainly more distinguished than many. Like most of the other headstones in the cemetery, it faced east, in the direction of sunrise.

I felt profound satisfaction in that moment, along with a sense of relief that prompted a lengthy and audible sigh. "So there you are, A.J.," I told myself in vindication as I gazed at the headstone of the white man whose photograph and letter to Pearl had filled me with so many hours of torment and wonder. Here was the last resting place of the English immigrant and Confederate veteran whose life had been the focus of so much of my reflection and ambivalent rumination in recent years. If I found out nothing more about him or the whereabouts of his white descendants, I knew that at least I had the satisfaction of that moment, of finding his grave that way, just one out of thousands in the old southern cemetery.

Then I glanced at the monument next to Beaumont's, that of his widow. It was much more modest, about half as tall, smaller in size, and in granite. It read on its face:

In Memoriam
Mary A. Beaumont, May 2, 1859, June 15, 1914.
In Heaven.

Part of the short headstone was oddly in the shape of a tree trunk, with the words "Woodsmen Circle" and the likeness of a hammer and ax carved into its side. I had no idea what those words meant. I jotted them down and drew a picture of the monument in my notebook while making a mental note to research

what the Woodsmen Circle was. I ran my hand over the headstone, feeling the rough, mottled surfaces where time had left its
marks.

I couldn't tell when anyone had visited the site last. There
were no flowers, not even dead ones. I did notice atop Mary
Ann's grave an ancient, badly weathered, and discolored stone
flower urn resting upside down. I reached over to right it, but
when I did a horde of red fire ants charged out. I quickly stepped
back.

The two graves were the only ones in the plot. No other
Beaumont family members were interred there.

I had driven 502 miles from Atlanta to find the cemetery that
day, Sunday, October 12. I had discovered the graves right at
sunset, about 6:30 P.M. It was an eerily beautiful scene, utterly
quiet and still.

As I gazed at the sun setting in a blaze of orange and violet
over the Mississippi River to the west, I reflected not just on the
Beaumonts, their white descendants, and the task still ahead of
me in the courthouse at Vicksburg. I also contemplated the
many paths our black family had taken all over America in the
years since A.J. and Laura loved in the 1870s. And as I waited to
watch the sun brilliantly flame out of sight, I thought not so
much about the dead white couple at my feet as about Laura,
Pearl, Fredda, and Mary, my mother. Especially my mother.

We had traveled so far from the South since that time long
ago.

CHAPTER FOUR

Jim Crow's Shadow

My mother hated the South at the time I was born. She hated the constant struggle of simply trying to endure and raise a young family under the pervasive oppression of segregation. It was bad enough that my father was absent from our home in Nashville for days and weeks at a time in the years between 1954 and 1956, that he often traveled somewhere deep in Mississippi, filling her with loneliness and dread. She had almost grown used to that.

In fact, on the cold, snowy night I was born, January 28, 1954, in Nashville's "colored" hospital, my father was on surgical duty in Mound Bayou and she was alone. Years later, when I was growing up in Seattle, she loved to talk about that night, filling the story with vividly dramatic detail. "A comedy of errors from the start!" she'd begin, recalling how she was alone in our house on Hawkins Street when the labor pains started coming on strong.

She put my brothers, Bobby and Wayne, in the care of a housekeeper, then waddled outside to our car and drove herself to Hubbard Hospital, Meharry's teaching facility, gripping the wheel of the stick-shift car as it made its way through the slush and snow. "Then," she would go on, her eyes growing wide with excitement, "as soon as I got there, the nurse told me I had to wait. Can you believe it? They told me I couldn't deliver."

The nervous and inexperienced nurse informed her that her obstetrician, Dr. Carr Trehern, a Meharry teacher, was attending an Arthur Rubinstein piano concert across town and that it would take a while for him to rush back to the delivery room. "So the nurse pointed me to a bed," my mother would continue, "and she said, 'Just lie down right here, Mrs. Henry. And whatever you do, make sure you keep your legs together *real* tight.'"

My mother would start laughing then, her bright eyes narrowing, her straight white teeth glowing, recalling how she did her best to keep me inside her despite the pain, demonstrating with her tan-colored hands the way she grabbed her belly tight. When Dr. Trehern finally rushed in, she would conclude, she squeezed me out in no time flat.

"The nurse wrapped you in a blanket and handed you to me. And you just sort of lay there on top of me late into the night with your eyes wide open, looking at me like the 'feetis' sang' that ever lived," my mother would say, as she slipped into her old St. Louis drawl, magically transforming words like "sweetest thing."

She was thirty-one years old that year, the mother now of three little boys, working full-time as a librarian at Fisk University to support us and my father in his surgical training. Her life was nothing if not a whirl of obligations. She was, like many black women in America's long history, a "working mother" long before white feminism claimed and celebrated the term. Adding to her busy-ness was the tension she felt over my father's absences and the sheer terror of the times. The racial strife breaking out across the South made it seem to her as if we were living in the middle of a war zone. Boycotts. Firebombings. Lynchings. She didn't want to see our family hurt and was particularly fearful that her kids might become fodder in the coming struggle in Nashville over court-ordered desegregation of the public schools, which promised to be bloody.

The pressure she felt in those years was always keenest whenever she got word of a new gain or setback in the movement for equal rights. In her job at the Fisk University library, she worked once as a researcher for a noted black sociologist, Charles S. Johnson, who was also the president of the university. Dr. Johnson was an expert on race relations, had written many sociological studies of the black South, and spent a lot of time giving lectures around the country and interviews on the radio. Working for him was often like being a witness to history, my mother said. She especially remembered May 17, 1954, a warm spring day four months after I was born, when the U.S. Supreme Court announced its momentous decision outlawing racial segregation in the public schools. She felt thrilled to field telephone calls that day from reporters at newspapers around the country seeking comments from Dr. Johnson. And she vividly remembered the cheers that erupted all over the black campus as the news spread among the Fisk University students, faculty, and staff who were listening to the radio bulletins. Fisk was located right across the street from Meharry, and the *Brown* decision soon set off a spontaneous celebration on those hallowed corners of black Nashville.

But at the same time she rejoiced, my mother felt terrified. Even then, in the back of her mind, she knew that my brothers and I were among the ones who ultimately would be in the middle of all the rage and fury when the transition at the public schools in Nashville came. And she knew that many white people in Nashville would not go along with such radical change without a violent fight.

Within two years her worst fears were realized when white extremists threatened to bomb Nashville's public schools and published fiery petitions in the city's newspapers calling for white people in the state to stand together to fight racial integration. The following example was published in the *Nashville Banner* on March 5, 1956:

RALLY TENNESSEANS!

Something CAN Be Done!

Stand with Virginia, the Carolinas, Alabama, Georgia, Mississippi and our other sister states of the South in the fight to preserve our constitutional rights, including the right to maintain a fair and just separation of the races in our schools and parks.

Let It Never Be Said That Tennessee Weakly Surrendered!

One day as the Montgomery bus boycott unfolded in December 1955, my mother's stress openly erupted while she was at work. She was listening to a radio in the library with a friend, Alva Johnson, as an announcer broadcast news about a clash between the black boycotters and the white police. Her friend pumped her fist in the air in solidarity with the protesters, repeatedly interjecting, "Give it to 'em, just give it 'em! This is great!" as she heard the news.

"I don't think this is great at all, Alva," my mother shot back in rage. "You can sit there and say all this because your husband is right across the street. Do you know where John is? He's in

Mississippi, where all this stuff is going on. I'm not happy about
this at all."

"Why, Mary!" her friend replied, rendered nearly speechless
by the anger in my mother's voice. "You should be ashamed of
yourself."

"You send your husband down there while those white people
are shooting folks," my mother answered bitterly, "and then tell
me how you feel about it."

White people. White people and the old system of inequality
were the bane of my mother's existence in 1956, the source of
nearly every sorrow. She hated everything about the personal
degradations she had to endure in our everyday life in Nashville,
where we were barred from most restaurants and public parks and
relegated to the back "colored" seats of public transports and the
decrepit "colored" public restrooms. Most of all she hurt deep inside witnessing us, the next generation, having to suffer under the
same burdens endured by so many previous generations in our
family.

She had known Jim Crow very well all her life, from the moment she was born in Peoples Hospital in St. Louis, a private black
hospital established in 1903 to serve the city's African American
population under segregation. So it wasn't that the system was
new to her. It was just that the Jim Crow that she had known in St.
Louis, a cosmopolitan city at the crossroads of North and South,
where Laura and Pearl had moved to establish the family in the
1890s, was a more genteel form of racial separatism than the oppressive kind that characterized the Deep South.

In the St. Louis of my mother's happy childhood, there was
a lot that a black girl could do. She and her friends could freely

attend cultural events like the municipal opera, exhibits at the art museum, and musical concerts at Forest Park. She could ride the St. Louis streetcars wherever she wanted, along with everybody else. Racial segregation was a comparatively discreet form of evil in which the city's restaurants, movie theaters, and other amenities were rigidly separate but many other civic offerings, including the public libraries, museums, and restrooms, were not.

Her segregated schools were all quite good, and her teachers among the best and brightest of their generation of black Americans, for few other professions and opportunities in society were open to them. And these teachers were nothing if not demanding in pushing my mother and her contemporaries toward achievement.

Nevertheless, the hypocrisy of American life was ingrained in her mind from the time she was a child, so much so that she, like many young black people, often looked at the racist society with a sarcastic humor. My mother remembered the way she and her black classmates at Sumner High in St. Louis used to recite the Pledge of Allegiance every morning: "I pledge allegiance to the rag of the United States of America," they would say, holding their hands over their hearts. "And to the Republic for which it stands, one nation, under God, indivisible, with liberty and justice for all," they would conclude, making sure to mutter "them white folks" as they took their seats.

My mother ran into the real Jim Crow for the first time at age twenty-two, when she left St. Louis to attend library school at Atlanta University, in the very heart of the South. The shoe stores, department stores, buses, restrooms, drinking fountains— everything was segregated, even the beloved libraries where she had found such peace and happiness in her childhood. Life among black people in the South was pervasively insulting and bleak.

Connecting St. Louis with the South were the trains that she traveled back and forth to attend school, and it was on these trains that she often encountered the starkest contrast between her native Midwest and the South. The routine for black people was always the same, no matter which railroad she took—the Southern, the Norfolk and Western, or the Nashville, Chattanooga, and St. Louis. The Ohio River represented the racial demarcation, the Mason-Dixon line. North of this line black passengers enjoyed equal treatment on America's railroads. South of it they entered hell. When the train crossed the Ohio River from Cincinnati into Paducah, Kentucky, the conductor went up and down the aisles making sure all the black people had headed up front to the "colored" cars. These invariably were the most decrepit cars on the train and were usually located just behind the coal car that supplied the fuel.

My mother carried a bottle of rubbing alcohol in her purse to wipe the coal soot off her face. For more than thirty hours on these rattling rides, she held her bowel movements and urine in check, so she wouldn't have to use the train's unattended and unkempt "colored" lavatory, which usually overflowed with trash, chicken bones, fish bones, and sewage. By the time she arrived at her destination she was nearly always sick with fever and nausea, vomiting out of one end and having diarrhea out the other, a Jim Crow disease that could last for days.

Traveling by rail in the shadow of Jim Crow during the 1940s was like going to war for my mother. When, on a starlit night in 1944, an old high school friend named Clarence Jefferson handed her a "White–Colored" sign that he had unscrewed from a Jim Crow train before shipping off to war as a GI in the Pacific, she kept the gift close to her soul, her equivalent of a Purple Heart for the struggle that was still going on at home.

Once in 1945, when she arrived home in St. Louis for the Christmas break from her job at Bennett College in Greensboro, North Carolina, she lay hot and feverish in bed for days after the Jim Crow train ride. At this point her mother, Fredda, insisted she do something. That she fight the system. The granddaughter of the English immigrant A.J. Beaumont and the daughter of the light-skinned Pearl, Fredda had so much white blood in her that most strangers would have sworn she was white. She had straight brown hair, light hazel-colored eyes, and fair skin, so fair that no one ever bothered her or even thought twice about her when she broke the color line to shop at department stores or shoe stores on her visits to my mother in the South.

When, as a child, my mother accompanied Fredda on trips to downtown St. Louis, where Fredda would pay the family's bills, she never failed to notice the way the white clerks at the gas, electric, and telephone offices would look up in shock upon seeing her and her mother together. The two visions didn't seem to go together. Why was this white woman with this little black child? Such puzzled reactions by white strangers constituted some of my mother's earliest and most vivid memories.

Indeed, Fredda or her own mother, Pearl, could easily have passed over to the other side and lived as a white woman, married a white man, raised a white family, and disappeared into white America leaving hardly a trace, as many very light-skinned black people did for centuries to get a fairer shot in American society. But, though they appeared white outside, both Fredda and Pearl were ebony black inside. Pearl would never have left the world of her darker-skinned mother, Laura, and Fredda felt the same. She had always known somehow, from her earliest years growing up in her grandma Laura's boardinghouse in St. Louis, that there was no happiness or love for her on the other side of the color line.

And love was all that mattered. *Love.* That's what the Bible said, didn't it? Passing outwardly as something she was not, forsaking all that she loved just to live a little better, was out of the question. And when in 1918, at age twenty-three, Fredda met the handsome, amiable, dark-skinned man of her dreams, Edward Clifford Turner, a postman who came from a big and happy black farming family in Lebanon, Illinois, she knew her life's path was set.

Once when my mother was about fifteen, she asked her mother if she had ever considered living as white, even for an instant. "No, never," her mother replied. "I always knew I'd rather live my life as a middle-class colored woman than a poor white any day."

And that's what Fredda did. Throughout her adult life A.J. Beaumont's granddaughter never moved from her beloved Ville, even as it rapidly decayed in the 1960s and 1970s, as so many of America's inner-city neighborhoods did with the exodus of the black middle class to the suburbs. Into her eighties Fredda insisted on walking and traveling by bus in the increasingly mean, abandoned streets of the Ville to go to the grocery store and run errands downtown. On more than one occasion she encountered tough black youths who didn't know a thing about her and spat and cursed at her, calling her a "honky" and an "old white bitch." The degeneration of her beloved Ville was the greatest sadness of my grandmother's long life.

It was in the Ville in 1945 that Fredda devised a plan for my mother to trick Jim Crow. Angry and tired of seeing her daughter suffer constantly from her train travel, Fredda urged her to masquerade as a white woman on the southern railroads, securing better accommodations and treatment in the White Only cars.

"You've got to act like you *belong* there. It's your attitude," my grandmother admonished my mother, whose thicker, wavy hair and tan-colored skin made her more noticeably black than either Fredda or Pearl. Fredda sat my mother before the bedroom mirror and proceeded to dab face powder all over her face and arms, then pulled a hat down low over her head to cover her hair.

"Oh, Mama, this'll never work," my mother protested.

"It will *too* work," Fredda answered, her voice filled with indignation. "But you've got to act like you belong there, do you hear? It's your attitude. You just sit in your seat and you stare straight ahead and don't you let those white people bother you. They won't make you move."

So my mother tried it, more to mollify Fredda than for any other reason. On her trip back south she remained in the White Only car. By the time the train crossed into Kentucky heading south into Dixie, it was the middle of the night and my mother found herself dead asleep on the shoulder of a white man sitting beside her. He was asleep as well.

But then the conductor came along checking to see that all the white and black people were in their right places on the train. He lifted my mother's hat to see her powdered face, then shoved his index finger into her shoulder. "Forward," the white man ordered. "Forward," to the Jim Crow car.

"I did exactly what you said," my mother later wrote Fredda after she arrived back in Greensboro in January 1946, sick with Jim Crow fever once more. "I sat in that car and acted like I belonged.

I really did. I had on the white powder and I was even asleep on the shoulder of a white man. But it didn't do a bit of good."

My mother said she vowed she would never again try to pass as something she was not. But now, ten years later, she was watching her own children grow up under the same oppression, the same racial meanness, the "same ol' shit," as she put it when she was feeling her most discouraged and depressed.

What made it worse was that she knew damned well that life could be much better. She had glimpsed a bit of the "other side" of the mountain in American society just a few years earlier in Germany, between 1951 and 1953, when my father served in the U.S. Army. Equality was enforced by law in the newly integrated U.S. armed forces, and my parents had thrived under a system in which white enlisted men crisply saluted my father as "Captain," a white soldier escorted my brother Bobby to school each morning, and my mother was respectfully addressed as "Mrs. Henry" and "Madam" wherever she went. My father found himself working side by side with white surgeons and nurses. For the first time in their lives they felt *free* from the constraints of segregation.

It was especially fantastic to be stationed in Heidelberg, a city rich in intellectual and cultural history, home of Europe's oldest university, built in 1386. Set in the valley of the Neckar River and surrounded by thick forests, the picturesque eight-hundred-year-old city had been the birthplace of German Romanticism and an inspiration to centuries of great thinkers and writers, Hegel and Goethe among them. Mark Twain, too, had rhapsodized about Heidelberg in his 1880 book, *A Tramp Abroad*, calling the enchanting city "the last possibility of the beautiful." Twain had traveled across Europe on a Grand Tour to find release from a protracted case of writer's block he was suffering during his creation

of *The Adventures of Huckleberry Finn*, the classic American novel of
race, youth, and life on the Mississippi. The year of his visit was
1878, one year after the freed slave Laura gave birth to Pearl.

Despite Heidelberg's role as a center of fascist "brown shirt"
support for Adolf Hitler, the city had been spared bombing by
the Allies during World War II. Just a few years removed from
the war, and three-quarters of a century after Twain, my mother
and father found inspiration of a different kind. My mother
gushed about the liberties they discovered in Europe in numerous letters to her family in St. Louis. In late June 1952 she wrote
to Fredda:

> *We went to one small Austrian club one night and John and I
> were sitting at the table alone while Alice and Foster were dancing.
> And get this: A white fellow came over to our table and said in all
> sincerity—out of the clear blue sky—"God, am I glad to see you
> people. I just got over here today from the States and it does my
> heart good to see somebody from home—and to see you here doing
> the things you should be able to do back there." He emoted for
> about ten minutes and I became convinced that he sure must have
> been homesick, to carry on that way. John had on civvies, but the
> white guy said right away, "You're in the medical corps, aren't
> you? I can tell." He was from Minnesota and asked where we were
> from. We said North Carolina, and he said, "God, what a hell of a
> place to be from!"*
>
> *That white man never would have approached us like that in
> the States. Can you imagine? But here, in Heidelberg and across
> Europe, we are suddenly Americans.*

Yet back in Nashville just two years later, life was as hard as
ever. My mother was "Girlie" and "Missy" once again to all the
white shopkeepers, and all of us were relegated to a second-class

citizenship. Meantime, my father was struggling to find a place for himself as a trained black surgeon in an America that was far from ready to accept one. He agreed with my mother that they needed to find somewhere far from the South for our family to live. Unlike so many black people caught in the maw of terror and change in the region, we were fortunate to possess the means and opportunity to escape. But to where?

My father's specialty was abdominal surgery, a skill he sharpened at the rural clinic in Mound Bayou and under steady fire at Hubbard Hospital's busy emergency room in Nashville, where he tended to shooting, knifing, and car accident victims, gaining the sort of priceless medical training only an inner-city hospital could provide. The plan my parents soon decided on was that once he finished his training in 1956, we would try to settle somewhere in the Midwest or farther east, between her family in St. Louis and his in Winston-Salem. My parents wanted to stake out a new place for us but didn't want to settle too far from the people they loved.

Most important, they hoped to find somewhere in America that offered good public schools, livable neighborhoods, and especially an accepting atmosphere for a young black surgeon to practice his skill. The prospective city and its medical community would have to possess a high degree of racial tolerance, since a black surgeon was a rarity in America then. Indeed, according to census data, 4,026 black physicians were practicing medicine in the United States in 1950, less than two percent of the nation's total. While I could find no available breakdown of these statistics into medical specialties such as surgery, the numbers were clearly quite small. Meharry's postgraduate surgical training program was begun only in 1941, and the first board-certified black surgeon to be trained under director Dr. Matthew Walker finished the program in 1948. According to Meharry records, my father was just the sixteenth surgeon to finish the school's still-fledgling residency program. When he completed his training in 1956, he was among the first fifty black surgeons in American history to graduate from one of the two surgical residency programs affiliated with black medical schools and accredited by the American Medical Association and the American Board of Surgery. (Howard University Medical College's surgical program, begun in 1935, was the other.)

My father's biggest dream was to pioneer, to put his skills and training to work in a topnotch hospital in the mainstream of American medicine, to pursue a dream often expressed by a trailblazing black surgeon of his era, the renowned blood plasma researcher Dr. Charles Drew—to take advantage of the new age of "equal" opportunity and set new standards of black possibility. As my father once told me years later, he wanted "to see what I was made of." The problem was that few places in America seemed to possess all the civic qualities my parents were looking for. It was one thing for the government and the courts to begin to outlaw racial segregation in schools, public transportation, and other areas, but it was another for civil and professional societies—white people themselves—to bend with the new ways.

Just as Jackie Robinson had found it hard to gain acceptance from many of his white peers in his chosen profession when major league baseball integrated in 1947, my father found very few hospitals in the Midwest ready or willing to take on a black surgeon in 1956. In some ways my father and other black surgeons may have faced greater difficulties in integrating mainstream medicine than Robinson did in baseball. My father and his black contemporaries were not, for the most part, blessed with the help of a white visionary like Branch Rickey, someone who possessed the desire or the power to force the issue of racial integration and acceptance on his white peers. In fact, the American Medical Association—the preeminent professional organization in the United States—historically barred black physicians from membership in many state and local branches, particularly in the South. Since membership was required by most hospitals for surgical and other hospital privileges, black physicians were effectively kept out of these hospitals until 1968, when the AMA finally voted to amend its constitution to bar racial discrimination at both the local and the national level.

So, in 1956, despite his excellent and fully accredited surgical training at Meharry and his U.S. Army medical experience, my father was either denied surgical privileges outright or actively discouraged from seeking them at white-run hospitals throughout the Midwest because he was black. He and my mother traveled that year to Louisville, Cincinnati, Lima, Indianapolis, Omaha, and many other places in search of a place to call home, but at each hospital the message was essentially the same: "Whites Only."

The reasons had far more to do with fear, ignorance, and bigotry than with science, of course. The system did not want the hands of black doctors healing the bodies of white people. "White society was scared to death in particular of the idea of a black doctor treating white women," explained my uncle, Dr. Frank Demby, a 1957 graduate of Meharry and retired longtime medical director of Napa State Hospital in California, one of the largest public hospitals in America. "It's that simple. That's why they didn't want any of us in their hospitals. It was the same old racial stereotype, the same old fears about sex, the same old racist stuff that guided America all along."

"In those days, in the 1950s, some of America's bigger cities— Washington, New York, Chicago—were beginning to see black surgeons obtain hospital privileges for the first time," noted Dr. William E. Matori, professor of surgery and director of continuing medical education at Howard University Medical School, when I called to ask him about the difficulties black pioneers faced in medicine in the postwar era. Matori was a contributor to a remarkable two-volume history of black surgeons entitled *A Century of Black Surgeons: The U.S.A. Experience*, published in 1987, in which my father is listed. "But if you were starting out somewhere new, in a place that hadn't really seen a black surgeon before," Matori continued, "you absolutely had to have the support and acceptance of your white fellow surgeons. And most of these white people who were approached just feared the reaction of their other colleagues. It's like the white man who says, 'I'd love to have you over to dinner, but you know the neighbors would object.' That was the real hurdle we all had to face."

Without a hospital to operate in and without the support of the white medical community, my father couldn't practice his skill in the places he and my mother wanted to live. They realized they would need to expand the scope of their search greatly.

And then, in March 1956, something else happened, something wretched and terrifying that made their search for peace and opportunity in America even more of a pressing and desperate concern.

I was sick with an earache on the cool March night that it happened, a two-year-old toddler lying fast asleep on the bed next to my mother in our house on Hawkins Street in Nashville.

It was late on a Friday night, my mother recalled. My parents had gone to the movies with another black couple earlier at a "colored" theater and afterward invited the friends over to the house for drinks. Then, as often happened in those days during my father's surgical training at Meharry, the telephone rang. It was a nurse at Hubbard Hospital's emergency room. There had been a shooting, and the hospital needed my father in the operating room.

"Will you be long, John?" my mother remembered asking him.

"I don't think so," he said, pulling on his jacket.

"I'll wait up for you, then."

My father hurried off, and the visitors said good-bye too. My mother checked on my brothers, who were sleeping in their bedroom near hers in our single-story house, then got into bed with me to read a magazine.

The house was still.

Half an hour after my father's departure, she heard a squeak in the hallway outside her bedroom, a sound she recognized as a footstep in a particular place on the wooden floorboards. Thinking it was my brother, she called out, "Bobby?" but got no response. Then she heard the squeak again. Before she could make another sound, a stranger appeared in the doorway and quickly approached the bed with a foot-long knife in his hand.

"Don't you say a word," snarled the intruder, a tall, dark-skinned black man with a bushy head of hair, cursing at my mother as he placed the knife first against her throat, then against my back as I slept beneath the blanket.

She stayed as still as she could.

"Please don't hurt my baby," she said to the man. "Please

don't hurt my baby. . . ." Over and over during the next long minutes, she repeated the words like a religious incantation, "Please don't hurt my baby," as he kept the knife on my back and attacked her.

When the man was finished, he slowly backed away from the bed and pulled up his trousers, still clutching the long-handled knife in his hand. He demanded her money and grabbed the few coins that spilled from my mother's purse after she managed to hand it to him. A moment later he turned his wild-eyed glare on her again. "Don't you open up your mouth, bitch," he said, cursing at her again before disappearing into the night just as suddenly as he had appeared.

My mother listened for one second. Five seconds. Ten, she recalled. Then she got up and reached for her bathrobe on the chair next to the bed. She pulled it on, held it closed tightly with her hands, and dashed on her tiptoes into the living room. She flicked on the ceiling light switch. The attacker was gone.

She could hear herself breathing each breath, loudly and deeply. She locked the front door latch, ran through the kitchen to make sure the back door was locked, then raced to Bobby and Wayne's bedroom.

How did he get in? The doors had all been locked, she knew.

She checked to make sure the boys, nine and six, were safe and still fast asleep in their beds. Then she noticed their bedroom window was wide open, wider than it had ever been, as the cool air of the Nashville night filled the room. She pushed the window down, locked it tight, and returned to the living room, where she picked up the telephone and slumped on the couch.

Tears ran in hot streaks down her face. She wiped her eyes with her trembling hands. She struggled to stop shaking. Her legs, her arms, her hands, nearly every part of her seemed to quiver without control.

She picked up the receiver and dialed o for the operator. "Please, can you give me the police?" she remembered saying through muffled sobs.

She heard several clicks on the line, then the sound of ringing. Then a connection. She took a deep breath. "I want to report . . . a crime," my mother heard herself saying into the phone, still overcome by the eerie sense of separation in time and space she first felt when the attacker tore away her nightgown. She felt as if her mind had somehow separated from her body and that they were now two completely different and disconnected things.

"What sort of crime?" a voice asked her.

"It's . . . a rape," she remembered stammering. "I've been raped."

She heard the white police operator's voice grow excited. Rape was the sort of crime that many women in 1956 hesitated to report because of stigma and fear. The policeman said he would have someone at our house right away.

My mother took a few more deep breaths, then reached to switch on the lamp on the stand beside her. Then she got up and went around the house flicking on lights everywhere, in the dining room, the hallways, and the kitchen, killing every speck of darkness she could find.

She then called my father at the black hospital where he was chief resident surgeon, the same hospital where she had given birth to me on the snowy night two years earlier. It was located a mile northwest of Tennessee's state capital downtown, not too far from our house on Hawkins Street, which was located barely a block from Twelfth Street, in the heart of the city's ghetto.

Most black people lived in this part of the city because of racial segregation, and Twelfth Street was a commercial hub everyone had to live with, a sometimes dangerous street after dark.

My mother began crying again as she waited for my father to come on the line and couldn't stop when he picked up the phone moments later in Hubbard Hospital's emergency room. She told him what had happened through her sobs. He said he would return home immediately.

The rest of the night was a blur to her. First the Nashville police arrived in a flash of red and white lights that lit up the neighborhood. White detectives with thick southern accents tried to reassure her as they pressed her for information. My mother didn't know if she was making any sense. The words just came tumbling out as if she had no control over them. The next hour was almost like a fantasy, a weird nightmare with one strange scene blending into another, little of it comprehensible to her.

"I was lying in the bed with my baby . . . I was reading . . . I heard a noise . . . I saw a man . . . he had a knife . . . he came to the bed . . . he put it against my neck . . . then he put it against my baby's back . . . then . . . ."

"Did he hurt the child? Did he hit you or cut you with the knife?"

She shook her head no. She answered all their questions, and the lead detective grew especially concerned upon learning that her husband, a surgeon, was away working at the hospital when the attack occurred.

"A man out doing good for his people in the dead of night, and this happens," the white man said. "Don't you worry, Mrs. Henry. We're going to find this man."

My father soon arrived. He wrapped my mother in his arms as

the police finished checking the house, inside and out, for evidence. After the police were done, my father called a fellow physician at Meharry who lived in our neighborhood, and he soon arrived to examine my mother. He checked her thoroughly and reassured her that she was okay. He also told my mother and father not to worry, that he would perform an abortion if she was pregnant.

And my mother began to weep uncontrollably anew.

"You're the third victim I've seen in the last two weeks," my father's colleague said. "But you're the only one who reported it to the police."

Late that night my father ran a hot bath for my mother, and after taking me out of their bed and placing me in my crib, he took the bedclothes and threw them in the trash. He telephoned Fredda in St. Louis, told her what had happened, and asked her to please come to Nashville as soon as she could. Then he changed the sheets, turned out all the lights in the house, and held my mother closely in his arms as she quivered and sobbed through the night.

For weeks afterward my mother and father struggled to cope with the rape. My mother couldn't sleep without all the lights on in the house and often went to bed fully clothed. She shook uncontrollably for weeks. The Nashville police frequently visited her at work in the library at Fisk to show her mug shots of suspects, none of whom resembled the man who had attacked her.

The more she thought it about, though, the more she thought it might be best, in a perverse sort of way, if the man simply got away and never had to face the justice system. She knew that if they did catch him, the white cops would hurt him, and that if he was found guilty, the court system could kill him. She didn't want that on her conscience. And she felt deep down that the man needed help, mental help of some kind, more than he needed to be punished. In time she began to wish that the police would just leave her alone. She wished she could just pick up her life and start somewhere else.

But my father's behavior troubled her just as much. He didn't trust the white Nashville police to do what needed to be done, and in the weeks after the rape he tried to seek justice himself. He bought a gun and spent hours searching Twelfth Street for the suspect, my mother recalled. Three times he brought strangers to our house at the point of his gun, each time asking my mother if this was the man. Each time she answered no and pleaded with him to stop trying to take the law into his own hands.

Not long afterward she received a call from Dr. Matthew Walker, my father's surgical idol and the mentor to many generations of black American surgeons at Meharry. He was checking to see how she was doing and wondered if there was anything he could do for her. My mother told Dr. Walker she was doing okay but was terribly worried about my father. "Please tell him not to try to hunt for this man," she said.

My father stopped his search soon after.

Time passed. Wounds began to heal—or at least to hurt somewhat less. And my parents' search for a new life somewhere far away from Jim Crow and the harsh despair of Nashville continued.

Frustrated by the discrimination he kept encountering at midwestern hospitals, my father decided to look farther west. My parents had heard wonderful things about the Far West from a white army colleague, a warrant officer from Minnesota, whom they had met in Germany in 1951. The white officer and his wife used to rhapsodize especially about the beauty of the Pacific Northwest, describing the rivers, the mountains, the fishing. It sounded so clean, fresh, and different that the images stuck in my parents' minds when they returned to the States.

That summer, in 1956, my parents dropped my brothers and me off at our grandparents' house in the Ville in St. Louis and, following the path of Lewis and Clark, headed across the Mississippi River and the Great Plains states on a long expedition west, with plans to visit Denver, San Francisco, Los Angeles, Portland, and Seattle. It was Seattle that my mother and father visited first, and they never went any farther. My father drove our old cream- and orange-colored Oldsmobile up and over the Cascade Mountains, across the Lake Washington Floating Bridge to the sparkling city by Puget Sound, and they were astonished by what they saw. The scene that spread before them was so idyllic, so blessed with clear air, freshwater lakes, tall pines, Douglas firs, and majestic snowcapped horizons, that it reminded them of Stockholm, of Salzburg, and especially of Heidelberg, where they had enjoyed a taste of freedom and equality for the first time in their lives as black Americans.

Like Heidelberg, Seattle was a small, peaceful, and provincial city back then, but one populated by many different kinds of people, Scandinavians, Italians, American Indians, Chinese, Japanese, and a small but growing number of blacks—1.7 percent of the population in 1950. Many of the newer residents had come to Seattle for work during the war years. To my parents the city certainly seemed, on its face at least, much more tolerant of human differences than the South ever could be because it was so diverse.

My father interviewed at all the hospitals in and around Seattle's First Hill medical district—"Pill Hill," people in Seattle still call it. After passing the Washington state medical and surgical board examinations, he found to his surprise that he was quickly invited to join the surgical staff at Doctor's, the Sisters of Providence, and St. Francis Cabrini hospitals.

The small but growing city—whose population expanded nearly 20 percent from 467,591 in 1950 to 557,087 in 1960—needed good surgeons, and it apparently didn't matter what color the surgeons came in. Or, at least, no one had thought to explicitly exclude nonwhites from the city's medical community, since there were only a handful of nonwhite physicians in the entire state anyway. Of Washington's 2,754 licensed physicians practicing medicine in 1950, just three were listed in census data as "Negro" and ten as "other nonwhite."

My parents stayed at a lovely place, the Sorrento Hotel, high atop Madison Hill near the hospitals overlooking the city, and for both it was a wonderful experience simply to register at the front desk and not have to worry about being turned away because of their race. One night, while my mother and father admired the view of Elliott Bay at sunset from their hotel room window, watching the ferry boats cross back and forth from Bainbridge Island, they realized almost simultaneously that the city possessed practically everything they could ask for.

"Why don't we just stay, John?" my mother remembered asking softly.

Dad took only a moment to reply: Why not?

So it was that in July 1956 my parents decided that Seattle was where we would live. My mother traveled by rail back to St. Louis to pick up my brothers and me from the old house in the

Ville, having meantime arranged to have our furniture and household goods, including the beloved china dinnerware she had purchased in Germany, shipped to Seattle from Nashville. Soon we all boarded a westbound Great Northern Pullman to join my father in the Pacific Northwest for good.

My father had arrived in Seattle at about the same time as a Meharry classmate from Louisiana named Philip V. Lavizzo, the father of the girl who would become my first sweetheart fifteen years later. Together that July, Dad and Dr. Lavizzo became the first black general surgeons in the history of Seattle, and the city, so far away from everything we had ever known, became our new hometown.

During all the years I was growing up in Seattle between 1956 and 1972, my parents never mentioned the sexual assault on my mother. Not once. They certainly never discussed it in front of us, their children, if they did mention it at all to each other. I guess they figured there was no reason to talk about it, given all the other bewildering things going on in our family's life as we came of age during the vexing era of racial integration.

As far as I, my brothers, and my sister, Sharon (born in Seattle in 1959, three years after my mother's rape), knew, a stranger had once tried to break into our house a long time ago on a cool March night in Nashville when I was a baby, but that was it. A burglar. A thief. A "bad guy," just like all the bad guys Eliot Ness and Matt Dillon were trying to catch each week on our black-and-white television in the 1960s. But the bad guy didn't get a thing from us. He was foiled somehow. Right had prevailed. That's what we always thought.

To us, the attempted break-in was just a factual event in our family history. My brothers, sister, and I knew it had happened, but we figured that it wasn't especially important, though it did produce certain repercussions in our daily lives. My oldest brother, Bobby, who was nine when it happened, vividly re-membered the burly Nashville policemen who came to dust for fingerprints on his bedroom windowsill the next day—the first white people he had ever seen in our house. He also recalled seeing a worker erect iron bars on all of our windows soon thereafter.

The break-in led to a new addition to our family, a gentle-tempered boxer who moved with us to Seattle later that year. We named him Sang because he seemed just "the feetis' sang" to Mom. Another result of the break-in was that we had to avoid playing anywhere near Dad's clothes closet, for Dad had a gun in there somewhere. And the break-in was why we all had to make sure to shut and lock the doors and windows tight each night on Lake Shore Drive, why my mother always felt uneasy, perhaps more so than we figured was warranted, if my father had to leave her alone in the house at night.

From the time I was a little kid, I knew that my mother and fa-ther had migrated to the Pacific Northwest from the Deep South to make a better life for us, to get as far away from the evils of Jim Crow and institutionalized bigotry as they could. I knew that that very quest had fueled much of our family's spirit, providing its lifeblood in the second half of the twentieth century. What I didn't know until many years later—what none of my siblings knew—was that Nashville had held even greater evils for my mother and father, evils that were deeply personal and painful.

It wasn't until the mid-1980s, when all of us were grown, out of the house, and leading our own lives in different parts of America, that my mother revealed what really happened that night in Nashville. By then I guess she had come to peace with it herself. She was retiring from her twenty-six-year career as a public school librarian in Seattle, proud that her four children were happy and independent, and keen on tying up the loose ends in her life.

My mother had always been open and honest about most things in our family and didn't like keeping secrets from us. The rape was the biggest secret of her life, and I guess she felt that letting us all know about it then, so many years later, would help fill in some pictures from our childhood for us and complete her own sense of healing.

I was thirty-one years old, living and working as a reporter in Washington, D.C., when my mother, on a visit from Seattle in 1985, told me almost offhandedly about the attack. We had gone for a walk near Dupont Circle one afternoon when she noticed the iron burglar bars over windows in the row houses on Nineteenth Street Northwest, near my apartment. She said they reminded her of the bars that were put up over the windows of our house on Hawkins Street in Nashville the year Dad was finishing his surgical training at Meharry.

"For that guy who tried to get in," I said.

She paused a moment and slowed her gait before speaking again. "He did get in, Neil. We never told you kids, but he did get in," she said. "He raped me. He held a knife on your back while you were sleeping next to me and he raped me."

I felt my breathing stop as I heard her words. I remember feeling as if I were frozen in place and sick inside, as if time and life and the earth had suddenly stood still. All I could stammer was "What?" and then question followed question after question.

We went to a coffeehouse and she told me the whole story, very calmly and matter-of-factly, from beginning to end, noting the attack was even covered in the Nashville newspapers. Rapes weren't often reported to the police in those days, and the rape of a black surgeon's wife had seemed especially newsworthy.

During that visit, she and I took the subway one morning to the Library of Congress to try to find the Nashville newspaper articles on microfilm. The library's periodical holdings, located in an office building across Independence Avenue from the Capitol, included microfilms of nearly every day's issue of nearly every newspaper in America, dating back to the eighteenth century. My mother wasn't sure of the exact date of the attack but knew it had to be near St. Patrick's Day. She had always associated St. Patrick's Day with her nightmare, she told me.

So we searched the March 1956 issues of the *Nashville Tennessean* and the *Nashville Banner* that morning, and within minutes we came upon the week of St. Patrick's Day in the reels of microfilm. My mother's face radiated anxious curiosity as we looked through the news pages, scanning each story in the columns of type. She discovered the article first. Suddenly, pointing to a small item on page 2 in the March 19 issue of the *Nashville Tennessean*, she exclaimed, "There! *There* it is, Neil."

The article was surrounded by larger news stories about the smashing of Joseph Stalin statuary in the Soviet Union, the acceptance of the first black students at the University of Texas, and a debate by southern newspaper editors over the pace of racial integration. Headlined "Attack Reported by Doctor's Wife," it read simply:

The wife of a Negro physician reported to police that she was raped in her bedroom shortly after midnight yesterday by a tall, bushy-haired man who threatened her with a knife.

The Negro attacker entered the South Nashville home after removing a storm window, according to Sgt. Carney Patterson of the city police department.

He slipped through a bedroom where two small sons were sleeping to enter the woman's room, Patterson said. The doctor was on call when the attack occurred. A third child was sleeping in the room with the woman, police said.

"Why didn't you ever tell us?" I said after reading the article slowly, over and over, on the microfilm reader. "Why didn't you let us know?"

"You all didn't need to know. For goodness' sake, what purpose would it have served to tell you?" she answered softly. "My word, you were having challenges enough when you were growing up. You didn't need to know about that."

For many minutes I couldn't speak. I felt tears welling in my eyes. I stumbled over my words. "How did you ever get over it?" I asked. "How did you cope?"

"You probably never get over it, honey," she replied after a pause, her brown chin resting in her hand as she sat back in the chair, her dark curly hair sprinkled with gray, her eyes reflecting a soft serenity. "I guess I haven't still. It's only been in the last year or two that I've started to feel safe again, and it's been, what? Nearly thirty years now."

She said it could have been a lot worse, all things considered. The crime wasn't murder, after all. The attacker didn't beat her or stab me with the knife. We were alive. We had survived it. And wasn't that the most important thing? Then, as she read the article again, she suddenly chuckled slightly and turned to me with an inexplicable smile on her face, a smile that seemed so out of place.

"You know what was really funny? It sure wasn't funny then, but I find it hilarious now," she said. "This ugly man, when he's finished, he climbs off me and he says, 'Give me your money.' So I go get my purse on a chair next to the bed, and there's practically nothing in there, just coins. I've got no cash at all. So I tell him, 'Can I write you a check?' Can you believe it? I mean, how *dumb!* I said, 'Can I write you a check?'"

And then, right there in the main reading room of the Library of Congress, my mother put her palm over her heart and started laughing so hard that tears came to her dark brown eyes. It was the same beautiful laugh I remembered from my childhood whenever she heard a good joke from one of her friends or a funny story from one of our crazy days at school with the white kids—a laugh that was so full and infectious. Soon I found myself starting to laugh with her, purely by reflex. We laughed and laughed for several minutes together like that, releasing ourselves to the irony and strange liberation of the moment. As I gazed at my mother next to me, I felt more respect for her than I had ever felt for any human being.

A couple of years later I summoned enough nerve to ask my father about the rape. We were having coffee together one morning in Seattle, where I was visiting on vacation. "Who told you about that?" he asked with a start, his eyes filled with fire, only nodding slightly and looking away when I told him that Mom had.

My father was never very forthcoming about his emotions or reflective by nature, and he certainly found it difficult, visibly so,

even to think about the attack when I mentioned it to him. After
a long pause he sighed and glanced out a living room window.
For a moment I thought he wouldn't answer at all. But then he
started to speak in a voice so soft I had to edge closer to hear him.
He told me that for a long time, even after we had moved to
Seattle, he would find himself taking a second look at strangers
he ran across who even remotely resembled the man my mother
had described to the police. Somehow, in the back of his mind,
he feared that the rapist had followed us to Seattle.

It was crazy, he told me. There was never any reason to suspect that the rapist had followed us or to suspect anyone in
Seattle, but suspect these strangers he did, especially the aimless,
rough, unemployed black men he ran across in the city's Central
Area slum. He couldn't get over the maddening mental picture of
a stranger casing our house in Nashville that night, witnessing
him leave for the hospital, and then committing the assault while
we were unguarded. He told me he was obsessed with the rape
for years and only began to get over it when he saw how my
mother, determined to get on with life, had slowly gotten over it,
had stopped being so afraid—at least outwardly. "She was very
strong," he said as he sipped his coffee with a sad and distant look
in his eyes. "That's the only reason we managed to make it. She
was just incredibly strong."

As I listened to my father that morning and remembered my
mother's words, I realized how impossible it would be for anyone
to ever get over such a thing completely. How could you? Like
most hurts in our family, this one, too, had been buried, swallowed, pushed somewhere deep within, probably in the same
place where the racial hurts went. That was our longtime method
of emotional survival, after all. The hurts had to be stowed away

somewhere if my mother and father were to get on with the struggle, raise their children, and survive the various challenges society presented every day of their lives. There were more important things to do than obsess about the past. It was over. Done.

In the years that followed, I often thought about my mother's rape by the black man in Nashville, turning her nightmare over and over in my mind and trying, in retrospect, to make it fit into the emotional fabric of our family life and my childhood. I realized the repercussions were many and powerful, not least of which was its role in shaping my brothers' and my attitudes toward a central challenge in our lives—growing up as black males in a racist society.

"Thugs," I vividly remember my mother muttering during my childhood in Seattle. "Jackson Street *thugs*," she'd say under her breath with venomous scorn as she drove us in our station wagon through the city's impoverished Central Area and International District, glancing balefully at the jobless black hustlers and idlers spilling out of bars and hobnobbing on drizzly cold street corners. I realized years later, in hindsight, that it was at such times, when she pointed out bitterly how empty and desperate life was for the vast majority of black men in our society, that life's choices were made painfully and graphically clear to us. Those choices, always quite clear in our mother's mind, and my father's, were doubtlessly greatly sharpened by the Nashville assault.

We could choose to skip school, fritter away opportunities, and escape into drugs, alcohol, or sexual conquest, like the black "bums" we passed in the inner city. We could choose to fill our insides with rage, self-loathing, and resentment about society and the hurts black people suffered and seek release in vengeance.

We could choose to end up in jail or jobless, dead at an early age or strung out in a gutter somewhere on any number of Jackson Streets in America, like so many millions of our kind. We could easily choose all that.

Or we could do better, my mother implicitly told us. We could turn the fire on itself and defeat the infernal demons. We could reach inside ourselves somewhere and rise above the base stereotypes and pitifully low expectations society placed on black men. We could strive to replicate in our lives the perseverance and vision of the people who came before us—Frederick Douglass, Sojourner Truth, Jackie Robinson, Martin Luther King, Jr. We could take advantage of the rare opportunities they worked to give us and pursue what we wanted in life despite our country's abysmal expectations.

We could do it. If we chose.

We could turn the fire on itself.

Or we could succumb to the depression and rage that every black person in America must feel at various points in life, regardless of background or class or skin tone. We could sink inexorably toward the nadir.

One or the other.

That was it, really. That was the ultimate truism about black opportunity that shaped our childhood during integration in Seattle. Whether it was really *true* didn't matter. It was this chilling observation about black existence in America that we were compelled to take in from our middle-class vantage. The stark reality seemed to be that there was precious little gray area, few other options, no middle ground of forgiving ambiguity or room for error for people like us. There never had been. There was no time to pause, to let up the fight, no chance to drop one's guard.

That was the clearest reality in a society that feared, despised, disrespected, and distrusted so many of us and harbored such low expectations of us. For black men in American society, there was essentially no middle ground—certainly not in A.J. Beaumont's time, not in my grandfather's or father's time, and likely not in mine.

As I contemplated the repercussions of the attack on my mother so many years later, I reviewed all that I had been taught about race in America. It was true, on the one hand, that my mother and father had sought escape from the South because they felt deeply menaced by white racism. But it was also true that they had felt menaced by the incomparable desperateness and self-loathing of black existence there. Indeed, I realized, by transplanting themselves as far away from the South as they could get, to largely white Seattle, my parents were seeking escape from *black people* in a certain sense—or, to put it more precisely, from a pathological "element" festering in the black South. That was the word my urbane, St. Louis–bred mother often used. "That *element*," she told me many years later, with bitterness and resentment in her voice—an amoral, criminal element bred by the sick system of entrenched black poverty, ignorance, hopelessness, and alienation that white racism had created and perpetuated, one represented graphically, she felt, by the wild-eyed black man who had raped her.

The most chilling irony, of course, was that it was the very fear of the nightmare she had experienced that simmered at the heart of white racism in America. The stereotypical vision deeply ingrained in the mind of white America was of a black male sexual predator on the loose, *unchained*, attacking a defenseless woman in her home in the night. That singular fear had helped fuel so many laws oppressing black people and given rise to Jim Crow separatism. That demented fear had sparked thousands of gruesome lynchings and other insane acts of mob terror and violence. And yet that racist nightmare—so evil, so insidiously harmful, and so false—had nonetheless materialized for my mother that night in Nashville, with certainly lasting emotional and psychological consequences.

My mother's attacker was never captured. My father believed the Nashville police did not do everything possible to find him— "she was a black woman," was all he said, his voice not disguising the disgust and resentment he still felt for white southern cops. My mother, however, disagreed, at least as far as that investigation went. She said the white policemen were remarkably kind to her—kinder than she had ever suspected white southern policemen could be to black people—and persisted for weeks in showing her mug shots of suspects. The lead detective especially was outraged that something like that could happen to the wife of a "colored" man who, he kept saying to her over and over, was trying to do so much good for his people.

At one point, curious to know how the police had conducted their investigation, I tried to get a copy of the official police report about the attack. But the Nashville authorities told me all such "minor" records from the 1950s had been destroyed years ago and never put on film. The criminal investigation was simply marked unsolved sometime in the 1960s, a police official told me over the phone, and left open, likely for eternity.

In nearly every child's life there comes a time when he can't help feeling sharp defiance and hostility toward his parents, no matter how loving they are. Pent-up feelings from childhood get somehow jumbled up with the affection and respect. I certainly went through a period like that after I left Seattle to begin my own path in life in the late 1970s, feeling a sharp, lingering resentment toward my mother and father over the unnecessary hurts and strains they each had inflicted upon me and my siblings when we were growing up. I despised my father for the whippings he had given me and my brothers; I remembered the psychological terror those attacks had created, the pain and the tears we sometimes went to sleep with. I despised the emotional pressures both my parents had exerted on me to excel in my white schools, recalling the disappointment so obvious in my mother's expressive eyes and so devastating to me whenever I fell short at anything. I hated the bitter memory of the bandaged splint I wore on my finger in junior high school after she had beaten me in a rage with a clothes brush and fractured the finger one Sunday morning when I refused to attend church with her. I loathed the old pathology about race she harbored, the one she had grown up with in St. Louis, the destructive ideas handed down and absorbed by me and shared by millions in our culture, which favored "good" hair and "light" skin over everything black.

But as I grew older and began to contend with life on my own terms, I, like most grown children, came to see my mother and father not simply as my parents but as humans with understandable frailties, flaws, and vulnerabilities as well as strengths. I couldn't fairly blame them for my demons anymore, because God knew they had plenty of their own. It was odd, but as their brown faces wrinkled and their hair turned silvery gray, I saw them as a microcosm of their entire generation of idealistic and ambitious black Americans whose often anonymous struggles and accomplishments nonetheless loomed large throughout many sectors of our society. No matter where I traveled in America for my newspaper, I began to see my parents everywhere in the dignified faces of strangers, of old and retired black professionals, looking back on lives lived through the daunting challenges of their age, yet lived fully and so humanly.

My mother and father took as articles of faith such basic things as racial integration and equal opportunity and the other great promises of their era. They believed so strongly that they cleared a trail from the South to the Pacific Northwest to see them come true, overcoming myriad racial and personal hurdles they found in their way. Such hurdles exacted a toll on them emotionally. They were, after all, human, and all humans are flawed. But when I thought about it at age forty-three, amazed by all that they had struggled with and overcome by the time they were forty-three, I wasn't sure if I could have done the same. I wasn't sure if I could have summoned the same emotional resolve, the same sturdiness of character, to see it through. I wasn't sure many people could have done that, given the same obstacles, hurts, and challenges to their souls.

But I was sure of a few things. I knew the results of their endurance. My parents stayed together through the toughest of times in our childhood during integration in Seattle and lived to see the day when their four children and seven grandchildren could take advantage of the openings in mainstream American society they and millions of others helped create. I knew that in 1997, forty-one years after my father migrated from Nashville to begin his practice in Seattle as a general surgeon, there were forty-seven black physicians listed with the King County Medical Society in Seattle, including experts in specialties spanning dermatology, urology, obstetrics and gynecology, ophthalmology, psychiatry, and surgery. And I knew that restrictive race covenants in residential neighborhoods, like the ones my parents were the first to fight in Seattle's south end in 1960, had largely been consigned to the ash heap of American history. And this was mainly because of my parents' ambitions and those of other, equally anonymous black parents of their era who had the courage to test the new laws of equal opportunity in their personal and professional lives.

Early on the morning of Monday, October 13, the day after I found the graves of A.J. and Mary Ann Beaumont in Natchez, I drove my rental car to the Old Warren County Court House in Vicksburg, my mind filled with our history, my heart pounding with anticipation. The day had finally arrived when I felt sure I would be able to find answers to all my questions about our family's racial past, about the white branch of our tree—answers that had eluded me for so many years.

I parked the car on a quiet side street. It was a drizzly, muggy morning on the banks of the Mississippi River, and as I walked along the stone path leading to the courthouse, I felt myself gradually coming to an understanding about my emotional struggles over race and my genealogical project. It was still an intellectual exercise for me, surely. I still badly wanted to satisfy my curiosity. I wanted to find my distant white cousins, to hear their family's story from the other side of the color barrier, and to compare their struggles over the past century to ours in order to draw a more complete portrait of our shared history.

But as I reflected on my mother's and father's lives, I also began to sense in a strange but unconscious way that in all my searching I also wanted to recognize what they and so many others had tried to do, to pay a small tribute to them, to reaffirm that despite the tough obstacles that still exist in American society, their generation's values of equality and struggle survive.

I didn't know what was ahead of me. I didn't know what kind of white people I would discover in my distant kin, if I could find them. I didn't know what changes America's racial progression and regression had brought to the Beaumonts' lives since the day in 1877 that our blood was joined by Laura, the former slave, and A.J., the white immigrant. But I felt an unusual clarity and strange tranquillity inside me that morning, a feeling that put into deeper perspective the old anger and disappointments over race and prejudice that my early middle age had brought out so sharply in the years after my daughter was born. For it grew clear in my mind that our family, too, had scaled a ways up the mountain that Martin Luther King, Jr., once dreamed of so vividly. And while the stark truth remained that none of us in America would ever be over the jagged peaks of racism, ignorance, and inequality until all of us were over them, I was nonetheless awed by the distance our black family had managed to travel.

My old rage was still there, somewhere inside. I supposed it would always be there, as long as I contemplated that my daughter would inevitably encounter some of the same racial hurts and struggles in her lifetime that we all had, throughout our family's time in America. I guess I was beginning to accept the inner fire as part of my being, as a fire that was not necessarily harmful if I could learn to control it, to harness it somehow, and use it to clarify things in my head. But I also felt a sense of confirmation, as only the South could imbue in me so deeply, that our long family journey from slavery had been worth it. And I had faith that my private project, too, would prove worthwhile somehow, that the common humanity my black ancestors had always tried to believe in despite the barriers of prejudice would see the search through to a meaningful end.

PART TWO

Discovery

CHAPTER FIVE

The Chase

The Warren County Court House was a magnificent old stone structure rising from a steep hill in downtown Vicksburg, overlooking the Mississippi River. From every mildewed corner, the building seemed to throb with history. Guarded by Civil War–era artillery pieces on its front and sides, it featured Greco-Roman granite columns supporting a pyramid-shaped roof and an imposing bell tower replete with clocks on all four sides.

During the Civil War the courthouse was a focal point in the siege of Vicksburg between 1862 and 1863, when the building stood as a defiant symbol of one of the last great stands of the Confederacy. Surrounded by advancing Union troops, Vicksburg's rebel defenders held out for many agonizing months before the army led by Ulysses S. Grant finally prevailed and returned the Stars and Stripes to the top of the courthouse bell tower.

For my family, too, the building held history. According to Louisiana military history, my great-great-grandfather's artillery

199

unit, the Cameron Battery, had fought Grant near this very place in defense of Vicksburg before being forced into retreat. Now, 135 years later, I was about to embark on a different kind of siege of this building. I felt certain that somewhere in its records, in the old ledgers, deeds, and microfilms cramming its ancient shelves, were clues to the whereabouts of A.J. Beaumont's white descendants.

I entered the courthouse at 8 A.M. from the drizzle outside and immediately found myself at the entrance to a small museum just inside the front door. The museum was dedicated to the Civil War, the siege of Vicksburg, and the building's storied past. I took a peek inside, where I saw glass cases filled with battle flags, muskets, pistols, and bugles. Several displays featured faded military uniforms and articles of period clothing, including a pair of tattered trousers once worn by a "plantation mammy." The walls, smelling sweetly of old pine, displayed brittle newspapers from the Civil War era and yellowing antebellum posters advertising auctions of slaves and land.

I wandered through the museum and soon found the room I was looking for, the office of Gordon Cotton, the archivist and curator of the Old Warren County Court House museum and library. I had spoken to him on the phone several times from my house in California in preparation for my visit and had been amused by his name the first time I heard him utter it in a drawl as smooth as velvet. I wondered what the Mississippi librarian looked like.

I knocked lightly on the open door and saw inside a pale, gray-haired man in his fifties seated at a delightfully cluttered wooden desk. The office was actually a small library filled from floor to ceiling with old leather-bound books, rare maps, and other ancient documents and tomes perched on wooden shelves anchored against the walls.

"You must be the fella from California," drawled the man, dressed in faded jeans and a plain plaid shirt, as he rose from his chair with a big smile. "Professor Henry?"

"It's a pleasure to meet you, Mr. Cotton," I said, shaking his extended hand. He invited me to take a seat at a table near his desk and offered me a cup of coffee. His office was a wonderful place, filled with the smells of fresh coffee and the sweet aroma of old books and ancient wooden floor planks.

"So you're doin' some investigatin'?" he asked as he took a seat at the table across from me.

As I told him the old story about Laura and Arthur and my long search for the Beaumonts, I found myself liking the historian instantly. His eyes reflected a bright twinkle that conveyed not just a quick wit but a genuine interest in what I was telling him, and when he spoke, it was with a smooth, gentle, and very likable Mississippi drawl that reminded me of the Civil War historian Shelby Foote.

"And you've got documents too," he commented, smiling as he glanced at the photos of A.J. Beaumont, his 1901 obituary, and the letter he wrote to Pearl acknowledging the mixed-race woman as his daughter. "Remarkable. Extraordinary," he muttered softly. "We see a lot of folks come through here trying to research their heritage, but not a lot of them have the kind of material you do. You're lucky."

"Well, yes and no," I answered. "I'm stuck in the year 1914. I know the Beaumont family was living in Vicksburg then, but that's as far as I've taken the trail."

I told the historian offhandedly about my visit to the Natchez city cemetery the day before, where I found the Beaumont graves. Suddenly I remembered the odd inscription on Mary Ann Beaumont's headstone—"Woodsmen Circle"—and I asked Cotton what it meant.

"Oh, that was a burial society in the old days," he answered. "You see, a lot of people paid dues to burial societies to ensure they were buried proper when they died. The Woodsmen Circle essentially guaranteed that its members would have headstones and proper funerals. Bereavement societies have always been very big in the South, for white people and black."

Cotton then rose from his creaky wooden chair and sauntered across the wood plank floor to a wall full of books on shelves behind his desk. There he reached up for one thin book among many similar ones, each protected by a white plastic cover closed with Velcro strips.

"These are the Vicksburg city directories from the period you're interested in. Telephones were pretty new back then, and the directories only began in 1905. They list pretty much everyone in town, even if they didn't have a phone."

He opened the plastic case and gently placed the 1914 directory on the table. Its pages were fragile and yellow with age. He carefully opened it up to the B's and stopped at page 128. He turned the book to me, and I ran my finger down the page to the name Beaumont.

"That's them, isn't it?" he asked.

I nodded in fascination, staring at the listing: "Beaumont, Arthur W." This was the sole surviving son of Arthur J. Beaumont. The listing also showed his wife's name, Anna, in parentheses and described him as a "foreman" for the Gotthelf Coal Company. The family's address was 728 Dabney in Vicksburg.

The listing also pointed out that Mary Ann Beaumont, Arthur W.'s mother, lived at the same address; she was described as "(wid Arthur J)."

"What's the Gotthelf Coal Company?" I asked, curious why the only son of a prosperous nineteenth-century cotton grower and plantation supplies merchant in Louisiana would be laboring as a coal worker in Mississippi barely more than a decade after his father's death.

"The Gotthelfs were one of our prominent Jewish families in the old days," Cotton explained. "That company was the big supplier of coal in town for many years. We don't have so many Jews in Vicksburg anymore. We used to have quite a few. But they all moved away to the bigger cities as the century moved on."

Cotton returned the volume to the shelf and came back with the issue of 1918, four years later. The listings showed the Beaumonts residing at the same address. But in the 1919 volume the Beaumont name did not appear. Cotton grabbed 1920, 1921, 1922, 1925, and 1929. No Beaumonts. I felt my heart sinking again as I scanned the telephone directories. The family seemed to have vanished again.

"Maybe there's something in the Fisher Funeral Home records," Cotton told me, reaching into another bookshelf for a large leather-bound tome. "Fisher was the big funeral home for many years in Vicksburg. These records go all the way back to 1854. If you had a little bit of money back then and died in Vicksburg, chances are Fisher put you in the ground."

He opened the old ledger and scanned the B's, turning the book toward me moments later, opened to page 10. It showed the record for the June 15, 1914, funeral of Mary Ann Beaumont, Arthur's widow:

Age 57. One black broadcloth casket and box, $140.00;
Embalming remains $25.00; Ladies burial robe $15.00;
Telephoning to Natchez 40 cents; Candles and hack to
train $3.00—$183.40.

I made photocopies of all the information I found in the directories and the funeral ledger before Cotton escorted me back
down the Old Court House steps and across the street to the
"New" Warren County Court House, which was built in 1935.
There he introduced me to clerks who would help me investigate
the probate, property, marriage, and other civil records in hopes
of finding more clues to the white family's history in the city.

But I was feeling stumped again, my head filling with doubt.
Every bit of information about the Beaumonts that I found with
Cotton was leading not to answers about the old riddle but to
more and more baffling questions. Where did the family go in
1918? Why was Beaumont's son working for a coal company?
Why did Mary Ann Beaumont feel the need to purchase burial
insurance after laying her prosperous husband in the ground in
Natchez and gracing his grave with such a distinguished marker?
What had happened to the immigrant's business, his plantation,
his fortune in St. Joseph?

I rapidly scrolled through probate records on microfilm,
searching for the case of Mary Ann Beaumont, hoping to find a
will of some kind that would have had to be registered with the
court. I found her probate record, case number 5680. It contained more than twenty-five documents, all photographed on
microfilm, each recording minor and perfunctory actions over
about a year's span.

"In the matter of the estate of M.A. Beaumont," read the first page of the record, dated June 15, 1914, written in the court clerk's flourished cursive handwriting. The documents revealed that Beaumont's widow died without a will, that her estate totaled $394.76, all of it in cash at a local bank, and that her son, Arthur Wilford Beaumont, was her only heir.

There were also records naming Arthur W. Beaumont the administrator of the estate. One document showed that most of the money in the bank went to pay for hospital fees at the Vicksburg sanitarium, where the widow had spent a month before her death, and for funeral and court costs. The document also showed that her headstone was provided by the Woodsmen Circle. The last document in the probate record was dated September 21, 1915, and in it the court abruptly expressed satisfaction that the Beaumont estate was administered properly.

I struggled to comprehend what I was seeing as I pressed the copy button on the court's microfilm reader to retrieve paper copies of the documents. The white family, whose lives by all appearance and description had seemed so prosperous and comfortable before the century's turn, appeared virtually penniless barely a decade and a half after A.J. Beaumont's death.

As I studied the documents in my hands, I couldn't help reflecting on my family's history during the same period. In 1915, the year the last document in Mary Ann Beaumont's probate record was being recorded by her son at the courthouse in Vicksburg, my grandmother Fredda—the granddaughter in St. Louis whom A.J. Beaumont never knew—was nineteen years old, deliriously happy, and being wooed by the beautiful black man of her dreams, postman Clifford Turner, a son of the distinguished ex-slave Young Turner in Illinois. My mother would be born eight years later. Also in 1915 my grandfather John

Robert Henry, Sr., was in medical school in North Carolina and about to begin his practice in Winston-Salem. He would meet Irma Neal in 1918, and my father would be born two years later.

I realized that my black family's foundation was being solidified and its unlikely rise in this century commencing at the same time that the white Beaumonts seemed to be in full descent, leaving hardly a trace in Mississippi. This was not the way I had expected the story, the saga of two American families, to unfold. It was not the kind of story that conventional wisdom and stereotypes about race in our country would ever tell. What were the records trying to say to me?

I had two more places to look for clues in the New Court House. I raced upstairs to a second-floor office containing marriage and divorce records, believing I might be able to find something about Arthur W. Beaumont or his children. A clerk escorted me into a small back room filled with bookshelves and large red leather-bound ledgers dating from the 1830s. Unlike the information in other departments, the marriage records were not on microfilm or microfiche. The records were originals, exquisitely written by hand in the red volumes. Until as late as 1970, the records separated all Warren County citizens into "white" and "colored" categories. The red volumes on the shelves read "Marriage Record White" or "Marriage Record Colored" for every year and were separated by race on adjoining shelves.

The clerk, a young brown-haired white woman, shyly asked me in a soft southern accent, "Is your party white or black?"

"White," I answered. "I'm looking for a white family."

"Okay, you'll find the years you want right here, Mr. Henry," she said, pointing to a shelf with red ledgers starting in 1915. "I'm sorry about that question. We have to ask, though."

I told her not to worry, that I understood. But I also made a mental note to spend a class session at Berkeley teaching my journalism students about the peculiarly fascinating things they could expect to encounter if they ever found themselves having to navigate county court records in a state like Mississippi.

I spent close to an hour in the book-crammed library, scanning all the white marriage and divorce records for Warren County between 1915 and 1949, but didn't find anything useful. I then returned to the first floor to hunt among the property records. The listings for the years 1915 to 1920 showed that the Beaumont house at 728 Dabney, which had been built in 1904, was owned by a man named Katzenmeyer. It was among several houses he owned on the block. The Beaumonts apparently were renters during the years they lived in Vicksburg.

My trail had turned cold as ice. It was close to 4 P.M. when I finished searching in the courthouse, and I was filled with far more questions than when I had started. Gordon Cotton sensed my confusion and disappointment when I returned to his office to thank him and say good-bye.

"No luck, huh?" the genial historian asked as he extended his hand to shake mine.

"I moved it up to 1918," I said. "But then the family simply vanished on me again."

Cotton nodded and clucked in sympathy. "Well, I'm sorry to hear that," he said. "I know how disappointed you must feel, especially after coming all this way."

He walked me to the courthouse door and looked briefly at

the darkening sky before saying good-bye. A storm was coming. "You never know, Mr. Henry," he encouraged me. "One thing we've learned around here is that skeletons have a way of rattlin' their bones when you least expect it. Keep the faith."

I had spent a full day at the courthouses in Vicksburg, from 8 A.M. until closing. As I drove all the way back to Atlanta on Interstate 20, retracing my path through Mississippi, Alabama, and Georgia in the driving rainstorm that began shortly after I left Vicksburg, I wondered what my next move would be. I was disappointed that I hadn't discovered as much as I had hoped, but intrigued by the nuggets of information I had mined. I realized the white family could have gone anywhere in America, but I didn't know where or how to search for them next. Through the rain, wind, and thunder I drove, racking my mind for possible new directions to explore.

"Four years. All this way, and all I was able to do was pull the story forward to 1918," I told Letitia over the telephone when I arrived back in my hotel room in Atlanta late that night. "They could have gone anywhere."

Letitia sighed and tried her best to boost my spirits. "Well, it sure sounds intriguing, doesn't it? I mean, this family went from the landed gentry to the lower working class in just a few years? That's pretty amazing."

"Seems so, but it's all so hazy, Tish. I mean, anything could have happened to them. There was a huge flu epidemic in 1918. It killed thousands of people in America. Maybe they just vanished. Maybe I'll never find out."

Letitia put Zoë on the phone then. My daughter immediately told me about her day in kindergarten—riding a tricycle, jumping rope, eating crackers, and singing songs. Within minutes I felt better just hearing her voice. Moments later we all said good-bye and I fell asleep instantly, exhausted by the discoveries and new puzzles of the day.

Early the next morning I attended the graduate and professional school fair sponsored by the city's historically black schools, which was the official purpose of my trip. I met scores of bright black students there and tried to recruit some into our journalism program at Berkeley. Late in the day I encountered an inspiring young woman who told me she hailed from a small town called Tifton in Georgia. She was graduating soon from Clark-Atlanta University, and I managed to excite her about the idea of coming west. The daughter of two schoolteachers, she was smart, committed to a career in journalism, and boasted a terrific academic record. She had a real spark in her eyes, and I knew she could be a fine addition to our program.

The young woman applied to our school of journalism and was accepted a few months later, our first-ever admission from one of Atlanta's historically black schools. I was thrilled. That Sherri was an honors graduate of the same black school my mother had attended for her library degree in the 1940s under the shadow of Jim Crow deepened my sense of elation.

My trip also turned out to be critically valuable for my genealogical research. I didn't know how critical until after I returned to California, where I soon visited a temple of the Church of Jesus Christ of Latter-Day Saints in Woodland, the county seat near our home. The Mormon Church operates family history centers at many of its temples, including the one in Woodland, where private citizens can conduct genealogical research using a host of valuable databases on microfiche and compact discs. These databases provide all kinds of census extracts and information from original birth, death, marriage, and military records from local jurisdictions across the country and around the world.

The Woodland center, located in a basement office near the church on the edge of a tomato field, also has U.S. Social Security indexes listing every deceased American citizen who ever registered with Social Security—from 1936, when Social Security was established, to 1995, when the indexes were issued. These compact discs contain hundreds of thousands of names and detail where each person resided at the time of his or her death.

I had been to the Woodland center many times before, hunting unsuccessfully for Arthur W. Beaumont's name in all of the files. Apparently, he either died before Social Security legislation was enacted or never applied after it was. But now, after my trip to the courthouse in Vicksburg, I had a new name to look up—his wife, Anna Beaumont, who was listed in the 1914 Vicksburg telephone directory with her husband.

I searched the Social Security index and discovered eight different Anna Beaumonts with dates of birth ranging from 1889 to 1926. Among the places these Anna Beaumonts died were Maryland, Texas, Indiana, and Illinois. One, though, was born in 1894 in Mississippi and died in Louisiana in March 1976. I thought she could be the right one and pressed a button on the computer to find the zip code of her place of death. It was listed as 71360, which encompassed nineteen jurisdictions in Rapides Parish in central Louisiana, near the town of Alexandria.

Later that afternoon at our house in Davis, while my daughter played with her friend Rachel amid the red and yellow roses in our backyard, I called central Louisiana telephone information to find out the name of the daily newspaper in Alexandria. The operator told me the paper was called the *Alexandria Town Talk* and gave me the number. I phoned the city editor to find out more about the newspaper. She told me it was 120 years old, the only daily in central Louisiana, and that the obituaries it published were very extensive and reliable, covering much of that part of the state.

The next morning at Berkeley I put in a request at the main library to see yet another small-town southern newspaper on microfilm, the *Alexandria Town Talk*, for the months of March and April 1976. Then I waited.

Shortly after the New Year, 1998, nearly two months later, the microfilms finally arrived on interlibrary loan from Louisiana State University. I picked them up at Doe Library on campus and immediately raced downstairs to a microfilm reader in the basement to see if one of the films contained an obituary for Anna Beaumont. I scrolled through the first roll of microfilm, turning the metal knob on the side of the reader with my left hand, checking each page in March 1976. I went slowly through the first five days of the month. The news pages were filled with happenings in the presidential primary season, featuring photographs of Ronald Reagan, Jimmy Carter, and Howard Baker, while the sports pages brimmed with news about the NCAA basketball tournament. I scrolled on through the microfilm, hunting, searching.

Then, on page A5 in the March 6 issue, among listings of the recently deceased in Rapides Parish, I found it. The obituary flashed before me like lightning in the night.

MRS. BEAUMONT

Mrs. Anna V. Beaumont, 81, of Pineville died at 7 a.m. today
in her residence. A native of New Orleans, she was a former
resident of New Iberia and was the widow of Arthur W.
Beaumont. . . .

It was her. My breathing quickened. I read on.

The obituary listed Anna Beaumont's memberships in numerous Catholic charity organizations, noted the time and place
of her burial in Pineville, and then listed her survivors, including
four daughters.

Four daughters.

I felt my heart pounding in my chest now. In a matter of seconds I had brought the white family forward in time all the way
to 1976, a leap of fifty-eight years. This was the white branch of
my family's ancestral tree coming to life before my eyes. But
the bigger question remained: Were any of the four Beaumont
daughters still living in 1998?

According to the obituary, the sisters all lived in Louisiana and
had assumed their husbands' surnames—Guggenheimer, Himel,
Guirard, and Decoux. Later that night at my computer at home
in Davis, I found three of their exact full names, addresses, and
phone numbers in an Internet telephone directory. The next
morning I mailed a letter to each of these three sisters explaining
who I was, my relationship to them, and my research. I also sent
them copies of documents, including A.J. Beaumont's 1901 obituary and his photograph.

I waited anxiously day after day, wondering what the white
families would think of my letter. Every time the phone rang, I
expected to pick it up and hear a Beaumont on the other end of

the line. But as each day passed and my anxiety mounted, I realized I could take only so much uncertainty for so long. When I didn't receive a reply by phone or letter after one week, I telephoned the Himel residence in Pineville. A housekeeper answered. I asked to speak to Mrs. Himel, but the voice replied that Mrs. Himel had died the year before. I felt my heart sink.

I told the voice I was searching for any of the Beaumont sisters and asked her if she or anyone else in the household knew of their whereabouts. The housekeeper replied that only two of the Beaumont sisters were still living and that one was suffering terribly from Alzheimer's.

"But Rita's still around," the voice said.

"Rita?"

"Yes, would you like her number?"

I answered yes, realizing that Rita was the one sister whose name I couldn't find in the Internet telephone directory, Mrs. Rita B. Guirard.

The housekeeper gave me her current name, Rita Beaumont Pharis, along with her telephone number and address in Pineville.

I debated the issue for hours in my mind, looking at it from every conceivable angle as if it were a prism refracting rays of light. I was unsure how to approach the white woman. In the end I decided to make my first contact by letter, not by telephone. I couldn't just call a white stranger out of the blue and introduce myself as a long-lost black cousin whose ties to the white family went back to the plantation era. That would have been just too nutty, too outlandish, too abrupt.

No, I decided that I would have to do it in writing. I would explain our historical saga, all of it, in a page or two. I would try to craft my request to meet her and to hear her family's story so that she would understand and not feel threatened in any way. I knew I had to play it as straight and as sincerely as I could, one human being to another. I would include copies of Beaumont's photograph and his 1901 obituary with the letter. Then I decided to tell her I would phone her after she received the letter and documents. I didn't want to have to wait, hoping for her to call or write me.

I sat down at our computer to type the letter. It took only a few minutes to write, the adrenaline rushing in a torrent through my fingertips to the keyboard.

February 6, 1998

Dear Mrs. Pharis:

    I am a professor of journalism at the University of California at Berkeley. For a number of years, as part of a personal writing project, I have been searching for the descendants of a man named Arthur J. Beaumont, an English immigrant who settled in St. Joseph, Louisiana, in the 19th century.

    Mr. Beaumont, a longtime merchant and cotton grower in Tensas Parish, died in 1901 and was buried in the historic Natchez City Cemetery. His obituary, published in the Tensas Gazette *in May 1901, is enclosed.*

    I have been searching for Mr. Beaumont's modern descendants in order to write a study about my family and his over the last century in America, for our families are very distantly related.

    In the 1870s, before he married, Mr. Beaumont had a relationship with a freed slave woman which resulted in a child. The woman and her child subsequently moved to St. Louis in the 1890s, where they remained the rest of their lives. These two women, Laura Brumley and Pearl Brumley, were my great-great-grandmother and great-grandmother.

Throughout these many years Mr. Beaumont's obituary, his photograph, and a handwritten letter he wrote in 1901 before he died, in which he acknowledged he was the father of the black woman's child, have been handed down as keepsakes in our family.

The study I am writing is largely about my family's experiences during this century, including the story of my great-great-grandmother after she moved to St. Louis. It also is about my mother and my father, a pioneering surgeon in Seattle, and my own experiences as a journalist in America and overseas. For many years I was a newspaper writer for the Washington Post *and* Newsweek *magazine before entering the teaching profession five years ago.*

I have been able to locate you largely through research I have conducted at libraries, courthouses, and census offices.

I know this letter must sound astonishing to you. Believe me, I am quite astonished myself, not least of all because I have been able to locate you.

As I say, I am a researcher and writer and want nothing more than to talk to you about the Beaumont family for my study. I would love to talk to you about your memories of your mother and father and your own experiences over this century. There are absolutely no legal or financial implications to this request. . . .

I will follow this letter up with a telephone call and will be glad to answer any questions you might have about me or my work. It would be an honor to meet you if you would consent to my visiting you in Louisiana at some point in the future.

I printed the letter on a sheet of my official university stationery. Then I signed my name with a ballpoint pen at the bottom and decided to send the packet of material via express mail, which I knew usually took just two days for delivery. I went to the post office with Zoë on that windy winter day and held her in my arms as I paid the $4.39 fee. Zoë asked the clerk to stamp her hand, as she always did whenever we visited the Davis post office on routine occasions, the purplish "First Class" stamp of ink staying on the back of her hand for days.

Then I waited nervously again, unable to eat or sleep much, my stomach knotting with each passing hour. I knew I was close to solving the puzzle. But how would the white woman and her family react?

One day passed. Two days. Three. I hoped to hear something from her first, before I had to call. But I heard nothing.

Late on the third day, Monday, February 9, I couldn't stand it any longer. I was baby-sitting my daughter that afternoon while Letitia was teaching her class on African politics at the Naval Postgraduate School in Monterey. Zoë and her pal Alex were playing a pretend game in her room, both of them dressed up in princess costumes—Zoë as Pocahontas, Alex as Cinderella.

"Zoë, I'll be on the phone for a few minutes, okay? You guys play here quietly and let me talk."

"Okay, Daddy," she said.

I retreated to my bedroom, picked up the telephone, dialed the number for Rita Pharis's house in Pineville, then sat down at my desk with my pencil and a yellow notepad in hand. My gaze fell on Letitia's roses outside our window as the call went through.

The phone rang once, twice, three times. I inhaled deeply to calm my nerves. For an instant I pondered whether I should leave a message if an answering machine picked up. But then the ringing stopped. The receiver had been picked up. I heard a moment of silence, then a woman's voice.

"Hello?"

I felt a sick nervousness in my stomach, very much like the

kind I always got before my lectures and other public speaking events.

"Mrs. Pharis?" I said.

"This is Mrs. Pharis."

"Mrs. Pharis, this is Neil Henry. I'm a professor at the University of California."

"Yes," the voice answered. It sounded a bit guarded, distant.

"I was wondering if you got a package of material I sent you. You should have gotten it over the weekend."

"No, I haven't gotten any package," the voice answered, the sound of a lush southern accent more obvious to me in this longer sentence.

A moment of silence followed. I was speechless. Now what? The scene I had so feared, the one I had tried so hard to avoid, was now unfolding inexorably before me like a nightmare. I realized I would have to explain everything by voice to the strange white woman listening in puzzlement on the other end of the line.

Where would I begin? I felt panic for a second, but then I took a deep breath and told myself to get to work.

Concentrate. Keep her on the line. Be professional. Explain what you want and fast.

"I'm sorry about that," I said. "Let me try to explain, Mrs. Pharis. I'm a teacher and I'm doing research for a book that your family might have something to do with. What I mean to say. . . ."

Tell it straight. Don't confuse her.

"Our families are very distantly related, Mrs. Pharis. For a number of years I have been searching for the descendants of a man named Arthur Beaumont. . . ."

"That was my daddy!" she interrupted. Her voice sounded intrigued then, her tone a bit stronger, firmer.

Keep going. Get to the point. Tell her about Laura and Pearl, but do it smoothly, clearly, succinctly.

"Yes, I thought it was," I said. "Your father's father was named Arthur Beaumont too, I believe. And a long time ago, you see, back in the 1870s, your grandfather had a relationship with a freed slave woman that resulted in a child. And that child and her mother were my great-great-grandmother and great-grandmother."

"I see, yes," she said.

Keep going.

"What I've been doing is researching and writing about my family history, Mrs. Pharis. And I was hoping I could include in this story some information about your family."

"Well, you see I'm the youngest of my sisters," she answered then, coughing slightly but seeming not in the least put off by my request. The tone of her voice was even, strong. "Goodness, my sisters could have really helped you if they were still living. . . ."

She paused.

Let her keep going.

"You see, the others are gone now. Except for one. And she's got Alzheimer's."

"Is that Mrs. Decoux?"

"No, she's passed. Mrs. Guggenheimer is the sick one."

"Well, that's sort of how I found you, Mrs. Pharis. With their names. You see, I sent letters to three of the four sisters I found in a 1976 obituary of your mother. And I called the Himel residence on Friday and got your name and address and number. That's how I found you."

"Yes, I had a different name back then when Mama died."

"Right, it was Guir . . ."

"Guirard, yes."

"And you know, I think that's why it's been so difficult for me finding all of you, because the Beaumont name hasn't lived on."

"Right, my mother and daddy only had girls."

"I have so many questions I don't know where to start."

Start with the easy ones. Don't scare her off.

"Look, I was wondering about something," I said. "Your father and mother at one point lived in Vicksburg back in the 1910s."

"Yes, that's right."

"And your father worked for a coal company. . . ."

"I thought it was a steel plant. . . ."

"Well, telephone directories back in the 1910s list him as the foreman of a coal company. Do you know why the family moved from Vicksburg to central Louisiana?"

"No, they didn't move here. They moved to New Orleans. They spent most of their lives in New Orleans."

"Oh, I see. And what did your father do there?"

"Oh, a lot of things," she said. Her voice was sounding freer, unguarded. "He was self-employed for a while. Then he got disabled in a car accident. . . ."

"Your mother was involved in a lot of things according to her obituary. Catholic organizations and the like. . . ."

"Oh yeah, she was a real pepper pot."

"Can you tell me when your father died?"

"Let's see, I was seventeen when he passed. Which means that would have been in 1947."

I did a quick calculation in my head as I listened to her. She was born in 1930, which made her just sixty-eight years old, seven years younger than my mother—her unknown second cousin. The two women, one white, the other black, were a generation apart in the family tree but as close in age as siblings.

A part of me had always wondered if the Beaumont I found would be too old to remember much of the family story. Instead, to my amazement, I was discovering that Rita Beaumont Pharis was much younger than I ever could have expected or hoped.

"Mrs. Pharis, in this packet of material I sent you, there's an obituary of your father's father from the *Tensas Gazette* in 1901...."

"Oh my goodness!" She sounded thrilled and started to chuckle.

"Yes," I continued, "it's been in my family all these years. And it talks a bit about the origins of your family in England. It mentions that the Beaumonts are descended from a long line of British military men. Did your folks talk much about this family history?"

"Oh, well, my Daddy did. He wrote a book about it."

"A book?" I exclaimed, feeling a jolt in my stomach. "What was the title?"

"Well, it was just a book he put together on his own. It wasn't published or anything like that. It's lying around here somewhere. I've given most of these things to my daughter. She's got all kinds of family papers. She's even got a photo of the house Daddy grew up in, in St. Joseph."

"Really!"

"Yes, indeed. Maybe we can collect this stuff for you."

Elation!

"That would be outstanding, Mrs. Pharis," I answered.

But I knew I still had to ask the most important question while

I had her on the line, the one that had been burning inside me all these years whenever I thought about the white family, *this* one white family out of the millions in America.

"Mrs. Pharis, I was wondering, did anybody in your family ever talk about your grandfather's relationship with a freed slave? Was anything like that ever discussed in your family when you were growing up?"

"Well, not that exactly," she answered after a pause. "It was not talked about openly. But my mother did for a very long time correspond with a child of my grandfather whom she cared about very much. We always understood her to be an Indian woman, though. That was the story we had always understood, you see—that my granddaddy Beaumont had had an affair with an Indian that produced this child."

"An Indian? Where did she live, do you know?"

"I think it was California, but I'm not sure. Her name was Pearl."

I felt a lump in my throat.

"Pearl," I said. "That was my great-grandmother's name."

"Yes? What was her last name?" she asked.

"Well, that's a good question. I believe she went by Beaumont for a while. . . ."

"No, that wasn't it. I would have remembered that."

"She also went by Hall. Pearl Hall. She was married a few times."

"No, that's not what I recall."

"She was also known by Brumley. That was her mother's name, Laura Brumley. She was born a slave on a plantation in St. Joseph."

"Brumley!" Rita Pharis exclaimed. "That was it. Brumley. Yes, my mother and Aunt Pearl corresponded all the way into the 1940s. I do remember that. I never met her, but we always knew her as Aunt Pearl, the half sister of my daddy."

"Oh my!"

My heart raced. I doubted that anyone in my family was aware of this information, of how hard Pearl had tried throughout her life to maintain contact with her white family, despite her white father's rejection of her, of how many overtures she had made and of how she had largely kept these overtures secret from her black loved ones, knowing they would feel ashamed of the connection and disapprove. Black was black and white was white, with no room in a racist country for middle hues. In that instant of revelation, as I listened to Rita on the phone, I marveled at how Pearl must have struggled in the 1920s and 1930s, with such evident loneliness, to navigate her own course along the color line—all in an effort to keep meaningful ties to both her white and her black families and to nurture those ties somehow, despite the monumental countervailing pressures of a racist society and culture.

"Mrs. Pharis, you say your mother talked about Pearl a great deal and kept in touch with her. Did any of that correspondence happen to be handed down? Did it survive the years?"

"Oh, no. I'm pretty sure not."

"Did your father ever talk about her?"

"Oh no, not at all," she said, chuckling.

"Why, do you think?"

"Well, you know, in those days it was just not talked about. People considered those kinds of things best kept swept under the rug, you understand, those relationships between the races. My mother was the kind of person who was very understanding and welcoming because she knew what it was like to be something of an outcast. She was poor and came from an Italian immigrant family in New Orleans. She was the one who kept in touch with Aunt Pearl. She was the one who loved her.

"But my daddy," she continued, "goodness, he would never have talked about such a thing, that his daddy had had an affair outside marriage, even if it was before he married. Especially if it was to someone who wasn't white. We are a very southern family in that way. The old way. . . ."

Her voice trailed off.

"But somebody in your family did recognize her. You say your mother kept in touch with Pearl," I said.

"Yes," she replied, "but Aunt Pearl was always an Indian to us. That's how she was described. And I suppose that's why it was understandable or partly acceptable."

"I wonder why," I said before thinking, puzzled. "Why was she described as an Indian?"

"Well," Rita Pharis said after a short pause, measuring her words. She coughed slightly. "I don't mean this in the wrong way, Mr. Henry. I hope you understand. But as far as my family was concerned, knowing my daddy and how he felt about race, well—better Indian than black."

I sighed, suddenly feeling stupid. Extraordinarily, terrifically stupid. Of course. That's exactly what a white southerner would want his people to believe, I thought. To a white southern man was there anything lower on the scale of humanity than a black woman? Was there anything more abhorrent to a white man than having to admit to a loving relationship with a black woman and to siring a mixed-race child with her? *Of course not.* Better Indian than black.

I contained my emotions and a few moments later thanked Mrs. Pharis for her time. I told her I'd call again in a few days after she had gotten my packet of documents. I mentioned I would very much like to visit her in Louisiana at some point, to meet her in person and talk to her about her family history.

She was quiet for a moment. She then told me she had been very sick lately, with nerve problems in her legs and back, and was under heavy medication. But she didn't reject the idea out of hand. "Let's just wait and see," she said hesitantly.

I decided not to push it and simply said good-bye. But I ached with anxiety as I hung up. I wanted so much to meet her and her family in person, to see what they looked like and how they lived in Louisiana, and to hear how they felt about so many things in American life.

I knew I was close to realizing my goal and was inexpressibly hopeful. Yet at the same time I knew that the white family could easily close themselves off to me, leaving me in a painful intellectual quandary from which there might never be an escape. Much of my dream rested on what Rita Pharis and her family would decide after reading my letter.

I waited a few days to give the white family a chance to receive and digest my letter. All the while I went about my normal routines at home and at school almost in a total daze. Several times during that period Letitia just hugged me tight without saying a word, to bolster me more than anything else. I was so excited and yet a mess of worry and confusion.

A few days later, after delivering a morning lecture to the ninety undergraduates in the "Mass Media and Society" course I teach each spring at Berkeley, I was sitting at the desk in my office when I decided to make a second call to Pineville. It was about noon Pacific time, two hours later in Louisiana. I dialed Rita Pharis's number, then took a deep breath as I sat back in my chair gazing at the sunlight dancing on my daughter's finger-paint pictures on the wall alongside a photo of Letitia smiling and holding Zoë.

She picked up after several rings, saying, "Hello?"

"Mrs. Pharis. It's Neil Henry in California again."

And then, as if by magic, a huge weight was suddenly lifted off my shoulders, for I instantly detected in her voice not distance or guardedness anymore but a brightness and cheerfulness upon hearing mine. She immediately told me that she had gotten my package and that she and her daughter were simply enthralled with it, especially the photo of her grandfather, Arthur Beaumont, and his obituary from the *Tensas Gazette.*

"It's just so thrilling to know we have a cousin we didn't know about," she said, her southern accent clear and her voice warm and delighted. "Especially on my father's side of the family."

I was puzzled by her use of the word "cousin" at first, so much so that for a moment I wondered whom she was referring to. Then she used it again—"My daughter Bobette's little boy wants to know if his new cousin likes Batman," she said with a chuckle—and it was only then that I realized she was talking about me. *I* was the cousin.

I realized that the door to the white family was opening. I was eager and satisfied, yet at the same time I felt a vague new worry about what I was getting into with these white strangers in a small town in central Louisiana. What sort of connection was I making? What sort of connection did I really want to make? What sort of connection were they expecting?

But I held those thoughts in abeyance, for I was so excited by what I was discovering. I was finally striking gold, the mother lode, in my long search. And I felt a sense of vindication and a renewed connection to Laura and Pearl—two women I never knew but whose lives had loomed so large in our family history.

"We're digging out all kinds of things for you around my house. And also my sister's house. We'll have them all here for you whenever you can make it out."

"Great, Mrs. Pharis. That's terrific."

"Call me Rita," she said good-naturedly.

I then decided to ask her a few more out of the endless questions I had for her about her family. Most important, I wanted to get an inkling about her family's quality of life. What did everyone do for a living? How well did they live? I told her that my family had moved all over the country since Laura left Louisiana back in the 1890s. I asked her if her people had stayed in Louisiana all those years.

She replied, "You know, I was thinking about that very thing myself just this morning, Neil. Mama always used to say she felt so wealthy inside her heart, knowing that all of her people—all the people she loved—were in the same part of the same state we always came from.

"We've never left Louisiana," she went on, "or done anything that anybody would consider great, I guess. I mean, there aren't any doctors or lawyers or writers in our family. Nothing like yours, I mean. We've had to get through some pretty hard times, to tell you the truth. We're just simple, ordinary people," she said. "But that's fine, too."

A moment later I asked again if I could visit her and her family. She said she'd like that very much but wanted to leave it up to her forty-one-year-old daughter, Bobette Coughlin, to decide when was best.

"She'll get in touch with you soon, Neil," she said. "I know she will."

When I hung up moments later, with energy and excitement coursing through me, I stepped outside my building to take a brisk walk on campus in the bright sunlight of that February day. I was thrilled, filled with the same sensation of discovery I had often felt in my journalistic work in Africa, in Washington, D.C., and so many other places whenever I believed I had a good story to tell and was about to sit down to write it.

As I paced toward the Campanile, the tall clock tower that stands over campus like a sentinel, I tried to fit the 150-year-old story of our two families together in my mind and felt bewildered by the unlikeliness of it all. On one side of our extended family tree was a white American family living an archetypal immigrant's dream during the era of Reconstruction and on to the turn of century, enjoying a prosperous way of life built on white supremacy and the plantation system. On the other was a tiny black family— a former slave and her child—possessing little but a dream at the start of the same era, an era oppressive to millions of black Americans. Yet during the century and a quarter that followed, the black family steadily climbed upward to somehow realize many of its dreams, with careers in medicine, engineering, education, and journalism, despite the obstacles of American racism. At the same time the far more advantaged white family seemed to suffer a mysterious and devastating fall after the patriarch's death in 1901—a decline I first began to glean in the courthouse records in Vicksburg and now badly wanted to find out more about.

I felt stunned and surprisingly elated by the paradox. Who could have predicted such a thing, given the stereotypes about race and low expectations for black people that have defined life in America? What would staunch believers in black inferiority have to say about these apparently contrasting black and white family stories?

Several days later, on February 22, I received an e-mail message from Rita's daughter:

> *Dear Neil:*
>
> *Hi. My name is Bobette Coughlin. My mother is Rita Pharis. We were very pleased to hear from you. Your letter was very interesting. We are gathering information that I hope you can use. It is Mardi Gras time here in La. My son and I caught a parade in Lafayette and caught many Mardi Gras beads and trinkets. It was a beautiful day and great fun. We are looking forward to hearing from you in the future. Wishing you all the best . . .*

I replied to her by e-mail and told her a little bit about my life in return, pointing out that I was a parent too, of a five-year-old girl. Then she answered with a second e-mail, telling me she had recently taken a new job as a speech pathologist and that she hoped my visit could be scheduled around her unusual work hours.

A few days later I telephoned her in Pineville to arrange the visit. She had a soft southern accent, just like her mother's, though her voice wasn't husky like Rita's.

We agreed on a date during my spring break from classes at Berkeley—the first weekend after St. Patrick's Day, Saturday, March 21.

"Hope you like seafood gumbo," Rita told me over the phone with a giggle later that same day. "It's our specialty 'round here."

"I love it. My mother cooked it from the time I was a kid."

"Well, good. We look forward to meeting you, Neil. My sister's daughter and her husband will be here—they're driving all the way up from New Orleans—and the husband of another sister too.

"We've got a lot of things to show you," Rita added shortly before we said good-bye. "A few surprises too."

CHAPTER SIX

"Welcome to the Family"

Named after the lush stands of pine that have grown in the fertile brown earth of central Louisiana almost since the beginning of time, Pineville is a sleepy southern town of about five thousand people on the banks of the famed Red River, which cuts a diagonal swath across the state from its entering point on the border with Texas to the Gulf of Mexico. The very tranquillity of this quiet hamlet belies the region's often troubled political and racial history.

During the Civil War numerous skirmishes and battles took place in this vicinity, including the burning of the stately Rapides Parish seat of Alexandria, just across the river, in 1863 by retreating federal troops. Later, this area became key to the rise of Huey Long, the populist Louisiana leader and champion of poor whites whose appeal to old southern values and conservative racial traditions resonated throughout the region in the 1930s. More than half a century later, Long, along with Ronald Reagan, remained a hero and beloved icon to most of the white population in central Louisiana.

Today, Pineville is perhaps most noted around Louisiana as the home of a state mental institution. Bordered by beautiful green forests growing along the banks of the rust-colored river drifting gently by, it is, like most towns in America, a place where most black people live on one side and most whites on the other.

To get to Pineville, I flew from Sacramento to Dallas, then made a connection to a thirty-six-seat propeller plane for the two-hour flight 240 miles southeast to Alexandria, the airport closest to Rita's house. As the plane soared high above the terrain, which gradually changed in color from the browns and reds of north Texas to the luxuriant greens and rust colors of central Louisiana, I tried to imagine what it must have been like to sink deep roots in one small region of America, this region, for more than 150 years, as the white Beaumont family had ever since A.J. Beaumont first arrived there from England.

I also thought about my years of research and how close to the white family, geographically, I had often been all along.

Natchez, where I had found the graves of Arthur and Mary Ann Beaumont five months earlier, was barely sixty miles east of Pineville. Vicksburg, where I had discovered several important clues in my search at the Warren County Court House, was one hundred miles to the northeast. Mound Bayou, where my father had saved the life of civil rights activist Gus Courts in 1955, was just 225 miles away.

I had been so close to the Beaumonts, I realized. Yet so many worlds apart.

I rented a car as soon as I landed at Alexandria's small commuter airport and checked into a Holiday Inn in town. I hadn't thought it necessary to call ahead from California to reserve a room, figuring Alexandria would not be especially popular as a destination for tourists. But the hotel clerk told me there was a state basketball tournament going on, along with a convention of the United Daughters of the Confederacy, and all the hotel rooms in Alexandria had been booked for months. "We got a cancellation just a few minutes ago," she said; "otherwise you would have been out of luck, Mr. Henry."

I found my room and immediately telephoned Rita after tossing my bag onto the bed. I took notes as she gave me directions to her house on Tudor Street in Pineville, which was located directly across the Red River from Alexandria.

After hanging up, I got back in my car, found the main artery connecting the two cities, MacArthur Boulevard, and soon crossed the Red River on an old iron bridge to Pineville. This road soon took me past a Louisiana state park with historical markers pointing out sites where Confederate troops had built artillery defenses on the Red River more than 135 years ago. Rita had told me her house was located on a short tree-lined street less than a mile from the state park, set among about a dozen other similarly styled, small, single-story homes built in the 1970s. Her neighborhood, which I soon found, seemed a humble, unostentatious enclave of working-class and retired whites.

It was a warm, overcast afternoon. Several front doors on the block were open to let in the spring air, brimming with the season's new life. Sweet smells of honeysuckle filled the air as I drove slowly down the street, looking for number 130. One white man in overalls was cutting his grass with a push mower. At the curb in front of another house, an elderly white-haired man was bidding good-bye to a younger man and woman. Birds swooped and chirped overhead, and white butterflies floated amid hedges of azalea.

Rita's home was at the end of the block, a modest two-bedroom house with a short flight of stairs leading to a small porch. After making a U-turn on the quiet street to park in front of it, I turned the ignition off, got out of the car with my satchel on my shoulder, and walked up a short cement path through a well-clipped lawn to the porch. The porch was framed by beautiful blossoms of tiny white and yellow bridesweed flowers. On my right, out of the corner of an eye, I noticed a white couple working in their yard next door. The man looked up at me briefly, quizzically. I nodded my head slightly in greeting, then turned to the door.

The screen door was shut, but the front door to the house was wide open, revealing a darkened blur of furniture in the front room and bright sunlight from a lace-curtained window in the kitchen in the rear. I knocked lightly on the screen door, the sound of wood on wood echoing lightly but surely inside. In one hand I cradled a bottle of red California wine for Rita, in the other a San Francisco 49ers T-shirt for her nine-year-old grandson, Patrick Coughlin.

I waited, my ears listening for a sound, my eyes peeled for the opening of the screen door. I took a deep breath, hearing only the birds singing softly in the treetops and the clipping sounds of the neighbors working in their yard. Then, seconds later I heard a low cough and the sound of footsteps padding along the floor inside, growing louder and closer. I noticed the outline of a figure approaching. A hand—a white hand lightly speckled with age spots—pushed the handle of the screen door.

As the door opened, my eyes fell upon the face of a smiling slender white woman with short, wavy dark hair sprinkled with flecks of gray. She was dressed in plain slacks and a warm beige sweater embroidered with red, purple, and green flowers. Around her neck hung a pair of bifocal eyeglasses on a gold chain.

"Hello, Neil," Rita said in the husky yet dulcet southern accent I recognized from the phone, her smile growing wider as her eyes found mine. "Come on in."

She kept the door open for me to enter, and I suddenly found myself tripping over my words. I was so nervous. I told her I had so much to show her from the documents and photographs I carried in my satchel.

"Me too. But let me do this first," she said. She stepped closer, then and folded her arms gently around me. I found myself returning her hug. "Welcome," she said.

Years of keepsakes filled her living room, which was furnished in early American–style pieces of solid wooden furniture. It was a very comfortable room with a well-worn carpet on the floor. Portraits and ceramic figurines of angels and Virgin Marys decorated the walls and bookshelves, testimony to her family's Roman Catholic faith.

As I followed Rita to her bright kitchen in the rear of the house, I found myself remembering all the times I had imagined this scene, this very moment, when I finally met the white Beaumont descendant in person. I had always envisioned the descendant as a white man, not a woman, for some inexplicable reason. I also had imagined family pictures filling the walls, including photos of the English immigrant and Confederate war veteran, Arthur Beaumont. But as I passed through Rita's living room, I noticed only one prominent photo, set atop a large console television set sitting in a corner. It was a black-and-white portrait dating from the 1930s, of Rita's beloved sisters—the granddaughters of Arthur Beaumont. Taken in the prime of their Louisiana youth, it showed them smiling gaily into the camera.

As we entered the kitchen, I was enveloped by the warm aroma of tomato sauce, seafood, and gumbo filé. Rita apologized for the smell of tobacco also lingering in the house. "I smoke," she confessed with a slight blush. I replied that I didn't mind in the least.

We then sat at a small kitchen table to share our treasures, our words spilling over themselves and our old keepsakes—photos, documents, letters—mixing together on the tabletop amid the salt and pepper shakers, spices, and a big tray of napkins. Things happened so fast and we spoke so quickly that it was hard to keep track in my notes, which I scribbled furiously in my notebook.

I pulled out my photos of A.J. Beaumont and my copy of the letter he wrote to Pearl in 1901. In addition, I pulled out a family tree I had sketched in pencil on the airplane from Dallas showing our relationship to the Beaumonts, along with photos of my family, including Laura, Pearl, Fredda, my mother, and Zoë.

Rita seemed fascinated by the photos, examining them closely through her bifocals, and instantly identified the former slave Laura as Pearl's mother without my telling her who she was.

"How did you know?" I asked her.

"I don't know," Rita said, nearly as stunned as I was. "Something inside me just said that must be Aunt Pearl's mother." Then, pointing at the photos, her bifocals perched on her nose, she instructed me, "Look—doesn't it look like they could be taken for Indians if you were told they were?"

"I suppose," I said. "I never thought about it."

Indeed, I hadn't. Laura to me had always been the beloved matriarch who had established our family's foundations in St. Louis so long ago, the woman who had raised Pearl on her own after leaving Beaumont behind. That's what I saw whenever I glanced at her photo, which had hung on the brick wall in our living room throughout my childhood in Seattle.

But to the Beaumonts, Laura had been little more than the mysterious, nameless, faceless "Indian woman" in Arthur Beaumont's past. The contrast was staggering when I thought about it. I had never considered race as a way to identify either Laura or Pearl. But for the white family all these years, race evidently was the only identifying mark.

Then Rita, opening a folder containing a pile of documents, showed me old photos from Arthur J. Beaumont's life in the late nineteenth century, when the family enjoyed its finest days in America. Among them was a large black-and-white picture of the two-story office of his flourishing plantation supply firm on Plank Road in St. Joseph. It seemed a bustling, thriving business in the old photograph, with numerous workers, black and white, posed out front.

Another photo showed Beaumont, his wife, Mary Ann, and his young boy, Arthur W., standing with a bicycle in front of a rambling country house featuring intricate wood latticework, one of two houses and plantations Arthur J. Beaumont farmed, Rita said. I instantly recalled the short 1894 account about Arthur W.'s ninth birthday, which I had found in my microfilm research of the *Tensas Gazette* nearly a year earlier.

MASTER ARTHUR BEAUMONT entertained his young friends on Monday night at a charming birthday party, which was largely attended and highly enjoyed by the young folks.

Seeing the picture before me now of nine-year-old Arthur W. and his parents gave me visual evidence of the family's lifestyle that the newspaper had hinted at so tantalizingly in words. This and the other photos seemed to mirror a comfortable, genteel way of life befitting a rags-to-riches English immigrant's story, as he and his family enjoyed his twilight years amid all the trappings of the Gilded Age in a typical small town in the American South.

"What happened, Rita?" I asked as I examined the old photos carefully. "The family seemed to be doing so well. What happened after that?"

"Well, they were. They truly were," she answered in her husky voice, softened by the gentle southern accent, a cigarette perched in her fingers, her eyes gazing at the photo of her grandfather's plantation. We both were sipping from cups of coffee.

"What can I say? My daddy always used to talk about how wonderful those years in St. Joseph were when he was a boy. But then, after Grandpa Beaumont died, things just went to pot. The story is that the boll weevil destroyed everything we had," Rita explained, referring to the insect pestilence that swept up from Mexico and wiped out thousands of cotton farms in the South, beginning at the turn of the twentieth century.

Of course, I thought to myself. The boll weevil! That explained everything. For the scourge did indeed change a way of life for millions of people, black and white, ruining the fortunes of many and ending the tight economic hold "King Cotton" had had on the South for decades. The devastation wrought by the voracious plant-eating beetle cut across the cotton states of Texas, Louisiana, Mississippi, Alabama, Georgia, and South Carolina like a scythe, prompting many farmers to diversify into other crops, such as peanuts. The scourge also spurred the northern migration of millions of suddenly unneeded black sharecroppers whose lives in the South's labor-intensive plantation system had revolved around cotton for generations. In A.J. Beaumont's beloved Tensas Parish in Louisiana, the population as a whole fell nearly 30 percent between 1900 and 1920, from 19,070 to 12,085.

For our bifurcated family, too, the boll weevil scourge surely had had a lasting effect. For the white Beaumonts, it resulted in the destruction of everything that the immigrant Arthur Beaumont had built over his half century in America, barely a few years after his death. For my black family, although the pestilence may not have triggered Laura's decision to leave Louisiana, she benefited from the burgeoning black migration to the North. It probably helped fill the rooming house that she ran for years in St. Louis for black workers and travelers, the house in which my grandmother Fredda was raised.

"It was certainly the boll weevil, but alcohol played a part too, I suspect," Rita continued. "You see, my daddy wasn't trained to do anything with his life except inherit what his daddy had built and to enjoy it. And when that fell apart, when the plantations fell away—well, there was little left except the memories. Dust and memories. It was all gone."

In *Trouble in Mind: Black Southerners in the Age of Jim Crow*, historian Leon F. Litwack notes that black sharecroppers and farmers, who suffered from the ravages of the boll weevil every bit as much as white plantation owners, nonetheless felt a grudging respect, even admiration, for the insect, not least because of its extraordinary ability to "render white men powerless [and] exert controls over white men," as blacks could not. Litwack quotes Mahalia Jackson as saying, "They were a proud and selfish people, those plantation owners and I believe . . . that God finally sent the boll weevil to humble them. . . . Thanks to the boll weevil, a lot of those thieving plantation people died out, too."

Still, for the black man, the bug's rapaciousness was in the end "no match" for the white man's, Litwack claims, and he cites the words of a black farmer, Ned Cobb: "What the boll weevil can do to me ain't half so bad to what a white man might do. I can go to my field and shake a poison dust on my crop and the boll weevil will sail away. But how can I sling a man off my back?" It was an era in which many poor blacks saw righteous justice in a natural disaster that crippled the white man as surely as the white man had crippled blacks through so many generations.

I watched as Rita rose from her chair to stir a pot of rice on the stove, and I realized I was liking her more and more as the minutes swept by. It was funny, but I had imagined for a long time that if I ever got the chance to meet a white Beaumont descendant in the flesh like this, somewhere at the end of my long search, I would feel the old resentment rise up deep inside me— feelings rooted in old hurts my family and I had endured at the hands of white people for so many years. I imagined myself focusing this bitterness on the descendant, the white cousin, I found.

But that wasn't happening with Rita at all. Far from it. With each passing moment I was finding myself drawn closer to her, appreciating her extraordinary candor about her life and her family's saga—along with the treasures she had unearthed for me— in a way that seemed to transcend our contrasting color and histories. It's difficult to explain. Perhaps impossible. But I stopped feeling so much like a black man sitting as a guest in her kitchen and stopped seeing her so much as a white woman acting as host.

We were just two people, two human beings linked by blood long ago and by a racial history peculiar to America, who were meeting in her small house in a small southern town on a spring afternoon simply to talk about it.

Rita carried herself with ease and physical grace. Her soft brown eyes reflected a genuine warmth as they looked into mine whenever she spoke, and her face was lined with wrinkles that spoke of dignity more than age. She laughed easily as she described her life to me that afternoon and evening, flashing a delightful, radiant smile and letting loose a low, infectious chuckle, usually punctuated by the words "What can I say?" Yet she also had a vague sadness deep in her eyes that never really went away.

The smells of crab and roux and steamed rice, familiar from my childhood in Seattle, filled the kitchen as Rita prepared dinner for the family gathering several hours away while we shared our stories. We were to be joined by Rita's niece, Carolyn Layne, and Carolyn's husband, Jack, who were driving to Pineville from New Orleans, five hours away, to meet me. Also coming were Rita's daughter, Bobette; Bobette's husband, Robert Coughlin, who was a special education teacher ; and their nine-year-old son, Patrick—they lived nearby in Pineville. One other family member was going to join us at the table: the elderly widower of one of Rita's sisters, Newton Himel, who also lived in Pineville. Like most residents of central Louisiana, he had worked in the oil and gas industry all his life.

Rita had asked me to come to the house early so we could talk and share our treasures before dinner. And as she spoke, I began to realize that much of the story she had to tell me was punctuated by sorrow. Ask most people about the major turning points in their lives, and invariably they mention some of life's traditional transitions—happy ones like marriage and the birth of a child or terrible ones like the death of a loved one. For Rita, there had been too many turns of the latter kind, particularly in recent years.

These were difficult days for her, she told me as she sat back in her kitchen chair, an apron tied around her waist. Within the last several years she had lost her three older sisters to death and disease. Rita had also been widowed twice and told me she never really got over the first time, in 1975. That was the year her young husband, an electrical worker named Alfred Patrick Guirard, succumbed to brain cancer after an agonizing seven-year battle. His fight against cancer sent the family into a turbulent fall that not only severely tested their economic well-being but also shattered Rita's long-held faith in the Roman Catholic Church, which she found less than supportive or sympathetic.

The disaffection she described to me eerily resembled my mother's feelings in 1968 when her Episcopal church in Seattle failed her in her hour of spiritual need in the wake of Martin Luther King's assassination. Indeed, it was in the same year, 1968, that Rita, who had been married for seventeen years to a man she loved deeply, found herself suddenly having to work full-time in a low-paying job at the Central Louisiana Electric Company to support her family while caring for her incapacitated husband and raising their eleven-year-old daughter, Bobette. Tears glistened in Rita's eyes as she described the loss of her second husband and of her sisters within the last two years. In recent months, Rita said, the losses had become overwhelming and she began to suffer panic attacks. Her doctor put her on anti-depressants, the first time she had needed medication of any kind.

"It's not been easy," she concluded softly, looking toward the bright sunlight outside her kitchen window, her words trailing off. She dragged on her cigarette until it glowed red on its end.

A moment later I heard the porch screen door open and turned to see a stout young boy and a bespectacled woman with reddish blond hair and piercing eyes stride into the kitchen. "This is Bobette," Rita announced, sounding brighter, "and that's my grandson, Patrick."

Bobette smiled as she took my hand in hers. "It's wonderful to meet you," she said. As a welcoming gift, she handed me a T-shirt reading "Louisiana," and I gave Patrick the 49ers shirt I had brought from California. Bobette then kissed her mother's cheek and took a seat at the table with us, while Patrick was given permission to watch television in the living room. For a moment there was an awkward silence.

"It's been a very hard time for my mother, for a very long time," Bobette finally remarked. (A speech pathologist at a local nursing home, Bobette had worked to put herself through college in the 1970s and 1980s after her father's long illness and death, earning a master's degree from Louisiana Tech.) "She hasn't been feeling well, physically or emotionally—have you, Mom? We've gone through so many sad things in our lives lately, but your call to Mama, just out of the blue like that—it was the best thing that's happened to her in a really long time."

"The whole thing has been a blessing," Rita's daughter added, glancing and smiling at her mother again. "Just a wonderful surprise."

I had always wondered what emotions I would feel upon meeting the Beaumonts in person. Would I rage at my white cousins? Would I cry? Would I dare to confide? But as I sat at Rita's kitchen table listening to Bobette, I realized how little I had ever thought about the effect I might have on the white family. Bobette, whose French name was a tribute to her father's Cajun heritage, told me over and over that my call had immensely bolstered and renewed Rita's spirits, which had fallen desperately low after her sisters' recent deaths.

My long search was leading me to places I never could have expected. Among the many surprises that day, my sympathy for Rita, the closest living blood link to A.J. Beaumont, was one of the biggest surprises of all.

She had been a mistake. A terrible mistake. An "oops" of providence, she told me. A child born in 1930 during the darkest days of the Great Depression to a thirty-seven-year-old poor white mother who could ill afford another mouth to feed. The last granddaughter of A.J., Rita Mary Beaumont entered the world in New Orleans, long after his death, with three older sisters, the youngest of whom was thirteen years her senior.

The family had fallen far and fast. So much so that another baby was simply the last thing in the world Anna Ventura Beaumont wanted or needed. It was bad enough that Anna was poor. What was worse was that, at the time of Rita's birth, she was in the throes of a final separation from her incapacitated and sickly husband, Arthur Wilford Beaumont, after nineteen years of heartache, betrayal, and alcohol abuse.

When Anna Beaumont found out she was pregnant with her fourth daughter, she cried and cried for weeks. As a devout Roman Catholic, however, she would take responsibility for her new child, doing the best she could. She would carry on in the face of adversity as she always had, from the time she was a poor immigrant girl from northern Italy known as Anna Sophie Ventura, whose parents, Joseph and Crucifixia, had struggled mightily to adapt to the new world after their arrival in New Orleans at the turn of the century.

That's how Rita had entered the world sixty-eight years ago, she told me, as we sat with Bobette at the kitchen table, our keepsakes in a clutter in its center. And as Rita talked about her childhood in New Orleans and elsewhere in Louisiana, I couldn't help comparing it to my mother's, growing up in St. Louis. For they were contemporaries—one a white woman, one a black woman, related by blood but with two very different stories to tell.

Rita's childhood in Louisiana was colored by her mother Anna's strength, grit, and constant tears. It was a childhood crippled by poverty and a torn family. By contrast, my mother, born in 1923, enjoyed a wonderfully happy childhood in St. Louis, buoyed by a loving and close family life and a steady source of income, even through the harshest days of the Depression, thanks to her father's job at the U.S. Post Office.

"Mama used to tell me that she just cried and cried for weeks after I was born," Rita recalled. "So that kind of set the tone for my upbringing. I never was very close to my daddy, and I probably felt for him much of the same sort of resentment that Mama did. She felt terribly betrayed by Daddy. But I loved my mother."

"And when I think about it," she continued, "Mama is probably the only reason we're able to meet today. She believed deeply in family, you know. Nothing was more important than family, no matter what our circumstances."

Anna met Arthur Wilford Beaumont in 1910, according to Rita. Anna was fifteen then and suffering almost nightly beatings by her father, Joseph. Desperate to escape her father's terror, Anna was willing to do practically anything, including marrying the young Beaumont, who had first come to her house in New

Orleans to woo her older sister but had fallen in love with Anna instead.

Arthur W. Beaumont was twenty-five then, a pale, willowy man who told Anna that his family hailed from northern Louisiana, from St. Joseph in Tensas Parish. He said he was the lone descendant of a very distinguished family that had once owned a great deal and often talked about the splendor of his family's past, especially on his father's side. He claimed his family roots were sunk deeply in England, where his male ancestors had valiantly served the monarchy in the Battle of Waterloo.

"Daddy believed really deeply in those things, in bloodlines and the old southern ways," Rita said. She then pulled out a manuscript her father had written in 1941, a few years before his death in 1947. She had made me a bound copy of the original, which I opened and began to read as Rita returned to the stove to put the dinner together.

The manuscript was written in Beaumont's elegant and flowing script. He had titled these eighty-eight pages of family history "The Family of Beaumont, Memory Genus."

"He had beautiful handwriting, didn't he?" Rita said, turning from the stove. "You can tell that he was an educated man."

"Yes," I said, shaking my head in amazement. His handwriting seemed perfect—so beautiful and precise it reminded me of the cursive alphabet on the posters pinned above the blackboards in my elementary school in Seattle.

Arthur W. Beaumont dedicated his book, which included numerous quotations from scripture, Shakespeare, Kipling, Longfellow, and other great literary figures, to his daughters to "help them through life." "I trust that as they travel along the avenue of years that this history and the verses and sayings in this

Rita Mary Beaumont at eighteen, in 1948 in Louisiana. Born during the Great Depression, this white granddaughter of A.J. Beaumont grew up in poverty in a single-parent household. She was fortified, however, by the love of her mother, Anna Ventura Beaumont, and her three older sisters. Photo courtesy Rita Beaumont Guirard Pharis.

Rita Beaumont Guirard with her first husband, Alfred Guirard, and their daughter, Bobette, in 1959. Photo courtesy Rita Beaumont Guirard Pharis.

Anna Ventura Beaumont (1894–1976) at sixty-six, in 1960 in Louisiana. The wife of Arthur W. Beaumont and the daughter of an Italian immigrant, she believed that "family was family," no matter the bloodline, and stayed in touch with the nonwhite "Aunt Pearl" against the wishes of her bigoted husband. Photo courtesy Rita Beaumont Guirard Pharis.

Arthur W. Beaumont (1885–1947), the white son of
Arthur J. Beaumont, at four, ca. 1889. He was raised
to be a "gentleman," to lead a life of privileged ease
and prosperity. When the family holdings were
destroyed during the boll weevil plague at the turn
of the century, however, he spent the remainder of
his life longing for all that was lost, including the
structure of white supremacy. Photo courtesy
Rita Beaumont Guirard Pharis.

Arthur J. Beaumont, progenitor of a dual racial legacy in America, near the end of his life, at sixty, ca. 1899. Photo courtesy Mary Turner Henry.

A.J. Beaumont's plantation supply store and saloon, with workers out front, in St. Joseph, Louisiana, ca. 1889. Photo courtesy Rita Beaumont Guirard Pharis.

(left) The Beaumonts—Arthur J., Mary Ann (1857–1914), and son, Arthur W.—in front of one of the family's two plantation homes outside St. Joseph, Louisiana, ca. 1889. Photo courtesy Rita Beaumont Guirard Pharis.

subject, but his heart and soul a Southerner, carried on for four years, until the surrender of General Robt. E. Lee, at Appamattox Md., in 1865.

In rags and tatters and wearing what was once the uniform of a captain in the U.S. Navy (This uniform had been taken by my father from the cabin of the commander of the U.S.S. Indianola) that had been captured by my father's command.

Arthur John Beaumont (my father) surrendered to the U.S. forces at Minden La., in 1865.

A few days later, he rode into the small village of St Joseph,

Tensas Parish, Louisiana, astrid a white horse (one of the few possessions allowed in the terms of surrender)

Penniless and forlorn, he applied for work to Eli Tullis, a young planter, who had just returned from the War and was trying to bring back something from a one glorious and prosperous South. This same Eli Tullis, later became the father of Mrs. Joseph Curry Sr. of St Joseph, Tensas Parish, Louisiana.

Dean Lee Tullis of the Law School of L.S.U.

Hugh Tullis, a prominent lawyer and Judge of the 10th Judicial

Two pages (30–31) from Arthur W. Beaumont's handwritten family history, penned in 1941 for his daughters, in which he recounts his father's service for the Confederacy and extols the Old South and its lost ideals. Courtesy Rita Beaumont Guirard Pharis.

Pearl Brumley Hall, the author's great-grandmother, in front of
her house at 6422 Chatham Street in St. Louis, ca. 1925. The
photo was given to the author by Rita Beaumont Pharis when
they met. The author later copied and framed it as a gift for his
mother. Photo courtesy the author.

The author and his mother, Mary Turner Henry, in Seattle in 1988. Photo courtesy the author.

A lunch during a 1999 gathering of the "Tenth Man Classic." Left to right: E.C. ("Uncle Sonny") Turner, Jr., Bobby Henry (brother), the author, and Dr. John R. Henry (father). Photo courtesy the author.

little volume may suit their problems and afford them a great deal of consolation and happiness," he wrote.

As I read through the memoir and history at Rita's kitchen table, I realized with an eerie start that it had been penned more than fifty years earlier in a spirit not unlike the one I felt as I tried to piece together our black family story for myself and, I hoped, for my daughter one day. I had always wanted to produce a story for Zoë to read when she was older, something to help her understand race and racism in America through the lessons of our family tree. Like me, Arthur W. Beaumont was trying to explain to his daughters where his people came from and the things they believed in. Like me, he was proud of his ancestors and hoped his writing would help steel his children with a strong sense of identity and faith.

Yet the lessons this white man was trying to tell in those eighty-eight pages were almost exactly the opposite of what I wanted to convey to Zoë. Beaumont's family story boasted of the glories of white supremacy, of the greatness of enjoying regal bloodlines, and of the enduring values of the Old South that his family's immigrant history illustrated. By contrast, mine was a story of black faith, of the struggle for equal rights, and of progress in the face of bigotry. Their story celebrated traditions that resulted in the oppression of black people. Our story celebrated the overturning of such traditions. We shared the immigrant's blood, but the morals of our two family stories could not have been more diametrically opposed.

As I read the history, I found sorrow and wistfulness at the heart of the white family story. The author, writing in 1941, when he was fifty-six, seemed to be looking backward on things that had been lost instead of looking with hope toward the future. By contrast, Beaumont's half niece and contemporary, Fredda, then forty-five, was simply glowing about her life in St. Louis and her family's future, doing all that she could to prepare her three children to take advantage of it. Already, the next generation was gearing up for the great changes for black people that were on the horizon. In 1941 my father was about to enter Meharry Medical College in Nashville, and my mother was about to become an undergraduate at Harriet Beecher Stowe College in St. Louis. Both were full of youth and, despite the oppression of Jim Crow, brimming with the optimism of their generation. They had everything to look forward to, so many goals to pursue, so many dreams that they would live to see come true. How far removed they were from the small town in Louisiana where Arthur W. Beaumont seemed obsessed with glorifying the past, the splendors of the plantation era, and all that been lost.

I was mesmerized as I slowly flipped through the pages of family history and only slightly surprised by the greatest omission at its heart: that the author had a black half sister—my great-grandmother Pearl—whom he refused to acknowledge, in life or in print.

Beaumont's manuscript traced the family's blood origins to France in the seventeenth century, when a paternal ancestor named Pierre Gustave Beaumont de la Bonnier, who hailed from the province of Beaumont la Chartre, sailed to England as a young *chevalier* along with thousands of other French sympathizers to remove the despot Oliver Cromwell from power and restore Prince Charles to the throne. In thanks, Beaumont the Frenchman was given land in Kent, where he raised his family and became an English citizen.

Thus began, according to Beaumont's family history, a long

association over the next several centuries between the now-Anglicized Beaumont family line and the British military. This alliance saw succeeding generations of Beaumonts fight for Britain in numerous storied battles, from the Napoleonic Wars and the Battle of Waterloo to the Crimean War and the Charge of the Light Brigade. The handwritten family history was full of colorful detail about the suffering, derring-do, and bravery of various Beaumont ancestors on the battlefield.

Arthur J. Beaumont, Arthur W.'s father, was born in Kent in 1839, one of six sons of the Waterloo veteran Peter Alastair Beaumont, who had retired as a "squire and Magistrate and lived the life of a country gentleman." Like his brothers, A.J., as he was commonly known, was educated at Woolwich Military Academy, a privilege given to the sons of Waterloo veterans. But in 1856, when he turned seventeen, he left home and sailed to America in search of his fortune—an act of defiance that caused his father to disinherit him, for his father had planned a British military career for him. Indeed, two of A.J.'s older brothers did serve the crown in the armed forces: Peter Beaumont, whose legs were "shot off during the Kaffir War in Africa," according to the manuscript, and Douglas Beaumont, who earned the Victoria Cross for gallantry in the Crimean War, as a captain of artillery during the Battle of Balaklava in 1854.

A.J. was one of three brothers to emigrate from England to America in the mid-nineteenth century. Clarence Beaumont, a physician, served as a lieutenant in the U.S. Army's Fifth Illinois infantry during the Civil War, then disappeared in the West after the conflict was over. Another brother, Louis Beaumont, also disappeared, somewhere in California during the Gold Rush of 1849.

"My father first settled in Chicago, remaining for about a

year," Arthur W. Beaumont continued. "But hearing so much about the great plantations of the South and the great landholders and slave owners who lived in almost regal splendor, he headed there to seek his destiny." Gradually, before my eyes, the manuscript filled in the details about the white branch of my family tree I had long sought, like dabs of oil paint completing a long unfinished landscape.

"Great opportunities lay in this section [of America]," the younger Beaumont wrote. "He secured a position as one of the assistants to the overseer on the great Frisbee Plantation, of ten thousand acres, in western Tensas Parish, Louisiana. This was in 1858. My father, for whom I am named, remained here until April, 1861, when the thunder roared and the lightning of war struck the entire South."

Then, the arrogant words of the long-dead white man cut through my soul. "Becoming imbued with the spirit of the Southern people," he noted, "my father enlisted his services as well as his spirit in the cause of the Southern people and of course became a soldier of the Confederacy. In April of 1861 he enlisted in Cameron's Battery–4th Louisiana Heavy Field Artillery, Captain [Archibald J.] Cameron commanding, with a roster of 103 men. He was engaged in many battles of major and lesser degree; he was at First Bull Run, also saw the beloved son of Louisiana, General Mouton, killed at Mansfield, La."

As I read these lines, I remembered the years I had spent voraciously reading about the Civil War to understand the broader context of Laura's and Arthur's lives. I was never able to find Beaumont's name in the incomplete rosters of Confederate volunteers from Louisiana in the National Archives, but I did discover in several Louisiana military histories that Archibald

Cameron's artillery battery was well known throughout the state and was one of the first units formed in Tensas Parish after Louisiana seceded from the Union in 1861.

First Bull Run, often called First Manassas, was the first major battle of the war, occurring barely three months after the surrender of Fort Sumter. It was a bloody engagement involving some 28,000 Union troops and 32,000 Confederate soldiers, most of them volunteers under the command of Generals P.G.T. Beauregard and Thomas J. Jackson, who earned his nickname "Stonewall" during this battle. The fighting took place near the banks of a small stream called Bull Run in the Virginia countryside south of Washington on July 21, 1861. To the world's shock, the Union troops were quickly and decisively routed in one of the South's greatest victories, setting the stage for other rebel military triumphs over the next two years.

Arthur J. Beaumont, his son wrote, "suffered the extreme privations and hardships of all soldiers of the Confederacy. Many times having only a small tin cup of meal and small piece of half putrid meat. This was the ration for one day. In the evening, they had to go 'a-foraging.'"

"Barefoot and in rags," the white family history recounted, "this young man, a British subject, but his heart and soul a Southerner, carried on for four years until the surrender of General Robert E. Lee in 1865. In rags and tatters and wearing what was once the uniform of a captain in the U.S. Navy (this uniform had been taken by my father from the cabin of the commander of the U.S.S. Indianola, which had been captured by my father's command) my father surrendered to the U.S. forces at Minden, La. in April, 1865."

A few days later Arthur J. Beaumont "rode into the town of St.

Joseph astride a white horse, one of the few possessions allowed under the terms of surrender. Penniless and forlorn he applied for work to Eli Tullis, a young planter, who had just returned from the war and was trying to bring back something from a once glorious and prosperous South."

I couldn't help smiling as I read those words, my attention grabbed by the name Tullis. The historical portrait filled in as I read on in wonder. *Tullis*—that name was imbedded in the heart of our black family's lore. The Tullis family had owned the cotton plantation where Laura Brumley, my great-great-grandmother, had been born in slavery in 1850. It was the New England–born mistress of the plantation, Sarah Tullis, who had taught Laura to read and write as a child and saw to it that she acquired sewing skills. The same Tullis family had figured prominently in Louisiana's political and economic rebirth after the war. It included a state judge and newspaper editor, Hugh Tullis; business and society leaders; and Lee Tullis, a dean of the law school at Louisiana State University. Beaumont's manuscript detailed the things that I had already discovered in my research.

As I read about this part of A.J. Beaumont's life, I couldn't help but link it to Laura's. In 1865, the year the Civil War ended, she was fifteen—in the prime of her teenage years—still living and working on the Tullis plantation. Into Laura's life in St. Joseph was destined to come the white man, the English immigrant and war veteran who would turn out to be the only man she would ever love, the father of her only child, Pearl.

"My father worked for Eli Tullis for several years," Beaumont's son continued, "he saved his money, and in 1867 with a few dollars and lots of credit he engaged in the cotton planting and general merchandising business. Prospering slowly, owing to the readjustment of conditions during this period of Recon-struction, by 1870 he had become a man of influence in Tensas Parish. By 1875 he had prospered still further and become a nat-uralized American citizen."

And, according to his son, Arthur J. Beaumont worked tire-lessly, proudly, doggedly against black political rights in Tensas Parish and his adopted state. What I always had suspected in the deepest recesses of my mind about his political beliefs suddenly became clear as I saw it in black and white in the manuscript be-fore me: A.J. Beaumont took "an active part in the banishment of Carpet Bag rule and the elimination of Negro influence in the state, by the election of Francis T. Nicholls as the first Demo-cratic governor since the war."

What his son did not point out in the manuscript was that A.J. Beaumont enjoyed a long relationship with Laura Brumley dur-ing that very period, which resulted in the birth of Pearl, my great-grandmother, in 1877. A year later, in 1878 in St. Joseph, Beaumont married Mary Ann Sims, a white woman who hailed from Arkansas. While it was always part of our black family story that the relationship between Laura and Arthur was very affec-tionate and conducted with mutual consent over a long period in the 1870s, it was not clear whether the relationship continued after Beaumont's marriage. Laura and Pearl continued to live in the South until the early 1890s, when they moved to St. Louis.

Arthur the younger wrote that he was the only child of the marriage between A.J. and Mary Ann Beaumont to survive child-hood. Two other children, including Florence, whose name I had found in the 1880 census records in Washington, died at an early age.

"My mother and father lived for many years in St. Joseph

where they enjoyed the respect, esteem, and confidence of all who knew them," the son continued, echoing all that I had discovered in the microfilms of old Louisiana newspapers. And it was during the last two decades of the century that the family became quite prosperous, turning the immigrant's dream of prosperity in America into reality. In the son's words: "During this maelstrom of events and kaleidoscopic changes in the affairs of the nation, my father acquired two great cotton plantations—Lakewood and Gladstone—which he operated successfully for many years. . . . [In 1901] my father died as he had lived—a man true to the ideals of the land of his adoption."

True to the ideals of the land of his adoption.

How true that was, I thought, as I read the white man's words. For Beaumont believed in slavery so deeply that he staked his life on it in wartime. He believed that black people did not deserve rights equal to those of white people, and like millions of other white men of his age in the South, he worked to erect a system of separatism and inequality that oppressed blacks by law through numerous generations. The evil system lasted all the way into the era in which I, his great-great-grandson, was born. And like many white men of such "ideals," A.J. Beaumont was a hypocrite, siring a mixed-race child in loving union with a black woman in private while maintaining in public his belief in our racial inferiority and enforcing our lower-class citizenship.

Arthur Wilford Beaumont wrote that he was destined to inherit his father's estate, along with the trappings, and traditions of the prosperous plantation life his family had grown to enjoy. But several short years after his father's death, disaster struck. In 1908, he revealed, the boll weevil scourge wiped out not only the family's extensive planting interests in rural Tensas Parish but also the plantation supply business on Plank Road in St. Joseph that his father had worked so hard to build after the Civil War. Arthur W. and his mother, Mary Ann, were ruined.

"Daddy wasn't trained to do anything with his life except to inherit what his father had built," Rita explained as we sat at her kitchen table, drinking soft drinks and awaiting the arrival of the other dinner guests. "He considered himself an aristocrat, a real dandy. I can remember from my childhood that he even used to carry around a pair of dancing shoes. Can you believe it?"

Bobette laughed as she heard this. "You're kidding, Mama. Dancing shoes?"

"He didn't have a penny to his name," Rita said, dragging on her cigarette softly and chuckling huskily as she shook her head slowly from side to side. "But he had dancing shoes."

As she showed me pictures of her father as a pale-faced child, Rita began to talk about her difficult relationship with him. "My mother had grown to despise him by the time I came along, and I think I did too, mainly because I loved my mama so much," she said, sipping her soda from a clear drinking glass, glancing at me over her bifocals. "I remember that I used to love to disobey him. I remember when I was going off to high school—my parents had separated years before—he sat me down to warn me about a few things. He said, 'Now, Rita, high school is a major turning point in a girl's life. And no matter what you do, don't you ever read the works of Guy de Maupassant.'"

She smiled, her face looking younger, brighter. "He said it the French way, you see. He was Cajun that way. 'Gie deh moh-peh-SAWN.' He was very proper. I guess he figured Guy de Maupassant was too sexy for my own good. But, of course, you know the first thing I did as soon as I got to high school was look up the books of 'Gie deh moh-peh-sAwN,'" Rita said, slapping her hand on the tabletop, throwing her head back, and laughing as Bobette and I laughed with her.

"It wasn't sexy at all," she sighed. "Maybe in the nineteenth century it was considered sexy, but I found it pretty dull."

Her father considered himself a very refined gentleman and aristocrat, Rita reiterated, and like many aristocrats he was not imbued with a great deal of worldly ambition. She said her father loved nothing better than to fish for trout and bass, raise prize roses, and read great works of literature. He wrote poetry, short stories, and novels in his spare time and frequently contributed short essays and letters about ethical issues of the day to the editor of the Louisiana Knights of Columbus magazine. He was a dreamer and an artist, his daughter explained, a man raised to live no other role but that of a white southern gentleman.

"Kindness is one of the most potent of God's medicines. It makes no distinction in race, creed or color," Arthur W. Beaumont stated in a verse published by the *Jeanerette, La. Enterprise* in October 1944 and pasted into his book of life's memories. "If it were prescribed more for the ills of this tired and weak old world, I am sure it would be just as effective as of yore and would bring about peace and goodwill to all men."

The manuscript was filled with such clippings from his writing, along with a list of more than twelve novels he said he had written, with titles like "The Last of the Fairmonts," "A Tale of Old Russia," and "The Master of Ravenswood," none of which were ever published.

And like his father, who had worked in the Democratic Party in the 1870s and 1880s to fight Reconstruction, black suffrage, "Negro influence," and carpetbag rule in Tensas Parish, Arthur

W. Beaumont believed deeply in the old southern way of life. He valued racial separatism and the cherished ideals of the Confederacy. Until the day he died, he considered his dearest possession a bronze medal, the Southern Cross of Honor, which the state's Daughters of the Confederacy chapter bestowed on him in 1920 at a ceremony in New Orleans, in recognition of his proud standing as a direct living descendant of a valorous veteran of the War Between the States.

When I read that passage in his family history, on page 45, I couldn't help comparing it to my family's story, for the differences between us suddenly became starkly apparent in my mind. Arthur W. Beaumont's most cherished keepsake all those years had been a medal representing the ideals of the Confederacy, white supremacy among them. My family's most cherished keepsakes also included a medal, but one of a far different kind—the lifetime NAACP membership pin that my grandfather Clifford, Fredda's husband, earned through his many decades of work for and paying dues in the civil rights organization in St. Louis. He had been so proud of it that when he died in 1971, Fredda— Arthur W.'s niece—lovingly insisted that the medal be pinned to the lapel of the suit he wore when he was laid to rest in our old family plot in Illinois.

So valued was his Southern Cross of Honor that in his manuscript Arthur W. Beaumont specified a line of succession for its possession after his death, from his oldest daughter to his youngest, Rita Mary, and from her to the oldest child of his oldest daughter. "It is strictly understood," he stipulated, "that the Southern Cross of Honor is never to be worn publicly, loaned, nor sold."

But today, Rita told me, the medal is missing, along with

much of her father's writing—lost or misplaced somewhere in the line of succession. "I wish I knew where it was," she indicated. "He wanted us all to keep it, but I don't know for the life of me where the thing is."

Near the end of the family history Arthur the younger provided an intricate color painting of what he called the Beaumont coat of arms, which showed a British lion rampant on a field of blue studded with the fleur-de-lis of France. Its motto read: "Erectus non elatus"—Lofty not proud.

While Arthur the younger was a dreamer all his life, a white aristocrat without a plantation to call home, his Italian wife, Anna, seemed always to have her feet firmly planted on the ground. It was Anna who got the family through the trials and hardships of the next forty years, Rita told Bobette and me. "My mother meant more to us as a family than Daddy ever did," Rita asserted. "She was the one who kept us all together."

The Beaumont family holdings were gone by 1910, when Anna first met Arthur, who was working then not as a prosperous landed gentleman but as a foreman for the coal company in Vicksburg, Mississippi. One spring night Arthur asked this fiery daughter of an impoverished Italian grocer to marry him, and she instantly said yes. However, Arthur W.'s mother, Mary Ann, didn't like the young woman and vociferously opposed the marriage. It was bad enough that the girl was just fifteen years old, and worse still that she was dirt poor and could offer little to the family. But what was infuriating to Mary Ann was that her only son wanted to marry an Italian, of all races, a people she considered crass and coarse and unworthy of the proud English blood that flowed through the veins of the Beaumonts.

Nevertheless, marry the young couple did, and soon children

were born: Marie Therese in 1912, Anna Elva in 1915, and Virginia Grace in 1918. Marie gained the nickname "Muggins," or simply "Muggie," after her adoring father told her she looked like a poor ragamuffin as she ate breakfast one morning with her face smeared with dirt. Certainly, Arthur W. was proud of his girls, especially because they were healthy and full of life. Born in 1885 in St. Joseph, he was the only surviving child of a couple who lost two other children to disease, and he believed deeply in his destiny to maintain the Beaumont bloodline in America.

Arthur W. knew his father had had another child by a woman his father had known shortly before marrying Mary Ann. And while the child of that relationship, Pearl Brumley, was his half sister, eight years his senior, he did not regard her as such because she was not white, and he refused to have anything to do with her whenever she tried to contact the family in her letters. In Arthur W. Beaumont's mind Pearl was little more than a half-breed. A mongrel. An old "Indian" woman. She was not white, and therefore her link to him was not valid or real. To Arthur W., the inheritor of his father's ideals, the "colored" relative simply did not exist.

"Daddy didn't even want to discuss such things, these relationships that were outside the formal structure of family and society, you know," Rita murmured softly as she flipped through her father's manuscript looking first at me, then at Bobette. "That just wasn't done. It was bad form. Aristocrats," she noted, holding her nose up to imitate an aristocrat's style and bearing, "never talked about such things. It was beneath them."

Anna looked at Pearl quite differently, though, Rita said. And it was Anna who, on her own, welcomed Pearl as a member of the

Beaumont family, as best she could under the circumstances—almost as an act of rebellion against her husband. No one knew when or how they met.

"I just wish you could have found us five years earlier, Neil," Rita interjected wistfully at this point, placing her hand on my forearm for emphasis. "My gosh, the stories my sister Muggie could have told you. She always knew so much more than me. And she would have loved to talk to you." I, too, felt the loss powerfully—if only I had been able to find the Beaumonts two or three years earlier, Rita's older sisters might have told me so much.

Somehow Anna and Pearl, who was living in St. Louis, did meet, and they became very friendly and corresponded regularly in the mail throughout their adult lives, Rita said. Her sisters had told her Pearl also visited the family on at least two occasions in the years before Rita was born. Anna was a very welcoming sort of woman, Rita emphasized. Anyone of common blood to her and her family was certainly family to her.

Her husband called Pearl an Indian, and maybe she was. Anna herself was not immune to judging people by their bloodline. She made sure to point out to anyone who cared to ask that her ancestors came from the *north* of Italy, where people were blessed with lighter skin and fairer features—unlike the southerners and the "Sicilianas," whom her family scorned. "No marry Siciliana! No Siciliana!" her Italian-born mother had often warned her as a child in New Orleans.

But in the end, when it came to family, those things didn't seem to matter to Anna. Once someone was a part of your blood, they were *family*, no matter the shade or color. And that included Aunt Pearl, Rita said—"always, no matter what Daddy felt."

Anna, the daughter of the poor Italian immigrant, found that she had something else in common with Pearl, Rita added—a sense of feeling like an outcast, like a stranger in a hostile land. So Anna knew the importance of feeling linked to people. To Anna, the beautiful and exotic-looking woman named Pearl, who sent photographs along with her letters from St. Louis, was simply Aunt Pearl, the sister of Anna's husband. And she became known that way to Anna's children, despite Arthur's firm opposition to maintaining any contact with her. Rita admitted it didn't hurt matters that Anna got some joy out of defying her husband that way.

"When my Aunt Muggie was dying almost two years ago, she would talk a lot about our family history," said Carolyn Layne, Rita's sixty-year-old niece, when she arrived later for dinner after making the long drive from New Orleans with her husband, Jack. "And she always remembered Daddy's half sister fondly. That's the way she described her—Daddy's half sister, Aunt Pearl. We always knew her that way."

Arthur W. and Anna Beaumont moved to New Orleans from Vicksburg in 1918, where Arthur got work in a department store called Maison Blanche. He was not a very dedicated worker, though, and labored sporadically, much to his wife's discontent. He began to drink and they began to argue more and more. They separated and reunited, only to separate again. This happened repeatedly. It was during one of those reunifications that Rita, the last child, was conceived in 1929.

Times were already difficult enough. There was no work, and Arthur W. had suffered internal injuries and a broken pelvis in a car accident, leaving him disabled and sickly for the remainder of his life. A devout Roman Catholic whose mother was named

Crucifixia Aragnona Ventura—"That ought to tell you enough about her faith," Rita chuckled—Anna knew she would never be able to divorce Arthur W. That would have been unthinkable. Still, not long after Rita's birth, she separated from her husband for good.

Anna needed to get to work to support her family, so they moved to Jeanerette, in the heart of Cajun country, where she managed to get a loan to open a grocery store a few years later. Times were tough, not only economically, but socially as well, Rita remembered. A single mother in those days, especially a single white mother, was frowned upon and looked at with deep suspicion and revulsion in the conservative southern culture. Rita used to make up stories when she was a child in elementary school to hide the fact that her mother and father were not living together. "I'd say, 'Daddy's away on a big ship. He's a captain,'" she recalled, with a distant and sad look in her eyes. "Or 'Daddy's traveling and won't come back for a long time.' Anything to avoid the stigma, you know? It just wasn't right in those days that we didn't have a daddy in the house."

They were poor, so poor they sometimes had to rely on handouts from charity. Unlike her husband, who was disabled and never worked after the early 1930s, Anna, as a small shop owner and faithful Democrat, promptly registered with the Social Security Administration after Franklin Delano Roosevelt signed the act into law in 1935.

As Rita remembered her childhood during the Depression, I realized that it was only because of Anna, the mother she loved so deeply, and a quirk of historical fate that I had been able to find the white family at all after so many years of searching. Had it not been for Social Security records, for the "mistake" that brought

Rita into the world as the "cow's tail" in the family line in 1930, and for Anna Beaumont's acceptance and love of my great-grandmother Pearl, I likely never would have heard this story of the white family I was distantly related to—an intricately woven story of human experience and tragedy that stood as a complement, in many ways, to the saga of my family. I was awed by the contrasts between Rita and me but also strangely moved by the human connection we were making.

Still, despite the common ground we were finding, the two of us were products of our separate racial pasts—a reality that struck me again in a flash when Rita confided that one of her sisters had married into a family that was active in the Ku Klux Klan in central Louisiana in the 1950s. She mentioned it almost offhandedly while we were looking at family photos. But from that point on in our gathering, I felt myself withdrawing slightly, becoming wary, more ill at ease than when I had arrived.

When the rest of her family gathered at Rita's house for dinner later, I was welcomed warmly by all and asked to join their circle around the kitchen table as they bowed their heads and held hands to hear Newton Himel, a gray-haired widower in his eighties who was suffering from cancer and heart trouble, lead us in a Catholic prayer. "Bless us, O Lord, for all of our gifts and for these we are about to receive," the elderly man recited in a deep southern drawl, and we joined in to close the traditional prayer with soft "Amens."

Then, clustering around the dining room table, we filled our white Styrofoam plates with Rita's seafood gumbo, crawfish salad, and Boston cream pie and traded stories about our lives.

Jack Layne, Carolyn's husband, a retired records analyst, was especially fascinated to hear about my years working in daily journalism in Washington, D.C., and overseas. "Did you know Bob Woodward when you were in Washington, Neil? Ben Bradlee?" asked Layne, a soft-spoken man with gray hair and a very pleasant demeanor, as he looked up from his bowl of gumbo with eager and expectant eyes.

My years writing for the *Post*, the years in which I finally came into my own as a reporter and as a man more comfortable in my own skin after the lonely years at Princeton, flashed through my mind. I especially remembered a windy autumn night in 1983 when I first spoke to Woodward, my editor in those days, about my idea to try to find my white cousins somewhere in America. He had been intrigued that I had historical documents to begin my hunt, but he cautioned that the sheer effort I would have to put into the search for the mythical Beaumonts might not translate into a good story in the end. And what was journalism if you didn't have a good story to tell? "What if the people you find after years of searching aren't particularly interesting?" he had asked me, leaning back in his chair with his hands folded behind his head. "What if the white guy you find is Joe Six-Pack working on an assembly line or something somewhere? What have you got then?"

I smiled to myself hearing his words in my mind again as I sat at Rita's dining table in Pineville. The irony was that Woodward had turned out to be right, at least in one way. The Beaumonts seemed to be the ordinary white Americans he had warned me I might find after years of searching. But God, how infinitely fascinating these people were to me.

"Yes, I knew both Woodward and Bradlee fairly well," I answered Layne as his eyes grew wide with surprise. "They were my bosses for a few years at the *Post*."

I also was fascinated by Carolyn, a striking woman with reddish hair and piercing, luminous brown eyes. Not long ago, after decades spent as a housewife and a mother raising her two children in New Orleans, Carolyn had started a career as an emergency room nurse at an inner-city hospital. She told me she had always been something of a rebel among the Beaumont clan, very independent by nature, and had married her husband, Jack, partly because his attitude about life was so laid back and tolerant and similar to hers. Despite their conservative southern white backgrounds, each had had black friends for as long as they could remember, she informed me, relationships that consternated their families to no end. "I can't tell you why I was different," she reflected, sitting back in her soft white sweater and smiling over her plate of green salad. "It's just the way I turned out."

She said she and Jack had raised two sons, one of whom was working as a Pep Boys auto mechanic in Baton Rouge, the other as a sales manager in New Orleans for Nextell, a communications company. The two sons had given them four grandchildren so far, distant cousins of my daughter's generation.

An avid skier, Carolyn had traveled around the globe in pursuit of her sport. But at the center of her life now, she told me— her true passion—was her new career in nursing at Charity Hospital in New Orleans. There every weeknight until long after midnight she helped save the lives of shooting victims and the sick in the hospital's trauma ward, where 90 percent of the patients and most of her fellow workers were black. "It's a different sort of life I have now than I ever knew," Carolyn said slowly in her elegant southern accent. "And I wouldn't trade it for a minute."

At the head of the table, observing all this chatter with a studied reserve, the old man, Himel, sat eating his dinner slowly, struggling noticeably and evidently in some pain from his illnesses, including the cancer that would spread to his liver in coming weeks. He sat at the table's edge with his back rigidly against the back of the chair, his pained breathing audible. After a few minutes the old man turned his head toward me. Peering at me through his eyeglasses, he began to speak about his political beliefs. The rest of the gathering listened as Himel talked about Ronald Reagan, the glories of the Reagan presidency, and the age-old conservative politics that he and his people in central Louisiana still believed in strongly, his viewpoint providing a sharp contrast to the moderate, progressive attitudes espoused by Carolyn.

"I probably don't need to tell you this," added the old white man in a thick drawl, coughing twice, his cane resting on the arm of his chair, "because I suspect you already know. But up here we got a lotta rednecks, Neil. Highway 190 is what we call our Mason-Dixon line in Loos-iana. North is redneck, and south is considered Cajun. Oakdale, just south of here, is considered the redneck capital of the state, so that ought to give you an idea of where you are."

Himel (pronounced "ee-mell") sipped some lemonade from his drinking glass, wiped his lips with a napkin, and stared at me through his eyeglasses. "I'm a staunch American," he continued, "and I believe in the rights of man. Huey Long was raised just thirty miles from here, don'cha know. He had his faults, but I always considered him a very good man. We also have a lot of Baptists in these parts—or at least they call themselves Baptists."

The rest of the table giggled.

"Yes, they call themselves Baptists, but I call them hypocrites.

You see, Pineville is supposed to be a dry city—you can't buy alcohol here—but you see more bottles lyin' around here on Sunday mornin's than anywhere else in the state, I reckon."

The gathering laughed again.

"I guess the point I'm trying to make is we believe in things here. We always have. We think people's rights are important and worth protecting."

I knew he was talking about race. I was certain that he was saying to me in a roundabout way that conservatism—conserving the old ways and traditions in the South—was something he and his people continued to believe in deeply, just as they had since the days of A.J. Beaumont in the 1850s. I assumed that when he said his "people" he meant either his family or white people or both. It didn't matter.

I felt a sudden tension in the air and a knot form in my stomach. I gently put my fork down and folded my hands in my lap. I felt my back stiffen, not knowing whether I should challenge the old man at the dinner table—to talk about the rights of *black* people since the days of A.J. Beaumont—or let him continue with his soliloquy.

The elderly white man paused, still eyeing me through his horn-rimmed spectacles, and sipped again from his glass. "But times change," he went on. "Lord knows times change. Circumstances change. And I suppose people do too. So I just want you to know I'm glad you found us. I'm very glad you spent the time and effort to find us. I'm especially glad because you've made Rita so happy."

I felt the tension ease. I didn't press the political point, though it remained awkwardly in the air. I didn't challenge the old man, didn't feel up to a fight, didn't think it was worth it. Inside I knew that fighting and arguing weren't really what I had come all this way to do. I was working, after all. And my work was succeeding in ways I never could have imagined. For one by one the old questions I had long wanted to ask the white family about their lives and feelings about America—the questions that had fueled my search for so long—were being answered in ways both cryptic and clear, and extraordinarily compelling.

It was a short, cordial dinner, after which Himel, feeling ill, expressed his regret at having to leave early. I and several others walked him to the door. Then, as I said good-bye to him there, the old white man suddenly did something unexpected. He placed his dark wooden cane on the crook of his arm, looked at me for a moment, then folded his arms awkwardly around me. He said, "Welcome to the family," in his gruff drawl before slowly heading out into the night.

The words echoed in my mind as the door was closed: "Welcome to the family."

I pondered how unreal and otherworldly the words had sounded coming from him and how uneasy they made me feel. Indeed, for the rest of the night the words reverberated in my mind.

"Welcome to the family"—that wasn't what I had come to Louisiana to hear. It was certainly not what I had expected, and I hoped the Beaumonts weren't mistaking my intentions. I wasn't an orphan or an illegitimate distant heir, and I felt a strange revulsion, at first, over Himel's use of the expression. I couldn't explain exactly why. But, as I mulled all this over nearly six hours later, I wasn't sure what I was feeling anymore in my heart. The intense feelings that had filled me throughout the afternoon and evening were turning into a state of self-protective numbness.

My senses were being pulled in so many directions at once that I felt myself closing off inside in an almost instinctive reaction of self-protection.

Carolyn came up to me a moment after Himel departed and said, "I thought you should know that Newton's the one who insisted that Jack and I come from New Orleans to meet you tonight. He was really insistent about it."

We were standing in Rita's living room then, watching as Rita and Bobette set up a projector to show old slides of family gatherings dating back to the 1950s. "You know, he called us in New Orleans," she continued, "and he said to me, 'Carolyn, if you love me, you'll be there. If you love me, you'll come.' He never said anything like that to me before. He felt really deep emotions about your coming."

"What makes it more surprising," Rita interjected then, almost offhandedly, her southern drawl tinged with remorse, "is that Newton and his family were KKK in the old days." Rita looked at me over her bifocals. "He is the one I was telling you about before, Neil. He is the man whose family was active in the Klan."

The room instantly fell into silence again.

"Oh, come on," Carolyn exclaimed softly after a moment, the shocked disbelief slowly spreading on her face, her bright eyes widening as she stared at her aunt behind the projector. "Come on, Rita."

Rita looked up again. "True," she said softly.

"Oh, you don't *mean* it!" Carolyn insisted, her face reddening with surprise and embarrassment over the knowledge about her uncle.

"It's true. You ask him, Carolyn. He was in the KKK."

"In those days," Bobette interrupted apologetically, "it was more a social thing than anything else, wasn't it? I mean, it wasn't always evil. . . ."

Carolyn glanced first at Bobette, then back in disbelief at her Aunt Rita, as the latter sorted through the pile of family slides.

"What's KKK?" asked Patrick, the nine-year-old, sensing the fierce emotions behind his mother's, aunt's, and grandmother's words. He tapped his mother's arm.

"What's KKK?" he repeated.

I felt myself backing up against a wall near the old photo of Rita's sisters, unable to speak as I witnessed the tense scene unfold.

"Oh, please, Bobette," Carolyn lashed back. "That's just shameful. I can't *believe* we had family in the Klan. It *was* evil. A terrible evil. I get so mad just thinking about it. It's outrageous."

"What's KKK?" the little white boy continued to ask each of the women over and over, finally pulling gently on his mother's sleeve. "What's KKK?"

Bobette placed her hand on her son's head to gently smooth his brown hair. She looked down at him with a sad smile. "Shhhh," she hushed him softly, telling him to never mind.

Rita continued to put her slides together in the eerie silence that filled the living room for several moments. I put my notebook and pen aside, then sat back on a couch, feeling a mixture of surprise, fatigue, and disgust.

"Welcome to the family."

I couldn't get over the feeling of Himel's arms around my shoulders, the awkward welcome the elderly man had issued to me, the emotional reconciliation he had wordlessly sought. It was as if I were reliving something our family had already gone through many years before, something atavistic. I recalled that nearly one hundred years earlier, shortly before his death, A.J. Beaumont had penned a letter of regret and apology to his mixed-race daughter, Pearl, and sought her forgiveness for not acknowledging her as his own for so many years. Now Newton Himel, a white man of similar background, had made an eerily similar gesture to me—and under eerily similar circumstances. (Indeed, he would die barely a year later.)

I felt torn in two different directions as I contemplated all this, desiring renewed connection, yet unable to get over the revulsion I felt. Why were we the ones who always had to understand and struggle to forgive, generation after generation? Most of all, though, I felt an almost overwhelming sense of sorrow.

For the first time in a long time, my parents' words of advice about white racism from my childhood in Seattle returned to my mind with a clarity I hadn't known before: *"It's their problem. It's the white people's problem. Not yours."* It was true, I began to understand just then. For the first time I saw that at least a small part of it was true. White racism was their problem, their legacy in this case, and they were the ones who would have to grapple with it somehow in a way that ultimately had to count. They would have to explain to nine-year-old Patrick what KKK meant. They would have to confess their connection to such evil to a child who didn't understand. Either that, or bury the shame in a tortured, cancerous silence.

I felt deep sorrow. And some sympathy for Bobette, as a parent. But these feelings were also mixed with relief that I would not have to explain such a dark thing from my people's past to my daughter. For the first time I realized, in that sad moment in Rita's living room, that at least one aspect of white racism wasn't my problem at all.

Rita broke the silence a moment later. "I won't lie and tell you we don't have these old feelings in our family," she said, looking up at me from the projector, her voice steady but subdued. "I remember the first time I saw an interracial couple, sometime back in the 1940s. I couldn't believe it. I was a teenager and I was absolutely speechless. I was at a restaurant. I was flabbergasted. I told my companion, 'Gosh, would you look at that!' And my friend said, 'They must not be from around here, because that's illegal.' It was just so unbelievable. I wasn't brought up to accept things like that."

Carolyn nodded, adding, "It's so true. It doesn't make it right, but it's true. When I was child we had a black maid named Rose. Remember Rose, Rita? We loved her like family. When she got sick we took her in and took care of her." Here Carolyn paused slightly, looking at me through her beautiful and intensely deep brown eyes.

"But," Carolyn went on, "my parents made it very clear to us that we could not call her *Miss* Rose, or call her by her last name. Ever. Because there were certain things, certain social rules, that you always had to obey about black people. You couldn't show them the same respect you showed white people. That was clear. That was the order of things."

Whoopi, Kobe, Denzel, Spike . . .

Rita nodded. "To this day I still have some of that feeling inside," she admitted, looking up at me from her slides. "I won't lie. It's a part of me. Like, I'll come up behind someone black in a car, and I'll hear myself saying, 'Come on and move, you black so-and-so. . . .' It's in me. You can't divorce yourself from your past."

"But it's also true," Rita reflected, "that things have changed—

for the better, I think. It's not like it used to be. I've had a couple of black friends in my life. And I promise you, in my little circle we don't have what we used to have—that old animosity toward black people. When I told my white friends about your coming to meet us, they were pretty thrilled. They said, 'I just can't believe you've got a black cousin.' Times change, you know? We probably never could have done this twenty-five years ago."

Rita was right, I knew. There was very little chance that our meeting and attempt at understanding could have happened in an earlier era, before the gains of black civil rights and all the other social changes in America over the last half century, especially the advances that allowed for closer personal relationships between the races. While the very word "miscegenation" remained as emotionally charged as any in our cultural lexicon, and while antebellum laws against interracial marriage had remained on the books in several southern states until 1967, interracial relationships in America—as just one small measure of change—were more common, tolerated, and accepted than they ever had been when Laura and A.J. first loved in the 1870s, even in tiny Pineville in Louisiana, the heartland of Huey Long and Newton Himel.

The fact was our society had changed drastically from the plantation era of A.J.'s and Laura's time. Certainly attitudes and perceptions had changed. A few of the most popular figures in our culture, from sports heroes like Tiger Woods and Derek Jeter to pop singing idol Mariah Carey, were products of loving interracial homes in an America far different from the country A.J. Beaumont arrived in in 1856. Who could have imagined back then or even as recently as twenty-five years ago that Americans would see a black man take the oath of office for the U.S.

Supreme Court with his white wife holding their family Bible at his side?

So Rita was certainly right, in a way. It was true that we had progressed as a society to a point where she and I could meet as social equals, white and black, as we certainly did on that long and emotional March day in the house on Tudor Street in Pineville. It was true that the tentative bonds we forged there, especially those between Rita and Carolyn and me, simply could not have been attempted had it not been for our respective experiences and learning during the era of integration and through other great changes in American society since the 1950s.

But it was also true that a gulf still existed between us as people, as it did between most blacks and whites across our country. We were once joined by blood from a taboo relationship in America's distant past, and some 120 years later we remained two families and two peoples with particular histories and backgrounds, representing two very different branches of a shared tree. Between us there was still a wary divide that awkward hugs could not disguise.

Bobette dimmed the lights in the living room, and soon more than forty years of the white family's memories began to illuminate a wall near the front door. There were slides of Rita laughing joyfully as a young bride in the 1950s, an era coinciding with my birth in the black hospital in Nashville. Rita was truly beautiful when she was young, raven haired, with pretty eyes as dark as coal. Next came pictures of Bobette as a gurgling baby happily eating prunes in a high chair in the late 1950s—about the time my family was settling into Seattle after making the long move from the South. Then the wall was splashed with pictures of Bobette's father and Rita's first husband, Alfred Guirard, a dark-haired fellow wearing a zoot suit at a Damon Runyon costume party from the same period. He was working at the time for United Gas and Electric, like many white blue-collar men in the region.

Photos from countless happy Christmases, Easters, Thanksgivings, Halloweens, Mardis Gras, and Sugar Cane Festivals and from summer vacations at sunny segregated beaches on the Gulf of Mexico flashed on the wall, along with portraits of Rita's cherubic mother, Anna, and her three sisters. Bobette, Carolyn, and Rita laughed hysterically at times, remembering the scenes as if they were yesterday. As I watched, I couldn't help reflecting on where I was and what my family was doing during the same period that our white cousins were leading their lives on the other side of the color barrier.

"These were the happiest days of your life, I guess," I remarked offhandedly to Rita as another photo of her laughing and hugging Alfred and baby Bobette filled the wall. "You all look so happy."

"Yep," she replied softly over the low hum of the projector. "They sure were."

On into the 1960s the photos and family memories hurtled. That was the era of racial integration I grew up in, in the white neighborhood in Seattle. Then Rita came to the year 1968. It was the family's last Christmas before Alfred, the husband she loved so deeply, was incapacitated by the brain disease that killed him seven years later. The room grew quiet, save for the sound of Rita clicking her projector from one slide to the next, as the late sixties dawned on the wall.

Then Rita apologized to me. She said she was too tired to go on.

"That's okay," I told her. It had been a long night. "I'm beat too."

We snapped a few rounds of new pictures then, some for me to take home to Letitia and Zoë and some for them to keep of me. Then, just as we all gathered our things to file out into the night, Rita remembered she had a surprise for me. She beckoned with her finger for me to return to the kitchen. I followed her and watched as she reached into her folder of keepsakes lying on the kitchen tabletop. She pulled out seven small black-and-white photos, each about three by five inches in size. Several displayed old yellow strips of Scotch tape on their borders, as if the pictures had been plucked from an album. The edges of a few others were dog-eared. The pictures were slightly blurred with age.

Rita gently placed the photographs on the table before me. They showed a light-skinned black woman with lustrous straight hair in various poses and scenes. They seemed to have been taken in the 1920s and 1930s, judging by the woman's haircut and style of dress.

"We've had these for such a long time," Rita said, gazing at the photographs through her bifocals, the brown and gray strands of wavy hair atop her head shining in the light over the table. "My mother saved them all those years. We kept them too after Mama passed. It's Aunt Pearl."

I looked closer at the photographs, my eyes disbelieving. I felt the blood of excitement racing to my face once more. There in the pictures before me was my mother's beloved grandmother. They were photos my family never knew existed.

Pearl evidently had sent the pictures to the Beaumonts to share her life in St. Louis with her white kin in Louisiana. One photo showed her smiling in the backyard of her house among shoots of blooming hollyhocks. Another showed her smiling and waving her hand from a bridge in Forest Park. Several others showed her posing on her front porch and in her front yard behind a pretty white picket fence. The backs of two of the photos bore Pearl's cursive handwriting in blue ink faded by time. The jottings read, "In the back yard with the hollyhocks" and "Duck pond, Forest Park."

I couldn't take my eyes off the pictures. Each one offered such a poignant glimpse from the life of a mixed-race woman who seemed to be trying, perhaps vainly, to keep a bridge to her white relatives.

"They're yours, Neil," Rita told me as I peered intently at the photos. "If you could make copies, I'd appreciate it. But they're yours."

I looked up at Rita to thank her, but all I could do was exhale. I couldn't summon a word, not even the simplest expression of gratitude. Rita seemed to understand. All she could do was smile back.

It was then that I began to understand that Rita and I were perhaps more alike than we knew. The revelation hit me with sudden and powerful force, for I began to see clearly that, in a way, Rita had been paying tribute to her mother, Anna, by welcoming me so warmly and by bestowing me with her gifts—just as I had perhaps been trying to pay tribute to my mother all these years, without even realizing it consciously, by searching for answers to the old questions in our family history. We were such different people, Rita and I, from such completely different backgrounds and histories. Yet in the end, despite our differences, we were oddly alike in the heart.

I stared closely at the photos. Then I asked Rita if she had a magnifying glass. I wanted to see something in one of them. The picture showed Pearl standing on her front porch in a pretty sundress. She seemed to be in her middle age. Rita directed me to a reading glass near the living room. I turned a light on and held the picture under the glass to make out the street numbers hung in the porch above her head.

What I saw banished any lingering doubt about our connection. The numbers on the porch of the trim, white wood-frame house with the picket fence read "6422" under the magnifying glass. This was the address on Chatham Street in St. Louis where Laura and Pearl lived in the 1920s and 1930s—and where my mother spent some of the happiest years of her childhood.

I gingerly placed the photos in an envelope, then slipped the envelope into my black canvas shoulder bag along with the Beaumont family history manuscript and the nineteenth-century photos from A.J. Beaumont's family life in St. Joseph that Rita had already given me. Rita walked me to the door. I was still virtually speechless by the time I got there, stunned by her act of kindness, numbed by the experiences of the night.

"You don't know how much this means to me, Rita," I told her as I stood in the entryway under the shining porch light, placing my arms around her to return her hug. "All of it."

"I'm so glad you came," she said.

A moment later we all said good-bye.

CHAPTER SEVEN

Tenth Man Classic

A few weeks after I returned to California from my trip to Pineville, I took Rita's old photographs of Pearl to a professional copier in downtown Davis, who enlarged the pictures for me on a color printer. Next I found a pretty cut-glass picture frame sitting on a silver stand at an art store, which I purchased for thirty-two dollars. When I got home, I slipped the finest photo—the one from the mid-1930s of my mother's grandmother standing proudly in her front yard behind the picket fence—inside the shimmering frame. As I gazed at it, the old black-and-white picture appeared so beautiful and so luminous, despite the blurriness of age, that it almost took my breath away.

"Who's that, Daddy?" my daughter asked me when I brought the framed photo into the living room and placed it on our coffee table to show her and Letitia.

It took me a moment to try to figure the relationships out. "Let me see. It's your great-great-grandmother, Zoë. Yeah, that's right. Two greats," I said. "Her name was Pearl. It's a very old picture. She isn't living anymore. But she was very special."

My daughter gazed at the photo, running her finger over the edge of the frame's silver border. For a moment, with her brown eyes, light brown skin, and curly brown hair, she reminded me almost exactly of pictures I had seen of my mother as a child and of my mother's mother, Fredda, a generation earlier in St. Louis.

"I didn't know her either," I added. "But some people still remember her really well."

It had been some time since I returned from Louisiana, and I had spent a great deal of it in deep reflection about my emotionally complicated odyssey, the story I had heard in Pineville, and what my search meant in the end. I found myself thinking more and more about how it had started in the first place years earlier with the oddly simple intellectual challenge I had posed for myself: try to find out what happened to the white family on the other side of my ancestral tree.

All along in that quest, a part of me had hoped and perhaps expected that I might uncover some earthshaking revelations about race relations and American history—lessons that might help me see my own experiences in this country, and those of my family and other black Americans, in a clearer light. I wanted to discover something so extraordinary and hitherto unknown about ourselves as Americans that it would be worth shouting about to the heavens. It was what kept me going in the search really, the sense that there just had to be some great intellectual treasure at the end of the trail.

There was a part of me too that had secretly hoped that my white kin had faired more poorly than my black kin over the past century. It was the same part of me that had secretly and perhaps vengefully wanted to rub the evil of white supremacy and bigotry in its face. I guess I wanted to show white people—especially the white family I was related to by blood—that blacks were just as smart, courageous, and strong, if not more so, than any people in America, and that all of us could prove it—as my family had through the generations—if given a fair chance.

In the end, as I contemplated my journey's lessons and ultimate meaning for me, none of those things really seemed to matter much at all. I didn't think I had uncovered any clear and definitive truth of universal significance—nothing as profound, sparklingly pure, and important to American race relations as $E = mc^2$ was to the world of physics, say, or the quadratic formula or the law of gravity. No flash of light or searing revelation suddenly exploded in my head, transforming my life forever. In some ways, race and racism in America remained as profoundly complex to me months after my visit to Pineville as they had when I began my search for the white family years earlier. I wasn't sure I understood the roots and anatomy of racial bigotry and ignorance any better, though I did continue to be sensitive to their effects on me, my students, and my family. To be certain, the topic still vexed me deeply, as much as it ever had, and as much as it likely always would.

Nor was I sure I had learned significantly more about the context of my family's struggles and successes in the face of racism—though I did appreciate my family even more in light of the Beaumonts' lives. I had been proud of all my people before the search and was just as proud afterward. And while I did at first feel elated to discover that my family's progress in the twentieth century contrasted with the Beaumonts' downfall after the boll weevil plague, that feeling was momentary, vain, and shallow. The term "poor white trash" in the context of the Beaumonts seemed, in the end, as hollow, useless, and malicious as any black slur or stereotype. For the truth was that Rita had generously opened the door to her house and to her family's remarkable life story to me, and I was grateful, having found parts of that story as moving and admirable as any I had run across in my life and career. Rita's struggles, inner strength, love for her family, and life experiences were no less profound, no less resonant, no less meaningful than those of anyone in my own close family—and don't such things constitute the true measure of a life and human existence?

In the Beaumonts I found a white family that certainly was every bit as human as we were, people who had struggled with their own brand of demons. Both of our families had been crippled to some degree by prejudice, personal trauma, and tragedy, but in the most important ways both branches had endured. So it wasn't what we did for a living that counted, nor what kind of china we dined on, nor what our houses and neighborhoods looked like. Nor, in this one sense, did our skin color even matter very much. What counted most through the generations, far more than any other factor, regardless of our race, was how we treated those we loved and how well we loved. That seemed the transcendent lesson or moral that my search had revealed. And it held true whether the figure was my mother or Fredda on one side of our family tree, or Rita or Anna Beaumont on the other. Simple as it was, it was my $E = mc^2$.

I emerged from my search with a complex web of emotions:

pride, a deeper understanding of human complexity, a sense of professional accomplishment. But I also felt a lingering sadness, sharper than any I had felt previously, over the cancerousness, the sheer wastefulness, of racial prejudice and bigotry, and the sinister way they can replicate themselves from one willing generation to the next.

Yet even in this stark sadness there was an overarching complexity. For I also began to recognize, grudgingly, that racism itself, while oppressing us and limiting our potential for generations, had also deeply challenged us as individuals, pushed us to strive harder, to compete better, to believe in ourselves more fully. That had certainly been true for my father, and it was true for me. Racism was a hurdle, but the pathology also stoked our inner fires to attempt to rise above it. To the extent that challenge and personal struggle are ingredients for a fulfilling, productive, and complete life, it was strangely true that racial prejudice, in a singularly American fashion, had pushed my family to be far better than society expected or even desired us to be. It had presented us with a unique form of challenge that the Beaumonts had never had to face really. And generation after generation, many of us proved ourselves in facing up to it. Indeed, this ceaseless contention with prejudice had concentrated our minds through the generations, helped forge our family bonds and identity as black Americans, and forced us to exceed ourselves at times in ways we perhaps wouldn't have otherwise. It was a thorny truth I was beginning to see, one I had a hard time reconciling with the pathology's pain and crippling evil.

It was also true that my family's advances in the twentieth century, while mirroring the rise of the black middle class across

America in the wake of the civil rights struggle, could not be separated from the chilling reality of abject poverty, failing schools, poor housing, meager opportunity, and hopelessness in which most other blacks in this country remained. Such suffering, inequality, and injustice constituted the most salient and overriding social context of our lives. Within this context my family story was something of an anomaly, I knew, one whose lessons were difficult to reconcile with the greater African American experience. What good was such progress, such success for our country as a whole, I often thought, if, with each succeeding generation, so many more of our kind were left in the mire with little or no way out?

During the years I pursued my project in the mid-1990s, a new generation of white conservative analysts authored widely publicized books asserting the racial inferiority of blacks. Richard J. Herrnstein and Charles Murray's *The Bell Curve* in particular was the focus of discussion for weeks in the national press and broadcast media, the stepchild in many ways of the work of the 1970s race theorist William Shockley, the Nobel Prize–winning physicist whose views on black genetic inferiority and sterilization had so disturbed me during my college years at Princeton. Often as I stood at my lectern as a professor at Berkeley, scanning the crowd of undergraduate faces before me, I made special note of the brown and black ones sprinkled among the white. At such moments I couldn't help envisioning my own face as a much younger man among them and feeling, as I did so many years earlier, the dull ache of unease and aloneness, the extra psychological burden I remembered having to bear. I began to see a clearer and deeper sense of meaning in my work—not just in teaching but also in trying whenever I could to shore up the souls on the edges, to help them believe in themselves and their promise. In this regard, my research helped to crystallize my thinking about the enduring evil and burden of prejudice and the fragile nature of human potential, especially among the young.

It also refueled my dedication and belief in our continuing struggle as a people, I realized. For it was during my research trip to the South in 1997 that I recruited a promising young woman from all-black Clark-Atlanta University to my journalism program at Berkeley. Sherri Day had had little journalism experience in her undergraduate training, but she showed a deep passion for questioning, learning, and writing. I was excited by her potential, and she did not disappoint. During her two years at Berkeley the bright young woman from rural Georgia succeeded beyond all measure, finishing at the top of her class and delivering the valedictory address at her May 2000 graduation before going on to work as a reporter for the *New York Times*. Such were the hidden, almost inexpressible joys of teaching in the difficult post–affirmative action age in California, feelings that carried even greater psychic meaning for me in the wake of my project.

The end of my search did not produce any major changes in the rhythms of my daily life, however, nor did it greatly adjust the mental prism through which I viewed life and American society. When I got back from Louisiana, I picked up my life right where I had left it. I taught my classes, delivered my lectures, researched and wrote, coached Zoë's softball team in Davis, refereed her soccer games, read her stories at bedtime, and went to sleep each night with Letitia, all of us enduring life's small challenges and taking pleasure in life's little joys from one day to the next, like most American families. Still, there were a few small changes as bits of information accrued in the wake of my discoveries, each lending new wrinkles to my life and to the story I had discovered on the other side of the tree. The truest value of my search lay not so much in how it transformed my life but in how it deeply informed it in so many ways.

When I called Carolyn in New Orleans a few months later to get information to fill out a fuller family tree, encompassing the complete span of the white and black sides, she sounded delighted to hear from me. "You'll never guess what happened," she said, struggling to contain her laughter. "The word got around about you among our cousins all throughout the state, but you know how word of mouth can get distorted—it turns out some of them completely misunderstood. They said, 'Did you hear the news? We're *black!*'" Carolyn chuckled. "I had to straighten it all out, to clarify the story for them. But it sure was funny."

I learned from Carolyn then that at least one member of the white Beaumont family, a young man, had recently left Louisiana to settle elsewhere, in San Francisco. He was a rarity, as hardly any of the white Beaumonts had strayed far from Louisiana since A.J. first settled there in 1856. Much as my black ancestors long ago, the young white man had felt somewhat stifled and oppressed by Louisiana's conservative culture and had yearned to branch out on his own to realize his dreams. He was an architect, Carolyn told me, and gay.

Our families stayed in touch occasionally, sending e-mail messages and greeting cards to each other on holidays and at other special times. Rita promised at one point to make a dress for my daughter, remembering the time when she herself was a little girl in the 1930s and her mixed-race Aunt Pearl in St. Louis designed and sewed her a dress that she had adored. But it would be a stretch to say we considered both sides of our tree one "family." Our lives continued much as before, separately, quietly, distinctly white and black.

Still, I think the small victories in life are important—just finding and meeting the Beaumonts was, I realized, significantly fulfilling. When I thought about it months later, it was almost as if all the old keepsakes—A.J. Beaumont's photo, his obituary, his 1901 letter to Pearl—had been handed down for one hundred years in my family not just for sentimental reasons but to bedevil, perplex, and provoke some descendant down the line. I had turned out to be that someone. In the end, if part of God's life plan for me was to unearth and tie together the forgotten and long-concealed threads in my family's racial past, I had at least gained the simple gratification of knowing that I had done so, that I had solved the old puzzle and solved it well.

Researching family history is, for most Americans, an effort to restore links to an old country and culture of origin. We are a restless, transient people by definition, hailing from many places around the planet, and in our sometimes disquieting alienation from our own country and modern society, we seek identity and perhaps solace in the old places we came from and the ways our people once knew. In my case, however, researching my family history was inspired by a deep desire to document, understand, and strengthen ties to my native land, a land that has done much through the centuries to deny black people a basic sense of birthright and belonging. I investigated the past in order to make a more meaningful connection to America, one that many of my fellow citizens perhaps take for granted, yet one that racial division through the generations has made murky, nebulous, ambiguous, fractured. I was interested not in my genetic ties to Africa, the old and disconnected place, but in my hard-earned and far more meaningful roots here, in this dirt, in the country I call home. Indeed, the black and white roots I unearthed proved to be as strong, compelling, and deeply affirming in a human and archtypically American fashion as I knew they must be when I started on my quest.

It was funny, but as the months went by after my visit to Pineville, I began to realize that perhaps my most precious discovery wasn't an intellectual revelation about the anatomy of race and racism in America, or even about white people. It was a slightly surer, purer, and better sense of myself and my own identity—as an American and, far more important, as an African American. That was the treasure I had unearthed. It was as if after all that searching, I had found a kind of mirror on the far side of the family tree. I had set out to explore the white side of my ancestry, but I came back with a stronger sense of my black roots and a deeper awareness and appreciation for those who had made my family history so meaningful and rich.

When I was a kid growing up in Seattle, I didn't know many black people. So the ones I did know I held closely in my heart, as if they somehow carried important keys to life's meaning and my own identity. I didn't realize, though, how tightly and dearly I held them inside until after completing my search for the Beaumonts, when I began to reflect on the deep influence these black people had had on me from the very start. My brothers, Bobby and Wayne, my sister, Sharon, and of course my parents were central figures in this regard. But so were my parents' closest friends, a group of black professionals who, like them, had migrated from the South to Seattle in the 1950s and 1960s and begun to form the backbone of an emerging black professional class in the city. Some were physicians, most of whom had graduated from Meharry in the same seminal era as my father.

I remember cocktail parties and Saturday night card games at our house, where young black families would gather amid loud laughter and a haze of cigarette smoke to unwind, trade stories, and party together while Nat King Cole, Nancy Wilson, Sarah Vaughan, and Billy Eckstine crooned from my father's record player. Often I would stand at the living room table next to my mother, my chin resting on the edge, soaking it all in as my parents played Tonk and bridge with their friends. I remember gales of laughter, ice cubes clinking in drinking glasses, cold cans of Rainier and Olympia and Heidelberg beer sweating in the heat, and moths circling the ceiling light fixture on warm summer nights. I would listen, smiling happily to myself, as they sprinkled their conversations with soulful southern expressions that seemed to melt like chocolate in the air. But most of all, I became mesmerized by everyone's faces and especially their hands—by my father's, by Drs. Earl and Rosalie Miller's, by Drs. Blanche and Phil Lavizzo's—smooth, strong, beautiful brown hands with slender fingers and immaculate nails, hands that worked in human blood and guts every day healing sick people, hands that were skilled, noble, and unafraid. These same hands were there before me, dancing in the lamplight, doing ordinary things—flipping cards, lighting cigarettes, grabbing drinks, covering yawns—and looking for all the world just like mine, except bigger.

Of all of those black figures in my youth, few were more special than Uncle Sonny, my mother's younger brother, who still lived in our ancestral house in the Ville in St. Louis. Throughout my childhood Sonny represented one of the last living links to our history there, to the city where Laura had moved in the 1890s.

Sonny was born in 1929, three years before the death of Laura, who had held her infant grandson in her arms the week of his birth and exulted that her small family finally had a "man baby" to celebrate. Years later this "man baby" became something akin to the Hope diamond among the jewels in my childhood world—although God knows few other people would have seen him that way. Uncle Sonny visited us often in Seattle, bringing with him all the beautiful jargon, mannerisms, and street culture of the old colored world in St. Louis, which seemed so far away growing up in the Pacific Northwest.

A confirmed and committed bachelor, he was named Edward Clifford Turner, Jr., after my grandfather. But everybody in our family had called him "Sonny" or "Stink" from the time he was a toddler. He had plump lips, skinny legs, a balding pate, and a round pot belly from years of good beer and soul food. Sonny both smoked hard, enjoying his Salems, and drank hard, becoming a connoisseur of Scotch and water on the rocks. He talked loud and didn't care a bit about his appearance when he was on vacation from his work as an architectural engineer in St. Louis, often going for days without a bath or a shave if he felt like it. God, how I loved him and wished I could be as free and seemingly easygoing as he was.

Sonny also was blessed with a rough and ragged vocabulary

that simply thrilled me as a child. He said stuff with his untamed mouth that neither I nor my brothers could even *think* about saying out loud. Despite my mother's protests at his language, the word "motherfucker" would regularly roll off his lips in a smooth Missouri drawl in a way in which every consonant was rounded to perfection—*"muh' fugga."* And he would use it as a verb, noun, adverb, or adjective, and sometimes all four in the same sentence.

To my impressionable ears Sonny was a true virtuoso when it came to the spoken word. He used language the way Willie Mays clubbed a homer, sped around the bases, and caught a fly. He used words the way Jim Brown barreled over tacklers and stormed to paydirt. He played with speech in his deep and resonant baritone the way B.B. King strummed his guitar. He brought such color, life, *blackness* to my world on Lake Shore Drive.

It wasn't ever just "cold" outside to Sonny. It was always "cold as a witch's tit" or "frigid as a whore's heart." When it rained hard it wasn't just *rain*—it was "frog strangler weather," the kind of downpour that sounded like "a cow pissin' on a flat rock." When it was hot, it was as hot "as little sister's wee-wee."

But he saved his best lines for women and sex. A woman wasn't just ugly to my uncle. She was as ugly as "a frog peepin' through buttermilk" or "as homely as ten yards of uncooked chitlins." If a woman was really attractive, she wasn't just sexy—she was "built like a ceramic defecatorium" and might "kill somebody if she got all that shit in mo'shun." If she looked sexually inclined, she was described by my uncle as able to "suck the chrome off a trailer hitch." And if he wasn't getting enough intercourse, Sonny would gruffly complain to no one in particular, "My dick's so clean you could cook greens with it."

I didn't understand half of what Uncle Sonny was talking about when I was a kid, but the *way* he said it—with such flair and animation and gruff theatricality—utterly galvanized me. His words were magic.

"The whole country went to hell when they integrated the armed forces, you know that?" Sonny mused one night as he dragged on a Salem cigarette, me and my brothers at his knee watching television. "Before that, we had a way'a doin' things and white boys had a way'a doin' things, you understand?"

We nodded.

"Back in the old days, if you wanted sex, you'd say, 'I gotta get me some cock.' That's the way we said it. 'I need me some cock.' Cock meant sex back then. Wantin' a little sex meant wantin' a little cock. You understand?"

We nodded again.

"Then they integrated the armed forces after the war, and everything's been fugged up ever since. Black men *never* ate pussy before integration, you know that? Only white boys did that. Then niggas started doin' it, and our whole goddam vernacular changed. Hell, you say, 'I want me some cock' now and people look at you like you're *queer*."

Bobby, Wayne, and I would nod our heads in almost perfect unison again, as if in complete understanding and agreement, although we did not comprehend half the exotic words our uncle was using.

"Don't you ever eat pussy, you hear?" Sonny would sagely go on, his booming voice lowering an octave. "Black men should *never* eat pussy. It's bad for your teeth."

Uncle Sonny might be loud, obnoxious, and crude, but I

loved him dearly for his stories, his independence, and the stark and beautiful contrast his very being presented to the white world I was coming to know. Indeed, it was Sonny whose passionate storytelling first opened my mind as a boy to the proud heroism of the Tuskegee airmen, the courage of Jackie Robinson and Marion Motley, the legends of Josh Gibson and Dr. Charles Drew, the incomparable beauty of Dorothy Dandridge and Lena Horne, and the creative genius of scores of black artists, from Duke Ellington and Louis Armstrong to Miles Davis and Thelonious Monk. My uncle was a veritable window to an enchanting world of blackness my white world in Seattle could not offer.

White people were many things to Sonny—"ofays," "honkies," "peckerwoods," "paddies," "Mr. Charley," even "Mr. and Mrs. Lynch," depending on his mood and circumstance. But "crackas" and "cracka muh-fuggas" were his pejoratives of choice. Black people enjoyed a similar variety of appellations in his Old World lexicon—"ziggaboos," "splibs," "cheegroes," "spooks," and his personal favorite, "club members," which he uttered with a loving drawl. That's what all of us were, even me. Club members!

I coveted the soul of the language my uncle brought from St. Louis on his visits to us nearly every summer. But no matter how hard I tried to mimic him, in private to myself, under my breath, I could never make "muh-fugga" or "nigga" or any of those other words trip off my tongue quite the way he could, my boyhood diction having been shaped forever by the clear, precise, upstanding English of the hopelessly white Pacific Northwest.

My uncle considered himself an expert on fishing, cooking,

hunting, fighting, engineering, politics, and practically every-thing in between. He was a blowhard. A blowhard's blowhard. But he was a true troubadour of opinion when it came to the op-posite sex. My uncle was married once. To an abrasive woman named Ethel, who I guess yelled at him a lot and made his life miserable. It was a mistake he rued for years. The marriage didn't actually last very long. Sonny remembered the duration exactly: "Ten months, ten days, thirteen hours, and twenty-five minutes," he would soberly intone every time the subject of marriage, in any context, came up. He recited those numbers so often that we, his nephews and niece, knew the marriage's duration by heart, as if it were a sacred psalm from the Old Testament.

His experience of marriage had left Uncle Sonny feeling much wiser about male-female relationships, especially black male–black female relationships. He rarely used the expression "black women" in ordinary conversation with us, preferring instead to use the word "Sapphire" to sum up that half of our race. "Sapphire" was akin to another all-encompassing term he used for black people— "The Ten Percent," as in ten percent of the American population. "Sapphire" and "The Ten Percent" con-stituted a special kind of shorthand for him.

After his fateful but blessedly brief marriage to Ethel in the 1970s, Uncle Sonny said he had a good working title for the book he intended to write someday about his life and times as a black man in America: *The Sapphirization of the Tenth Man*. He claimed it was sure to be a national bestseller.

Our family was blessed in having a colorful figure like Sonny in every generation, around whom so much of our story could be told. But there was one person in particular, Pearl, whose story seemed the most colorful of all, the one that joined together the black and white branches of our extended family tree.

I never knew Pearl. She died ten years before I was born. But Pearl's story loomed large in our family, a true morality tale about black and white in America. I knew that she was born in 1877 in St. Joseph, Louisiana, and died in 1944 in St. Louis, and that she was the daughter of a black woman born in slavery and an Englishman who had come to America to seek his fortune before the Civil War.

Pearl was married once, in the 1890s, to a black man, Frank Hall, who fathered her child Fredda in 1896. But she enjoyed numerous relationships with men of both races after the marriage ended in divorce, for she did love men very much. At one point, in the 1910s, she ran away with a jazz singer, but that affair eventually fell apart.

Pearl spent many happy years in the 1920s with a Jewish man named Jacob Bronstein, her second husband, an immigrant from Russia, who worked as a carpenter in a St. Louis clothing factory. In his jovial Russian accent, Bronstein used to tell Pearl exciting stories about his unusual arrival in America through a cold and distant place called Sitka, Alaska. Like Pearl, Bronstein was a figure not fully accepted in the mainstream of American society, an ethnic Jew relegated to the fringes. But the Russian immigrant and his mixed-race American wife, both orphans from their past, loved each other well and found great comfort in their strange alikeness.

After "Mr. Jake" died, Pearl became involved in the 1930s and 1940s with a white handyman named Charley James, who lived with her in her white frame house on Chatham Street. Charley used to call her "Poyle" in a heavy Brooklyn accent and loved her dearly until the day she died.

A gorgeous, vivacious quadroon, Pearl lived her life in the lonely twilight between the white and black worlds, never feeling fully accepted in either. At that time there was little or no room in American society for very light brown when it came to race. Pearl never felt fully comfortable in her own skin, and because of this, people who loved her remembered a kind of sadness always hovering over her. "She just never fit in," my mother recalled about the grandmother she loved so deeply. "She just never felt at ease with herself."

Pearl was even estranged at times from her daughter, Fredda, who viewed her mother's inexplicable fondness for the South and her secretive attempts to maintain contact with her white relatives there, the Beaumonts, as beneath her. "Those white people never did anything for us," Fredda used to chide her. "Those people don't want anything to do with you. Stop living in the past."

"I'm just an orphan girl. A poor little orphan girl," Pearl once moaned in Fredda's living room when she was feeling especially sorry for herself in the early 1940s, not long before she died.

Fredda exploded: "You ought to be ashamed, Mama! Here you have a daughter, grandchildren, great-grandchildren for goodness' sake, a family that loves you, and you sit here in my living room talking like an old fool. You ought to be ashamed!"

But despite her sense of isolation, one thing remained constant in Pearl's life: her undying love for and devotion to her grandchildren, Fredda's kids—Vivian, Sonny, and Mary—who adored her just as much. They knew her by her beloved nickname, "Mam-ee," a derivation of the French *ma mère* ("my mother"). And Mam-ee, to the children, was the cat's meow. They idolized this woman who dressed and walked like a Paris model and loved to tool around St. Louis in her Model T Ford. It didn't bother them that she could curse a blue streak—so much so that Fredda's husband, Clifford, used to call her the "old battle-ax."

Pearl doted on the kids, especially on holidays. Whenever she visited, Pearl promised a nickel to little Mary, my mother, if the little girl could put just one curl in her grandmother's straight and silken hair, anything to make Mam-ee look a bit more "colored." It was ironic. While many black people at the time were processing their coarse hair in a struggle to make it look "white," Pearl insistently headed in the opposite direction, trying her damnedest to make her hair look "black."

As a little girl, my mother would go at this unusual task with all her energy and creativity, filling Mam-ee's hair with curlers and pins. But no matter how long the curlers and pins were kept on Mam-ee's head, her hair would return to its natural straightness once they were taken out. Mam-ee just had too much white blood in her.

During the Depression my mother and her family moved in with Mam-ee and Charley in the tidy little house at 6422 Chatham Street. It was there, in her adolescent years, that my mother discovered the joy of books, of the public library, of reading and writing—a joy she passed on to me many years later in Seattle. The house on Chatham Street also figured in my mother's earliest memories when, as a toddler in the mid-1920s, she and her mother would visit Pearl and her mother, Laura, then in her twilight years. My mother remembered sitting on Laura's lap and watching the old woman sip coffee from a saucer, then retiring with her later to a second-floor bedroom, where they would fall asleep together watching the white lace curtains ruffle in the afternoon breeze.

Some of my mother's most cherished memories, long before her years in Atlanta, Nashville, and Seattle, came from those years on Chatham Street in the 1920s and 1930s. And no person figured more prominently or lovingly in those memories than Pearl, my mother's beloved Mam-ee. It was Pearl who showed her how to use elbow grease to clean the grime from the bathtub, Pearl who taught her what class and style meant in fashion and music, Pearl whose language was so salty that my mother and Uncle Sonny used to practice saying "shit" in just the right soulful, southern way she did—"sheeee-it."

And it was Pearl who showed my mother and her brother how to stand up to white people when they messed with them, how to put them in their place—like the time a white boy repeatedly took Sonny's tricycle from him, reducing him to tears. "You go out there and beat that little cracka's ass," Pearl told her five-year-old grandson, "or I'm gonna beat yours." And Sonny did just that, because he feared Mam-ee's wrath more than any white boy.

Pearl, the daughter of an Englishman and a woman born into slavery, may have looked white, but she taught all of her family a great deal about what it meant to be black.

Memories of Chatham Street and Pearl, I knew, occupied some of the dearest places in my mother's heart. Once on a visit to St. Louis she, Bobby, and I tried to find the graves of Laura and Pearl at an old black cemetery near Lambert Airport. The cemetery had been neglected for many years, though, making the task impossible. At the end of our long, unsuccessful search that chilly February day, my mother concluded, "It just goes to show—all this doesn't mean anything." She waved her arms toward the expanse of lonely headstones, many of them chipped or broken or fallen over in the mud and overgrown with weeds and wildflowers. "Folks don't live on in graveyards. It's what you remember in your heart that counts."

On Thursday, May 14, 1998, after my classes at Berkeley were finally finished for the term, I flew from Sacramento to Seattle for a small family reunion. Every six months or so, my brother Bobby, Bobby's grown son, David, Uncle Sonny, and I would get together to play golf on various courses in California and Washington. We called this regular gathering of black males in our clan "The Tenth Man Classic" in honor of Uncle Sonny's favorite expression for black folks, "The Ten Percent." We usually played miserably. And Uncle Sonny often won these informal tourneys, despite his advancing years. But winning or losing was never the point, despite the intensity of our competition. Drinking lots of beer, smoking good cigars, eating soul food, celebrating the latest accomplishments of Tiger Woods, and joking around with each other were.

This time our weekend gathering was set for the golf courses of Seattle, and I was looking forward to seeing everyone even more than usual, especially my mother and Sonny. The plane flew northward high over California in the bright blue afternoon sky, which turned gray and cloudy by the time we entered

Oregon over the Cascade Mountains. All the while, brimming with excitement and eagerness, I thought about how much time had passed and how much our family and American society had changed since 1956, when my parents migrated from segregated Nashville to make a new start for themselves in the Pacific Northwest.

My father, so stern, unyielding, and hard-working throughout my childhood, had changed, becoming far more reflective in the years since his retirement in 1988. "If I had to do it all over again," he had told me during one of my more recent visits, "I probably never would have even gone into medicine. I probably would have enjoyed forestry or oceanography a lot more. But in my day and age there was never even an option like that for black men, as there is now." That, he said, was the reason the larger struggle by his generation and the push for racial integration had been worth it. The mere fact that talented black men and women could aspire to success and greatness in so many different fields these days, not just a few, was to him the greatest and most worthwhile change he had seen in society in his lifetime.

My father had also become a surprisingly emotional man in more recent years. During my visits, whenever he and I hugged to say good-bye, he would begin to cry. I could feel his frail body tremble almost uncontrollably in my arms. It was amazing. This old black man, who had rarely betrayed any real emotion or pain for so many years, for fear of betraying any weakness to his children, suddenly began to display a great deal of emotion in his old age. During those partings in Seattle, I could literally feel my father releasing the great sadness inside himself. Finally, in a life spent with such tight emotional restraint and guardedness, he seemed to be allowing himself to let loose all kinds of hurts and sorrows he had kept pent up inside for so long. In those moments I felt closer to him than I ever had as a child.

After my plane landed in Seattle, as I slowly walked into the terminal with the legions of other travelers, my satchel on my shoulder, I heard a familiar voice. It was unmistakable over the din of greetings, as gruff, loud, and obnoxious as it ever was in my childhood.

"Hey dummy, you ready to get your ass kicked?"

I smiled as soon as I heard it.

"Sonny, I brought my driver this time," I informed my sixty-eight-year-old uncle, punching him gently on his soft, round shoulder. "And I'm not takin' any prisoners. So be prepared for your whuppin'."

"All right, that's enough of that," my mother said smiling, joining us amid our laughter and placing her arms around my neck. "You're looking good."

"So are you, Mom."

She was looking fabulous, in fact. But of course, she always looked that way to me. Her dark hair was short, curly, sprinkled with silver and gray, her twinkling eyes a deep brown, her face tanned and elegantly lined with age. She was wearing a blue sweatshirt, sweatpants, and running shoes—her usual outfit for her morning exercise, a four-mile walk along the shore of Lake Washington—but she managed to carry even the most ordinary clothing with singular personality and style.

"Flight okay?"

"Yeah, sure was," I said, kissing her on the cheek. "Zoë and Tish say hi."

"Let's go get something to eat, okay? Wanna?" she asked, slipping her arm inside mine.

"Yeah, I'm starved."

"Good," Sonny growled as we went to retrieve my golf bag and then headed for my mother's car. "You can pay for it too. We're senior citizens."

In the years since our move to Seattle, perhaps the one thing that had stayed mostly the same was Sonny, I realized. Retired from his engineering career, my uncle now loved to monitor the world's happenings through the satellite dish he had installed on the roof of the old house where he and my mother had grown up in the Ville. But he remained a frequent visitor to Seattle, still carrying a potbelly on his stovepipe legs, still loving his Scotch and water, still cursing about the "Sapphires" and "crackas" who made his life hell. He had stopped smoking, though. And while the top of his tan-colored noggin was still as shiny and bare as a cue ball, he had decided several years back to grow the remaining hair on the sides of his head as long as he could and then pull the strands back into a hip little ponytail that he bound with a tie. With his ever-present Greek sailor's cap on his head and the ponytail down his neck, Sonny looked like he had a full head of hair underneath, which I suppose was the effect he desired.

We piled into my mother's green Honda Civic, and she drove us through the rain-soaked streets of Seattle to a favorite restaurant, a seafood grill about a half hour away from the airport on Lake Washington, in the city's Leschi Park section. As we caught up with each other's lives, I felt like a nervous kid again, harboring an amazing secret and badly wanting to share it but not knowing how or when.

Years earlier I had confided my idea of searching for the Beaumonts to my mother, but the quest had been so fruitless for so long that I had long ago stopped discussing it with her. I was almost certain I would fail, and I figured she felt the same way after a while. And I had certainly never discussed my search with Sonny, not since the first time back in the 1980s when my uncle had growled his disdain and disapproval of any attempt to find the white family. "Forget them goddamn people," he had muttered to me over the phone when I told him I was going to search for his white cousins. "If you wanna write about something, write about the black folks in your family. What the hell's wrong with you?"

Now, years later, I finally had the full story to tell and the priceless photos of Pearl in my satchel. But for the life of me I didn't know where to begin or how. I realized I was feeling almost as hesitant and apprehensive about the prospect of telling my mother and uncle about their white cousins as I had been in making my first telephone contact with Rita.

The Seattle I saw passing outside my mother's car window that night certainly was remarkably different from the city I had known as a boy in the 1950s and 1960s. Back then Seattle called itself the "Queen City of the Pacific Northwest," but in reality it was little more than a sleepy backwater in a far corner of the continent, an afterthought in our national consciousness. For decades Seattle was known for Boeing aircraft and Weyerhaeuser lumber and little else, except its climate, in which rain fell seemingly year-round. It was a happily unsophisticated place that reveled in its provinciality, a town where folks liked to wear lumberjack outfits and hats with floppy ears in the winter, à la Elmer

Fudd, and where there was no such thing as a traffic jam or a car horn honked in anger. I still saw Seattle as it used to be. I remembered the summer fishing trips my father and I took to catch salmon off the Pacific coast. And I recalled the minor league baseball games my brothers and I enjoyed as we sat high in the wooden bleachers at Sick's Stadium in Rainier Valley, where, by night, we could watch the stars and moon peek between the clouds, and where, on clear sunny afternoons, Mount Rainier loomed majestically beyond the right field wall like a giant snow-capped sentinel.

Now, however, the city I grew up in called itself the "Emerald City," a place where Oz-like fortunes were indeed being made. Gone were the days of 1969, when Boeing ordered massive lay-offs at its manufacturing plants and plunged the city into a terrible recession, prompting the cynical refrain, "Will the last person leaving Seattle please turn out the lights?" Now Seattle had much bigger shoulders of economic might and a population that had more than quadrupled since the days of my boyhood. Distant hillsides once green with virgin firs and pines were gradually being replaced by growing satellite towns like Bellevue with skyscrapers of their own. Multimillion-dollar homes, golf courses, and developments had been carved into these hillsides. The once sleepy backwater I had known as a child was now a city of international renown, one that had seen the birth of new technologies that were fueling the longest sustained period of economic growth America had ever known. Traffic clogged Seattle's streets and freeways now, smog poisoned its air, and sport fishing for coho, king, and silver salmon off the coast was now much more tightly restricted because so many species of the fish were endangered.

One thing hadn't changed. The rain that seemed to fall relentlessly on the pretty city when I was a boy was falling now, and my mother's windshield wipers flipped back and forth in a steady lament as she turned her car onto a quiet street called Lake Washington Boulevard. We arrived at the Leschi Grill after a few minutes, and as we waited in the entryway for the waitress to show us to a table, I put my arm around my mother's shoulder and gave her a quick, warm hug.

"You don't get older. You just get better, right? Isn't that what they say?" I said smiling.

"Maybe," she chuckled, her hands shoved into her windbreaker. "But old age isn't for sissies, just the same. You remember that."

In recent years my mother had thrown herself into an array of travel and writing projects that had made her retirement one of the busiest and most creative periods of her life. She had journeyed to Africa, Europe, and around the country over the past decade and found herself growing in ways that went far beyond the social. In 1985 she was awarded a highly competitive humanities fellowship for educators to spend a month studying the works of Alice Walker, Flannery O'Connor, Eudora Welty, and other southern writers at the University of Mississippi at Oxford. It was a privilege that would have been unthinkable for a black woman in the era of racial segregation, some forty years earlier, when she had attended college.

For much of her life, my mother had been fascinated by minority history in Seattle, and in 1983 she joined the Black Heritage Society of Washington State, a group of black educators dedicated to preserving artifacts and commemorating the achievements of the state's black population. In 1997, at the age

of seventy-four, she authored a book that told the personal sto-
ries behind the parks, swimming pools, and other landmarks in
Seattle named after twenty-three distinguished black Americans,
Medgar Evers, Martin Luther King, Jr., and Thurgood Marshall
among them. Published under a grant by King County, *Tribute:
Seattle Places Named for Black People* was lauded by reviewers in
Seattle and appeared on shelves in libraries and bookstores
throughout Washington. One reviewer, a columnist for the
Seattle Times named Jerry Large, wrote this about my mother on
December 7, 1997, in a long column devoted to her book:

> Henry was the librarian at South Shore Middle School in the
> midst of a 27-year career when she noticed how much children
> struggled with a black history quiz. Many of the children were
> cared for at the Odessa Brown Clinic and swam at Medgar Evers
> Pool, but had no idea who the people were who lent their names
> to those landmarks.
>
> Henry is of that generation of black people for whom dignity
> was paramount. Her home is immaculate and tastefully deco-
> rated. Her bearing and her language are gracious and graceful.
> She is the product of segregated schools whose teachers saw
> each child as a great hope not just for herself but for a whole
> race of people.
>
> This country's movement forw ard and the people who kept
> it moving mean something to her.

After we took our seats in the restaurant, my mother, Sonny,
and I toasted each other with martinis—still their drink of
choice, dating from the 1950s—and we laughed long into the
night as we recalled events from my childhood in Seattle and
from theirs in St. Louis. It wasn't until the next morning that I

was able to begin to tell them about the story on the other side of the tree.

I showered and dressed for our "Tenth Man Classic" golf game while Sonny prepared breakfast. The day was cloudy and overcast, but the sun was beginning to peek through the mist in the east. It promised to be a clear and sunshiny day for our outing.

As I entered the kitchen, where my uncle was cooking scrambled eggs, I noticed my mother seated nearby in the dining room. Dressed in her walking clothes, she was eating a bowl of cereal in skim milk and reading the morning paper. I took a seat across the table from her and watched for a moment as she chewed her raisin bran. She continued peering at her newspaper through her tortoiseshell eyeglasses.

"Whatcha doin' today, Mom?" I asked.

"Oh, nothin' much. I've got a doctor's appointment at noon," she replied idly, her eyes still skimming the front page. She took another bite of her cereal. "Annual checkup. Then, well, I guess I'll cook a salmon for you all and Bobby. I think Sharon and her kids will be by too."

"But you're more or less free for the day? You have some time maybe to read some things?"

She nodded. "Yep. Reckon I'll just relax."

"Good. I've got somethin' to show you. You too, Sonny."

I felt my heart beating in my throat as I went to the bedroom, quickly returning to the dining table with my satchel. I sat down with the bag in my lap and looked up at my mother, who had finished one newspaper article and started to turn the page.

"You know I've been researching all this time for my book," I began, reminding her about the research I had been doing about

Meharry, the family's move to Seattle, and the white neighborhood I grew up in—research in libraries, courthouses, and archives.

"Yeah, I know," my mother answered softly, looking at me for a moment, then returning her gaze to the newspaper's world news page.

"And you remember a long time ago I also had an idea to try to find the Beaumonts, to compare their story to ours."

She nodded again. But then, as she began to turn the newspaper page once more, she looked up and cast a brief glance at my face.

"I found them, Mom. In Louisiana."

She fixed her eyes on mine, holding the newspaper page suspended with her left hand. Her expression was quizzical.

"They never left, after all these years. I found them and I got in touch with them."

"Say, what?" I heard Sonny mutter in disbelief in his gruff baritone as he stood behind her now.

"And they invited me down there to have dinner with them."

"Oh shit," Sonny grumbled.

"What?" my mother exclaimed, echoing his disbelief as she dropped the newspaper and softly tapped her left hand on the table.

"And I did. I went there," I told them, feeling my words catching in my throat and hearing my voice quaver with emotion. "In March. I flew to Louisiana. I met them and I heard their story."

"*What?*" she exclaimed again, leaning forward now, her face electric with surprise. "You've gotta be joking, Neil."

I pulled out my copy of the fifty-six-year-old handwritten history of the Beaumonts and placed it on the table before her, along with the photos from the white family's life in St. Joseph before the turn of the century. Sonny looked on with her, standing over the table with a cup of steaming coffee in his hand, his brow furrowed as his eyes scanned the material.

"Why, you little shit . . . ," he said, starting to laugh in spite of himself.

"Here are the Beaumonts in front of their house in the country, at about the same time Laura moved to St. Louis," I indicated, my finger pointing at the old photo before them. "The little boy with the bike is Beaumont's son. That's the half brother Pearl never knew."

My mother pushed her empty cereal bowl aside. She touched the photo with her finger and placed her other hand on her heart as she leaned forward to look closer.

"And this one," I went on, pointing to another picture that Rita had given me, "this is A.J. Beaumont's store in St. Joseph. But they had a hard time after that. After Beaumont died. A really hard time."

I told Sonny and my mother about the fall of the white family's fortune, about their suffering after the boll weevil plague and on into the Depression, about the tragedy and heroism of both Anna's and Rita's lives. I told her about Newton Himel and about Carolyn too, and Carolyn's work at the black hospital in New Orleans.

"This is their story. This is what happened to the Beaumonts after Laura and Pearl moved to St. Louis," I said then, pointing to the manuscript before her. "It's a family history that was written by Beaumont's son in 1941."

My mother opened the small bound book, just as I had weeks earlier at Rita's kitchen table in Pineville. She couldn't take her eyes off the family history as she slowly turned from page to page, with Sonny leaning closely to peer over her shoulder.

"They had some very hard times after 1900—broken marriages, alcohol abuse, personal tragedies," I continued. "But the book isn't about that really. A lot of it is about how wonderful slavery and the plantation era was for them."

"And I bet there's nothin' in there about Mam-ee, right?" Sonny interjected, still leaning over but raising his eyes to mine. "Nothin' about the child that was born on the wrong side o' the blanket."

"Right. Not a word," I replied. "But they do remember her down there, Sonny. That's what's most amazing."

I looked at Mom again as she leafed through the book. Her eyes seemed riveted on each page she turned. I reached across the table to place my right hand on my mother's left.

"All those years, Mam-ee stayed in touch with them. Throughout her life in St. Louis. She tried her damnedest to stay in touch. She wanted them to know her."

I looked back at Sonny.

"And all this time they thought she was an Indian," I added. "They called her Aunt Pearl and thought she was Indian . . ."

"Typical whities!" Sonny exploded, his laugh booming now.

". . . because Beaumont figured 'better Indian than black.'"

"Typical!"

My mother still seemed too surprised to speak. All she could do was shake her head from side to side, an uncomprehending look frozen on her face. She alternately moved her gaze from the old photos to the manuscript and back. Her reaction seemed to suggest that something in her universe had suddenly, weirdly, shifted, but she wasn't sure exactly what had happened.

"But . . . how? *What?*" she stammered, focusing her deep brown eyes intensely on mine. "What was it like, Neil? What happened? What was it like to be with them?"

I answered as best I could, but no matter how hard I tried, I couldn't find the words that would do justice to what I had experienced in Pineville, or to what I was feeling then.

"They were an ordinary southern white family," I said slowly, finally, emphasizing each word distinctly. "And here I had come from out of nowhere, a black cousin suddenly flying across the country to meet them, representing a family of doctors and teachers and engineers."

Sonny began to chuckle again. "You sneaky little shit."

"And we sat together and ate gumbo at their dinner table. I learned some things I really despised. I found out one of those people was in the Klan. . . ."

They continued to study me with their eyes.

"So it was emotional. That's what it was, most of all. It was just like you always used to say, remember? Race in America is never a simple thing to understand or to explain to anyone. But one thing is always true: being black in America can be a powerfully rewarding experience. Remember how you used to say you wouldn't want to go through life any other way? Because being black in this country is such a meaningful and *interesting* life? That's exactly what it was like. That's what I felt."

I looked up at Sonny again, then back at my mother. They waited for me to go on.

"I found out so much that was different about us. We're so incredibly different. But I also found some things that were the same."

And then I looked down at the satchel in my lap again and remembered the gift I wanted to give her. I reached into the bag and pulled out the framed photo of Pearl.

"They had pictures, Mom. They had pictures of Mam-ee," I exclaimed, spreading all of the old photos of their grandmother on the table before them, placing the prettiest one in its frame near a vase of tulips at the table's edge.

My mother stared at the images for a moment. Then, as it dawned on her what exactly was before her, she gasped with delight. The enchantment began to spread on her face.

"Sonny, look!" she cried.

And it was in that instant, seeing the happiness in her eyes, hearing the laughter in her voice, that I knew my long search was finally reaching its true end and that it had been worth all the effort in ways far dearer to me than I could ever have expected. She and my uncle remembered every detail of every old blurred picture I showed them, just as I knew they would. And for a moment I felt myself once again joining them in their childhood some sixty years earlier in the house behind the white picket fence in St. Louis.

My mother would spend much of the rest of that sunny spring day lost in reading the book and looking at the old black-and-white photos Rita had given me, marveling, she would tell me later, in the memories they evoked, the questions they inspired, and the new knowledge about the past they offered. But for now, as we hovered together over her dining room table in Seattle, her gleeful words and memories tumbling out, there was simply the wonder of discovery.

"I love you, Mom," I heard myself saying as she and my uncle took turns cradling in their light brown hands the old photograph of their grandmother glimmering in its cut-glass frame.

"I love you guys. . . . ."

I'm not sure they heard me above the laughter.

COMPLETE FAMILY TREE

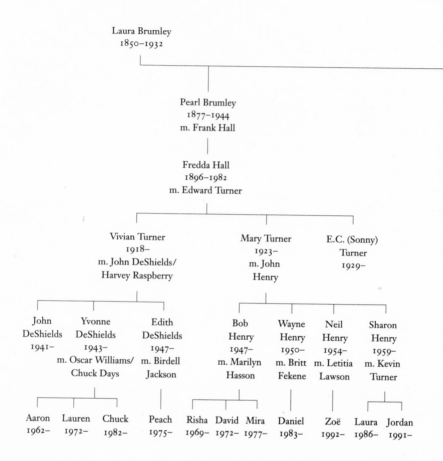

Laura Brumley
1850–1932

Pearl Brumley
1877–1944
m. Frank Hall

Fredda Hall
1896–1982
m. Edward Turner

Vivian Turner
1918–
m. John DeShields/
Harvey Raspberry

Mary Turner
1923–
m. John
Henry

E.C. (Sonny)
Turner
1929–

John
DeShields
1941–

Yvonne
DeShields
1943–
m. Oscar Williams/
Chuck Days

Edith
DeShields
1947–
m. Birdell
Jackson

Bob
Henry
1947–
m. Marilyn
Hasson

Wayne
Henry
1950–
m. Britt
Fekene

Neil
Henry
1954–
m. Letitia
Lawson

Sharon
Henry
1959–
m. Kevin
Turner

Aaron
1962–

Lauren
1972–

Chuck
1982–

Peach
1975–

Risha
1969–

David
1972–

Mira
1977–

Daniel
1983–

Zoë
1992–

Laura
1986–

Jordan
1991–

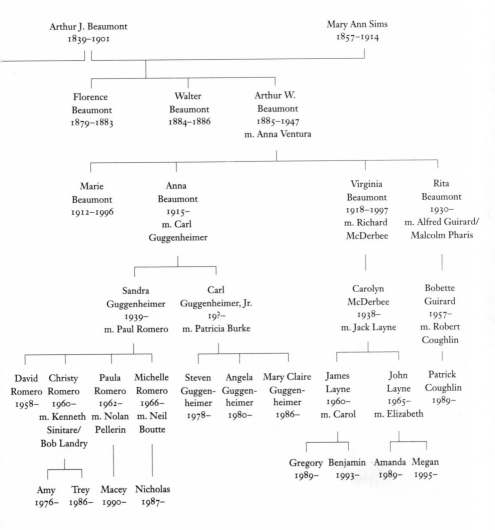

Arthur J. Beaumont
1839–1901

Mary Ann Sims
1857–1914

Florence
Beaumont
1879–1883

Walter
Beaumont
1884–1886

Arthur W.
Beaumont
1885–1947
m. Anna Ventura

Marie
Beaumont
1912–1996

Anna
Beaumont
1915–
m. Carl
Guggenheimer

Virginia
Beaumont
1918–1997
m. Richard
McDerbee

Rita
Beaumont
1930–
m. Alfred Guirard/
Malcolm Pharis

Sandra
Guggenheimer
1939–
m. Paul Romero

Carl
Guggenheimer, Jr.
19?–
m. Patricia Burke

Carolyn
McDerbee
1938–
m. Jack Layne

Bobette
Guirard
1957–
m. Robert
Coughlin

David
Romero
1958–

Christy
Romero
1960–
m. Kenneth
Sinitare/
Bob Landry

Paula
Romero
1962–
m. Nolan
Pellerin

Michelle
Romero
1966–
m. Neil
Boutte

Steven
Guggen-
heimer
1978–

Angela
Guggen-
heimer
1980–

Mary Claire
Guggen-
heimer
1986–

James
Layne
1960–
m. Carol

John
Layne
1965–
m. Elizabeth

Patrick
Coughlin
1989–

Amy
1976–

Trey
1986–

Macey
1990–

Nicholas
1987–

Gregory
1989–

Benjamin
1993–

Amanda
1989–

Megan
1995–

Acknowledgments

I thank my mother, Mary Turner Henry, and my father, Dr. John Robert Henry, Jr., of Seattle, for their love, support, and assistance with the research that led to this book. With patience, wit, and infinite understanding my mother in particular endured many hours of questioning in which I tried to piece together the narrative of my parents' lives in St. Louis, Winston-Salem, Heidelberg, Nashville, and Seattle. Without her consent, criticism, and generous help this book would not have been possible.

I also thank my brothers, John Robert Henry III of Seattle and Wayne Turner Henry of Boston, and my sister, Sharon Theresa Henry of Mercer Island, Washington, for their friendship and constant good humor. My siblings remember as well as I the unusual racial journey we experienced during childhood, an adventure that continues to the present day, and their keen insights along the way have proved extraordinarily helpful and reassuring at many turns, not least during the period of my research and writing.

I extend special thanks to Rita Beaumont Guirard Pharis and her family in Louisiana, who opened the door to their lives and shared their remarkable family history with me that eventful March evening in

Pineville. By doing so they allowed me a chance to reap the full rewards of my project. For that, I will always be grateful. I also express special thanks to Carolyn M. Layne of New Orleans for her help in constructing the Beaumont genealogy.

I'm very grateful to my aunt, Vivian DeShields Raspberry, and my cousins, John DeShields III and Yvonne DeShields Days, all of St. Louis, for their generous support of my work and the use of photographs and other historical documents in their possession. I also thank my uncles, Dr. Frank Demby of San Rafael, California, for sharing his wisdom, especially his recollections of his teaching and training at Meharry Medical College, and Edward Clifford Turner, Jr., of St. Louis, for his storytelling skills and exquisite taste in single-malt Scotch, soul food, and Cuban cigars.

As a kid growing up in Seattle, I was fortunate to count as family friends a number of black professionals, many of whom pioneered like my parents from the Deep South to the Pacific Northwest in the 1950s. I thank them for their family friendship, love, and example. They include the late Philip and Toby Burton, Frank and Janice Fair, Hon. Judge Charles and Lazelle Johnson, Dr. Bill and Helen Lacy, the late Drs. Philip and Blanche Lavizzo, Drs. Earl V. and Rosalie Miller, and the late June Smith.

I'm also grateful to three brilliant teachers who inspired me in my school years: the late Lee O. Schmalbeck at Sharples Junior High School in Seattle, the late Professor H. H. Wilson at Princeton University, and Professor Penn Kimball at Columbia University.

Numerous libraries and historical societies were very helpful at many turns in my research, including the University of Washington, Louisiana State University, the University of California at Berkeley, the University of California at Davis, the Yolo County Public Library in Davis, the British Imperial War Museum and British National Army Museum in London, the Church of Jesus Christ of Latter-Day Saints Family History Center in Woodland, California, the Tensas Parish Public Library in St. Joseph, Louisiana, the National Archives and Library of Congress of the United States in Washington, D.C., and the historical societies of St. Louis, Missouri, and Tensas Parish, Louisiana. I especially thank Gordon A. Cotton, curator of the Warren County Court House Museum and Library in Vicksburg, Mississippi, for the public records expertise and assistance he offered during my visit, and Quinton L. Jones, curator of the Archives of Meharry Medical College in Nashville, Tennessee.

Many friends, professional colleagues, and students played an invaluable role in supporting and encouraging me to complete this book. I am very grateful to them and will attempt here to name all of them, apologizing in advance for what may be an incomplete job. I thank my colleagues, first, on the faculty at Berkeley's Graduate School of Journalism, including Joan Bieder, Lydia Chavez, Mark Danner, William J. Drummond, Clay Felker, Cynthia Gorney, Paul Grabowicz, Ken Light, Paul Mason, Marcia Parker, Susan Rasky, William B. Turner, and Carolyn Wakeman, for their unfailing good cheer and camaraderie. I'm especially grateful for the expert editorial eyes of Jon Else, Tom Goldstein, Thomas C. Leonard, and Orville H. Schell, all of whom offered valuable comments and criticism on early drafts of the manuscript. I also thank the administrative staff at the journalism school, including Roy Baril, Mimi Chakarova, Andre Des Boine, Johnny Dong, Ida Fowler, David Martinez, Paulette Powell, Michele Price Rabin, and Kean Sakata. I especially am grateful to former staff members Mitsuru "Mitch" Ikuta and Natalie Smolensky, who never tired in their assistance to me in my transition from newspapering to academia.

Leon F. Litwack, the Alexander F. and May T. Morrison Professor of American History at Berkeley, offered a keen eye and terrific suggestions for improving the book at a critical time in its creation, and for that I will always be thankful. I'm grateful, too, to Naomi Schneider, James Clark, and Ellie Hickerson at the University of California Press for believing in this book, to copy editor Virginia Croft and designer Nicole Hayward, and especially to project editor Sue Heinemann, who made timely suggestions and wielded a terrific pencil during the editing process. I also thank my agent, Jill Kneerim, for her literary expertise and counsel.

Among the hundreds of undergraduate and graduate students who have passed through my "Mass Media and Society" lectures and my news reporting and writing seminars in the seven years I have taught at Berkeley, a number have supported me in my work as well as assisted me in my teaching. They include Lauren Barrack, Gregg Bell, Anita Chabria, Sherri Day, Karen D'Souza, Charlotte Fadipe, Eric Gran, Emelie Gunnison, Damon Hack, Tyche Hendricks, Matthai Kuruvila, Andrea Lampros, Harry Mok, Suzanne Pardington, David Pescovitz, Rob Selna, Jackie Spinner, Jessica Thaler, and Elliot Zaret. I also thank the many students in my Journalism 200 classes through the years, who provided the grist for informing and improving my work as an educator. My respect and affection to all you guys.

I also express appreciation to the following San Francisco Bay Area journalists, whose work I have come to admire and who have generously assisted me on occasion in my Berkeley classroom and lecture hall: John Diaz, Richard Gonzalez, Adam Hochschild, Tim Keown, Ann Killion, Gwen Knapp, Teresa Moore, Carl Nolte, Lori Olszewski, Bob Porterfield, Manuel Ramos, Dennis Richmond, Gary Rivlin, Joan Ryan, Barbara Shulgasser, and Ruthe Stein.

Professional colleagues and dear pals from my days in Washington, D.C., and Africa when I wrote for the *Washington Post* supported me consistently, through the bad times as well as the good. I thank, above all, David Maraniss, Bill Hamilton, and Janet Philips. I also treasure the support and friendship of these kindred spirits: Paul Addison, Jeffrey Bartholet, Jerri Eddings, Johanna Janssens, Jennifer Parmelee, and Rehana Rossouw. In addition I'm grateful to Leonard Downie, James V. Risser, Roger Wilkins, Juan Williams, and Bob Woodward for considering and commenting on early drafts of the manuscript. Thanks, too, to editor Donna Frazier, my old friend from our days in graduate study at Columbia's Journalism School; Dr. William E. Matori; and Tansey Thomas.

During my formative years as a reporter and writer in New York City and Washington, D.C., I was very lucky to be surrounded by colleagues and counterparts whose camaraderie I treasured, whose excellence I admired, and whose zest for the craft inspired me. I thank them for demonstrating from the very start how rewarding journalism could be. They include my splendid brethren from the *Washington Post* summer intern class of 1977: Sandra G. Boodman, John Feinstein, Ted Gup, Carla Hall, Vanessa Barnes Hillian, and Lexie Verdon. I also thank Charles R. Babcock, Gene Bachinski, Karlyn Barker, Jamie Baylis, Dudley Brooks, Warren Brown, Milton Coleman, Denis Collins, Leon Dash, the late Herbert Denton, Jackson Diehl, Lewis Diuguid, Maureen Dowd, Bill Elsen, Patrice Gaines, Joyce Gemperlein, Michael Getler, Dorothy Gilliam, Donald Graham, Nell Henderson, Craig Herndon, Michael E. Hill, Alison Howard, Gwen Ifill, Michael Isikoff, the late John Jacobs, Janis Johnson, Robert G. Kaiser, Laura Kiernan, Athelia Knight, Charles Krause, Steve Luxenberg, Jim Malone, Dennis McAuliffe, Michelle McQueen, Eugene L. Meyer, Reid Miller, Courtland Milloy, Morton Mintz, Thomas Morgan, Beth Nissen, Angus Phillips, William Raspberry, David Remnick, Eugene Robinson, Wendy Ross, Ann Rutherford, Mike Sager, Deborah Schwartz, Jane Seaberry, the late Howard Simons, Molly Sinclair, Dita Smith, Christine Spolar, Valerie Strauss, Fred Sweets, Karyn Taylor, Pat Thompson, Vernon Thompson, James M. Thresher, Loretta Tofani, Judith Valente, Paul Valentine, Elsa Walsh, Martin Weil, Benjamin Weiser, Michael Weisskopf, Larry Whiteside, Tom Wilkinson, and Brad Wye.

I am grateful, too, to the following wonderful souls whose companionship and confidence in me I found deeply rewarding and nurturing at different times, and in many different ways, since I moved west and made Davis, California, my home: John and Melissa Gates, Robert B. Gunnison, John Samples, the late Richard C. Sinopoli, Andrew and Melissa Skalaban, and Dave and Cindi Unmack.

Finally, I thank my wife, Letitia Lawson, whose editorial assistance, endless patience, sympathy, common sense, laughter, and loving support saw me through this odyssey in one piece, sane and whole. To her I owe everything.

Text: 10/15 Janson
Display: Rotis Serif
Design: Nicole Hayward
Composition: BookMatters
Printing and binding: Haddon Craftsmen